THE EQUILIBRIUM OF WIT

FRENCH FORUM MONOGRAPHS

36

Editors R.C. La Charité and V.A. La Charité

THE EQUILIBRIUM OF WIT

ESSAYS FOR ODETTE DE MOURGUES

EDITED BY
PETER BAYLEY
AND
DOROTHY GABE COLEMAN

FRENCH FORUM, PUBLISHERS
LEXINGTON, KENTUCKY

Copyright © 1982 by French Forum, Publishers, Incorporated,
P.O. Box 5108, Lexington, Kentucky 40505.

Library of Congress Catalog Card Number 81-71433

ISBN 0-917058-35-6

Printed in the United States of America

CONTENTS

PREFACE

We wish to preface our volume with thanks and with apologies. The apologies are to the many friends and colleagues of Odette de Mourgues whom we have, inevitably, not contacted or whose contributions we have not been able to include. By choosing a theme and a period for this book which might give it critical and historical unity, we found ourselves obliged to impose a stricter selectivity than is perhaps usual with *Mélanges*. We are grateful for the forbearance and understanding of those who accepted these limitations.

Our thanks go to the friends and colleagues of our own who have been generous with their experience, advice and time—in the first place, of course, our contributors and our publisher. In particular we wish to record our indebtedness to Girton College for a grant towards the expenses of publication, to the Department of French at Cambridge and its head, Professor Peter Rickard, for the use of its facilities, and above all to the patience and skill of its secretary, Miss Veronica Freemantle.

PJB
DGC

Cambridge, March 1981

Rawsley Murfmett
Camberell

FOREWORD

If one word had to be chosen to sum up the intellectual and the personal gifts of Odette de Mourgues, it might be *élégance*, in the sense given by Littré: "Distinction dans le langage et dans le style qui, sans affectation, résulte de la justesse et de l'agrément." Yet anyone attempting a summary of her achievements will necessarily be haunted by the specter of her own mistrust of unexamined generalizations and her particular sense of their comic potentialities and paradoxical possibilities. Can any commentator match her special ability to combine lightness of touch with penetrating insight into substance? The brief remarks appended here are simply those of a colleague recalling with gratitude long years of shared experience.

The year 1946 was fortunate for Girton. While College and University were adjusting to post-war possibilities, an application for admission as research student was received from a French Agrégée d'anglais with unusual qualifications. K.T. Butler as Mistress and Henriette Bibas as Director of Studies in Modern Languages, both skilled talent-spotters, suggested to a raw recruit as College Lecturer (the present writer) that she interview Odette de Mourgues in Paris about the possibility of combining research with a post as College *lectrice*. The encounter might well have provided material to a semiologist concerned with non-verbal assumptions: the interviewer, desperately determined that College Traditions should be suitably upheld, contrived, after untold complications, to provide tea and cakes in the fifth-floor bedroom of a minor Quartier Latin hotel; while the interviewee responded with puzzled politeness to the exotic habits of the English who can allow no intellectual activity to prevent the sacred tea-hour.

On coming to Cambridge as a research student, O.M. had already impressive qualifications in different disciplines. She had begun by studying Law, obtaining the Licence en droit of Grenoble in 1934, and the Diplôme d'études supérieures de droit of Aix-en-Provence in 1938. She recalls appearing as a barrister on a case concerned with bathtubs—but, rapidly, personal pleasure and love of a challenge turned her energies to the study of English language and literature. In 1942 she was placed second of all candidates in the examination for the Certificat d'aptitude à l'enseignement des langues vivantes; in 1945 she came first in the major competitive contest for the Agrégation d'anglais. Meantime, she had held teaching posts at schools in Valence, Digne and Marseilles, and an Assistant Lectureship at the University of Aix-en-Provence; after the liberation in 1944 she was attached to the Ministry of Information in Marseilles. The circumstances of the War and of the Resistance had caused many interruptions to study or teaching. Friends from the early Girton years will remember an outstanding short story which Odette could very occasionally be persuaded to read, where she evoked with characteristic subtlety and concentration the central problems at stake and the sharply individualized landscape in which they were set.

In the late 1940's, Lectureships in Cambridge, whether in College or University, were particularly few. Girton elected O.M. to a Research Fellowship in 1948 and to a College Lectureship in 1949. To both undergraduates and colleagues she had from the beginning given a threefold stimulus: intellectual, personal and practical. Her contacts with the Director of the newly-established Maison française in Oxford, Professor Henri Fluchère, and with the French Embassy in London and its successive Cultural Attachés, brought many French experts in very varied disciplines to address a lively College French Society; in later years the University French Society was to benefit greatly from her advice as senior member.

In 1950 she was awarded the Ph.D. for her dissertation on *Metaphysical, Baroque and Précieux Poetry*, to be published by the Oxford University Press in 1953. This work stood out on three counts. First, the determination to introduce "idées claires et distinctes" into "the welter of terminology" (typically, for years after publication, O.M., having proposed a firm definition of the slippery term "baroque," refused to use that term in any of her lectures); second, the illuminating comparisons drawn between French and English poets of a given period; third, and especially, the sensitive and suggestive analyses of particular poems.

1950 was also the year of her first University appointment, as Assistant Lecturer; to be followed by a Lectureship (1952), a Readership (1968) and a personal chair (1975). Successive Drapers' Professors, as Heads of the French Department (Professors L.C. Harmer and L.J. Austin), rapidly recognized the range of her contribution to French studies in Cambridge and beyond.

Meantime, between her first critical study and the many which were to follow, O.M. published two highly original novels, each showing the interest in structure, in selection, in creative stylization and especially in the borderlines between the serious and the comic which inform so many of her critical works. In *Le Jugement avant-dernier* (1954) a selected set of differing individuals meet in turn the often unrecognized testing-point on which a whole future will depend; in *L'Hortensia bleu* (1956), "le besoin d'ordre, ce désir de trouver autour de soi, et en soi-même, un dessein intelligible et satisfaisant" takes on unexpected forms and finds equally individual outcomes. A comment made on the second of these novels might well apply to both: "Un mélange d'humour, de savante ingénuité, de dépaysement dans le familier, donnent au livre une qualité rêveuse, un ton d'originalité, qui sont la marque d'un écrivain maître de son expression."

Five critical works on major French authors were to follow, as well as an anthology of seventeenth-century French poetry and many important contributions to periodicals, presentation volumes and colloquia. Several threads run persistently through all: the determined pursuit of a "nettoyage de la situation verbale"; the quiet but firm reexamination of preconceptions, whether centuries old or ultra modern, around Classicism; the wish to enhance enjoyment not by the kaleidoscopic shifts of anachronistic vision, but through a full sense of the problems and possibilities faced by a given writer in a particular period; and, above all, the ability to make perceptive judgments spring alive, whether in lapidary formulae or in the detail of finely suggestive textual analyses. It would be difficult to find, in any of these books, any page which tempts the reader to skip. It must be rare, too, to meet a critic with such a command of incisive and imaginative expression in two languages: the French volumes which follow O.M.'s initial publications in English are no mere translations, but her own rediscussion, in different terms, of basic issues.

The authors chosen—La Fontaine, Racine, La Rochefoucauld and La Bruyère—are among those most central to the French Classical tradition, and those least immediately accessible to many of the English. They are also those where the modern critic, French or English, may find it hardest to convey that complex balance between "plaire et instruire" which each author shaped from the conventions of his day. In *O Muse, fuyante proie* . . . (1962, preceded by a briefer English study in 1960), La Fontaine's subtle triumph as a poet is seen to emerge from his awareness and his personal conquests of the intertwining and partly forbidding poetic traditions of his time. In *Racine or the Triumph of Relevance* and in its French counterpart, *Autonomie de Racine*, both 1967, the indivisible interdependence of Racine's resources (any one of which—metaphysical, moral, dramatic, or poetic—might so easily be given undue pre-eminence) is worked out in a series of finely-planned chapters and close commentaries, to reach the quiet culmination: "Une étude de la tragédie racinienne n'a de conclusion que dans l'effacement du commentateur." Her most recent study, *Two French Moralists, La Rochefoucauld and La Bruyère* (1978), again tackles problems of definition (here, those of the term "moralist" in its variations across the centuries and between France and England); reassesses the persistent provocation offered by two outstanding original authors in relation both to the assumptions of their period and of subsequent commentators; analyses particular forms of tension (between moral and social criteria, or between sensibility and moral judgment); and penetratingly relates the expression of these problems to the resources available in the language of their age.

Cambridge recognized O.M.'s scholarly achievements by the award of the Litt. D. in 1968. In 1973 the French Government elected her a Chevalier de l'Ordre du Mérite. She specially requested that the formal ceremony be held in Girton College, and her father, a distinguished French medical consultant, conferred the award; one of her two brothers, both of whom are medical specialists and frequent welcome visitors to Cambridge, also came from France for the occasion.

It was fitting that her pre-retirement year, 1980-81, should be marked by her giving two public lectures remarkable for their lucidity and their wit: the Cassal Lecture in the University of London, on "Intelligence et comique chez Molière," and the Zaharoff Lecture in the University of Oxford, entitled "Quelques Paradoxes sur le Classicisme." Both subjects represent long-standing interests: among her many contributions to collective volumes (on Seneca and Garnier, on Scève and Shakespeare, on Théophile . . .) there figure probing evaluations of the comic in *Le Bourgeois gentilhomme* and in *Dom Juan*; while work about to be published includes investigations of "Le Comique de la Préciosité" and of "Voiture and the Question of Wit."

She has naturally been in demand as Visiting Lecturer, whether on single occasions in this country, or for a semester's teaching in the United States or in Canada. As a *comparatiste* she has enjoyed observing some contrasts between the pleasantly uninhibited immediacy of response from some students on the other side of the Atlantic and the sometimes more cautious, guarded expression of reactions from certain of the British; on the other hand, she has always rejoiced in collecting, whether in novels or in conversation, examples which undermine or explode the myth of "English understatement." Her first year of "retirement" from Cambridge will open with a visiting post in Washington, to be followed by wide journeys. Early experience of travel stemmed, in the pre-war years, from family car-tours across Europe, unusual at their date; as soon as post-war circumstances allowed, she shared hazardous expeditions in ancient cars over the then unremade roads in the Alpine passes or the mountains of Spain. Later years have provided round-the-world expeditions, with specially enjoyed pauses in Egypt, Greece or Sri Lanka, and many returns to favorite regions in West Scotland or the Iles du Levant, in Brittany or in Italy.

If hosts in many countries have found O.M. a welcome guest, her gifts as a hostess will be remembered by many others. Already, during her years as a resident Fellow in Girton, she initiated new possibilities both for celebrating special occasions and for regular entertainment. Her parents and brothers, both in Le Puy and in their country home at Le Mazonric, generously received many English visitors. In more recent years, the house she shares with Sheila Gillies—a Life Fellow of Girton whose multiple contributions to the College as Steward and Tutor will be warmly and widely remembered—has offered a constant welcome to colleagues, undergraduates, research students, official visitors from France and many friends. The garden echoes the qualities of its owners: meticulous planning, the art of selection, and a sense of how to blend tones and contrasts so as to give unusual pleasure at any season of the year; it is, to quote the last phrase of *Two French Moralists*, "a perfect exemplification of carefully achieved naturalness."

Among those who have enjoyed this hospitality, research students may keep a special memory. O.M.'s influence on sixteenth- and seventeenth-century studies has built a considerable school, not so much of "disciples" (she has always preferred argument to dutiful absorption) as of individuals grateful to have been guided towards new means of discovery. Many important implications stem from her incitement, and her past pupils lecture in many universities.

Those who know her only through her writings will appreciate the skill and sensitivity through which she shows how each creative writer both fulfills and transcends the traditions of his time or of his country. Those who have worked closely with her will specially value her intellectual and personal loyalty to principles, to institutions and to friends. Any over-solemn interviewer might well be met by her enjoyment of parodic self-definition: "can't draw, can't sew, can't cook . . . can't distinguish a rugby bat from a cricket racket"—and also by the persistent creative purpose lightly indicated in: "ambitions—to be a novelist and to speak English like a native." No meeting with Odette, whether in person or in print, can have lacked the stimulus of wit or the impulse to imaginative reassessment of preconceptions. Her especial gifts, which will continue to inspire colleagues, students, friends and readers, might best be summed up in the concluding words of *O Muse, fuyante proie* . . . : "La discipline de l'imagination, un grand respect du langage, le culte de la grâce et beaucoup de tact."

Alison Fairlie
March 1981

A LIST OF MAJOR PUBLICATIONS
BY ODETTE DE MOURGUES

CRITICAL BOOKS

Metaphysical, Baroque and Précieux Poetry. Oxford, 1953.
La Fontaine: Fables. London: Arnold, 1960.
O Muse, fuyante proie. . . . Essai sur la poésie de La Fontaine. Paris: Corti, 1961.
Racine, or the Triumph of Relevance. Cambridge, 1967.
Autonomie de Racine. Paris: Corti, 1967.
Two French Moralists: La Rochefoucauld and La Bruyère. Cambridge, 1978.

FICTION

Le Jugement avant-dernier. Paris, 1954.
L'Hortensia bleu. Paris, 1956.

ANTHOLOGY

Anthology of French Seventeenth-Century Lyric Poetry. Oxford, 1966.

ARTICLES

"The European Background to Baroque Sensibility." In *A Guide to English Literature*, vol. 3: *From Donne to Marvell*. London: Pelican Books, 1956, pp. 89-97.

"Reason and Fancy in the Poetry of Théophile de Viau." *L'Esprit Créateur*, 1 (1961), 75-81.

"Poésie baroque, poésie classique." In *Trois Conférences sur le baroque français*, Supplemento al n. 21 di *Studi Francesi* (settembre-dicembre 1963).

"Originalité." In *Actes du IVe congrès de l'Association internationale de littérature comparée* (Fribourg). Paris, 1966, pp. 1259-64.

"Tragedy and Moral Order in Racine." *French Studies*, 20 (1966), 123-33.

"La Fontaine et la distance poétique." *L'Information Littéraire*, 20 (1966), 103-08.

"*L'Hippolyte* de Garnier et l'*Hippolytus* de Sénèque." In *The French Renaissance and Its Heritage: Essays Presented to Alan Boase*. London, 1968, pp. 191-202.

"*Le Bourgeois gentilhomme* as a Criticism of Civilization." In *Molière: Stage and Study: Essays Presented to W.G. Moore*. Oxford, 1973, pp. 170-84.

"Deux Triomphes de l'hyperbole." In *De Shakespeare à T.S. Eliot. Mélanges offerts à Henri Fluchère*. Paris, 1976, pp. 73-79.

"Dom Juan est-il comique?" In *La Cohérence intérieure: Etudes . . . présentées en hommage à Judd D. Hubert*. Paris, 1976, pp. 33-45.

"Phèdre: A Search for the 'Hidden God.' " In *Racine: Mythes et réalités* (Actes du colloque Racine tenu à l'université de Western Ontario, London, Canada, en mars 1974). 1976, pp. 87-100.

"Voiture and the Question of Wit." *L'Esprit Créateur*, 20 (1980), 7-18.

Article on D'Aubigné in *Mélanges offerts à Henri Weber* (in press).

Article on Molière in *Mélanges offerts à Georges Couton* (in press).

LECTURES

Cassal Bequest Lecture, *Intelligence et comique dans le théâtre de Molière*. University of London, 1980.

Zaharoff Lecture 1980, *Quelques Paradoxes sur le classicisme*. Oxford: Clarendon Press, 1981.

Dorothy Gabe Coleman

Scève: A Virile Intellect Aerated by Sensibility

Since Grierson's characterization of Donne, Herbert and Marvell as "metaphysical" poets in 1921[1] with the famous phrase "strain of passionate paradoxical reasoning" and Eliot's definition of their kind of wit as a "tough reasonableness under the slight lyric grace,"[2] there have been numerous important studies analyzing closely the imagery, language, conceits and juxtaposition of words in these poets: studies like the brilliant one of James Smith,[3] who considered the elements in a metaphysical conceit—"they can enter into a solid union and at the same time, maintain their separate and warring identity . . ."—or Rosemond Tuve,[4] who examined the force of Ramist logic on the poetry of the seventeenth century in England. Alan Boase[5] made a first step in comparative criticism when he discovered Sponde, whom he called "un Donne manqué." He was followed by Odette de Mourgues,[6] who posited a French metaphysical "line" in the light of Grierson's definition. Of course, the first French poet she alighted on was Scève: his qualities, she argued, are akin to those of Donne—"investigation of experience, compressed passionate reasoning, functional rather than merely decorative conceits, special awareness of the metaphysical problems underlying the problems of his love" (p. 21).

This argument is the beginning of this volume, a volume which occupies the temporal span 1544-1700. In this essay I propose to look at Scève anew from the point of view of "wit," stressing his virility, allusiveness, sensibility, syntactical articulation and his manipulation of language.

Wit is defined by Miege's dictionary[7] as *esprit* and *entendement* or understanding. The OED goes further: "intellectual ability, genius, talent, cleverness, mental quickness or sharpness, acumen." A second meaning is "That quality of speech or writing which consists in the apt association of thought and expression" emphasizing the intellectual character of wit and hinting that it is the variety and quickness of putting together thoughts that characterize wit. These definitions of wit make me ponder about the sharpness of invention, the intellectualization of reality, the acumen or subtlety of an author's technique, Johnson's *discordia concors*, the niceties of distinction and Scève's acute and always analytical mind. Implicit in wit is a sense of proportion and balance in the discipline of art.

First, Scève was writing from the 1520's onwards; he was among the first who gave attention to the Roman literary colonnade and one of the last who inherited the linguistic conjuring tricks of the *grands rhétori-queurs*. Undeniably, there is a verbal wit in him. The punning in his Neo-Latin epigram to Ducher,

> Delia si laetis blandum mihi ridet ocellis:
> Non mirum: mea nam *Delia delitiae est,*[8]

shows already a certain liveliness and awareness of the sound of words. (See the poem to Rondelet.) This pun is echoed through *Délie* (dizain 9: *delices de mon Ame*) and can be compared to the verbal gymnastics of dizain 2,

> Par les vertus de sa vertu guidées
> S'esuertua en œuvre esmerueillable . . . .

The pun in dizain 417, "Fleuue rongeant" on Petrarch's *Rime*, 208, 1-2, *Rhodanus/rodens*, is doubly attractive: as a pun and as an allusion to Petrarch's affair in Avignon,

> Ou ce Thuscan Apollo sa ieunesse
> Si bien forma, qu'a iamais sa vieillesse
> Verdoyera a toute eternité . . . .

The irony brought in to dizain 19 (which is on the defection of the Conné-table de Bourbon) by a consciously used archaic word: "Mais celle part, comme on dit, la greigneur," is a kind of apology neatly said through the "if I may put it like that." This "alliance of levity and seriousness" (Eliot) demands a participating reader and thus establishes the point that the culture of readers is crucial.[9]

Second, Scève is one of the first allusive poets in France, and allusive-ness was seen by Eliot as essential for the quality he called wit.[10] I shall take one dizain to demonstrate this allusiveness:

Pour me despendre en si heureux seruice,
Ie m'espargnay l'estre semblable aux Dieux.
Me pourra donc estre imputé a vice,
Constituant en elle mes haultz Cieulx?
 Fais seulement, Dame, que de tes yeulx
Me soient tousiours toutes nuisances lentes.
Lors vous, Nuisantz, Dieux des vmbres silentes,
(Me preseruant elle d'aduersité)
Ne m'osterez par forces violentes
Non vn Iota de ma felicité.

                                        (dizain 75)[11]

The word *Dame* is the pivot of the poem: isolated by two commas, it is typographically central.[12] Furthermore, it is the fifth syllable of line five: was Scève aware of this? Surely.[13] Again, punctuation picks on the third and fourth syllables of line seven—on *Nuisantz*. These two forces—*Dame* and *Nuisantz*—dominate the dizain: the battle between the powers of good and evil, the struggle between light and darkness, the opposition between the Heavens and the Underworld and the hammering out of a closed position where *heureux seruice* ends on *ma felicité* and the whole circle moves around *Dame*. It brings to mind the last two lines of the first dizain,

Piteuse hostie au conspect de toy, Dame,
Constituée Idole de ma vie . . . ,

where there is a similar punctuation around *Dame* and the use of *Constituée* echoes the Latin sacrificial term (e.g., Vergil, *Aeneid*, VI, 244: *constituit* means "made to stand"; and *Aeneid*, V, 236 ff.: *candentem in litore taurum / constituam ante aram voti reus*).[14] The legal nuance is brought out by Cotgrave: "*Constitu*, an order, institution, decree, sentence, constitution, ordinance, act, statute."[15] The poet is making, creating, ordaining and establishing as a ritual his Paradise within his *Dame*. Propertius' argument that since Cynthia loves him he knows the supreme joy and ecstasy, the feeling of being on a level with the Gods, "nunc mihi summa licet contingere sidera plantis" (I, 8a, 43), is in fact the model for this traditional theme. But Scève is in some doubts as to whether his love is being fully returned. The question is followed by the imperative movement of the second part of the dizain: *Fais*. Délie is impelled to be his tutelary Deity with very clear associations of not only preserving him against adversity but also against death since the allusions point in the same direction: *Nuisantz, Dieux des vmbres silentes* and *forces violentes*—all suggesting death.[16] I think that we cannot realize the full force of the poem until we introduce into our interpretation of it all the harmonics of *Délie/Hecate/Persephone/Libytina* and *Diana*. The resonances behind *Dieux des vmbres silentes* are vast: the prayer to Hecate in *Aeneid*, VI, 264 ff., is very much in keeping with this dizain:

> Di, quibus imperium est animarum, umbraeque silentes
> et Chaos et Phlegethon, loca nocte tacentia late,
> sit mihi fas audita loqui, sit numine uestro
> pandere res alta terra et caligine mersas.

Or the further explanation that Vergil gives of *umbra*—phantom-like things in insubstantial silence,

> Ibant obscuri sola sub nocte per umbram
> perque domos Ditis uacuas et inania regna.

The poets invoke the gods of the spirit world, gods who rule the ghosts and the silent ghosts themselves, ghosts of the silent dead. Or we may remember the prayer to Persephone in Tibullus, III, 5:

> At mihi Persephone nigram denuntiat horam:
> immerito inveni parce nocere dea . . . ,

or Tibullus' address to the shades themselves:

> Parcite, pallentes undas quicumque tenetis
> duraque sortiti tertia regna dei.

Or we may "hear" in the dizain the *Manes* of the Graeco-Roman underworld gods, gods such as Dis, Orcus, Hades, Mors—the daughter of Erebus and Nox—and Persephone.

Scève's control comes out in the structure of this dizain: four lines asking a question which expects the answer no; lines 5-6, a gentle prayer to Délie and the last four affirming very boldly that even death will not damage his faith and love. The sound associations of line 6, "Me soient tousiours toutes nuisances lentes," seem to color the *lentes* which Cotgrave gives as "gentle, soft, meeke and patient." The *oi*, the *ou* (three times) and the *ui* make it a line of very slow delivery and the last line is an absolute: not "a iot, point or pricked" (Rabelais quoted by Cotgrave); being disyllabic (the same as its Latin form) and being the second negative (line 9 has the first), it assumes maximum force. In this example there is not so much erudition, but a depth of knowledge precisely because Scève was steeped in Latin literature and his allusiveness is in trying to force language into his meaning. As Eliot said about Marvell, "[Wit] is confused with erudition because it belongs to an educated mind, rich in generations of experience."

Thirdly, the sensibility of Scève. The perfect poise between the play of intellect and the depth of emotion can be demonstrated by one device— that of the clash between adjective and adverb—which seems to dominate *Délie*. The depiction of a feeling where literary and personal experience are intimately linked up in order to dislocate, shock and disrupt the reader of *Délie*. At times the clash between adjective and adverb seems to control the dizain. For example, dizain 269:

> Ces deux Soleilz nuisamment penetrantz,
> Qui de mon viure ont eu si long Empire,
> Par l'œil au Cœur tacitement entrantz,
> Croissent le mal, qui au guerir m'empire.
> Car leur clarté esblouissamment pire
> A son entrée en tenebres me met:
> Puis leur ardeur en ioye me remet,
> M'esclairant tout au fort de leurs alarmes
> Par vn espoir, qui rien mieulx ne promet,
> Qu'ardentz souspirs estainctz en chauldes larmes.

The love is long, *si long Empire*, and it is the presence of Délie's eyes that is the crucial experience: the hyperbole of the two suns is linked by the first clash—*nuisamment penetrantz*—where the adverb is a neologism, then to the second—*tacitement entrantz*—another coining of the adverb, and leads to the fifth line giving as a logical reason what is not connected to logic in another clash and another neologism, "Car leur clarté esblouissam-ment pire," which may be compared to this line, "En la clarté de mes desirs funebres" (7, line 8), which intensifies the paradoxical reasoning of the poem.[17] Light and darkness hover through dizain 269, the heat of ardor playing against the heat of tears until we reach the last, "Qu'ardentz sous-pirs estainctz en chauldes larmes," where one feels engaged in a metaphysi-cal shudder.

In the paradox of adverb/adjective combinations it is the context that is important. For example, this line in dizain 444: "Crea Amour saincte-ment phrenetique," where there is a clash between holiness and frenzied-ness through a verbal juxtaposition. The argument of the poem is that in Platonic terms Nature created Love,

> Pour me remplir d'vne melencolie
> Si plaisamment . . . ,

and here there is another clash between melancholy and merriness. In other dizains—for example, number 403—it is a single word *meurdryerement* which hits at *benigne*: and the key to the poem is the goddess Libytina:

Tout le iour voyant celle presente,
Qui m'est de soy meurdryerement benigne.
Toute nuict i'ars la desirant absente,
Et si me sens a la reuoir indigne,
Comme ainsi soit que pour ma Libytine
Me fut esleue, & non pour ma plaisance.
Et mesmement que la molle nuisance
De cest Archier superbement haultain
Me rend tousiours par mon insuffisance
D'elle doubteux, & de moy incertain.

Primarily she is the goddess of death but with one strange aspect: "Les Latins ont mis en rapport *Libitina* avec *libet* d'où les formes *Lubitina* et *Lubentina, Libentina,* et ils en ont fait une Vénus infernale."[18] The whole poem is around the uncertainty: the poet does not know whether he is worshipping the corpses of the dead or the libidinous delights of Venus. Thus the clash is one small unit of Scève's technique which echoes the ambiguity of love.

When the clash comes in a passionately reasoning poem, the effect is magnificent: the perfect dizain 367 offers the reader in the seventh line a strong *Car* combined with the clashing paradox of adverb and adjective:

Car en mon corps: mon Ame, tu reuins,
Sentant ses mains, mains celestement blanches,
Auec leurs bras mortellement diuins
L'vn coronner mon col, l'aultre mes hanches.

We participate in the miracle of love: it fixes a stable world which though small is in itself totally independent of the general impermanence and mutability of the universe and of life. And yet, Scève is pursuing the *puzzling* nature of things and is forcing the intellect and feelings of the reader to get the balance of the last four lines.

Line 8 repeats the *mains* so that we have a very vivid sensation of Délie's hands touching the poet; he sees them as *blanches* and feels the touch; yet at the same time the hands enlock the adverb *celestement*. The very concrete clashing with the heavenly. Line 9 reverses the earthly and the heavenly; this time *mortellement* carries the lingering knowledge that this is a human affair, that it is momentary, that it too is tinged with death and yet, the adjective *diuins* seems to cancel this death forever *within* the poem, which ends with a vision of an eternal embrace through two concrete human beings—hands and arms, neck and thighs. This dizain is a concentrated one: the argument is paradoxical and tight and yet, there is no sense of strain here but rather a "passionate reasoning" on the problems which surround love.[19]

I have elsewhere[20] examined Scève's sensibility from the point of view of the *emblesmes* and concluded that the woodcuts give us some essential features of Scève's *paysage intérieur*. A reappraisal of the role of sensations in Scève is badly needed,[21] and here I shall just take one example of his success in communicating sensuality, indeed carnality:

> Plus pour esbat, que non pour me douloir
> De tousiours estre en passions brulantes,
> Ie contentois mon obstiné vouloir:
> Mais ie sentis ses deux mains bataillantes,
> Qui s'opposoient aux miennes trauaillantes,
> Pour mettre a fin leur honneste desir.
> Ainsi, Enfant, comme tu peulx saisir,
> Et (quand te plait) hommes, & Dieux conquerre:
> Ainsi tu fais (quand te vient a plaisir)
> De guerre paix, & de celle paix guerre.
>
> (dizain 309)

A single word *bataillantes* evokes a visual impression of Délie; it is in a rhyming position and thus calls attention to itself. Corresponding to *bataillantes* is *trauaillantes* in the next line and through these two lines,

> Mais ie sentis ses deux mains bataillantes,
> Qui s'opposoient aux miennes trauaillantes . . . ,

we feel the immediate relationship of the two partners, both straining in a physical combat. The two adjectives are taken from battle terminology. *Bataillantes* is used only once in *Délie*; so too is *trauaillantes*—thus forming a shock point of density in the whole cycle. Yet the first line *Plus pour esbat* and the later phrases (*quand te plait* and *quand te vient a plaisir*) are "playful," deliberately playing down the intense seriousness of the two adjectives. This levity intensifies the seriousness and makes the dizain something very different from Marot's playfulness, for in him the *badinage* is not set against a seriousness. I am suggesting here that Scève is the first modern European to use the "wit" of, say, Propertius or Horace for his own vernacular poetry.

This leads me in to my next point: the Latin virility of Scève's style. Throughout the Renaissance and the seventeenth century in France and England, the Latin force of masculinity, the muscular imagery, the intellectual character of virility and the dense vigor dominated in their poetics. Scève, in the preliminary poem, talked of his *durs epigrammes*, meaning hard-hitting compactness, the difficulty, the turning away from Petrarchan *dolcezze* and the implication that he was going to write in a tough, heroic and harsh style. The hardness, the harshness (what Odette de Mourgues called "unfrench characteristics," p. 22) of his style strike one forcibly. Take the articulation of the dizain which has been often commented upon. Since the publication of Jerry Nash's Concordance[22] we are able to test some hypotheses: for example, his use of conjunctions like *mais* (182 times of use), *car* (108 times), *donc* (45), *affin* (15), *ainsi* (74), *doncques* (11), *certes* (16) and *alors* (16). Scève, by choosing to articulate so often a dizain around intellectual terms, shows acuteness of intellect. Through language he is able to be introspective in a lucid and creative way. That the hardness and even severity of Scève's technique is akin to Donne's is based on several pieces of testimony. Jonson's phrase that "Done himself, for not being understood, would perish," is the same as Charles Fontaine said about Scève's poetry:

> Brief, ilz ne quierent un Lecteur,
> Mais la commune autorité
> Dit qu'ilz requierent un Docteur.

And secondly, we have Carew's fine piece of literary criticism on Donne in *An Elegie upon the Death of the Deane of Paul's, Dr Iohn Donne*. Donne, argued Carew, had cleared pedantry and servile imitation away; he brought fresh invention and masculine expression to poetry; he had steered towards hardness,

> Since to the awe of thy imperious wit
> Our stubborn language bends, made only fit
> With her tough thick-ribbed loops to gird about
> Thy giant fancy, which had proved too stout
> For their soft melting phrases.

The manly style of Donne is at one with his "strong" lines. Donald Davie[23] gives a very interesting comment on the "strong" lines of metaphysical poetry: "Verse may be 'strong' or it may 'aspire to the condition of music'; it cannot do both." Is this not equally applicable to Scève and Donne? The former "never aims at musical effects or at loveliness for loveliness' sake" (Odette de Mourgues, p. 22), while the latter uses roughly accented, almost tuneless lines: "I sing not Syren-like to tempt; for I am harsh . . . ." They both, in my opinion, go against the "platonic" tradition of poetry which Ronsard or "the hony droping Daniel" subscribed to, and prefer a more "Roman" tradition. They both address themselves to an intellectual élite who have their sensuality aerated by intelligence. Both hold that, in Seneca's phrase, "Non est ornamentum virile concinnitas," and they both demand participation on the part of the reader.[24]

In one sense all poetry demands a reader. But in another sense metaphysical poets require one imperiously and urgently to be ready to tackle serious and difficult problems. I shall end this essay by reading slowly aloud to myself dizain 48 and see what happens:

> Si onc la Mort fut tresdoulcement chere,
> A l'Ame doulce ores cherement plaict:
> Et si la vie eust onc ioyeuse chere,
> Toute contente en ce corps se complaict.
> A l'vn aggrée, & a l'aultre desplaict
> L'estre apparent de ma vaine fumée,
> Qui tost estaincte, & soubdain rallumée,
> Tien l'esperance en lubrique seiour.
> Dont, comme au feu le Phœnix, emplumée
> Meurt, & renaist en moy cent fois le iour.

That stunning line—*L'estre apparent de ma vaine fumée*—strikes and shocks me in almost the same way as "Je hume ici ma future fumée" in Valéry's *Le Cimetière marin* or Reverdy's "Le délire aux doigts de cristal." This intimate fusion of concrete with abstract, the idea of "besmoaking" thrust on the reader makes the mental configuration visible and palpable: indeed the poets translate almost voluptuously abstract, intellectual thoughts. The poets give one the emotive shock which stings one to explore further the content of the poems—to reach more than an emotive stage, to experience an aesthetic emotion. The argument of the Scève dizain describes the conflicting attractions of life and death to his body and soul respectively with the result that the poet's existence constantly vacillates and his hope is "en lubrique seiour." The first four lines "play" with death and life: for example, the paradox in the first line, *Mort . . . tresdoulcement chere*, where the adverb occurs only in this poem; the *chere* is thrown across to the adverb *cherement* in the second line, which thrusts it back as an adjective in the third line. Similarly, the adverb *tresdoulcement* becomes the adjective *doulce* in line 2. The alliteration in line 4 is strongly marked. The whole section strongly depicts an uncertain position where the "playful" elements intensify the theme. The next few lines play around the brilliant line (mentioned before) two sets of opposites: *aggrée* and *desplaict*, and *estaincte* and *rallumée*. At this point the comparison with the Phoenix enters: the last two lines evoke the perpetual dyings and rebirths of this fabulous bird. The Phoenix is an attribute of hope since it rises continually from the dead ashes of its former body. The strength of the image here lies in the fact that the two things being compared are the vacillating hope within the poet and the dying-renascent Phoenix. The attributes of the Phoenix are concretely transferred to the poet's hope: thus, *esperance* becomes *emplumée* and *meurt & renaist en moy*. The acceleration of this dying-rebirth process expressed through the phrase *cent fois le iour* conveys the constant tension of the poet's life and expectations as well as the tumul-tuous and sudden vicissitudes in his experience of love. The poem has blos-somed from abstraction into a rich world of legendary associations. The very timelessness and grandeur of the Phoenix also serve to amplify and make more significant the poet's hope.

Scève has intellectual subtlety and sophisticated use of imagery and paradoxical reasoning in a passionate way. What he does not have is the homely language and the natural utterance of the spoken language. It is the aristocratic characteristics of sixteenth-century French poetry as it was inherited from Rome that mark Scève. In the same way as Eliot, who detects, rightly in my opinion, a kind of "wit" in Marvell, may I suggest that we look for and find a "wit" in Scève: a quickness of intellect with powerful expression which succeeds, sometimes, in shocking and disturb-ing the reader. The discipline of art, the sense of proportion, the intellec-tual subtlety and the fiery clarity of his intense vision stir in me mental and physical excitement as I enter his puzzling world of love and life. An intellectual poet who is constantly inspecting and criticizing his experience by means of an intellect aerated by sensibility.

NOTES

1. H.J.C. Grierson in the introduction to his *Metaphysical Lyrics and Poems of the Seventeenth Century* (London, 1921).

2. T.S. Eliot, *Selected Essays* (London, 1932), p. 293.

3. His article "On Metaphysical Poetry" first appeared in *Scrutiny*, Dec. 1933, and can now be found in the posthumous book, *Shakespeare and Other Essays*, ed. E.M. Wilson (Cambridge, 1975).

4. *Elizabethan and Metaphysical Imagery* (Chicago, 1947).

5. "Then Malherbe came," *The Criterion*, 10 (1930), 286-306.

6. *Metaphysical, Baroque and Précieux Poetry* (Oxford, 1953).

7. Guy Miege, *A New Dictionary French and English with Another English and French* (London, 1677).

8. *Oeuvres poétiques complètes de Maurice Scève*, ed. B. Guégan (Paris, 1927), p. 312, my italics.

9. This verbal wit in Scève would bear further analysis, for it is one of the ele-ments of Latin poetry—e.g. Propertius—and is going to be a quality in metaphysical poetry—e.g. Marvell.

10. Especially in his essay on Andrew Marvell, in *Selected Essays*, pp. 292-304.

11. The edition used throughout is The *"Délie" of Maurice Scève*, ed. I.D. McFarlane (Cambridge, 1966).

12. Note the number of times *Dame* is isolated by two commas in the whole cycle: for example, 81, 1: "Ne t'esbahis, Dame, si celle foudre": 194, 1: "Suffise toy, ô Dame, de dorer"; 216, 3: "Dedans mon Ame, ô Dame, tu demeures"; 238, 1: "Ta cruaulté, Dame, tant seulement"; 364, 2: "Prendre congé, & te dire a Dieu, Dame";

377, 3: "Et de moy, Dame, asseurance te baille"; and 408, 5: "Mais bien me soit, Dame, pour tumbe humide." There is something lapidary about Scève's use of punctuation which could well deserve analysis.

13. See dizain 8, where *Dame* is the fifth syllable of line 5; dizain 12 has *certes* in the same position; dizain 36 has *possible*; dizain 316 has *moy miserable* as the center. One could say that Scève's punctuation was crucial.

14. See other examples in *Délie*: 36, 8: "Constituer en serue obeissance," and 330, 6: "Constitua en ce sainct lieu de viure."

15. *Dictionary of the French and English Tongues* (London, 1611).

16. Compare dizain 378, where the poet, in the last few lines, is certain that she—above all she—can give him immortality. Note too the strong punctuation on line 7: "Mais toy, qui as (toy seule) le possible / De donner heur a ma fatalité, / Tu me seras la Myrrhe incorruptible / Contre les vers de ma mortalité."

17. Valéry, in *Je disais à Mallarmé (Oeuvres complètes,* Pléiade edition [1957], I, 652), characterized some poets—among whom I would place Scève—as composing "dans une même œuvre les qualités de séduction immédiate qui sont essentielles à la poésie, avec une substance précieuse de pensée sur quoi l'esprit puisse revenir et s'arrêter quelque peu sans regret."

18. A. Ernout and A. Meillet, *Dictionnaire étymologique de la langue latine* (Paris, 1951, 3rd ed.), *sub* Libitina.

19. See the clash of adverb/adjective in the following examples: 130, 1: "Tant me fut lors cruellement piteuse"; 188, 4: "Craingnant tes mains piteusement cruelles"; 372, 7: "Celle doulceur celestement humaine"; 143, 4: "Ie me nourris de si doulce mensonge"; 421, 10: "Ma volonté sainctement obstinée"; 424, 5: "Mesmes son œil pudiquement peruers"; and 212, 4: "Furent le mal tressainctement inique."

20. *An Illustrated Love 'Canzoniere': The 'Délie' of Maurice Scève*, Bibliotheca franco-italiana (Geneva-Paris, 1981).

21. I give here some examples that have not been discussed: 439, 2: "Alimenté est le sens du doulx songe"; 366, 7: "Pour m'allaicter ce pendant qu'il croissoit"; 166, 10: "Apouriroyt l'odorante Sabée"; 155, 2: "Cuysant le Corps, les mouelles consume"; 227, 1: "Pour m'efforcer à degluer les yeulx"; 76, 6: "M'entreclouit le poursuyvre du cy"; 285, 7: "Ame enyurée au moust d'vn si hault bien"; 65, 7: "Car, savourant le ius de tes saueurs"; 420, 3: "Ne prenne, apres long spasme, grand deffault"; and 174, 10: "Strigile vain a mes sueurs perdues."

22. *Maurice Scève: Concordance de la "Délie,"* 2 vols. (Chapel Hill, 1976).

23. *Articulate Energy: An Enquiry into the Syntax of English Poetry* (London, 1955).

24. For the English background of sixteenth- and seventeenth-century poetics and Donne, see Arnold Stein, "Donne's Harshness and the Elizabethan Tradition," *Studies in Philology*, 41 (1944), 390-410.

François Rigolot

Prosodie et sémantique: Une hypothèse sur le sens des quatrains atypiques dans la *Délie* de Maurice Scève

Il ne semble pas qu'on se soit jusqu'ici interrogé sur la présence de dizains à forme atypique dans la *Délie* de Maurice Scève.[1] On sait qu'à l'exception du huitain initial ce recueil est constitué de 449 dizains en décasyllabes sur quatre rimes. Or, si l'auteur a adopté pour la grande majorité d'entre eux la disposition des rimes la plus courante à l'époque (celle de deux quatrains croisés, réunis par un distique, selon le schéma ABAB BC CDCD), il a néanmoins introduit quinze exceptions à ce schéma en substituant à l'un des quatrains croisés un quatrain embrassé, soit en position initiale soit en position finale. Ces dizains anormaux se répartissent de la façon suivante:

—11 dizains à quatrain embrassé initial: 27, 46, 51, 60, 171, 190, 196, 198, 218, 224 et 264 (*ABBA* AC CDCD);
—4 dizains à quatrain embrassé final: 280, 331, 334 et 336 (ABAB BC *CDDC*).

Ces quinze exceptions à une pratique courante de la prosodie posent un problème d'interprétation que le stylisticien ne peut esquiver. En effet, chez un poète aussi "dur pour son génie" que Maurice Scève (et Odette de Mourgues n'a pas pour peu contribué à renouveler l'intérêt que nous lui portons),[2] il est impossible de mettre ces variations formelles sur le compte du hasard ou de la négligence. Pour un artisan du vers aussi scrupuleux ces déviations devaient avoir un sens dans l'économie complexe du recueil. C'est à propos de la recherche de ce sens que nous voudrions formuler ici une hypothèse qui s'appuie à la fois sur les données de l'histoire littéraire, sur l'étude des poétiques de l'époque et sur une analyse précise de la fonction de cette forme atypique dans l'économie du recueil.

L'étude des poétiques de la fin du quinzième et du début du seizième siècles nous apprend que l'emploi des formes croisées et embrassées est étroitement solidaire de la pratique des deux grands poèmes à forme fixe, la *ballade* et le *rondeau*. Ainsi les *arts de seconde rhétorique* tendent tous à associer le schéma croisé à la ballade alors qu'ils voient dans le schéma embrassé la caractéristique principale du rondeau. On parle de "rimes de rondeaux" pour désigner la strophe ABBA et de "croisure de balades" pour caractériser la disposition ABAB.[3] Dans son *Art de Rethorique vulgaire* Jean Molinet remarque que les rimes "se croisent" à propos de la "ballade commune";[4] en revanche, il donne des exemples de schémas embrassés au chapitre des "virlais," le virelai n'étant qu'une variante du rondeau.[5]

La même tendance s'observe chez Clément Marot. La disposition croisée qui gouverne ses épigrammes en forme de dizains est également la règle dans ses ballades de dix vers décasyllabiques: ABAB BC CDCD. C'est d'ailleurs pourquoi les poéticiens parlent de "dizain marotique" ou "dizain de ballade" pour désigner ce type de poème.[6] Cependant, lorsqu'il écrit ses rondeaux (et le "rondeau simple" est celui qui se rapproche le plus du dizain puisqu'il se compose de deux quatrains reliés par un distique), il recourt à la rime embrassée selon le schéma: ABBA AB ABBA.[7] Dans son *Art poétique françois* (1548), Thomas Sebillet, le législateur du Parnasse marotique, reprend dans sa définition du *dizain* le modèle "régulier" du schéma croisé: "Entens donc que reguliérement au dizain lés 4. premiers vers croisent, et lés 4. derniers."[8] Il donne, en revanche, une description du *rondeau simple* fondée sur la définition de la rime embrassée: "Le Rondeau simple ha quattrain en premier couplet, et quattrain en dernier, unisones, dont lés premiers et derniers vers symbolisent, et lés deus du mylieu demeurent en ryme platte" (ibid. p. 123).

Tout porte donc à croire qu'au moment où il va écrire sa *Délie* Maurice Scève se trouve devant une situation prosodique sans ambiguïté: s'il veut écrire son recueil en dizains, il doit se conformer au modèle marotique qui fait autorité et utiliser la fameuse "croisure de balades." Cette présomption est si forte que Sebillet, citant la *Délie* dans sa définition du dizain, croit pouvoir affirmer qu'il en est effectivement ainsi dans *tous* les poèmes du recueil scévien. Après avoir donné la règle des quatrains croisés, il ajoute à l'adresse de son lecteur: "comme tu peus voir en ce dizain pris de la Delie de Scève, *et en tous les autres dont ell' est pleine*" (ibid., p. 111). Autrement dit, les quinze quatrains embrassés de la *Délie* constituent bel et bien une *infraction à la norme* dont il est tentant de vouloir rendre compte; et cela d'autant plus qu'ils semblent s'immiscer sournoisement dans le texte sans raison apparente.

La première solution qui se présente à l'esprit est évidemment celle de la *contamination des genres*. Scève aurait voulu introduire une des caractéristiques, reconnue comme majeure, du rondeau dans l'économie du dizain balladique. On est alors amené à se demander quelles sont les connotations poétiques particulières qu'attribuent les théoriciens au rondeau et que Scève aurait voulu récupérer, au moins partiellement, dans sa *Délie*. En fait, les manuels de *seconde rhétorique* sont unanimes à insister sur la *circularité* du genre: "Fault que les lignes [soient] *retournantes* et sugites a la premiere ligne," lit-on dans les *Regles de seconde rhetorique* (Langlois, p. 20); et Jacques Legrand, dans son traité *Des Rimes* précise: "[Rondeaulx] vont en rondelant et en respondant baston [c'est-à-dire: vers] a aultre, et pour tant sont ilz ainsi nommez" (Langlois, p. 4). Même si cette étymologie est fantaisiste, elle témoigne d'une métonymie sémantique fort intéressante: c'est le mouvement tournant du poème sur lui-même qui est perçu comme caractéristique du rondeau.[9]

Le Grant et Vray Art de pleine Rhetorique de Pierre Fabri, dont les six éditions au moins—de 1521 à 1544—attestent le succès,[10] ne parle pas autrement au sujet du rondeau. Il reprend d'ailleurs plus d'un de ses exemples à l'Infortuné, autrement dit à l'auteur du *Jardin de plaisance et fleur de rhetorique* (publié, rappelons-le, par Antoine Vérard vers 1500). On y lit des déclarations de ce type: "Qui veult faire rondeau, il le doibt faire *rond*," "Tout rondeau doibt estre *clos en soy*" (ibid. p. 63). Sans doute cet effet de rondeur, de fermeture sur soi est-il dû en priorité au refrain dont la répétition fait l'originalité du genre.[11] Mais le schéma embrassé contribue à renforcer cette impression de retour du chant sur lui-même. C'est bien d'ailleurs ce qu'exprime le verbe *symboliser* lorsque Sebillet l'emploie pour définir la rime du rondeau.[12] "Symboliser" c'est s'accorder, se ressembler, avoir des rapports d'affinité. Synonyme de "convenir," ce verbe, jugé à la mode par d'Aubigné, suggère la conformité, la concorde; de là son emploi par les poéticiens pour signifier: *rimer avec*.[13]

Ainsi l'insertion de schémas embrassés dans le dizain marotique pourrait s'interpréter comme le désir, de la part de Scève, de produire, par intermittence et en des points déterminés du texte, un *effet de rondeau* caractérisé par le mouvement tournant, le retour sur soi, la *circularité* et la *fermeture*.

Pour avoir quelque vraisemblance, cette hypothèse doit évidemment pouvoir s'accorder avec la thématique du recueil; car les lois de la prosodie restent toujours des guides extérieurs qui demandent, pour devenir valides, la confirmation d'indices textuels particuliers.

Telle que nous venons de la définir, la fonction du quatrain embrassé est, de toute évidence, en accord profond avec l'esthétique scévienne de l'*enfermement*. Le thème de la "liberté . . . asseruie" (6), de la captivité heureuse (207), du "doulx seruage," trouve son expression graphique et phonique dans l'étau constitué par la disposition des rimes: A BB A. On croit entendre la voix même de l'amant prisonnier qui désigne l'instrument de son supplice: "Voyez comment [la rime] en prison nous vient mettre!" (276). La rime n'est pas le "bijou d'un sou," mais le joujou d'un fou. Fou génial qui fait *symboliser*, comme dirait Sebillet, sa prison textuelle avec sa prison mentale. La chevelure emprisonne par ses "laqz" (296), ses "noudz" (135, 386), ses "rhetz" (46, 324, 411), et, parallèlement, le poète cultive une forme poétique qui traduit cet asservisssement thématique.[14]

Il serait alors tentant de vérifier dans les quinze dizains atypiques l'existence de signaux thématiques précis qui *surdéterminent*, pour ainsi dire, la sémantique du schéma embrassé et offrent une justification textuelle à l'infraction qu'ils représentent. Plutôt que de considérer, l'un après l'autre, chacun des quinze dizains en question, nous examinerons d'abord le dizain 224 qui offre la particularité d'occuper le centre exact du recueil et jouit, de ce fait, d'un statut poétique tout spécial. Il n'est pas question de revenir ici sur un phénomène connu qu'illustre particulièrement la tradition médiévale. On sait l'importance du centre, du point médian (la critique de langue anglaise parle de "midpoint") dans la composition des romans et des poèmes épiques.[15] L'emploi délibéré d'une telle structuration ne devrait pas étonner chez Scève, si méticuleux dans ses constructions formelles et si désireux de maintenir une double allégeance vis-à-vis des traditions italienne et française.

Il n'est d'ailleurs pas besoin de faire intervenir ces éléments relatifs à la théorie de l'imitation pour justifier l'importance du dizain 224 dans l'économie de la *Délie*. L'analyse attentive du poème suffit en soi à prouver sa fonction métaphorique dans le défilé métonymique du recueil. Mais rappelons-en d'abord l'énoncé:

> Nouelle amour, nouelle affection,
> Nouelles fleurs parmy l'herbe nouelle:
> Et,ià passée, encor se renouelle

> Ma Primeuere en sa verte action.
> Ce neantmoins la renouation
> De mon vieulx mal, & vlcere ancienne
> Me detient tout en celle saison sienne,
> Ou le meurdrier m'a meurdry, & noircy
> Le Cœur si fort, que playe Egyptienne,
> Et tout tourment me rend plus endurcy.
>
> (dizain 224)

Si l'on compte, comme on doit le faire, le huitain d'ouverture comme le premier poème du recueil (c'était le cas dans l'édition *princeps* de 1544, la seule qui doit être retenue),[16] la position centrale du dizain 224 ne fait aucun doute. On a en effet le décompte suivant: huitain initial / 224 dizains / 224 dizains / dizain final. En outre, cette centralité s'affirme par le double lien sémantique qui s'établit avec le huitain initial et le dizain final. Le thème de la *rénovation*, développé avec insistance dans le premier quatrain (*"Nouelle* amour . . . "*) reprend en l'accentuant la fameuse déclaration du huitain initial: "les morts, qu'en moy tu *renouelles* . . . " (v. 3). Le parti-pris pour la *dureté*, pour la difficulté de la forme, qui s'exprime, dans le huitain, "en si *durs* Epygrammes" trouve un écho au dernier vers du dizain mitoyen: "Et tout tourment me rend plus *endurcy.*" Cette dureté, gage de la durée, a été obtenue grâce à l'épreuve du feu:

> Amour (pourtant) les me voyant escrire
> En ta faueur, les passa par ses *flammes.*

Ces derniers mots de la dédicace (huitain initial) annoncent les premiers mots de la conclusion (dizain final) qui reprennent le jeu sur durée/dureté: "*Flamme* si saincte en son cler *durera.*" Le renouvellement des "mortz" (huitain initial), devenu rénovation du mal d'aimer (dizain mitoyen), s'avoue finalement nouveauté perpétuelle par l'immortalité poétique (dizain final). C'est bien le sens des deux derniers vers:

> Nostre Geneure ainsi doncques viura
> Non offensé d'aulcun mortel Letharge.

L'éternel printemps du genévrier ne renvoie pas seulement à l'arbuste emblématique de l'Arioste;[17] il est aussi une notation *auto-textuelle*, une allusion à la "Primeuere" du dizain central qui, désormais, "se renouelle" pour toujours "en sa verte action."

Or c'est justement dans le quatrain atypique du centre que s'exprime la *Primavera* de Maurice Scève. Le printemps correspond au moment où le soleil arrive au point d'intersection de l'écliptique et de l'équateur; les jours y sont égaux aux nuits comme, dans la *Délie*, les poèmes qui précèdent

224 sont aussi nombreux que ceux qui le suivent. Ce quatrain embrassé est donc véritablement le *point équinoxial* du recueil. En lui se reproduit ce mouvement de retour sur soi du chant que nous avons signalé comme caractéristique des *rimes de rondeau*. Bien plus, à la circularité dynamique de ces quatre premiers vers s'oppose la linéarité statique des six vers qui suivent. Le contraste est frappant: dans le sizain tout n'est que vieillissement ("mon *vieulx* mal, & vlcere *ancienne*"), souffrance ("*playe* Egyptienne," "tout *tourment*"), détention ("Me *detient* tout en celle saison *sienne*"), durcissement ("me rend plus *endurcy*") et mort ("le *meurdrier* m'a *meurdry*, & *noircy*"). Pour reprendre la métaphore cosmographique, si 224 est le point équinoxial du recueil, alors le quatrain de la "Primeuere" correspond à l'équinoxe de printemps tandis que le sizain de la "saison sienne" signale l'autre équinoxe, celui de l'automne.

A cette lecture d'astronome, qui s'accorde d'ailleurs fort bien avec les préoccupations de l'époque et que Scève a certainement voulu inscrire dans le schéma plus vaste du conflit entre les principes lunaire (Diane-Délie) et solaire (Delius-Apollon), s'en ajoute une autre, non moins troublante. Le quatrain équinoxial peut en effet se lire aussi, selon toute vraisemblance, de façon allégorique: il porte alors un éclairage nouveau sur la création poétique au *milieu* de sa course, "nel *mezzo* del camin di nostra *via*," pour parler comme Dante. Tout se passe comme si, arrivé au centre de son ouvrage, le poète ne pouvait offrir la promesse de "nouelle amour, nouelle affection" sans signifier *aussi* qu'il annonce à son lecteur de nouveaux dizains, "nouelles *fleurs* parmy l'herbe nouelle." La triple apposition anaphorique de la rénovation, dans les deux premiers vers, prend d'ailleurs un sens encore plus nettement auto-référentiel dans les deux vers suivants:

> Et, ià passée, encor se renouelle
> Ma Primeuere en sa verte action.
> (vv. 3-4)

Un huitain et 223 dizains viennent de "passer" ("ià passée"); 225 dizains nouveaux sont annoncés ("encor se renouelle"). Comment, dès lors, ne pas lire "Ma Primeuere" comme "mon activité poétique" qui se déploie dans le printemps renouvelé de l'inspiration.

Il faut d'ailleurs s'arrêter sur ce mot "action" parce qu'il mérite un commentaire. Son abstraction même, et sa généralité, lui confèrent une polyvalence sémantique qui autorise une pluralité de lectures. Certes, à un premier niveau, on a raison de citer le *Dictionnaire* de Huguet et de donner pour "action: attitude, contenance, gestes."[18] Mais il ne faut pas oublier qu'à un niveau poétique ce terme a un sens beaucoup plus précis. L'*action*, c'est l'activité de l'*Acteur*, double de l'*auteur* (latin *actorem*: qui agit, par confusion avec *auctorem*). Scève qui, comme le remarquait déjà Parturier, "continue à certains égards l'école des rhétoriqueurs,"[19] n'ignorait certes pas ce sens du mot "action" dans le contexte littéraire où il l'avait rencontré. Il n'ignorait pas non plus la signification du latin *actio* dans les traités de rhétorique. Ce mot servait à traduire la figure qu'Aristote appelait *energeia (Rhét.* III, xi, 2-4), cette aptitude à rendre les choses vivantes par un style animé. Quintilien employait d'ailleurs le gérondif *agendo* pour signifier la même chose: la vertu de l'*energia* est de dire les faits en action ("est enim ab *agendo* dicta").[20]

En outre, on sait que depuis Dante le mot "Primeuere" se prête aux jeux de la "remotivation" sémantique. Dans la *Vita nuova* (chapitre XXIV) Amour explique que *Primavera* veut dire *prima verrà* (première elle viendra). A ce compte, on pourrait voir dans *primevère* une allusion phonique aux *premiers vers* et dans *verte action* une référence à l'*action en vers* du poète. Il y aurait alors une coïncidence troublante entre les numérologies de Dante et de Scève (chapitre XXIV *vs* dizain 224). Le premier quatrain du dizain central pourrait se lire ainsi:

Nouelle amour, nouelle affection,
(*le même thème continue, mais renouvelé*)

Nouelles fleurs parmy l'herbe nouelle:
(*on trouvera de nouvelles fleurs de rhétorique dans mes nouveaux dizains*)

Et, ià passée, encor se renouelle
Ma Primeuere en sa verte action.
(*et, aussitôt terminée la première partie de ce poème, la seconde lui succède, œuvre vivante de poésie*)

Cette traduction en prose est évidemment abusive, dans la mesure même où elle réduit un texte polysémique à une signification unique. Cependant, dans sa littéralité inadmissible, elle rend compte de l'existence d'un sens allégorique en ce moment privilégié du recueil où le poète fait *retour* sur son expérience poétique pour la signaler comme telle. Si, selon l'expression d'Alfred Glauser, chaque dizain est "comme un huis-clos dans lequel [le poète] a choisi de s'enfermer,"[21] alors le quatrain embrassé du dizain central est la signature de cet enfermement puisqu'il exhibe la "rime de rondeau" pour en faire la théorie.

On peut alors se demander comment se situent les quatorze autres quatrains atypiques de la *Délie* par rapport à celui de la "Primeuere" et si leur fonction s'accorde avec celle que nous venons brièvement de décrire.

Observons d'abord que l'on peut répartir les dizains où ils apparaissent selon le tableau suivant:

A) 10 dizains à quatrain initial embrassé (ABBA):
—un groupe de 4 dans la série 1-100: 27, 46, 51 et 60;
—un second groupe de 4 dans la série 100-200: 171, 190, 196 et 198;
—un groupe de 2 dans la série 200-300: 218 et 264.

B) 4 dizains à quatrain final embrassé (CDDC):
280, 331, 334 et 336.

Il est remarquable que tous les dizains du modèle (ABBA) précèdent ceux au type (CDDC). Il y a là un placement voulu de la part de ce grand agenceur de rimes qu'est notre poète; et ce plan demande, bien sûr, à être interprété.

Observons ensuite que dans cette série de 14 éléments les sous-groupes s'ordonnent selon la proportion 4/4/2/4, ce qui présente un rapport d'analogie flagrant avec la composition du sonnet. En effet, si en théorie le sonnet se compose de deux quatrains et de deux tercets, dans la pratique qui s'instaure avec Marot il comprend: deux quatrains embrassés (ABBA), un distique (CC) et un quatrain final embrassé (DEED). Autrement dit, du point de vue de la disposition des rimes, le sonnet marotique se conforme au schéma 4/4/2/4 qui est celui que suit Scève pour répartir ses quatrains embrassés dans l'ensemble de la *Délie*. Cette adéquation des numérologies est assez troublante pour qu'on cherche à formuler une hypothèse qui l'explique au moins en partie.

Il est certain que la structure du sonnet marotique représente le triomphe du quatrain embrassé. Contrairement à Peletier qui propose de terminer par un quatrain croisé (DEDE), Marot—qui a sans doute introduit le genre en France[22]—généralise l'emploi du dispositif embrassé dans les trois quatrains du sonnet.[23] Or, lorsque Marot publie son premier sonnet (le seul d'ailleurs des trois "sonnets authentiques" qu'il ait publié), il ne lui donne pas ce titre: le poème figure au *Second Livre des Epigrammes* dans l'édition des *Oeuvres* de 1538.[24] Ceci montre bien que le plus grand poète de l'époque assimilait alors le sonnet à l'épigramme. Nous avons montré ailleurs ce que Scève devait à Marot et comment le poète lyonnais avait transformé l'épigramme marotique, écrite sous des formes strophiques extrêmement variables, en un poème à forme fixe, le dizain isostrophique et isométrique de la *Délie*.[25] Il serait maintenant tentant de considérer la pratique du quatrain embrassé dans les "durs Epygrammes" de la *Délie* comme un hommage à l'illustrateur de l'épigramme française et à l'inventeur du sonnet français.[26]

Clément Marot n'était d'ailleurs pas le seul à rapprocher le sonnet de l'épigramme. Dans son *Art poëtique françoys*, Sebillet place le chapitre sur le sonnet tout de suite après celui sur l'épigramme et commence en ces termes:

Du Sonnet

Qu'est Sonnet.—Le Sonnet suit l'epigramme de bien prés, et de matiére, et de mesure: Et quant tout est dit, *Sonnet n'est autre chose que le parfait epigramme de l'Italien, comme le dizain du François.*[27]

En outre, le théoricien de l'école marotique divise le sonnet en deux quatrains et un sizain, selon le rythme 4/4/2/4, en insistant sur la description de la rime embrassée dans le dernier quatrain. "Lés [vers] 4. et 5. [du sizain] fraternizent aussy en ryme platte, mais differente de celle dés deux premiers: et le tiers et siziéme symbolisent aussy en toute diverse ryme dés quatre autres" (ibid., p. 116). Il cite alors le sonnet de Marot, "Au ciel n'y a ne Planette ne signe" comme le modèle du genre.

On pourrait également citer l'étrange témoignage d'un Italien de Lyon selon qui Scève aurait composé et traduit de nombreux sonnets. Il y a certainement là une confusion avec les dizains de la *Délie* qui s'explique par l'assimilation, alors courante, du sonnet à l'épigramme.[28] Quant à Maurice Scève lui-même, on peut aisément comprendre pourquoi il n'a pas composé sa *Délie* en sonnets. Marot avait lancé l'épigramme française à Lyon en 1538; et la strophe qui dominait chez lui était le dizain en décasyllabes sur quatre rimes. On peut imaginer que, sous la pression de milieux humanistes lyonnais, le poète de la *Délie* ait voulu écrire un *canzoniere* d'épigrammes qui reprendrait à Marot l'illustration du genre antique récemment retrouvé.[29] Il semble bien d'ailleurs que Scève ait considéré, sa vie durant, le sonnet comme un *poème d'escorte*, servant de préface ou de dédicace à l'œuvre qu'ils introduisent. Des neuf sonnets que nous avons conservés de lui, six observent la disposition marotique (DEED), les trois autres adoptant un schéma de tercets irréguliers (CDE CDE).[30]

L'idée même que Scève pouvait se faire du sonnet comme *poème d'escorte* intéresse ici notre thèse. En effet, la fonction du système constitué par les quatorze dizains atypiques n'est pas sans analogie avec celle de cet autre système de quatorze vers qu'est le sonnet-préface ou le sonnet-épilogue. Dans un cas comme dans l'autre il s'agit de substituer à la continuité métonymique du discours une pause métaphorique qui sollicite l'interprétation. Il ne faut d'ailleurs pas sous-estimer la *valeur ornementale* de cette pratique. Les habitudes de lecture du seizième siècle rendent fort bien compte de ce goût du décor de l'œuvre littéraire. Cependant le souci de l'ornementation formelle n'est jamais cultivé pour lui-même dans les grandes œuvres poétiques, il doit aussi enrichir le *sens* du texte qu'il est chargé d'agrémenter. En somme, on pourrait parler de la *fonction décorative* des dizains atypiques dans la même mesure que l'on parle à propos des emblèmes de la *Délie*. Emblèmes et quatrains embrassés constituent des séries, plaisantes à l'œil, curieuses pour l'esprit, et dont le symbolisme visuel invite à l'interprétation.

Il n'est pas question de chercher ici une explication plus ou moins "cabalistique" sur le modèle de celle qu'on a proposé pour justifier la distribution des emblèmes dans le texte. Cela ne veut pas dire qu'il faille écarter, avant tout examen, la possibilité d'une telle interprétation. On pourrait très bien imaginer qu'il existe des correspondances secrètes entre la place des dizains atypiques et les étapes d'un itinéraire initiatique que le poème invite à reconstituer. S'il en était ainsi, les spéculations ésotériques sur la répartition des emblèmes trouveraient une vraisemblance accrue. Nous laissons à d'autres le soin d'enquêter dans ce domaine, préférant nous en tenir à la seule description objective des phénomènes de surface.

En conclusion, nous pouvons avancer que le choix et l'organisation des dizains atypiques de la *Délie* répondent à un project précis dont il est possible de reconstituer l'essentiel. L'hypothèse, tacitement tenue jusqu'ici par la critique, de la gratuité des schémas erratiques n'est plus désormais recevable, même s'il est illusoire de rechercher quelles furent les *intentions* (toutes les intentions) de Scève au moment où il procédait à la composition de son recueil.

La dette que contractait le poète envers Pétrarque et les sonnettistes italiens, compliquée par l'ambivalence de ses rapports avec Marot, permet d'expliquer en partie la constitution de ses quatrains embrassés en système signifiant. La lecture de l'*Art poétique* le plus célèbre de l'époque, celui de Sebillet, apporte d'ailleurs de précieux éclaircissements à ce sujet. En outre, la tradition littéraire qui tend à placer au centre du poème l'apparition d'un événement poétique majeur permet de préciser l'importance du quatrain atypique dans le dizain central du recueil: celui-ci joue le rôle d'art poétique interne, répondant à l'invite du huitain initial et annonçant la promesse du dizain final.

La thématique de l'*enfermement*, qui domine—comme l'a bien vu la critique—l'économie de la *Délie*, trouve sa justification prosodique dans le jalonnement du texte par les quatrains d'exception. Les *arts de seconde rhétorique* décrivent en effet la rime embrassée au chapitre du rondeau, genre strophique qui se caractérise justement par sa *circularité*. Les "durs Epygrammes" de Scève empruntent donc leur forme à la fois à la ballade (ce sont les 434 dizains atypiques à quatrain initial ou final embrassé), autrement dit aux deux derniers genres strophiques à forme fixe que l'on cultive encore au début du seizième siècle. Par le choix de cette forme, Maurice Scève affirme une continuité avec l'héritage poétique français; mais par la distribution de ses poèmes, il annonce aussi ce que sera l'*Olive*, ce que seront les *Amours*, des *canzonieri* où triomphera l'écriture d'un genre étranger.

Enfin, dans son rapport d'analogie avec l'emblématique déclarée du recueil, la pratique distributive des quatrains atypiques signale une tendance de la poésie scévienne à recourir à la symbolique visuelle, interrompant ainsi la métonymique du discours par des pauses métaphoriques que le lecteur (le critique) sera invité à interpréter.

NOTES

1. Comme nous le verrons, Thomas Sebillet est sans doute le premier à s'être trompé sur l'homogénéité de la *Délie* du point de vue prosodique. Voir son *Art poétique françoys* (1548), éd. F. Gaiffe (Paris, 1910), p. 111. Sa postérité est abondante parmi les poéticiens. Ainsi Philippe Martinon parle de Maurice Scève, "dont l'obscure *Délie* est écrite en *dizains de ballade*," autrement dit selon le schéma ABAB BC CDCD (*Les Strophes: Etude historique et critique sur les formes de la poésie lyrique en France depuis la Renaissance* [Paris, 1912], p. 30). I.D. McFarlane est le premier éditeur à parler de ces "dizains atypiques" et à en donner la liste, sans toutefois s'interroger sur leur fonction dans l'économie du recueil. Sauf indication contraire, c'est à cette édition que se rapportent nos références dans le texte: The *"Délie" of Maurice Scève* (Cambridge, 1966).

2. Voir *Metaphysical, Baroque and Précieux Poetry* (Oxford, 1953). Madame de Mourgues a souligné, avec justesse, la complexité d'une poésie qui cherche à transmettre un contenu intellectuel complexe dans une forme particulièrement difficile. Voir en particulier, pp. 10-12.

3. Voir *Recueil d'arts de seconde rhétorique*, éd. E. Langlois (Paris, 1902). Nous nous référons à ce recueil dans le texte en plaçant (Langlois) entre parenthèses. Ainsi le *Traité IV* oppose les "rimes entrelaissiées" aux "rimes desjoinctes," c'est-à-dire la "croisure de ballades" aux "rimes de rondeaulx" (Langlois, pp. 206-07).

4. (Paris, 1493), dans Langlois, pp. 235-36.

5. Ibid., pp. 231, 232. Molinet parle des "rondeaux doubles, qui se nomment simples virlais" (p. 231).

6. Clément Marot a en effet écrit au moins cinq ballades à strophes de dix décasyllabes. Ce dizain balladique est "composé de deux quatrains croisés, réunis par un distique qui leur emprunte leurs rimes voisines, répétant la précédente et amorçant la suivante" (Ph. Martinon, *Les Strophes*, p. 407).

7. Il faut bien sûr ajouter le refrain qui vient s'intercaler après le sixième et le dernier vers sous la forme d'une reprise du premier vers. On a donc: ABBA AB *R* ABBA *R*.

8. Pp. 110-11.

9. Langlois fait remarquer qu' "à l'origine le rondeau était un chant destiné à

accompagner les rondes, marquant par ses alternances de solo et de refrain les évolutions des danseurs" et que "dans les premiers temps on l'appelait aussi *rondet*, autre diminutif de *rond*" (p. 4, n. 4).

10. La première édition est précisément publiée à Lyon, en 1536, par Olivier Arnoullet et il est plus que probable que Scève la connaissait. Cf. l'édition d'A. Heron (1889-90; rpt. Genève: Slatkine, 1969), Introduction, p. xviii.

11. "Ce qui fait l'originalité du rondeau c'est la répétition du refrain," écrit Pierre Villey à propos de Marot. "L'art propre du rondeau est de choisir heureusement ce refrain, et de le *ramener* avec à propos sans qu'on sente l'effort ou l'artifice" (*Marot et Rabelais* [Paris, 1923], p. 55).

12. *Art poëtique françoys*, p. 123; voir aussi l'emploi de ce verbe dans les chapitres "De l'epigramme," p. 197, et "Du Sonnet," p. 116.

13. Cf. Edmond Huguet, *Dictionnaire de la langue française du XVIe siècle* qui donne des exemples de Sebillet et de Foquelin (*Rhetorique françoyse*, 28 vᵒ).

14. Cet emploi métaphorique se retrouve aussi au niveau onomastique. Le lien de servitude ("l'indissolubil nodo") se trouve en même temps *délié* par le jeu de la remotivation du nom propre de Délie. Voir notre *Poétique et onomastique* (Genève, 1977), p. 110.

15. Nous renvoyons pour la bibliographie à notre article sur Dante et Rabelais à paraître dans le numéro spécial de la revue *Littérature* (1981) qui reproduit les *Actes* du colloque de Columbia sur l'intertextualité au moyen âge. La coïncidence entre le numéro du canto central de la *Divine Comédie* et celui du chapitre médian du *Pantagruel* n'est sans doute pas non plus un effet du hasard.

16. Dans la seconde édition, celle de 1564, ce huitain est placé à la fin du recueil; mais cette édition n'a probablement pas été revue par Scève. Voir l'édition d'I.D. McFarlane, p. 104.

17. Contrairement à ce qu'écrit en notes Parturier dans son édition de la *Délie* (Paris, 1916), il s'agit beaucoup moins d'une allusion à la Ginevre de l'*Orlando Furioso* (canto V) qu'au "bel genebro" des *Rime* de l'Arioste (sonnet VII, v. 14) dont aucun éditeur n'a mentionné l'existence. Du Bellay reprendra d'ailleurs cette allusion dans l'*Olive*. Voir l'édition d'E. Caldarini (Genève, 1974), p. 8.

18. Voir McFarlane, p. 434, note sur 224.

19. Introduction, p. xxii.

20. *Inst. Orat.* VIII, iii, 89. Le *Thesaurus Graecae Linguae* de Henri Estienne traduira encore *energeia* par *actio*. Sur l'homonymie *energeia/enargeia*, voir T. Cave, "*Enargeia*: Erasmus and the Rhetoric of Presence in the XVIth Century," *L'Esprit Créateur*, 16 (1976), 5-19; Glyn P. Norton, "Rabelais and the Epic of Palpability," *Symposium* (1979), 171-85.

21. *Le Poème-symbole* (Paris, 1967), pp. 21-22.

22. Le débat sur la précédence de Mellin de Saint-Gelais reste ouvert. Voir l'édition des *Oeuvres diverses* de Marot par C.A. Mayer (Londres, 1966), p. 18.

23. Sans doute le sonnet "Voyant ces noms de veue si loingtaine" a-t-il un schéma atypique (ABBA ABBA CC DDDC); mais il est d'authenticité douteuse. Voir C.A. Mayer, Introduction, pp. 48-49.

24. Ibid., p. 17.

25. "L'Intertexte du dizain scévien," *Cahiers de l'Association Internationale des Etudes Françaises*, 32 (mai 1980), 91-106.

26. Sur l'invention de la première épigramme française, voir C.A. Mayer, Introduction à son édition des *Epigrammes* de Marot (Londres, 1970), pp. 9-10.

27. Livre II, chapitre 2, p. 115.

28. Sur le témoignage de Ridolfi dans l'*Aretefila*, voir V.-L. Saulnier, *Maurice Scève* (Paris, 1948), II, 290.

29. Il ne faudrait pas non plus sous-estimer l'influence de l'épigramme néo-latine, en particulier lyonnaise. La fameuse œuvre collective de 1536, le *Tombeau du Dauphin*, en est la preuve.

30. Maurice Scève, *Oeuvres poétiques complètes*, ed. B. Guégan (Paris, 1927), pp. 191, 274, 290, 291, 292, 299, 300, 301 et 302.

Richard Griffiths

Humor and Complicity in Ronsard's "Continuation des Amours"

Most love poetry which contains humor has tended to rely above all on parody; it is not love poetry in the normal sense of the term, but humorous poetry first and foremost. There is, however, one form of humor, of a subtle and less obvious kind, which emerges in the love poetry of the second half of the sixteenth century. It is very much concerned with the relationship between the poet and his reader and can be found in even the most apparently serious collections of love poetry. Its greatest exponent was Ronsard, though many of his contemporaries and his successors followed his lead, often less successfully; and the emergence of this practice can tell us much about changing attitudes to love poetry in the period.

In Renaissance love poetry, particularly in the sequences of sonnets based on the Petrarchan tradition, there was always a necessary complicity between poet and reader. The reader was fully aware that the poet was an author of "fictions." The poet, therefore, might or might not be writing about personal experience; indeed, the basic presumption would be that he was probably not. In any case, it did not matter. The conventions within which the love-experience was housed were sufficient unto themselves. A poet would choose the conventions within which to write; and these conventions, unreal in human terms, were considered to be real in essential terms. Thus, even if a lived experience lay at the base of a love-collection, it was transmuted into a more ideal form (whether the ideal be of purity or impurity), and reality was left behind. The objects of love who were chosen by love-poets were, therefore, in no way presumed by the reader to equate to real people (except to the extent that noble ladies might be flattered to be chosen to be the basis for a fiction).

There was, nevertheless, a complicity between poet and reader which consisted in the poet's presenting the love-experience as a coherent story which hung together in a real manner. Scève's *Délie*, for example, starts with the poet's first sight of his beloved; and all the emotions expressed, and the events depicted, relate coherently to each other. Poets, in the spate of love-collections following *Délie*, announced at the beginning of their collection the tone in which it was going to be written; and that tone remained constant throughout:

> Qui veut sçavoir en quante, et quelle sorte
> Amour cruel travaille les esprits
> De ceux, qui sont de son ardeur espris,
> Et, le servant, quel fruit on en rapporte:
> Qu'il vienne voir ma peine ardente et forte.[1]

Indeed, the reader is called upon, by Magny for example, to realize the truth of the poet's love through the sight of the poet and his mistress, rather than just through the "sincerity" of the verse:

> Qui le croira, bien qu'en vers je l'escrive,
> Que pour mon mal, difficile à celer,
> Un ardant feu se voye estinceler
> Dans la froideur d'une glace si vive?
>
> Je n'escri rien qui du vray ne derive,
> Mais si quelqu'un ne croit à mon parler,
> Voye ma Dame, et sans plus loing aller,
> Il trouvera la froidure nayve.
>
> Regarde après mon corps jà consumé,
> Il le verra vivement alumé
> Du cler rayon de sa beauté celeste:
> Et cognoistra que sa dure froideur
> Alume en moy la devorante ardeur
> Et le brazier qui me brusle et moleste.[2]

The poetic conventions are thus transposed into "real" life, and the reader is expected to accept these conventions in the spirit in which they are offered. The game between the poet and the reader has already started.

Where this game of complicity begins to depart from this norm is in the mid-1550's, and the best example of this departure is Ronsard's *Continuation des Amours* (1555). Here the poet, as well as writing playful love poetry to his mistress, extends that playfulness to his reader and to his fellow-poets and in the process calls into question the convention of complicity.

The *Continuation des Amours* differs from contemporary love-sequences in a number of ways. What must be stressed, however, is that it does *not* differ from them in its change from one style of poetic language and creation to another. Enough has been written about the years 1550-1555 for us to know that a considerable change came over the writing of love-poetry in this short period, mainly because of the greater popularity of certain "new" sources for inspiration. This change was common to a number of other contemporary poets; how, when they changed, did they explain *their* new stance to their accomplices, the readers?

Tyard approached the problem in a very straightforward way in his 1555 Third Book of *Erreurs amoureuses*: he had been exhausted by "burning" for his beloved in vain. If, therefore, his (Tyard's) beloved would become less fierce towards him, he, too, would write in a simpler way:

> Donq adouci la rigueur qui me touche:
> Car si je voy ta beauté moins farouche,
> Je te peindray d'un pinceau plus naïf.[3]

Baïf, on the other hand, claimed that it was because of a new mistress that he was writing differently. Not only that, but he broke the unspoken convention by proclaiming that his first collection, the *Amours* (1552), had been written to a purely imaginary woman, Méline, whereas now (1555) he was writing to a *real* person:

> . . . Des mon enfance i'ai sonné
> Une amour contrefaite.
> Afin qu'un iour i'eusse le pris
> Entre les Amans mieux apris
> A chanter leur detresse,
> Si vraiement i'etois epris
> D'une vraie maistresse.[4]

The reality of this love, he wrote, had made him write in less polished manner. He would have liked to have been able to write about her in a "stile plus haut":

> Mais lise, qui voudra, les liures pour aprendre
> Des auteurs anciens la science immortelle,
> D'aeles se garnissant pour uoler à la gloire:
> Quant à moy sans cela i'ose bien entreprendre
> Guidé de tes beaux yeux et de leur clarté belle
> Dresser de notre amour assez longue memoire.[5]

He surrounded this concept with all the commonplaces about "poésie feinte" which abounded in the mid-50's, more usually in an "anti-Petrar-

chan" context, and which are now generally accepted to have been not serious statements of "anti-Petrarchism," but one more arrow in the quiver of
Petrarchan conventions: "sous un nom feint . . . ,"[6] "Ni mon amour n'est
point imaginee, / Ni feindre un heur ie ne me veux aussi,"[7] "Croy pour
vray que l'Amour me tourmente . . . / Sans rien feindre au plus pres ie pein
l'heur maleureux."[8] Indeed, the word "vrai" occasionally gets over-played:

> Et ne soit leu rien emprunté
> Des passions etranges,
> En tout ce que i'aurai chanté
> De tes vraies louanges
>
> Rien pour moy ie ne mentirai
> En ces chansons, que i'écriray
> De notre amitié vraie,
> Tout ainsi que ie sentirai,
> D'amour la vraie plaie.
>
> Si que celui qui les lira
> Vraiement tout raui dira,
> Combien une amour nette
> En mes chansons s'eloignera
> D'une amour contrefaite.[9]

In the famous poem addressed by Baïf to Ronsard, the poet defends his
simple style against Ronsard's criticisms that it is not "learned" enough
and accuses him of being unaware of the effect of love upon the writing
of poetry:

> Las amy las, las de quelle matiere
> Le cueur as tu, si Cupidon autant,
> Qu'il fait mon cueur, le tien est pincetant
> Et tu flechis si doctement ta fiere?

Baïf himself is so much in love that he has forgotten all that he has learned,
and is subdued by Cupid, who "chanter ne me permét / Que comme enfant,
ce qu'enfant il me ditte."[10] All that matters to him is that Francine should
enjoy his verse: "Ce que i'écri te plait, tu aimes bien mon stile: / Aussi i'écri
pour toy / C'est pour toy que ie chante."[11] The four books of the *Amour
de Francine* end with a firm statement of the simplicity of Baïf's approach,
in a passage owing much to Horace, and in words that were to be taken up
in Du Bellay's *Regrets* three years later:

> Le pis que lon dira c'est que ie suis de ceux
> Qui à se repolir sont un peu paresseux,
> Et que mes rudes vers n'ont etté sur l'enclume
> Remis assez de foys: aussi ma foible plume

le crein de trop erner, et ie crein d'effacer
Et r'efacer ma rime et de la retracer:
Et pour n'en mentir point mes ongles ie ne ronge
Pour r'agencer un vers que cent fois ie resonge.[12]

What is fascinating is that Baïf, as well as finding an excuse for his own "naïf" style, later ascribed exactly the same reason to Ronsard. Ronsard described in simpler style his love for Marie, says Baïf, because it was possibly "amour non feint" (as opposed to his previous love poetry):

... puis en stile divers,
(Possible outré d'une flechade vraye
D'amour non feint) pour soulager sa playe,
Va moderer en plus douce chanson
Son braue cœur sous un moins graue son.[13]

Ronsard himself, as we shall see, gives some very different reasons for the change. And whereas Baïf, and Tyard, despite the new-found self-consciousness in relation to style, maintain in their different ways the old complicity in relation to the coherence and reality of the love-experience, Ronsard, engaging in a subtle and complex dialogue with his reader and with his fellow-poets, connives at a playful mockery of the convention, in that the inner workings of it are laid bare.

The first thing that strikes one, on reading the 1555 *Continuation des Amours*, is that the coherence of the traditional love-sequence has apparently disappeared. Where Baïf, Tyard, Peletier, were still attempting to maintain this inner coherence, and occasionally having to produce the kind of self-justification we have already seen, Ronsard includes poems which contradict each other; Petrarchan attitudes rub shoulders with other traditions, poems on constancy are interwoven with poems on inconstancy, some poems are even addressed to Cassandre still. The easiest solution would be to presume that Ronsard had just thrown into this collection all the love-poems that he had on hand at the time: "Ronsard publie ses poésies quand elles sont achevées, dans le premier recueil à venir, sans avoir un rigoureux souci d'homogénéité," as a critic has recently said.[14]

Now, while this is certainly true of collections such as the *Bocages* and the *Meslanges*, which have no claim to be "sonnet-sequences," the *Continuation des Amours* is a different matter. Everything points towards specific intentions, in a collection which makes a coherence of incoherence.

In the same way as his contemporaries, Ronsard had decided to modify the style of his love poetry; and, like them, he set about self-consciously announcing this decision. The first and last sonnets of the collection[15] are not, as in collections like *Délie*, statements about love, but statements about style. A change of style has been elevated into the most important concern of the collection.

How, to keep his complicity with the reader, does Ronsard "justify" this change of style? Like Baïf, he dedicates his collection to a new mistress. Unlike Baïf, he does not claim that the previous mistress was pure imagination, and that the new one is "real." Instead, he creates a different character, a simple country girl; in Sonnet VIII, for example, this is made clear implicitly, without need for explicit statement. It does not matter that, as Desonay, Gadoffre, and others have pointed out, the simple country girl courted by a nobleman is a "lieu commun de la littérature courtoise"; it does not matter that the actual class system and conventions of the sixteenth century in France would have made such a liaison unthinkable, and its expression in print doubly unthinkable if it had been real; the reader is aware of the convention, and its coherence makes it "real" within the complicity that has already been established.

But how, then, can the Cassandre poems of only three years before be "justified"? Only by the introduction of a new theme, that of inconstancy. The theme was already "in the air," and on the way to becoming a convention. La Tour d'Albenas, for example, in his "Conférence de deux damoiselles" of 1551, had addressed his love to two women, Anne and Claude.[16] In Sonnet IX of this collection Ronsard tackles the problem head-on, and justifies the shift from Cassandre to Marie with an arrogant, and humorous, praise of inconstancy which goes far further than any of his predecessors:

> Je le veux estre aussi, les hommes sont bien lours
> Qui n'osent en cent lieux neuve amour entreprendre . . .
> . . . Les hommes maladifs, ou mattés de vieillesse,
> Doivent estre constans: mais sotte est la jeunesse
> Qui n'est point eveillée, et qui n'aime en cent lieux.[17]

Once the theme has been introduced, it is extended even further. Other women are introduced:

> Je ne suis seulement amoureus de Marie,
> Janne me tient aussi dans les liens d'Amour.

> Je ne dy pas si Jane estoit prise de moi,
> Que tost je n'oubliasse et Marie et Cassandre.

> D'une belle Marie en une autre Marie,
> Belleau, je suis tombé.[18]

Alongside these poems, of course, one finds many poems extolling the poet's constancy to one woman, in the Petrarchan vein: and the poet even points out at one stage that:

> Je ne suis point de ceus qui changent de fortune,
> Comme un tas d'amoureus, aimans aujourd'huy l'une,
> Et le lendemain l'autre.[19]

The constancy-inconstancy theme is even introduced in relation to the poet's mistress, who is accused of inconstancy.[20]

Now, despite these contradictions, the collection does not appear to be a random gathering together of disparate poems, as some critics have suggested. The treatment of the constancy-inconstancy theme, in the form it takes, could not have been produced in such a random way. It begins to look as though the contradictions are intended. The picture is built up of a poet who addresses different women in different ways, and even the same woman in different ways according to his mood, the situation, and how she can be won over. (In the process, of course, this *does* allow him to throw into the collection any love poetry he has been writing recently.) A new complicity between poet and reader is being forged, in which the artificiality of the conventions, from being implicit, has become explicit.

That this is the intention is underlined by those poems which actually refer to the poetic process: sonnets I, XXIV, and LXX. The first two are addressed to fellow-poets, the third to "Marie"; but they are in fact addressed to the poet's partner in complicity, the reader. We know that the readership for love poetry in the mid-sixteenth century was very restricted. This small, elite audience must have read most of what appeared; one sometimes gets the impression that it consisted mostly of the poets themselves. The exchanges between poets, from collection to collection, have a coherence in themselves. The reader is quite clearly presumed to have a complete knowledge of what has been written by those who are being addressed,[21] and to understand the allusions that are being made; he is also presumed, naturally, to know any classical sources that are used, and to pick up allusions there as well.

The poets whom Ronsard addresses on this question are Baïf and Tyard, whose approach to the same problems we have already seen. The covert allusions to their own statements lead to a delightful game of double or triple bluff, which is then rounded off by the themes being gathered together in a statement to the imaginary Marie which underlines her unreality.

The introductory sonnet, addressed to Tyard, gives one reason for Ronsard's change of style: that he had been criticized by the public for his former style. The final sonnet gives a completely different reason: that he had changed it because of Marie. (Note that there is, as yet, no trace of the "anti-Petrarchism" which is introduced, to muddy the issue further, in 1556.)

The very title of the collection points towards Tyard, whose *Continuation des erreurs amoureuses* had appeared in 1551, as his second volume of love poetry. Ronsard's first sonnet, based heavily on Horace, casts Tyard in the role he had forged for himself, both in the *Solitaire premier* (1552) and in the *Continuation des erreurs amoureuses* (1551). In the latter he had, on various occasions, railed against the "vicieux peuple, ô vile peuple ignorant,"[22] though the main reason for his anger had been their attitude to his love. In the *Solitaire premier*, however, Tyard had defended contemporary love poetry against criticisms of obscurity and learnedness. His interlocutor, Pasithée, asked him:

Que respondrez vous à ce qu'ils dient, que si par estranges façons de parler vous taschez d'obscurcir et ensevelir dans voz vers vos conceptions tellement, que les simples et les vulgaires, qui sont (jurent-ils) hommes de ce monde comme vous, n'y peuvent recognoistre leur langue, pource qu'elle est masquée et desguisée de certains accoustremens estrangers, vous eussiez encor mieux fait, pour atteindre à ce but de non estre entendus, de rien n'escrire du tout?

Tyard's reply was "que l'intention du bon Poëte n'est de non estre entendu, ny aussi de se baisser et accommoder à la vilté du vulgaire (duquel ils sont le chef) pour n'attendre autre jugement de ses œuvres que celuy, qui naistroit d'une tant lourde cognoissance."[23]

The only example given, in this text, of such obscure poetry is Scève's *Délie*, which is naturally highly praised by Tyard, who owed so much to Scève's example: no reference to Ronsard is made,[24] and the criticisms appear to have been those leveled at the Lyons school.

Was objection eventually made to Ronsard, too? Quite possibly, but not necessarily. He himself was to voice the kind of objections to Scève that so annoyed Tyard. In the *Bocage* of 1554 he called on his lyre not to "chanter tousjours le haut," but "sonne, et laisse à la France dire / Cela que dire elle voudra: / L'homme grave qui ne prendra / Plaisir en si basse folie / Aille fueilleter la Delie."[25] At the same time, we must remember that Ronsard himself was accused of looking down on the "unlearned" poetry of others, as Baïf pointed out early in 1555:

Souvent, Ronsard, pour l'amitié sincère,
Qui nous conioint, tu dis m'amonnestant,
Qu'en mes amours ie ne decouvre tant
De mon sçauoir, que ie pourroy bien faire.[26]

The norm appears to have been for the poet to claim that he had been criticized for the new style, and the choice of critic does not seem necessarily to have had to relate to reality. In the case of this collection of Ronsard's, the first and last sonnets give them the same "real" message (that he has tried a new style, and is tempted to give it up) even though the message is not followed (see the *Nouvelle Continuation*), and even though the reasons given differ wildly from each other.

In the first sonnet Ronsard, despite the fact that the poems under discussion are just being published for the first time, informs Tyard already of "chacun's" response to them. Here "chacun" plays the role of "Ronsard" in Baïf's *Amour de Francine*, and is equally unreal. Ronsard is here heavily under the influence of the classical source he has decided to follow. In Horace's Satire II, 1, the poet consults his friend Trebatius about his writing of satire. Though the problem is different, the public is depicted as criticizing the poet, whichever path he takes in order to please them:

> Sunt quibus in satura videar nimis acer et ultra
> Legem tendere opus; sine nervis altera, quidquid
> Composui, pars esse putat similisque meorum
> Mille die versus deduci posse.27

He turns to Trebatius (Tyard), and despairingly asks him: "Trebati, quid faciam, praescribe."28 In one of his Epistles, Horace refers to the public in the following terms: "Belua multorum es capitum . . . Quo teneam voltus mutantem Protea nodo?"29

Now Ronsard was placing his collection under the aegis of Tyard, a poet who had pioneered the way in France with a succession of love-sequences. Ronsard's title followed his; Ronsard addressed him as a fellow-poet in the first sonnet. Tyard, like Horace, abhorred the public. The conversation between Horace and Trebatius must have seemed a perfect model. Into that model was poured a discussion on poetry which does not necessarily need to be taken seriously. (Indeed, the two forms of criticism leveled at Ronsard in it are, as we have seen, unlikely to be true.) That it need not is shown by the response which Ronsard ascribes to Tyard ("Il le faut laisser dire, / et nous rire de lui, comme il se rit de nous"), which, unlike the Tyard of the *Solitaire premier*, does not take a firm line on the matter, praising the high style against its critics.

The extensive use of Horace in this first sonnet is also a hint to the reader of the tone which is going to underlie so much of the collection. But there is a further twist; the knowledgeable reader would know that Trebatius' response to the question had in fact been: "Quiescas." To Horace's further question, "Ne faciam, inquis, omnino versus?" the response had been "Aio"30 (Trebatius thus taking the same line as Pasithée in the *Solitaire premier*, rather than that of Tyard). This leads us directly into the theme of the sonnet to Baïf, XXIV.

The tone of this sonnet is, like so much of the rest of the collection, playful. Just as in the third sonnet in the collection, addressed to Du Bellay (and Du Bellay's poems addressed to Ronsard), there is a taking up of literary allusions, a teasing about the poet's choice of subject-matter, and even a parody of the poet's style. Here Ronsard starts with the parody of Baïf's style and language. The word "langoureux," for example, is a hallmark of Baïf's love poetry, and also sums up the tone of his verse.[31] Du Bellay, in his *Regrets*, parodies Baïf by much the same technique as Ronsard:

> ... Tu n'esprouves (Baïf) d'un maistre rigoureux
> Le severe sourcy: mais la douce rudesse
> D'une belle, courtoise, et gentile maistresse,
> Qui fait *languir* ton cœur doulcement *langoureux*.[32]

Ronsard, of course, piles on the parody even more strongly:

> Bayf, il semble à voir tes rymes *langoreuses*,
> Que tu sois seul amant, en France, *langoreus*,
> Et que tes compaignons ne sont point amoureus,
> Mais font *languir* leurs vers dessous feintes pleureuses.

He also takes up Baïf's obsession with "feintise" in the *Amour de Francine*, which we have already seen as being an unreal "justification" for a change of style; and in doing so, he appears to be replying both to the attack on "Ronsard"[33] and to the attacks which abound in the *Francine* poems against the kind of poet who "trop enflé le langoureux . . . feigne."[34] This, despite the fact that Ronsard himself was ostensibly turning his back on "learned" poetry, and (if this were to be taken literally) should have agreed with Baïf's strictures that "tu flechis si doctement ta fiere."[35]

This is, then, on the one hand, a playful mocking of Baïf's style, of his obsession with "feintise," and of his accusation that other poets wrote love poetry which was "imaginary." Given what we have already said about "complicity," the double-take is obvious. Ronsard proceeds to deny the accusation in ambiguous terms:

> Tu te trompes, Bayf, les peines doloreuses
> D'amour autant que toi nous rendent doloreus,
> Sans nous feindre un tourment.

It is ambiguous because of what follows: Ronsard accuses Baïf of writing verse "Qui se faignant un dueil se fait palir lui-mesme," and suggests that if one is *really* in love it is impossible to write love poetry:

> Non, celui n'aime point, ou bien il aime peu,
> Qui peut donner par signe à cognoistre son feu,
> Et qui peut raconter le quart de ce qu'il aime.

Though this statement is taken from Petrarch,[36] in its original context it was a fairly innocuous statement about the difficulty of expressing true love. Here, amidst the discussion of pretense and "feintise," it is much more striking. The message is a *reductio ad absurdum*; love poetry cannot be sincere, because it is written. There is a further subtle twist; the other poets are as "sincere" as Baïf (ll. 5-7), but Baïf himself is insincere. The whole convention is being mocked.

Another poem by Baïf ("Donques on dit que mon amour est feinte")[37] has sometimes been seen as an answer to Ronsard, together with the poem just after it, in which he declares "l'on dit que ie fai du transi."[38] There is a problem here, however. Ronsard is not mentioned. The *Second Livre* of the *Amour de Francine*, in which these poems figure, was printed at the same time as the *Premier Livre*, and Ronsard's poem shows an extensive knowledge of the themes of the *Amour de Francine* (on the basis of which most critics have dated Baïf's work as having appeared much earlier in 1555 than Ronsard's). The dating could, of course, have been wrong, and Ronsard, or Baïf, could have read the other's poems in manuscript. Far more likely, however, is that the two poems in question were a further elaboration of Baïf's extensive treatment of the theme of "feintise," and were unconnected with any actual accusation.

Ronsard has, then, in this poem, taken the ground from under any appreciation of the poetry in the collection as "real." His playful mockery of Baïf's obsessions has extended to a mockery of the very conventions which poet and reader should keep unstated.

The dialogue with Tyard and Baïf about the nature of love poetry extends into the final sonnet, to Marie. Both Tyard and Baïf, in their collections which appeared just before Ronsard's, had offered their new poetic style to their mistresses. Baïf claimed that he did not mind in what style others wrote, nor whether anyone "blamed" him for his song. He is not writing for the public, but for Francine. "I'ai tout ce que ie veu si tu veux m'estimer." She likes his style, and so his poetry has succeeded: "D'avoir touché le but de mes vers ie me vante, / Si mon chant amoureux est pour te contanter."[39] Note the similarity of the themes of "blame," and of the public, to Ronsard's poem to Tyard. Tyard playfully twists the same kind of theme with a promise to write with "un pinceau plus naïf" if she will "adouci[r] la rigueur qui me touche."[40] Style itself thus becomes a counter in the game of love.

Ronsard's sonnet LXX is a brilliant combination of these concepts within a game of complicity with the reader, who is aware not only of the real reason for the change of style, and of the unreality of Marie, but also of the reason for change, and the possible further change, which was given in Sonnet I. It turns around the concept of the style being capable of bending the rigor of the beloved, and suggests that it has been unable to do so and is therefore to be regretted. Further items incorporated in the poem are (1) the idea of the "high" style being appropriate to the great poet, which "pour chanter si bas n'estoit point destiné," and (2) the *inconstancy* of Marie: "vous me manquez de foy." It does not matter that Marie is here described as refusing not only the poet's touch but also his kisses (in contrast to earlier sonnets); the unreality of the convention has, as we have seen, already been underlined. This delightful end to the formal part of the *Continuation* sums up the tone of so much of the collection. As well as being playful with Marie, the poet is playful with his fellow-poets, and with the reader.

Throughout the collection, the reader has been presented with humorous turnings-around of poetic conventions of the same type. One of the best examples of this is Sonnet XIX, "Mais respons, meschant Loir . . . ," in which the water is addressed in the same way as Marie is later to be. The river is "inconstant," and thus shares the major theme of the collection:

> D'autant que je t'aimoi, je me fiois en toi,
> Mais tu m'as bien montré que l'eau n'a point de foi.

The poet believes that the poetry addressed to the river (as to his mistress) only entitles him to gentle treatment. Added to this, we have the theme of the river (as the mistress) only achieving fame through connection with Ronsard; and this grand theme is made ridiculous through the contrast of language ("au milieu de ta fange . . . ") and also through the futile event which is accorded the grand treatment.

In the *Nouvelle Continuation des Amours* (1556) further "declarations of intent" are made by the poet, both in the form of attacks upon "ces tomes enflez, qui n'ont rien dedans eux / Que des vers sourcilleux, et de gros mots venteux, / empoulez, et masquez," in the opening "Elegie,"[41] and also in the comic anti-Petrarchan vein of "A son Livre," which expands the theme of inconstancy from the *Continuation*. The unreality of both of these themes is shown by a number of factors. Firstly, a poem which reflects much of the content and language of the Elégie, and which contrasts Anacreontic love poetry with "un vers enflé plein d'arrogance haute, / Obscur, masqué . . . ," etc., the hymn to Christophle de Choiseul, which appeared in the 1556 edition of Belleau's *Odes d'Anacréon teien*, eventually found itself in the *Deuxiesme Livre des Hymnes*, among grand poetry far from the "description douces, et doucement coulants d'un doux stile" of Anacreontic verse. As always, Ronsard continued to write poetry in all styles, from high to low, according to the subject. Secondly, the introduction of anti-Petrarchism (in "A son Liure") at this point (and one must not forget how much in vogue this spurious attitude was) coincided with the introduction of far more poetry in the Petrarchan vein, often with close relationship to Petrarchan originals.

The changes between editions of what became the *Amours de Marie* did little to change this new kind of complicity. Indeed, the wry humor of "A son Liure" was pushed to the head of the collection, immediately followed by the sonnet to Tyard. The contrast between the answer to a critic that "les amours ne se souspirent pas / D'un vers hautement grave, ains d'un beau stille bas," and the complaint that Ronsard's main aim had been to please the public, is clear; as is the contrast between it and the claim in the Marie sonnet that the poet should never have abandoned his "grave premier stile, / Qui chanter si bas n'estoit point destiné." But the poet, far from trying to attenuate the contrast, accentuates it by changing the first line of the Tyard sonnet to relate it to "A son Liure," by using the word "blasmoit" in line 1, in relation to the public, as in that poem. Finally, the 1587 edition introduced the word "blasme" in line 4 as well. The unreality of the convention of complicity is consciously underlined.

A further twist, from 1560 onwards, is the introduction of "Le Voyage de Tours." This continuation of the dialogue with Baïf gives us a fantastic variant on the Marie theme, in an eclogue in which Baïf's "docte Francine" becomes a simple country girl (as, later, in Baïf's own Eclogues), and in which Francine's sister Marion becomes Marion/Marie (and for the first time attached to Ronsard) and they both move from the Clain to the Loire. The unreality of the "learned" Francine being depicted as a simple country girl accentuates the unreality of the Marie theme. Humor is added by the bathetic effect, after the highflown statements of love, of Ronsard's concern for comfort: "Mais je le retiray le menant d'autre part / Pour chercher à loger, car il estoit bien tard." Belleau's glosses on the collection give a straight-faced commentary which tries to make a real story out of what is known to be unreal.[42]

I have taken this one collection because I believe it to be the moment of departure for a new trend, towards which the close-knit body of poets in the early 1550's had already been moving. The new mood continued. Other writers entered the game, teasing Ronsard with the very conventions he had been mocking. Magny, and others, extended the theme of inconstancy: Tyard asked Cupid to grant Ronsard the favors of "Et Jane et Marguerite, et Marie et Cassandre."[43] But where Ronsard's wit, subtlety and "nerve" could, while mocking the convention of complicity, still avoid destroying it, later poets ignored the need to do so. In the later part of the century, poets like Durant mocked the conventions far more bluntly:

> . . . Sous un nom de Charlote,
> le me flate et me dorlote,
> Et me feins d'estre amoureux.
>
> C'est un beau mestier de feindre,
> C'est un plaisir de se plaindre
> Et ne point sentir le mal . . . .[44]

But we also find poets no longer caring to create coherence in their love-collections, not trying to "justify" their attitudes, not even trying to create the "coherence of incoherence" of Ronsard's *Continuation*.

The acceptance of the unreality of a poet's passion had always been part of the aesthetic experience of the century, but an appearance of credibility had also been essential. The new-found freedom from this could produce amusing poetry; but it also produced the decline in love-poetry which was to culminate in the games of Voiture and the *précieux*, and which was to exclude love-poetry from the respectable genres of the classical age of the seventeenth century.

NOTES

1. Tyard, *Erreurs amoureuses* (Lyons, 1549), vol. 2 of *Oeuvres poétiques complètes*, ed. Lapp (Paris, 1966), p. 10.

2. Magny, *Les Amours* (1553), I, ed. Mark S. Whitney (Geneva, 1970), p. 25.

3. Tyard, *Erreurs amoureuses, augmentées d'une tierce partie* (Lyons, 1555), IX, ed. Lapp, p. 135.

4. Baïf, *Quatre Livres de L'Amour de Francine* (Paris, 1555), III, 65.

5. Ibid., I, 32r.

6. Ibid., I, 4v.

7. Ibid., I, 20v.

8. Ibid., II, 56v. On the question of "feintise," Dr. Ian Maclean has pointed out to me a further possible layer of ambiguity: the use of "feindre" to mean "to create poetic fictions in the neo-platonist manner." An example of this usage is to be found in Ronsard's *Odes*, V, 3, "A Madame Marguerite," ll. 121-26 (Laumonier, III, 104): "Diray-je si quelqu'un soubhaicte / De se feindre nouveau poëte, / Il ne doit sinon epreuver / Quelle est ta gloire, sans qu'il songe / Dessus Parnasse, ou qu'il se plonge / Es flots menteurs pour s'abreuver?"

9. Ibid., III, 66.

10. Ibid., I, 19v.

11. Ibid., I, 29v.

12. Ibid., IV, 116v-117r.

13. Baïf, *A Monseigneur le Duc d'Anjou*, in *Les Amours de Ian Antoine de Baïf* (Paris, 1572), included in *Euures en rime* (Paris, 1573).

14. Raymond Lebègue, "Remarques sur la structure des recueils de Ronsard," in *Renaissance Studies in Honor of Isidore Silver (Kentucky Romance Quarterly*, 21 [1974], Supplement No. 2), p. 49. Cf. also, on the *Continuation des Amours*, M. Dassonville, "Pour une interprétation nouvelle des *Amours* de Ronsard," *Bibliothèque d'Humanisme et Renaissance*, 28 (1966), 251: "il semble bien que des circonstances particulières l'aient amené en 1555 à publier prématurément la *Continuation des Amours* et à réunir au plus tôt en un recueil des pièces diverses dont le seul mérite était d'être achevées."

15. The additional poems after the last sonnet can be taken as an additional section unrelated to the sequence.

16. In *Le Siècle d'or, et autres vers divers* (Lyons, 1551).

17. *Continuation des Amours*, IX, ed. Laumonier, VII, 126.

18. Ibid., XI, XXV, XL; ed. Laumonier, VII, 127, 142-43, 157.

19. Ibid., XV, ed. Laumonier, VII, 133.

20. E.g., ibid., XIV; ed. Laumonier, VII, 131-32.

21. For example, Ronsard's poem to Du Bellay (*Continuation des Amours*, III; ed. Laumonier, VII, 118) would be incomprehensible without such knowledge.

22. Tyard, *Continuation des erreurs amoureuses*, 1551, XXXIII; ed. Lapp, p. 122.

23. Tyard, *Solitaire premier ou, Prose des Muses, et de la fureur Poëtique* (Lyons, 1552), ed. Baridon (Geneva, 1950), p. 67.

24. Despite the affirmations by Laumonier (Ronsard, *Oeuvres complètes* [Paris, 1959], VII, 116), and Weber (Ronsard, *Les Amours* [1963], p. 613). It is worth noting that, at any rate, the *Solitaire premier* appeared in the same year as Ronsard's *Amours*.

25. "Le Fourmy," in *Le Bocage* (1554).

26. Baïf, *L'Amour de Francine* (1555), I, 19v.

27. Horace, Satire II, 1, ll. 1-4.

28. Ibid., ll. 4-5.

29. Horace, Epistle I, 1, ll. 76 and 90.

30. Horace, Satire II, 1, ll. 5-6.

31. E.g. *L'Amour de Francine* (1555), p. 13r: "d'estre ainsi langoureux"; p. 14r: "de son feu ie change langoureux"; p. 18r: "s'elle rit de me voir langoureux"; p. 19v: "Ayant eté tout un iour langoureux . . . / Madame douce a guery la langueur," etc.

32. Du Bellay, *Regrets* (1558), XXIV.

33. *L'Amour de Francine* (1555), I, 19v.

34. Ibid., I, 29v.

35. Ibid., I, 19v.

36. CLXX, *Piu volte gia*, in *Le Rime*, ed. Giosuè Carducci and Severino Ferrari (Florence, 1960), p. 257.

37. *L'Amour de Francine* (1555), II, 45v.

38. Ibid., II, 45v.

39. Baïf, *L'Amour de Francine* (1555), I, 29v.

40. Tyard, *Troisième Livre des Erreurs Amoureuses* (1555), IX; ed. Lapp, pp. 134-51. The "Dedicace" to this collection is dated 1554.

41. "A Jean de Morel, Ambrunois . . . Elégie,"*Nouvelle Continuation des Amours* (1556); ed. Laumonier, VII, 225.

42. The game is continued in Baïf's *Diverses Amours*, where certain sonnets respond to details from this poem. Needless to say, the details given in the "real"

biographies of both authors by modern critics are entirely based on these poems, and not on any external evidence.

43. Tyard, *Elégie à Pierre de Ronsard*, in *Les Oeuvres poétiques de Pontus de Tyard* (Paris, 1573).

44. Gilles Durant, *A Claude Binet, Lieutenant Général a Riom*, Ode XXXIII, in *Les Oeuvres poétiques du Sieur de la Bergerie* (Paris, 1594), II, 128.

Philip Ford

Ronsard and the Theme of Inspiration

Je n'avois pas quinze ans que les mons & les boys,
Et les eaux me plaisoient plus que la court des Roys,
Et les noires forests espesses de ramées,
Et du bec des oyseaux les roches entamées:
Une valée, un antre en horreur obscurcy,
Un desert effroiable, estoit tout mon soucy,
A fin de voir au soir les Nymphes & les Fées
Danser desoubs la Lune en cotte par les prées,
Fantastique d'esprit: & de voir les Sylvains
Estre boucs par les pieds, & hommes par les mains,
Et porter sur le front des cornes en la sorte
Qu'un petit aignelet de quatre moys les porte.[1]

It is in this way that Ronsard introduces an autobiographical section of 56 lines relating the details of his poetic calling at a time when he was a page in Scotland. Or at least, that is how Michel Dassonville views the section.

Tout pourrait être écossais dans cette scène . . . . Les roches basaltiques couvertes d'oiseaux de mer. Les landes effrayantes où dansent, au clair de lune, les sorcières du sabbat. Et les Nymphes, Fées et Sylvains bien étrangers aux dryades, pans, napées et oréades qui ne sont que personnages de papier surgis plus tard de la lecture des poètes de l'antiquité.[2]

Paul Laumonier, on the other hand, locates this setting in the Loir valley, and as for the nymphs and fairies, "En réalité ce sont les buées qui s'élèvent le soir et se dissipent le matin sur les prés du Loir; leurs formes mouvantes suggéraient au poète l'idée d'un chœur de Nymphes."[3] To what extent, then, are we justified in trusting Ronsard's apparently autobiographical verse? Or rather, how should we interpret it? For Ronsard has recourse a number of times to a scenario of this kind in connection with his vocation as a poet, and the details are seldom consistent. In the following pages, I propose to consider three of these descriptions and to show how beneath their apparent similarities their significance changes according to context and literary associations.[4]

Poetic imagery, by its very nature, is a highly complex and elusive phenomenon. Because the individual's reactions to a given experience differ, an image based on any experience, whether this be an actual event or the description of an event, will inevitably evoke varying feelings. In *The Gallo-Roman Muse*, Dorothy Coleman has spoken of the way in which, in sixteenth-century poetry, "images, allusions, parallels from Ancient literature and mythology, play their part in awakening the *right* body of associations needed to understand the piece of communication."[5] This calls for a reader who is almost as active and creative as the poet himself, and the process of interaction with the text cannot fail to be full of pitfalls. The poet is at only one remove from his field of reference. The reader, on the other hand, has to work back, via the allusions which have suggested themselves to the poet, to his original thought. In the case of a field of reference as wide as that of the divine inspiration theme, even the well-informed reader may have difficulty in picking his way through the complicated maze which the poet has created with his allusions to the tradition.

What is particularly disorientating for the modern reader is the compounding of uncertainty which results from Renaissance allusions to ancient writers. To understand a sixteenth-century poet, we must attune our own sensibilities not only to the world of the poet concerned, but also to his perception of the ancient world, which may not necessarily be our own (and which, indeed, was open to different interpretations in his own times). In addition, the multi-layered nature of the Ronsard poem, with its variously interwoven motifs and allusions, helps to produce an impression of elusiveness which is, perhaps, the essence of his poetry. We may understand an individual image and all its ramifications, but the total effect of the imagery of an entire poem often retains a certain mystery: "Certum est quia impossibile est."

The theme of poetic inspiration is one that preoccupied Ronsard throughout his career. Stripped of some (although not all) of its metaphorical trappings, Ronsard's theory concerning the Muses is expressed at the beginning of the *Abbregé de l'art poétique françoys:*

Sur toutes choses tu auras les Muses en reverence, . . . [et] les tiendras cheres & sacrées, comme les filles de Jupiter, c'est à dire de Dieu, qui de sa saincte grace a premierement par elles faict cognoistre aux peuples ignorans les excellences de sa majesté. Car la Poësie n'estoit au premier aage qu'une Theologie allegoricque, pour faire entrer au cerveau des hommes grossiers par fables plaisantes & colorées les secretz qu'ilz ne pouvoyent comprendre, quand trop ouvertement on leur descouvroit la verité ... Car les Muses, Apollon, Mercure, Pallas & autres telles deitez ne nous representent autre chose que les puissances de Dieu, auquel les premiers hommes avoyent donné plusieurs noms pour les divers effectz de son incomprehensible majesté.

(Laumonier XIV, 4 & 6)

Ronsard considers that the earliest poets—Eumolpus, Linus, Orpheus, Homer, and Hesiod—were divinely inspired, but they were followed by "les seconds poëtes que j'appelle humains," a group which includes all the Roman poets "excepté cinq ou six desquelz la doctrine, accompagnée d'un parfaict artifice, m'a tousjours tiré en admiration." Ultimately, therefore, Ronsard sees divine inspiration as proceeding directly from God, although pre-Christian thinking may have attributed it to the Muses, an image which even in this expository prose passage Ronsard is unwilling to abandon altogether. What, then, is the exact nature of "les Muses" in this passage— agents of God, or merely a metaphor for poetry? It is precisely because their exact significance remains so ambiguous that Ronsard's references to the Muses and poetic inspiration take on something of the nature of a mystic experience, and it is not given to the profane fully to understand the process whereby the poet receives inspiration. However, such descriptions are part of a long and fruitful tradition, going back to Hesiod, one of Ronsard's divine poets, and it is in this context that they must be viewed for their implications to emerge.

The texts under consideration here share a number of common points, of which the most important are the "poetic" landscape of the *locus amoenus*, the presence of mythical gods and demi-gods, and the initiation into the mystery of poetry. Together, they had formed enough of a commonplace in ancient literature for Persius, writing in the first century A.D., to devote the entire prologue of his *Satires* to rejecting the *topos:*

> Nec fonte labra prolui caballino
> nec in bicipiti somniasse Parnaso
> memini, ut repente sic poeta prodirem.
> Heliconidasque pallidamque Pirenen
> illis remitto quorum imagines lambunt
> hederae sequaces .... [6]

He goes on to say that it is the desire for money and not divine inspiration that turns men into poets, repudiating the Hesiodic tradition of inspiration to which Ronsard is alluding in the passages under discussion. Despite the very different uses to which Persius and Ronsard put this tradition, both poets rely on finding one thing in their audiences: the ability to recognize the tradition and its various ramifications. So, before examining Ronsard's use of this tradition in detail, let us first consider the development of the *topos*, and its function in the context of those ancient works where it is to be found.

As Hesiod is the earliest extant poet to introduce the theme, all subsequent references to encounters with the Muses tend to allude, at least implicitly, to the Hesiodic account, which is as follows:

Let us start our song with the Heliconian Muses who inhabit the great and hallowed Mount Helicon, and dance with dainty feet around the dark spring and the altar of the mighty son of Cronos . . . They once taught Hesiod the beautiful art of singing, as he was tending his lambs under hallowed Helicon. The goddesses first spoke these words to me, the Olympian Muses, daughters of aegis-bearing Zeus: "You rustic shepherds, base reproaches to your name, mere bellies, we know how to tell many lies which resemble the truth, but we know how to speak the truth when we want to." Thus spoke the glib-tongued daughters of mighty Zeus; and they pulled off a branch of luxuriant laurel and gave it to me as a staff, a wondrous thing; and they breathed into me a prophetic voice so that I might celebrate the things to come and what had come before. And they ordered me to hymn the race of the blessed gods that are immortal, and always to sing the Muses first and last.

(*Theogony* 1-4, 22-34)

Scholarly opinion is divided with regard to the exact nature of Hesiod's vision—religious experience, literary convention, or elaborate metaphor—but this need not concern us here. What is important is the rural setting, including a spring of water associated with divine inspiration (ll. 2-4); the address by the deities to the future poet (ll. 26-28); the initiation rite (ll. 30-32); and the promise of prophetic powers and a divine mission (ll. 32-34). All this points to the unique position of the poet as intermediary between the divine world and the human world, and the mystical nature of the poet's art. And as we have noted, the whole description serves as a point of reference for claims of divine inspiration in subsequent poets. Thus, Callimachus refers to the opening of the *Theogony* in *Aetia* 2, Vergil does likewise in *Eclogues* 6, 64-73, while a similar legend was associated with the father of Roman poetry, Ennius, related in Lucretius 1, 117-126:

> Ennius ut noster cecinit qui primus amoeno
> detulit ex Helicone perenni fronde coronam,
> per gentis Italas hominum quae clara clueret;
> . . . .
> . . . sibi exortam semper florentis Homeri
> commemorat speciem lacrimas effundere salsas
> coepisse et rerum naturam expandere dictis.[7]

(ll. 117-19, 124-26)

(The context of this quotation is a section in which Lucretius is demonstrating that there is no hell or life after death. It is significant, too, that elsewhere (4, 580-94) he gives a rational explanation for the belief in rural deities like the "capripedes satyros," nymphs, fauns, and Pan, demonstrating that to use a tradition is not necessarily to believe in it.)

In his use of the *topos*, Horace adds a new dimension to the tradition: the *odi profanum vulgus* theme. This makes its appearance, for example, at the end of *Odes* 1, 1, where the traditional poetic landscape is seen as a refuge from the preoccupations of more prosaic men:

> me doctarum hederae praemia frontium
> dis miscent superis, me gelidum nemus
> nympharumque leves cum Satyris chori
> *secernunt populo*, si neque tibias
> Euterpe cohibet nec Polyhymnia
> Lesboum refugit tendere barbiton.[8]
>   (II. 29-34)

In *Odes* 3, 4, Horace sees his whole life as being under the protection of the Muses (II. 9-36). Moreover, the poetic landscape in this poem is envisaged more in terms of an imaginary world than as a real one:

> auditis an me ludit amabilis
> insania? audire et *videor* pios
>   errare per lucos, amoenae
>   quos et aquae subeunt et aurae.[9]
>   (II. 5-8)

Propertius too relates a mystical encounter with the Muses and Apollo in *Elegies* 3, 3. Again, there is an implicit reference to the Hesiodic account, with the poet imagining he has been translated to Mount Helicon:

> Visus eram molli recubans Heliconis in umbra,
> Bellerophontei qua fluit umor equi . . . . [10]
>   (II. 1-2)

The Ennius legend is mentioned (I. 6), and the poet is then addressed by Apollo himself, who urges him to abandon all idea of epic poetry for amatory verse. (There is a direct precedent here in Callimachus *Aetia* 1 where the Hellenistic poet also receives a visitation from Apollo, urging him to keep a slender Muse—τὴν Μοῦσαν . . . λεπταλέην—and incidentally providing the inspiration for the opening of Vergil's sixth eclogue.) Calliope then speaks to the poet and, at the end of the elegy, gives him inspirational water to drink.

These, then, are the principal uses of the theme among ancient writers, and they serve three main functions. The most important one is naturally the affirmation of the poet's claim to have direct links with a divine source of inspiration, to be both poet and prophet: this notion underlies all uses of the theme. By implication, and in the case of Horace, at least, explicitly, this involves in the second place the rejection of the *profanum vulgus*. The third function concerns the divinely inspired justification for the choice of a particular genre of poetry. Ronsard would have been aware of the uses and interdependence of these themes, along with their contexts, and it is perhaps these which may throw some light on the ways in which the French poet means us to understand the allusions to his various encounters with the Muses.

To return to the opening of the *Hymne de l'Autonne*, Ronsard has in mind passages from several ancient poets in the composition of his own version of the theme. The first thirty lines of the poem deal with a neo-Platonic concept of poetic inspiration: protected by the δαίμων associated with the Muses (who in a later variant become Apollo himself), the poet who is of a pure and virtuous soul receives a divine *furor* which transforms him into a prophet, a philosophical justification of the theme whose sources may be found in the *Phaedrus* 245 and the *Ion* 534:

> Il [i.e. the Daimon] me hassa le cueur, haussa la fantasie,
> M'inspirant dedans l'ame un don de Poësie,
> Que Dieu n'a concedé qu'à l'esprit agité
> Des poignans aiguillons de sa divinité.
>
> (II. 9-12)

After this opening section come the lines already cited at the beginning of this essay, in which Ronsard describes the rural setting, peopled with demi-gods, which proved so conducive to his development as a poet, and he then goes on to describe his own meeting with the Muses:

> J'allois apres la danse & craintif je pressois
> Mes pas dedans le trac des Nymphes, & pensois
> Que pour mettre mon pied en leur trace poudreuse
> J'aurois incontinent l'ame plus genereuse,
> Ainsi que l'Ascrean qui gravement sonna,
> Quand l'une des neuf Sœurs du laurier luy donna.
>   Or je ne fu trompé de ma douce entreprise,
> Car la gentille Euterpe ayant ma dextre prise,
> Pour m'oster le mortel par neuf fois me lava,
> De l'eau d'une fontaine où peu de monde va,
> Me charma par neuf fois, puis d'une bouche enflée
> (Ayant de sur mon chef son haleine soufflée)
> Me herissa le poil de crainte & de fureur,
> Et me remplit le cœur d'ingenieuse erreur,
> En me disant ainsi: Puisque tu veux nous suivre,

Heureux apres la mort nous te ferons revivre,
Par longue renommée, & ton los ennobly
Acablé du tombeau n'ira point en obly.

(II. 43-60)

In a poem where Ronsard expounds on the theory of the "fabuleux manteau" ("comment / On doit feindre & cacher les fables proprement, / Et
à bien deguiser la verité des choses / D'un fabuleux manteau dont elles sont
encloses," II. 79-82), should one take *au pied de la lettre* the poet's description of his preferred world as compared with "la court des Roys"? Rather,
we are dealing here with the world of the imagination and of literary allusiveness, where Ronsard, in common with earlier users of the theme, is
describing poetic inspiration in mythological terms. Admittedly, Hesiod
refers to his encounter with the Muses as an actual event; but in the case
of Ennius, Horace (*Odes* 3, 4), and Propertius (3, 3), the encounter is
described in terms of a vision. Moreover, the agnostic Lucretius uses a
similar image to portray poetic inspiration:

> . . . sed acri
> percussit thyrso laudis spes magna meum cor
> et simul incussit suavem mi in pectus amorem
> musarum, quo nunc instinctus mente vigenti
> avia Pieridum peragro loca nullius ante
> trita solo. iuvat integros accedere fontis
> atque haurire, iuvatque novos decerpere flores
> insignemque meo capiti petere inde coronam
> unde prius nulli velarint tempora musae.[11]
>
> (I, 922-30)

He goes on to say that the whole point of his poetry is to sugar the pill of
his doctrine in order to render it more accessible (II. 943-47). It is perhaps
this Lucretian passage, combining as it does the imagery of inspiration, the
desire for poetic renown ("laudis spes magna," I. 923), the recognition of
the novelty of the task accomplished (II. 926-28), and the idea of the poet
as purveyor of Truth, that lies behind Ronsard's introduction of the
Hymne de l'Autonne.

However, within this framework there are references to other instances
of divine inspiration, notably to that of Hesiod himself:

> Ainsi que l'Ascrean qui gravement sonna,
> Quand l'une des neuf Sœurs du laurier luy donna,
>
> (II. 47-48)

compare *Theogony* 30-31. Ronsard also has in mind here the passage in the
sixth *Eclogue* where, in Silenus' mythological song to his young captors,

Chromis and Mnasyllus, Vergil's friend Gallus makes a totally unexpected appearance:

> tum canit errantem Permessi ad flumina Gallum
> Aonas in montis ut duxerit una sororum, . . .
> ut Linus . . .
> dixerit: "hos tibi dant calamos, en accipe, Musae,
> Ascraeo quos ante seni, quibus ille solebat
> cantando rigidas deducere montibus ornos."[12]
>   (II. 64-65, 67, 69-71)

Here, we are at most dealing with an elaborate allegorical compliment. The immortalizing use of water in Ronsard (II. 51-52) reminds the reader of the end of Propertius 3, 3:

> talia Calliope, lymphisque a fonte petitis
> ora Philetaea nostra rigavit aqua,
>   (II. 51-52)

while the physical act of inspiration (II. 53-56) comes from Hesiod (II. 31-32). In both cases, this results in the poets' acquiring prophetic powers, accompanied in the case of Ronsard by poetic "fureur" and its concomitant effects (II. 55-68). This section owes its general tenor, like the opening of the hymn, to Plato, although there is also an allusion to Horace, compare line 56, "Et me remplit le cœur d'ingenieuse erreur," and the description of the mad poet in the Ars poetica 453-54, "quem . . . urget . . . / . . . fanaticus error." A Horatian theme ends the Muse's speech to Ronsard: the poet should not expect to "amasser de grands biens en ce Monde" (l. 69), but in rural peace, untroubled by those in authority, he will live "tout paisible & coy" (l. 75), compare Horace Epodes 2.

The final section of the introduction, II. 77-86, refers to Ronsard's education under Dorat:

> Ainsi disoit la Nymphe, & de là je vins estre
> Disciple de d'Aurat, qui long temps fut mon maistre,
> M'aprist la Poësie, & me montra comment
> On doit feindre & cacher les fables proprement.
>   (II. 77-80)

The transition comes, perhaps, as something of a jolt: we are abruptly transferred from the pastoral bliss of the main section of the introduction to Dorat's classroom; and this is all the more disconcerting if the reader bears in mind the time gap between the Muse addressing the fifteen-year-old Ronsard, and the start of the poet's studies with Dorat at the age of twenty!

It is clear from this discussion of the opening lines of the *Hymne de l'Autonne* that Ronsard is establishing a very close connection between himself and the ancient poets by his allusions to their experiences of inspiration when portraying his own. The prominence assigned to Hesiod, one of the divine poets, by implication raises Ronsard's status to a similar level, while Lucretius is no doubt recalled because he, like Ronsard, is claiming to reveal important universal truths for the benefit of mankind. However, because of the overlapping of imagery within the whole tradition of the theme, the allusions are seldom uniquely associated with a single poet. This means that Ronsard's experience of poetic inspiration becomes a composite one made up of many different layers, so that a single phrase or image may conjure up associations with more than one source, mixing the mystical, the lyrical, and the rational portrayals of inspiration. Nonetheless, the allusions all tend to emphasize the poet's superior knowledge of the universe (whether in the Hesiodic or the Lucretian traditions) and thus provide the opening with a sense of unity in spite of apparent diversity.

Earlier, Ronsard had described his poetic calling in similar terms in the "Elégie à Pierre l'Escot." However, if the function of the *topos* in the *Hymne de l'Autonne* is principally concerned with the poet's role as intermediary between the divine and the human worlds, it follows a different course in the "Elégie" to present another theme, the inescapable nature of the artist's vocation and the lack of gratitude with which he is met. Inevitably in Ronsard, this is also linked with the idea that the Muses will ensure the artist's posthumous renown, cf. the opening lines:

> Puis que Dieu ne m'a faict pour supporter les armes,
> Et pour mourir sanglant au milieu des alarmes
> En imittant les fais de mes premiers ayeux,
> Sy ne veulx-je pourtant demeurer ocieux,
> Ains comme je pourray je veulx laisser memoire
> Que les Muses jadis m'ont aquis une gloire,
> Afin que mon renom des siecles non veincu
> Rechante à mes neveus qu'autresfois j'ay vescu
> Bien voulu d'Apollon & des Muses aymées,
> Que j'ay plus que ma vie en mon age estimées.

Although the inspirational *locus amoenus* is present in this poem (ll. 85-94), with Ronsard depicted as three years younger than in the *Hymne de l'Autonne*, the Hesiodic tradition does not this time play a particularly significant role:

> Je n'avois pas douze ans qu'au profond des vallées,
> Dans les hautes forets des hommes reculées,

> Dans les antres segrets de frayeur tout couverts,
> Sans avoir soing de rien, je composois des vers.
>
> (ll. 85-88)

Rather, it is to Ovid that Ronsard seems to be alluding in this poem. Because of his exile from Rome on account of a poem he had written,[13] Ovid was considered in the sixteenth century as an *exemplum* of the unhappy lot of the poet, with the *Tristia* and the *Epistulae ex Ponto* underlining this at great length.[14] *Tristia* 4, 10 is the last poem of book IV, in which Ovid rounds off the book with an account of his life. The main themes of the poem are the poet's reputation with posterity, the inevitable nature of his calling, and the comfort (if not physical well-being) which he derives from the Muses in his exile. The poem is addressed to his future admirers:

> Ille ego qui fuerim, tenerorum lusor amorum,
> quem legis, ut noris, accipe posteritas.
>
> (ll. 1-2)

After describing his early life and family background in some detail, Ovid moves on to his infatuation with poetry:

> at mihi iam puero caelestia sacra placebant,
> inque suum furtim Musa trahebat opus.
> saepe pater dixit "studium quid inutile temptas?
> Maeonides nullas ipse reliquit opes."
> motus eram dictis, totoque Helicone relicto
> scribere temptabam verba soluta modis.
> sponte sua carmen numeros veniebat ad aptos,
> et quod temptabam dicere versus erat.[15]
>
> (ll. 19-26)

Lines 17-70 of Ronsard's poem are an amplification of part of the above: witness the first two lines of this section:

> Je fus souventesfois retencé de mon pere,
> Voyant que j'aimois trop les deux filles d'Homere.

Other details also allude to the Ovidian text, witness lines 39-41:

> Homere que tu tiens si souvent en tes mains,
> Que dans ton cerveau creux comme un dieu tu te pains,
> N'eut jamais un liard

and Ovid l. 22; and the suggestion of Ronsard's father to turn to the law (ll. 45-52) may refer to the allusion in Ovid to his brother's profession:

frater ad eloquium viridi tendebat ab aevo,
fortia verbosi natus ad arma fori.
(II. 17-18)

Lines 77-84 in Ronsard go on to speak of the inevitability of the poet's calling ("O qu'il est mal aisé de forcer la nature!" [I. 77]), just as Ovid illustrates the fact by showing that even when he tried to write prose, it came out as verse (II. 23-26). The vocation of the dedicatee of Ronsard's poem, the architect Pierre l'Escot, is spoken of in similar terms (II. 105-26) before the poet concludes by looking back nostalgically to the artistic Golden Age under François Ier and Henri II. The death of the second of these two monarchs (I. 153) implicitly marks the end of this period of good fortune (which Ronsard always portrays in retrospect as rosier than when he was actually experiencing it); and this theme of loss is emphasized by the links with the Ovidian text, where exile has consigned the Roman poet to a cultural wilderness exactly similar to the one Ronsard finds himself in.

Ronsard also incorporates the *topos* into the "Complainte contre Fortune," addressed in 1559 to Odet de Coligny. Once again, the poet evokes the *locus amoenus* associated with the innocence of poetic creation (II. 79-80), cf.:

Il n'y avoit rocher qui ne me fust ouvert,
Ny antre qui ne fust à mon œil decouvert,
Ny belle source d'eau que des mains ne puisasse,
Ny si basse vallée où tout seul je n'allasse.
Phœbus au crin doré son luth me presentoit,
Pan le Dieu forestier sous mes flutes sautoit,
Et avec les Sylvains les gentiles Dryades
Foulloyent sous mes chansons l'herbette de gambades.
(II. 83-90)

Again, to what extent are we concerned here with any kind of real landscape? Propertius 3, 3 among other texts probably provides the answer, for it is there quite clear that the various references to geographical features on Mount Helicon are to be read metaphorically as allusions to different genres of poetry. Thus, the "tam magnis . . . fontibus . . . / unde pater sitiens Ennius ante bibit" (II. 5-6) are a reference to epic poetry, later represented as a river by Apollo:

Quid tibi cum tali, demens, est flumine? quis te
carminis heroi tangere iussit opus?
(II. 15-16)

Elegiac poetry, on the other hand, is seen in terms of a gentle meadow— "mollia sunt parvis prata terenda rotis" (I. 18). Further links with Propertius are provided by Ronsard's allusions to Apollo and Pan (ll. 87-90); compare, for example, Ronsard ll. 88-90 and Propertius 29-30:

> orgia Musarum et Sileni patris imago
> fictilis et calami, Pan Tegeaee, tui.

Thus, the evocation of Propertius 3, 3 sheds light on the function of the topographical imagery in the passage quoted: as a youth, Ronsard went through all the various genres of poetry.

The metaphorical nature of this imagery is made more explicit later in the same poem when Ronsard produces a prosopopoeia of the Muses, who are making their complaint to Fortune. Again, we are presented with the poetic landscape, for the Muses have nurtured:

> Un Ronsard Vandomois, luy permettans l'entrée
> (Qu'à bien peu nous faisons) de nostre onde sacrée,
> Luy permettans de boire en nos divins ruisseaux,
> De toucher nostre luth, de monter aux coupeaux
> De nostre sainct Parnaze, & comme pour conqueste
> Porter de nos lauriers un chapeau sur la teste,
> Et au raix de la lune entre cent mille fleurs
> Fouler l'herbe du pied au milieu de nos sœurs.
> (II. 165-72)

Once again, there seems to be a basic unity in this poem with regard to the way in which Ronsard uses the imagery of the inspirational landscape. The Horatian reminiscence (ll. 171-72) to *Odes* 1, 4, a poem on the pressing inevitability of death even in the midst of renewing life, perhaps emphasizes the unique role of the Muses to confer immortality on humans.

So, it is clear that, despite a superficial resemblance in details, the inspiration theme can fulfill very different functions in Ronsard's poetry, which the understanding of poetic allusions helps to elucidate. While this understanding may not provide us with all the answers—ultimately, the Ronsard text always retains a certain mystery, eschewing the perfect clarity of the classical period of French literature—it is nevertheless essential if false conclusions are to be avoided. The reference by Ronsard to a whole tradition of interrelated themes guides the reader's attention by evoking certain contexts in ancient writers, while at the same time leaving some scope to his imagination by alluding to not one, but several contexts simultaneously. The result is a text which is all the richer on this account.

NOTES

1. Quotations from Ronsard will be taken from *Oeuvres complètes*, ed. Paul Laumonier et al., 20 vols (Paris, 1914-1975). For this quotation, see Laumonier, XII, 47-48.

2. M. Dassonville, *Ronsard: Etude historique et littéraire*, I: *Les Enfances Ronsard* (Geneva, 1968), p. 83.

3. Laumonier XII, p. 48.

4. The poems under consideration here are *L'Hymne de l'Autonne*, Laumonier XII, pp. 46 ff.; the "Elégie à Pierre l'Escot," Laumonier X, pp. 300 ff.; and the "Complainte contre Fortune," Laumonier X, pp. 16 ff.

5. *The Gallo-Roman Muse: Aspects of Roman Literary Tradition in Sixteenth-Century France* (Cambridge, 1979), p. 90.

6. "I have not moistened my lips in the fountain of the horse, nor do I recall having dreamt on twin-peaked Parnassus, to account for my sudden appearance as a poet. I give up the maids of Helicon and wasting Pirene to those who have winding ivy encircling their busts . . . . "

7. "As our own Ennius sang, who first brought down from beautiful Mount Helicon a garland of evergreen foliage, which would win fame among the people of Italy . . . He tells of how the ghost of the ever-famous Homer appeared to him, and began to weep salt tears, and to expound upon the nature of the universe."

8. "*I* am associated with the gods above by ivy garlands, the reward of a learned brow; *I* am separated from the populace by the cool grove and the light-footed bands of nymphs and satyrs, so long as Euterpe does not restrain the pipes, or Polyhymnia shrink from tuning the Lesbian lyre."

9. "Can you hear, or am I deluded by a delightful madness? I seem to hear her, and to wander through holy groves where pleasant streams and breezes pass."

10. "I had seemed to be lying in the gentle shade of Mount Helicon where the streams formed by Bellerophon's horse flow . . . . "

11. "But a high hope of renown has struck my heart with its sharp goad, and at the same time has inspired in my breast a sweet love of the Muses. Fired with this and with a vigorous mind, I now pass through pathless regions of the Muses, previously untrod by any foot. It is delightful to come across untouched springs and to drink one's fill; it is delightful to pick fresh flowers and to seek a glorious garland for my head from flowers with which previously the Muses have wreathed no man's brow."

12. "Then he sings of how Gallus, wandering by the rivers of Permessus, was led by one of the sisters into the Aonian hills, . . . and how Linus . . . said: 'The Muses give you this reed-pipe—here, take it—which they previously gave to the old poet of Ascra [Hesiod]. He used to play it when he brought the unbending ash trees down the mountain.' "

13. Cf. *Tristia* 2, 207, "perdiderint cum me duo crimina, carmen et error."

14. For example, George Buchanan writes in his first Elegy, "Exul Hyperboreum Naso projectus ad axem, / Exilium Musis imputat ille suum" (ll. 97-98).

15. "But I loved the heavenly rites even as a boy and the Muse would stealthily draw me into her activities. Often my father said: 'Why do you attempt this useless occupation? Even Homer himself left no wealth behind.' I was moved by his words, and having abandoned Mount Helicon completely, I tried to write prose. But poetry came out spontaneously in appropriate metres, and whatever I tried to say was in verse."

Alan Boase

Quelques Réflexions sur les "Sonets pour Helene"

Chère Amie,
Je viens de relire récemment un article que j'ai écrit il y a cinquante ans. Il a présenté au public anglais, celui du *Criterion*, la poésie de Jean de Sponde. A vrai dire, je l'ai trouvé souvent un peu juvénile pour mes vingt-sept ans. Il lui manquait en somme la finesse et la précision qui ont caractérisé votre premier livre auquel je pensais bien souvent en me relisant. Selon vous, "the distinctive blend of passionate feeling and paradoxical rationalization which we call metaphysical poetry is essentially an effort to achieve the perfect poise between intelligence and sensibility." C'était bien le sujet de mon "Enfin Malherbe Vint." Je m'imaginais l'avoir trouvé chez Jean de Sponde, chez Jean Godard, chez La Ceppède, chez Etienne Durand même. Vous avez même poussé le scrupule jusqu'à demander de la poésie "métaphysique" qu'elle envisage les problèmes centraux de la métaphysique au sens philosophique. Malheureusement il s'est créé un malentendu. Comme j'ai moi-même montré en français[1] le terme "métaphysique" qui est discuté par le Chevalier de Méré et Madame de Sablé avait clairement pour eux la nuance de psychologiquement subtil, et cet usage est confirmé au siècle suivant par Marivaux. Ces observations ne diminuent aucunement votre excellente démonstration que Maurice Scève doit être considéré comme un poète métaphysique au sens anglais. Je dois ajouter même que Scève bientôt oublié par un seul enthousiaste comme Pontus, jamais réédité jusqu'au dix-neuvième siècle, fut enfin loué par un Anglais, le traducteur de Dante, qui, dans un de ses articles publié en 1821, a remarqué qu'on trouverait chez Scève "de belles choses dignes de notre Donne."

On me dit que je dois écrire sur l'équilibre de l'esprit, ce que vous avez vous-même si bien défini comme la facilité de changer de ton—du grave au frivole ou de l'ironie au sarcasme—dans un même poème. Le meilleur exemple, que je voudrais exposer à votre attention, est celui de Ronsard lui-même.

Il me semble qu'on n'a jamais rendu justice aux *Sonets pour Helene*, et plus particulièrement au second livre de ce recueil, tel qu'il sera remanié et augmenté par 34 sonnets, transférés des *Amours diverses* en 1584.[2]

C'est dans ce dernier recueil que Ronsard se met à évoquer pour nous une scène précise. Qu'on se répète certains débuts,

> Te regardant assise aupres de ta cousine
> Belle comme une Aurore, & toy comme un Soleil,
>
> (I, 17)

ou bien

> Nous promenant tous seuls, vous me dites, Maistresse,
> Qu'un chant vous desplaisoit, s'il estoit doucereux.
>
> (1, 26)

A vrai dire ni l'un ni l'autre de ces deux sonnets ne tiennent cette promesse. Le second se transforme en une épigramme amusante sur le crocodile,

> Mais vostre œil cauteleux, trop finement subtil,
> Pleure en chantant mes vers, comme le Crocodil,
> Pour mieux de desrober par feintise la vie.

Au premier cependant nous trouvons un croquis inoubliable, si toutefois entièrement externe, d'Hélène:

> Toy comme paresseuse, & pleine de sommeil,
> D'un seul petit regard tu ne m'estimas digne.
>   Tu t'entretenois seule au visage abaissé,
> Pensive toute à toy, n'aimant rien que toymesme,
> Desdaignant un chascun d'un sourcil ramassé,
> Comme une qui ne veut qu'on la cherche ou qu'on l'aime.

Ailleurs, c'est toute une scène évoquée, la scène d'un ballet de cour:

> Le soir qu'Amour vous fist en la salle descendre
> Pour danser d'artifice un beau ballet d'Amour.
>
> (II, 30)

La scène en est devenue célèbre, mais nous avons quelque chose de plus profond dans un autre sonnet. Le site est une chambre au grenier dans le Louvre; de la fenêtre on voit un endroit célèbre alors pour son couvent, et

ce qui suit possède du pathétique mais aussi de l'ironie comme Hélène
déclare que,

> La solitaire vie, & le desert sejour
> Valent mieux que la Cour, je voudrois bien y estre.
> A l'heure mon esprit de mes sens seroit maistre,
> En jeusne & oraisons je passerois le jour.

pendant que le poète la prévient

> Sur les cloistres sacrez la flame on voit passer:
> Amour dans les deserts comme aux villes s'engendre.
>
> (I, 29)

Et il s'agit de s'en contenter.

Le sonnet exquis (II, 23), malgré toutes les différences, revient au fond
aux mêmes conclusions,

> Ces longues nuicts d'hyver, où la Lune ocieuse,
> Tourne si lentement son char tout à l'entour.

Le rêve illusoire de trouver sa maîtresse entre ses bras—thème conventionnel et souvent dans le plus mauvais goût. Ici il est transformé, en partie par
le souvenir de l'insomnie (destiné à se répéter dans les *Derniers Vers* poi-
gnants du poète mourant),

> Où le Coq si tardif nous annonce le jour,
> Où la nuict semble un an à l'ame soucieuse,

et aussi par le contraste amer entre la véritable Hélène et son fantôme:

> Vraye tu es farouche, & fiere en cruauté:
> De toy fausse on jouyst en toute privauté.
> Pres ton mort je m'endors, pres de luy je repose,

transformé aussi par la note ironique de reconnaissance sur laquelle il termine le sonnet:

> Le bon sommeil ainsi
> Abuse par le faux mon amoureux souci.
> S'abuser en amour n'est pas mauvaise chose.

L'acceptation d'une situation sans espoir, contre son gré et pourtant volontairement, cela ne pourrait guère mieux s'exprimer.

Les faits évidents de la situation sont employés dans cet autre sonnet
(II, 24) que tout le monde connaît. On reconnaît mieux ses qualités en
supposant pour un moment une absurde accusation de vanité personnelle.

Comment un amoureux en cheveux gris pourrait-il répondre au mépris d'Hélène autrement qu'au nom de sa poésie et la célébrité qu'elle lui a apportée? Et pourtant quelle ironie de penser que lorsqu'elle reconnaîtra sa bonne fortune, il sera, lui, un cadavre sous terre, un fantôme pâle dans les limbes, et elle, une vieille édentée accroupie au foyer. Et si le poète résiste à toutes tentations de s'apitoyer sur lui-même tel qu'il sera, pour elle il y a un reste de tendresse, une réticence miséricordieuse plus évidente dès que nous tournons la page pour relire les vers où Ronsard évoque la *chair si moisie* d'une vieille Hélène grecque devant son miroir (II, 26). Seule la distance imposée par la comparaison antique justifie la brutalité du tableau.

Le *carpe diem* conventionnel qui termine "Quand vous serez bien vieille" peut se prendre comme le symbole même des *Sonets pour Helene*, où l'impression dominante reste celle d'un retour au ton galant mais respectueux de la tradition pétrarquiste et une préciosité épigrammatique. Ce serait un jugement incomplet. Six ans plus tard, quelques mois à peine avant la mort de Ronsard, une nouvelle édition de ses œuvres a paru dans laquelle 34 nouvelles poésies ont pris leur place parmi les *Sonets pour Helene*, toutes transférées des *Amours diverses*. Même en supposant qu'aucune parmi elles n'a jamais eu de rapport primitivement avec Hélène de Surgères—difficile à admettre—elles témoigneraient de la décision de révéler une vision complète de sa passion pour Hélène. Ces sonnets ajoutés au recueil comprennent, il est vrai, quelques compliments alambiqués—"La Poudre de Chypre," "La Saignée," "La Coupe vénéneuse"—ces titres semblent s'imposer. Cela dit, ajoutons tout de suite que la plupart de ces poèmes sont étonnants, à la fois pour leur intérêt humain et pour leur qualité poétique. Examinons-en quelques-uns:

> Quoy? me donner congé d'embrasser chaque femme,
> Mon feu des-attizer au premier corps venu,
> Ainsi qu'un vagabond, sans estre retenu,
> Abandonner la bride au vouloir de ma flame:
> Non, ce n'est pas aimer.
>
> (*Les Amours diverses*, 13)

Ajouter quelque chose ne pourrait qu'affaiblir l'indignation du poète devant une suggestion qui n'aurait été que trop caractéristique d'Hélène comme les sources contemporaines nous la montrent. Une telle division de rôles ne serait à ses yeux qu'une tricherie indigne. Le reste du sonnet dépeint les signes d'un véritable amour comme *inquiétude, soufre* et *braise*, une jalousie peu commode, il est vrai, et peu semblable à cette *flamme de Cour* dont elle est seule capable. Cette note de réalité, d'une impatience virile—de l'indignation plutôt qu'une simple ironie—se répète plus d'une fois dans ces sonnets ajoutés où Ronsard déclare: "Elle a de nos chansons & non de nous souci."

C'est elle qui est certainement le sujet de deux remarquables *sonnets d'aveux*. Les *Sonets pour Helene* primitifs ont laissé ses sentiments pour le poète totalement énigmatiques. Elle n'est vue que du dehors. Même le sonnet que nous venons d'examiner est une évasion de sa part. Regardons ailleurs:

> Prenant congé de vous, dont les yeux m'ont donté,
> Vous me distes un soir comme passionnee,
> Je vous aime, Ronsard, par seule destinee,
> Le Ciel à vous aimer force ma volonté.
>
> (*A.D.*, 34)

Comme il en arrive si souvent, l'attaque de ce début nous donne tout le thème, et pourtant la suite nous offre de nouvelles modulations. Ici cela prend la forme d'une raison négative pour l'affection d'Hélène. C'est ni son savoir, ni son âge, ni sa beauté. Le manque de raison est la preuve de la destinée. Le sonnet suivant (*A.D.*, 35), "Quand je pense à ce jour, où pres d'une fontaine / Dans le jardin royal . . . ," est la confirmation naturelle de l'aveu d'Hélène: "Je n'y veux résister, il le faut laisser faire," s'écrie-t-elle. Sa joie semble seulement mitigée par la présence d'une compagne (sans doute Diane de Cossé Brissac, la cousine mentionnée déjà).

De l'aveu nous passons au désaveu, tandis que la réalisation de l'indifférence d'Hélène se fait comprendre. Et alors une nouvelle forme d'ironie— une ironie tournée contre lui-même: "Amour, je pren congé de ta menteuse escole" (*A.D.*, 46), ou "J'ay honte de ma honte, il est temps de me taire" (*A.D.*, 27). De cette ironie nous passons à la flagellation de soi qui rend remarquable l'étonnant "Au milieu de la guerre, en un siecle sans foi" (*A.D.*, 30). Ronsard confronte ici son dilemme entier, et le résultat est totalement dissemblable à l'ironie des *Regrets* de Du Bellay. Le sonnet est presque baudelairien dans son intensité poétique, mais non sans une nuance de patriotisme. La toile de fond est ici la lutte fratricide des Guerres de Religion, une *Thébaïde* comme il le dit avec une allusion aux frères ennemis, Etéocle et Polynice. Il désavouе non seulement Hélène et l'amour, mais même les Muses. Ecoutons cette diatribe:

> Au milieu de la guerre, en un siecle sans foy,
> Entre mille procez, est-ce pas grand folie
> D'escrire de l'Amour? De manotes on lie
> Des fois, qui ne sont pas si furieux que moy.
>
> Grison & maladif r'entrer dessous la loy
> D'Amour, ô quelle erreur! Dieux, mercy je vous crie.

Tu ne m'es plus Amour, tu m'es une Furie,
Qui me rends fol, enfant, & sans yeux comme toy:

Voir perdre mon pays, proye des adversaires,
Voir en noz estendars les fleurs de liz contraires,
Voir une Thebaïde, & faire l'amoureux.

Je m'en vais au Palais: adieu vieilles Sorcieres.
Muses, je prens mon sac, je seray plus heureux
En gaignant mes procez, qu'en suivant voz rivieres.

La désinvolture du sonnet suivant n'est pas moins caractéristique—"Le juge m'a trompé" (*A.D.*, 31), sonnet d'une sagesse terre à terre:

Nud je vins en ce monde,
Et nud je m'en iray. Que me servent les pleurs,
Sinon de m'attrister d'une angoisse profonde?
Chassons avec le vin le soin & les malheurs:
Je combats les souciz, quand le vin me seconde.

Parmi ces sonnets ajoutés je constate encore que l'exacte parallèle au burlesque fantasque de John Donne—son poème sur la puce—trouve exactement son pendant dans le "Cousin, monstre à double aile, au mufle Elephantin" (*A.D.*, 9), semblable à la nature renverseée chère aux poètes baroques.

Il me semble qu'en face de ces poésies de la maturité de Ronsard, c'est un véritable appauvrissement qui s'annonce avec Malherbe. Le sens même du célèbre "Enfin Malherbe vint" dans l'*Art Poétique* de Boileau. La régularité des stances, la condamnation de tout enjambement, de toute élision, marquent une conception de la poésie qui allait dominer pendant plus d'un siècle à l'exclusion de l'*esprit*. Il suffit de penser au meilleur de Malherbe, tel que "Beauté, mon beau souci," pour se rendre compte que la mélodie des alexandrins équilibrés détruit le ton qui se veut badin dans certaines strophes. Par exemple, "Madame, avisez-y, vous perdez vostre gloire" fait imaginer l'index d'un pédagogue!

Cela me fait retourner à la dernière partie de votre premier livre. J'approuve pleinement la façon dont vous y traitez la préciosité. Cette tendance à une forme de poésie mi-sociale, faite pour une élite, je la vois commencer presque dès le début du siècle. Je parlais il y a un instant de l'*esprit*. Où peut-on tourner pour voir définir utilement l'*esprit*? Je me rappelle l'avoir fait autrefois un peu par hasard. C'est là ce qui m'a guidé à un charmant poète mineur—celui qu'on a appelé *le grand madrigalier* qui, comme dit Voltaire, a su écrire "avec une finesse qui n'exclut pas le naturel." C'est le Marquis de la Sablière qui a su trouver la finesse d'écrire en faisant "valoir l'esprit des autres."

Or le marquis dont la veuve est devenue plus tard l'amie de La Fontaine, fut lui-même membre du groupe d'amis de la jeunesse de La Fontaine, groupe dont Maucroix et Pélisson furent aussi des membres pendant les années qui ont précédé la Fronde. Celui qui semble avoir initié La Fontaine à l'usage du vers libre (ou libéré) qui est devenu le grand instrument des *Fables* semble bien avoir été La Sablière. C'était la grande trouvaille de La Fontaine et qui lui a permis de développer finesse et naturel comme vous avez si bien montré dans votre excellente *O Muse, fuyante proie* . . . .

NOTES

1. Voir mon article, "Tradition et révision de valeurs dans l'anthologie française (1692-1960)," *Annales de la Faculté des Lettres et Sciences Humaines d'Aix*, 46 (1962), 31-47.

2. Edition utilisée: *Les Amours*, ed. H. et C. Weber (Paris, 1963).

Elizabeth Armstrong

A Study in Montaigne's Post-1588 Style and Sensibility

Montaigne's vocation as an author was a late one. It is impossible to date any of his original writing before his thirty-eighth birthday, 28th February, 1571, when he commemorated, by an inscription in his library, his resignation from his post of *conseiller* or magistrate in the Parlement of Bordeaux and his determination to spend his remaining days in peace in the company of the Muses. Nonetheless, he was to know three great periods of creative activity in the twenty-one years of life which lay before him. The first lasted, with some intervals and fluctuations, from some time in 1572 until the beginning of 1580, and produced Books I and II of the *Essais* in their original form, published in two smallish octavo volumes in 1580 by the local Bordeaux printer Simon Millanges, Book I containing fifty-seven chapters, Book II thirty-seven chapters (including the exceptionally long "Apologie de Raimond Sebond"). The second resulted in the Fifth edition of the *Essais*, published at Paris in June 1588: it added numerous alterations and insertions, and a Third Book containing thirteen wholly new essays. This new material, which almost doubled the total size of his work, was not composed steadily during the intervening years, but mostly during 1586 and 1587, in an extraordinary bout of inspiration and energy. Montaigne had spent eighteen months travelling in Germany, Switzerland and Italy, had returned to occupy for two successive two-year terms the office of Mayor of Bordeaux, the last part of them deeply concerned with the civil wars and with the task of preserving some public order in the province in collaboration with Marshal de Matignon, the royal Governor of Guyenne. Another experience of a different kind had also had time to make itself felt: he had become a famous author. He had a new confidant: the general public. He had a new status: that of a great literary artist. But when he returned home later in 1588, with the completed Paris edition, the creative impulse renewed itself a third time—if indeed one should not think of it rather as the irrepressible continuation of the previous one. Between then and his death, 13th September, 1592, he read much and wrote constantly. Just as Montaigne had corrected and embellished some of the chapters of Books I and II, when he re-read and re-published them in the 1588 edition, so now in the 1588 edition itself he entered not only corrections but hundreds of additions and alterations. Some of these are merely supplementary examples and anecdotes, or smart quotations aptly introduced. Others are passages of great importance for both their content and their style. There were indeed no new chapters. But there was certainly a conscious new stage in his writing. On his copy of the 1588 edition, on the title-page, he crossed out "Fifth edition" and substituted "Sixth edition," and he entered in a blank space the motto *Viresque acquirit eundo*—"it gathers strength as it goes along," a tag from Virgil, *Aeneid*, IV, given—as Montaigne so often did with quotations from his favorite poets—a meaning remote from the context in which the quotation is to be found.

It is one of these instances of "gathering strength as it goes along" that I intend to examine here, as an example of Montaigne's mature wit.

To none of the essays did Montaigne return at his last period with more interest than the chapters he had written in Book I when he was studying Stoicism as expounded by Seneca in his *Epistles* and (in a lesser degree) by Cicero in some of his philosophical writings. Not naturally stern or melancholic, he had been obliged when he first retired in 1571 by a series of events in his life to ponder the prospect of death: the loss of his great friend Etienne de la Boétie, little older than himself; the death of his father, to whom he was much attached, leaving him head of the family; the death of a younger brother at the age of twenty-three as the result of an accident playing tennis; the death of his first child, much awaited after five years of marriage; a riding accident in which he himself had narrowly escaped death; the outbreak of civil war in which no one's life, freedom or property was safe. From these meditations sprang the chapter I, 20, "Que philosopher c'est apprendre à mourir," which takes as its text (as it were) a pronouncement of Cicero. Most eloquently, in the 1580 text, Montaigne demonstrated to himself and his readers that uncontrolled fear of death is incompatible with happiness, freedom and human dignity: thus, the man is truly a slave, whatever his position, who can be forced by the threat of death to plead for mercy from a tyrant or to act against his conscience. But his exposition of the Stoic way was never bigoted. In a final exhortation to the reader to accept death as part of the scheme of things, he did not hesitate to turn to one of his favorite poets, Lucretius, and paraphrase the address in which Mother Nature apostrophizes mankind, maintaining that he who accepts life from her must also accept death—an Epicurean rather than a Stoic doctrine.

When Montaigne began to re-read this chapter after 1588, he was immediately moved to make, after the first four sentences, a long addition, written across the top of the printed page, continued in short lines down the inner margin, and completed across the bottom of the page.

Already in the 1580 text, Montaigne saw overcoming fear of death not as an end in itself but as a means to a happier life, and claimed that all rational opinions had the same aim. Now, after 1588, he paused in his final revision to emphasize this point: "toutes les opinions du monde en sont là, quoy qu'elles prennent divers moyens . . . " he had written, and now he inserted after "en sont là" the words "que le plaisir est nostre but."

He dismissed summarily the apparent differences of the various philosophical schools, or "sects" as he affects to call them, as verbal—mere quibbling, showing more obstinacy and wrangling than befits so sacred a profession (is there a touch of irony about the use of sacred in this connection?). And he transcribed from Seneca's Letter 117 the words, "Transcurramus solertissimas nugas" ("Let us pass over these trifles"), perhaps pleased at being able to quote a revered philosopher against the shortcomings of philosophers. But his point is that all this verbal dissension does not prevent the philosopher from being human and therefore desiring (whether he admits it or not) inevitably to have pleasure and not pain as the object of his efforts: and he expresses this by a metaphor taken from the stage— whatever part a man plays he is always playing himself as well. Thus we are brought to the essential paradox, which Montaigne left implicit in the original texts but is now determined to dramatize to the utmost: "Say what they may, in virtue itself, it is *volupté*—voluptuousness—which is the ultimate target at which we aim." Montaigne momentarily becomes a disrespectful schoolboy, and the philosophers the ponderous teachers: "I *like* dinning this word[*volupté*] into their ears which so much offends them."

Who are the originals of this caricature? Chiefly the Stoics, whom Montaigne studied seriously but could also see at moments as arrogant and inhuman, even in the first stage of the *Essais*: *voluptas* was not necessarily a pejorative word, but it was spurned as an evil by extreme exponents of an ascetic philosophy, and Montaigne had quoted with disapproval in II, 2 the "Stoic sallies" attributed to Antithenes, "I would rather be demented than voluptuous," and to Sextius, "that he would rather be fettered by pain than by voluptuousness"—("qui ne juge que ce sont boutées d'un courage eslancé hors de son giste?").

Montaigne was quite aware that the word *voluptuousness* was most commonly used for sensual and especially for sexual enjoyment. He protests against this. If the word means the supreme pleasure, it is more appropriate to *virtue*. This voluptuousness—that of virtue—for being more sprightly, muscular, sturdy and manly, is but the more seriously voluptuous—a calculated paradox. *Virtue* is in fact a word which means in Latin vigor, force and manliness as well as moral excellence. Montaigne, following Cicero in *Tusculan Disputations* (II, 18), derives *virtus* from *vis*. He would prefer what we call "virtue" to be called instead by the gentler and sweeter name of "pleasure." But in that case what about voluptuousness as commonly understood, which Montaigne (who knew something about it) describes as "that *lower* voluptuousness"? Does it have any claim to the name, supposing that "voluptuousness" means a supreme form of pleasure? Montaigne boldly moves into the world of registered names and trade-marks and proprietory rights in them. If "cette autre volupté plus basse" wants to be called *volupté*, this should not be *par privilege*, that is, by holding a patent or monopoly in it, but *en concurrence*, that is, by competition in the open market. On these terms, what *does* it offer by comparison with Virtue? Montaigne finds it less free from disadvantages and drawbacks than Virtue: it has its vigils, its fastings and its travails, its expenditure of sweat and blood, it has acute passions (or sufferings) of many kinds, and it can bring with it a satiety[1] so heavy that it is the counterpart to penance. Why should we say of the "volupté plus basse" that these difficulties serve as a stimulus and a spice,[2] and complain, when it comes to Virtue, that the difficulties attending it make it austere and inaccessible? It is much truer of Virtue that the difficulties ennoble, whet and intensify the pleasure it procures for us.

And now the conception of Virtue which Montaigne advocates begins to come to life. It is no longer an abstraction. He begins to use words about it which can apply only to a person. "He who weighs up the cost as against the fruition of her is surely unworthy of her acquaintance [*accointance*]." He deals summarily with those writers who teach that *she* is desirable, only the *quest* for her is rough and painful: since no man can claim to have won her, what else is this but to say that she is always displeasing? For the most perfect men have been content to aspire to her and approach her without possessing her.[3] But such writers are mistaken. They ignore the human truth, that the pursuit of a worthwhile pleasure is itself pleasurable: the undertaking takes on the quality of the object it has in view. This finally leads Montaigne to conjure up the quality of Virtue, of which this is particularly true: "The joy and bliss which shines out in Virtue fills all her appurtenances and approaches, right up to the first entrance and the outermost barrier." A suggestion of personification if not of allegory hangs over this eloquent passage. The pursuit of Virtue is already more like the Quest of a heroine of romance than the painful observance of a moral code, and the final picture is of some great palace or sanctuary at whose very park-gates the visitor begins to feel the atmosphere of happiness and benignity radiated by the lady who inhabits it. One of her chief gifts to her devotees is in fact the power to scorn death, and so Montaigne returns to his original theme, that no true enjoyment of life is possible if fear of death is able to poison it.

There is much in this passage which is characteristic of Montaigne at all periods of his literary activity: the assimilation of ancient wisdom, inter-preted in a personal and sometimes critical way; the ready resort to meta-phors derived from games, from commerce, from cooking; the challenging questions to the reader; the impatience with any philosophy which claimed to raise man above the limitations of his nature; the tendency to preach a sort of superior hedonism as the highest good.

However, there is here a determination to speak out, an urgency to con-vince the reader, a lyricism in celebrating what he believed in, which gives an unusual momentum to this defense of Virtue as he understood it. He is no longer the detached observer, the cautious weigher up of probabilities. He rejoins naturally the fervor of his writing of twenty years before and adds the certainties he has learned by experience. "Mais ilz se trompent . . . ."

In an addition made at the same period to the famous chapter on edu-cation, "De l'institution des enfans" (I, 26), Montaigne introduced an impassioned defense of the attractiveness of Virtue. He had already, in the original 1580 text, claimed that philosophy had a place in the education of children, and that it was quite wrong to paint it as "inaccessible aux enfans, et d'un visage renfroigné, sourcilleux et terrible." Now he repudiates a sim-ilar misrepresentation of Virtue, in the passage beginning "Elle a pour son but la vertu, qui n'est pas, comme dit l'eschole, plantée à la teste d'un mont coupé, rabotteux et inaccessible." As he continues we recognize a traditional picture which is certainly at the back of his mind also in the defense of Virtue added to "Que philosopher c'est apprendre à mourir." This is the *topos*, both iconographical and literary, which opposed Virtue to Voluptuousness, showing Virtue at the top of a high rock approached only by a steep and narrow way beset by thorns and stones, while Volup-tuousness stood invitingly at the end of a smooth, wide and gentle path spread with flowers. Such a picture occurs, for instance, among the illustra-tions, many times copied and reprinted in France as in Germany far into the sixteenth century, of Sebastien Brant's *Ship of Fools*.[4] This shows a knight asleep who sees in a dream the rival goddesses thus placed: plain

Uoluptas.   **Uirtus.**

BRANT, Sébastien, Stultifera navis, Paris [Georg Wolf] pour Geoffrey de Marnef,
8 mars 1498: in-4.

Virtus, muffled in prudish veils and ostentatiously holding a distaff, stars in
the sky above her but thorns and thistles round her, glares down disapprov-
ingly from her rock at *Voluptas*, a provocative gothic nude surrounded by
roses, oblivious of the lurking figure of Death behind her or the hell-fire
descending on her from the wrath of Heaven. Montaigne on the contrary
gives the true Virtue "fortune et volupté" as her companions, and
reproaches those who have thought up "cette sotte image, triste, querel-
leuse, despite, menaceuse, mineuse" and perched it "sur un rocher, à
l'escart, emmy des ronces, fantosme à estonner les gens."

If the iconographical tradition which opposed *Virtus* to *Voluptas* was vividly and frequently renewed, the literary tradition had received fresh authority from the greatest French poet of Montaigne's time, Pierre de Ronsard. "La Vertu amoureuse," a long poem written as a compliment to Bishop Jerome de la Rovere, was published in the *Ve Livre des Poemes* in 1560,[5] and incorporated in all the collected editions of the poet's works. In it Ronsard represents Virtue as a beautiful and amorous goddess; she is not "effeminée" like the goddess born from the foam of the sea—Venus— but her glance is both gentle and proud, "her eye-brows are somewhat low," and her look similar to that of Pallas Athene in a peaceful mood. Except in thus using about Virtue terms normally associated with human charm, Ronsard's description differs in almost every respect from Montaigne's. In his vision of Virtue, he saw a huge rock, on the highest point of which she had her temple, attended by Study, Sweat, Labor, Honor and Uprightness. Those who seek her suffer "a hundred thousand travails, through rocks, through torrents, through plains and valleys, through thickets and thorns." At the foot of the steep way leading to her mountain, the alluring rival goddess *Volupté* lies in wait for passers-by, ridiculing Virtue and those who search for her, and preaching self-indulgence. Ronsard is thus clearly an exponent of the view (singled out by Montaigne for particular criticism in the addition to "Que philosopher c'est apprendre à mourir") that the *Quest* for her is rough and painful, the *enjoyment* of her pleasurable; no human being, in Montaigne's opinion, can claim to possess her. Ronsard, on the contrary, hymns the joys and rewards of those who have won her—"Toujours mes amoureux ont de moy jouissance"—particularly of course Bishop Jerome de la Rovere. Montaigne certainly knew Ronsard's poetry, and admired him as a poet, so it is quite possible that he had read "La Vertu amoureuse."[6]

Why did Montaigne go to the trouble of making this long addition to "Que philosopher c'est apprendre à mourir," criticizing the commonplace which treated *vertu* and *volupté* as incompatible?

There is perhaps one clue. He had already discussed Virtue, and already personified it, in 1580 in the chapter "Du jeune Caton" (I, 37), professing himself well able to admire virtue of a degree and kind which he himself could never emulate. He criticized two tendencies of his own time. One was to perform virtuous actions mainly for reasons of profit, vainglory or fear: "Virtue recognizes only actions done for her, and for her alone." The other was to credit the heroes of the past, whose virtuous actions have come down to us, with similar base motives. Those who show this tendency, to belittle the great deeds of others, do so, if not from sheer malice, because they judge others by themselves, or, more probably in Montaigne's view, they simply have not sight strong and clear enough to be able "to conceive of the splendor of virtue in its native purity," nor sight trained to do so. Montaigne intervenes here with a post-1588 addition showing how alive the subject still was for him: so hateful to him is the tendency to sneer at accounts of virtuous conduct that he now proclaims it to be the duty of right-thinking people to make a conscious effort to counteract it, by painting virtue as fair as possible, "and it would not become us ill were passion to carry us away in favor of forms so sacred" ("C'est l'office des gens de bien de peindre la vertu la plus belle qui se puisse; et ne nous messieroit pas, quand la passion nous transporteroit à la faveur de si sainctes formes").

There is certainly vehemence as well as wit in his defense of the attractiveness of Virtue in the post-1588 addition to "Que philosopher c'est apprendre à mourir," and to "De l'institution des enfans." The association of Virtue with the prig and the kill-joy seemed to him unjustifiable and thoroughly harmful in its effects. He saw nothing virtuous about self-denial for its own sake. He could, indeed, at least by the last period of his life, respect those who practiced self-denial as a Way, provided—it seems—that they were genuine and that they did not condemn others. "Without being chaste myself, I nonetheless sincerely approve the chastity of the Feuillants and the Capucines and I have a good opinion of their routine,"[7] he declared in another post-1588 addition to "Du jeune Caton." But condemning pleasure, and trying thereby to attain liberation from the limitations of the human condition, seemed to him an illusion. A long life of pleasure-seeking (not always so selfish as he would have the reader believe) had convinced him that the alternative to asceticism was not unbridled self-indulgence but integrity, humanity and a reasonable amount of self-control. The pursuit of Virtue, thus understood, seemed to him the highest happiness that mortal man could know. This apparently unromantic conception of Virtue had, for him, an almost romantic significance, and did not exclude a possible element of the heroic, as long as the truth was always borne in mind which he had expressed in one of the Third Book essays in 1588, "La vertu est qualité plaisante et gaye" (III, 5).

NOTES

1. Cf. "Le desir et la satieté remplissent de douleur les sieges au dessus et au dessous de la volupté" (post-1588 addition to I, 54). Florio, who translates this sentence in I, 54 correctly, rendering "satieté" by "satiety," makes the strange blunder in I, 20 of rendering "satieté" by "societie," altering the whole meaning. Did he misread the French text, or mis-hear someone reading it aloud to him or have a misprint in his copy, or think that "satieté" was a misprint for "societé"?

2. Cf. "Je ne suis guere adonné aux accointances venales et publiques: j'ay voulu esguiser ce plaisir par la difficulté, par le désir et par quelque gloire" (III, 3).

3. Cf. "nostre vertu mesme est fautiere et repentable" (post-1588 addition to II, 6).

4. First edition Basle (Johannes Bergmann von Olpe, 1494). First French edition Paris (Geofroy de Marnef, 1498) (in Latin translation).

5. Ronsard, *Oeuvres*, eds. P. Laumonier, R. Lebègue and I. Silver, 20 vols., (Paris, 1914-1975), X, 337-48.

6. In the case of Montaigne's protest in "De l'institution des enfans" against the misrepresentation of *Philosophy* as forbidding and austere, one is tempted to wonder whether Ronsard had not read Montaigne. In the original text of Ronsard's "Hymne de la Philosophie" (1555) there was a long allegorical passage giving just such a description of Philosophy as Montaigne criticized. In 1584, four years after the appearance of Montaigne's essay, Ronsard suppressed 37 lines forming the essential part of this description. See *Oeuvres*, VIII, 85-102 (lines 185 onwards). Was it Montaigne who had converted him to the view that philosophy was "Not harsh and crabbed, as dull fools suppose"?

7. Montaigne was buried in the church of the Feuillants at Bordeaux (his heart, according to a custom of the time, was buried separately in a place with which he had special connections—the village church at Montaigne itself). These arrangements were almost certainly in conformity with his express wishes.

Terence Cave

Desportes and Maynard: Two Studies in the Poetry of Wit

However one defines the term, wit depends on a high degree of linguistic self-consciousness in speaker and audience.[1] The "talent for saying brilliant or sparkling things" (OED) and the "discovery of subtle analogies, resemblances" (Grierson) both require a mastery of words—their sound, their rhythm, their semantic coloring, their accidental similarities and discordances. The language of wit draws attention to itself and consequently tends to distance or even hide what it refers to. The expressive energies it harbors may, of course, be released in such a way as to produce insights of an intellectual or moral kind: Pascal and other French moralists richly exploit this heuristic function of wit. But even in these cases it is obvious that the medium itself is more than usually indispensable for the communication of a message: successful wit is memorable because it depends on a particular order of words, a special act of linguistic equilibrium. In this sense it is already a form of literary expression, even when it occurs in apparently non-literary contexts such as *salon* conversation or modern publicity. It depends, too, on cultural allusiveness, whether the culture be "high" or "low." In order to be understood, it requires intimate familiarity with a particular set of conventions: commonplace metaphors, registers of language, social reference, and so on. Thus parody, which is a variety of wit, operates on a known body of materials, disrupting and inverting it. Where wit becomes one of the dominant procedures of a literature or of social discourse, one can infer that a powerful tradition of expression has already established itself, constituting a universe of linguistic and literary signs which wit can displace in patterns whose unexpectedness is directly consequent upon the stability of the system. Wit is a parasite which creates surprises, engineers explosions, from within the body of its host.

The two sonnets which have been chosen for analysis here were written during a period when the art of refining traditional poetic materials was at its peak. Unlike Ronsard, for whom the resources of tradition could provide an abundance of new styles and insights, Desportes and Maynard rejected cosmic vision and divine fury in favor of those modes of writing most accessible to an urbane society: for Desportes, sonnets and *stances* on the theme of love (and some elegant religious poems); for Maynard, the epigram, the philosophical ode in the manner of Malherbe, and of course the ubiquitous sonnet, amorous or encomiastic. Within these relatively limited fields, they aimed not at disconcerting the reader, at changing his focus (as Scève succeeds in doing, within a quasi-epigrammatic form and with an almost equally restricted range of materials) but rather at a kind of complicity: the game is to offer to the reader, without boring him, what he expects to receive. Hence "content" or "subject matter" becomes a pretext for the polished modulation of tones, rhythms and harmonies; the equilibrium of form and the play of wit remain wholly uncontaminated by any attempt to justify the *dulce* in terms of the *utile*. Such poetry sails perilously close to the banal, and there is indeed much banality in the verse of the late sixteenth and early seventeenth centuries; even the best of it, consumed in large quantities, can easily appear insipid (an adjective much used by critics of Desportes). Yet even such slight poems as these have their own authenticity. They are quintessentially poetic in that they suppress or disguise any reference to the extra-poetic realm, to the world of common experience, in order to operate within a closed and self-defining world of verbal gestures. Vertiginously empty of significance, they may at times achieve a perfection which is not accessible to poets who work with materials less precarious.

> Sommeil, paisible fils de la Nuict solitaire,
> Pere alme nourricier de tous les animaux,
> Enchanteur gracieux, doux oubli de nos maux,
> Et des esprits blessez l'appareil salutaire:
>   Dieu favorable à tous, pourquoy m'es-tu contraire?
> Pourquoy suis-je tout seul rechargé de travaux
> Or' que l'humide nuict guide ses noirs chevaux
> Et que chacun jouist de ta grace ordinaire?
>   Ton silence où est-il? ton repos et ta paix,
> Et ces songes vollans comme un nuage espais,
> Qui des ondes d'Oubli vont lavant nos pensées?

O frere de la Mort que tu m'es ennemi!
Je t'invoque au secours: mais tu es endormi,
Et j'ards tousjours veillant en tes horreurs glacées.[2]

Desportes's sonnet is built around an unstated subject: the overt theme of insomnia disguises yet implies its root cause, the pain of unrequited love. A delicate hint of this suffering is given in the first line by the word "solitaire," and the motif is taken up more and more insistently as the sonnet progresses: in the phrases "nos maux," "esprits blessez" and "rechargé de travaux," and in the rhetorical paradox (burning amid ice) of the last line. But love itself is never mentioned, still less the object of love. Since the sonnet is one of a cycle of love poems, and since Desportes could rely on the familiarity of his audience with the Petrarchan connotations of fire and ice (and indeed of the theme of insomnia itself),[3] he could afford to omit and understate. Similarly, the sense of *personal* suffering is overlaid by the successive personifications of sleep itself, which seems to be the principal protagonist of the poem: the first person singular is restricted to lines 5-6 and 12-14 and plays a passive role except in the last two lines. Even the torment of insomnia is presented in large measure in an inverted form, since it is the *benefits* of sleep which predominate in the first eleven lines. The word "oubli" (line 3, picked up more strongly in line 11) is as it were the pivot, the medial point between the sweet repose of sleep and the fantoms it eliminates. Indeed, Desportes throughout steers a finely adjusted course between positive and negative, between the "favorable" and the "contraire": for example, the question which shapes the first tercet ("où est-il?") is a delicate yet powerful means of indicating the absence of qualities stated ("silence," "repos," "paix") while nevertheless invoking them, a procedure akin to the rhetorical device of paralipsis.

These fundamental features of the poem's mode of operation can be traced also at the level of sound and image. The closely woven pattern of sound which begins to operate in the opening phrase of the poem and is sustained—with certain modifications—until the end, is centered on the vowel "i," usually in conjunction with sibilant and liquid consonants. These sounds, together with others marginally less prominent ("ou," or the darker nasals "en/an" and "on") form a series of shifting assonances, amounting at times to something like internal rhyme ("fils"-"nourricier"; "nuict"-"jouist"; "humide"-"guide"; "songes"-"ondes"; "vollans"-"lavant"; "Oubli"-"ennemi"; "mort"-"endormi"; "secours"-"tousjours"). Yet, by a careful process of separating the constituent sounds and reversing their order, as in the distribution of "s" "l" and "i" in line 1, Desportes succeeds in producing an effect which is all pervasive without being obtrusive. The harmonies are imitative to the extent that they evoke an impression of suavity and soft whispering; and one might also say that the obsessive quality which arises from repetition is appropriate to the parallel yet antithetical themes of sleep and insomnia. Thus the sound pattern itself, overlaying the thematic pattern, helps Desportes both to avoid direct statement and to maintain the balance between positive and negative.

The quasi-mythological image of sleep is invoked in the first quatrain by a series of epithets: the tone is that of a formal apostrophe, discreetly elevated by the latinism "alme" and the inversion of line 4. The dominant notations are carried by the adjectives, which, being abstract and similar in meaning (with the exception of "solitaire" and "blessez"), make the personification fluid, so that the faces of Sleep, while apparently differentiated ("fils," "Pere," "Enchanteur"), slide together beneath the mantle of sound. In lines 5-6, the blandness of the opening gives way to a question which polarizes the underlying tension in the most general and abstract terms: only the phrase "rechargé de travaux" carries a degree of concreteness. Line 8 is likewise generalized; but the intervening line 7, by means of a secondary personification, introduces something close to sensation into the transparent and virtually intangible texture of the quatrains. It is true that the sound-play ("humide"-"guide," "nuict"-"noirs") homogenizes the impression given by the line, both internally and in relation to the rest of the poem; yet there is no doubt that at this point the sensuousness of sound apparent from the outset is augmented by a more concrete sensuousness.

The first tercet opens once again in abstraction. "Silence," "repos" and "paix" offer virtually no obstacle to the reader's attention; the whole sense is conveyed by the inverted question and its rhythm, which represent perhaps the most finely calculated point in the poem. Here, for a moment, the negative abstraction "silence" is itself negated, so that the pause at the cesura is pregnant with the amorous complaint implied by the double negative yet still not expressed. When the flow resumes, "repos" and "paix" soon give way to a second concrete image, expanded this time over two lines. "Concrete" is in fact hardly an appropriate term for an image of dreams, clouds, and the dark waters of Lethe: the emphasis is once more on fluidity and a merging of disparate elements in which the interplay of sounds plays a major role ("songe" sharing a phoneme with both "nuage" and "onde"). On a first reading, this merging process conceals the fact that there are two images in these lines, that there is no self-evident link between the "nuage espais" and the "ondes d'Oubli."[4] The modulation from one to another becomes explicit if one conceives of the "nuage" as a rain cloud; but even this mild rationalization is hardly necessary given the overall consistency of sound and tonality.

The allusion to Lethe, the river of oblivion in the Underworld, constitutes a focal point in the structure of the sonnet. It resumes and intensifies the sense of the preceding lines while at the same time preparing a major shift in the personification (note also that in terms of the rhyme scheme, the last line of the first tercet is also the first line of a closing "quatrain"). In line 12, the "paisible fils de la Nuict solitaire," the "Pere alme nourricier de tous les animaux" becomes the brother of Death, a source of destruction rather than renewal;[5] "contraire" is replaced by the personalized "ennemi," which is reinforced by a secondary antithesis with "frere"; and the tone, having passed from vocative to interrogative, is now exclamatory: Desportes is concentrating his resources for the close of the sonnet. Line 13 describes ("Je t'invoque") and negates ("tu es endormi") the whole of the preceding development: the invocation and questioning of Sleep have taken place in a void, since Sleep himself is asleep. The touch of irony in "endormi" thus derives from a double negative not unlike that of line 9. In this instance, however, the resulting "positive" (the insomnia induced by the pain of love) is powerfully proclaimed: "J'ards," sharply contrasted both in sound and in tone-color with the rest of the sonnet; fire is antithetical to darkness and to water, both of which were central to the images of lines 7 and 10-11. This retrospective antithesis is intensified within the last line itself by the opposition between burning and freezing: the refreshing humidity of the night and the waters of oblivion are now metamorphosed into a frozen region amid which the flame of passion burns and cannot be quenched; the placing of the two elements at opposite ends of the line, separated by the notion of eternal consciousness (and hence of eternal suffering), reflects their incompatibility. The progression "Sommeil"-"Oubli"-"Mort" thus ushers in a powerful reworking of the traditional "icy fire" paradox in terms of infernal imagery.

The play of antithesis and inversion in the sonnet as a whole, and particularly at the climax, is by no means devoid of expressive functions: a sense of restless melancholy, of an abstract yet intense suffering, is undeniably projected to the reader. Yet there remains a certain distance between the feeling which the sonnet purports to describe and its enactment in poetic terms. Each gesture remains elegant, even at the close; the smooth surface of the poem is never broken. There is no violence in the cadence of line 12; the predicament defined in line 14, although ostensibly personal and infernal, is perceived by the reader above all as a superbly constructed pattern of formal elements. The poem is thus the literary equivalent of a "nocturne": Desportes is working in terms of given aesthetic quantities rather than in terms of experience; melancholy is the pretext for a certain register of poetic effects. He seems indeed to have discovered, in the theme of sleep and its absence, a reflection of his own poetic: he is at once the craftsman-poet, ceaselessly vigilant, and the "enchanteur gracieux" who overlays the disagreeable realities of life with his own suave harmonies.

If insomnia is a stock theme of love poetry, the *aubade* or *alba*, on which Maynard's sonnet is a variation, is no less so: indeed, the elegiac separation of lovers at dawn is one of the oldest of all amorous motifs in literature. Its erotic and emotive content is not exploited here; rather it becomes the pretext for a light-hearted and witty exercise of the fantasy:

> Demeure encore au lit, belle et pompeuse Aurore,
> Sans venir aux mortels ta lumiere apporter;
> Puisque ses plus doux fruits Amour me fait gouster
> Entre les bras aimez de celle que j'adore.
>   Mais quoy! c'est vainement que ta grace j'implore;
> Mes vœux ne peuvent pas ton voyage arrester;
> Voire mesme on diroit que pour me tourmenter,
> De ses plus clairs rayons ton visage se dore.
>   Si c'est le desplaisir de coucher au costé
> D'un jaloux à qui l'âge a tout pouvoir osté,
> Qui te fait si matin commencer ta carriere,
>   Pourquoy suis-je privé de ta douce faveur?
> Feut-ce par mon conseil, diligente Courriere,
> Que tu fus espousée à ce fascheux Reveur?[6]

Maynard, like Desportes, addresses his sonnet to a personification, pleading with her and questioning her to no avail: with some minor adjustments of style, lines 5 and 12 would not have been out of place in Desportes's poem. In both instances, too, the personification borders on the mythological, although no mythical figures are named. This element is however more central to Maynard: the sonnet cannot be understood unless one knows the fable according to which Aurora deserts her aged and impotent husband (Tithonus) every morning to seek some new lover. This mythological situation, evoked in the tercets, is complemented by the situation of the poet-lover, which is likewise far more explicit here than in the earlier poem: from the first stanza, it is plain that he is in bed with his mistress and resents the coming of dawn which will end his pleasures. Yet the interplay of these two situations is executed without reference to any "natural" or "landscape" features, other than the barest possible notations for the visual impact of dawn. "Lumiere," "voyage," "ses plus clairs rayons," "se dore"—none of these expressions suggests an interest in sensuous or concrete values; the vocabulary here, as elsewhere in the poem, is generalized and commonplace, while the only metaphor, other than that consequent upon the personification itself, is the well-worn reference to the "fruits of love" in line 3. No decor is provided for the mythological motif of the tercets,[7] whereas Desportes's nocturne, however stylized, does give a sense of darkness and includes embryonic elements of description and concrete metaphor.

To these denials of poetic "coloring," one may add the reduction to a minimum of assonance, alliteration, and internal rhyme. The alliterations of "coucher au costé" "commencer ta carriere," "conseil . . . Courriere" lend a certain insistence to the poet's argument, and the internal rhyme "voyage"-"visage" may not be wholly accidental; furthermore, the sounds are certainly calculated to avoid any harshness of texture. But the elaboration of a sensuous or imitative sound pattern is totally absent.

What resources, then, does Maynard exploit?

It is apparent from the first line that diction and tone of voice are essential to the engagement of the reader's attention. The diction remains relaxed throughout and the movement of the argument is clearly signposted, in contrast with Desportes's associative, conjunction-free syntax. Precisely because there is no lingering over poetic effects—except for purposes of irony—the movement is rapid, accelerating in the first tercet as the mythological burlesque reaches its climax. Maynard thus creates the illusion of a close correspondence to the rhythms, structures and inflections of ordinary speech: "Mais quoy!," "Voire mesme on diroit," "Feut-ce par mon conseil . . . ?" The correspondence is illusory to the extent that the mask of relaxation disguises a number of formal poetic devices, such as inversion, not to mention the whole apparatus of metre and rhyme required by the sonnet form: much of Maynard's wit—like Marot's—depends on the sleight-of-hand by which a complex poetic structure is made to appear simple. This deflation of art is prolonged in the materials of the poem by the deflation of myth: there is already a discrepancy, in the first line, between the casual intimacy of the address and the supposed dignity of the recipient, a discrepancy which undercuts with irony the formal epithets "belle et pompeuse." The quasi-mythological figures of Aurora and her husband are in fact reduced to the human level, notwithstanding the antithesis implied by "mortels" in the second line (itself ironic); and when the attention moves in the first tercet specifically to the mythological situation, the diction, perversely, becomes still less formal. Tithonus is simply "un jaloux à qui l'âge a tout pouvoir osté"; Aurora is credited with an undignified eagerness to leave his bed. As in the first line, the only concessions to "poetic diction" are made, ironically, in the closing lines: "diligente Courriere," "fascheux Reveur"—a neat antithesis which deflates both figures simultaneously.[8]

The wit of the conclusion, which the structure of the whole poem is designed to release, depends on an analogy and an incompatibility between Aurora's situation and the poet's. Her distaste for her impotent husband, and her presumed desire to join her lover (though this factor is not referred to), should imply sympathy with the poet's vigorous enjoyment of the fruits of love; but it also means that she gets up early, which has the opposite effect. Maynard thus creates a kind of antithesis dependent not so much on verbal polarization, as in Desportes, but rather on a witty conjunction of situations. Furthermore, the wit is gratuitous: no insights into the nature of love or the passage of time are suggested; indeed the reduction of myth to the level of a human comedy has the reciprocal effect of transposing the lover's situation into the realm of comic fantasy. This is particularly evident in the last two lines, where the poet abandons altogether his role as lover in a final attempt to deflate his mythical antagonist.

This sonnet, like many others of its day, is an exercise in social dexterity. It has a virtuoso quality, not only because of its poetic fluency—though that is striking enough—but also because it acts out the adroit handling, by purely verbal means, of an awkward predicament. The dawn will not change her schedule, but the poet extricates himself with wit and elegance from his losing position, turning disadvantage to apparent advantage. Not that the predicament is "real": far from it. The whole thing is a conjuring trick. But it enables the poet to assert that kind of superiority most applauded by a society in which competitive dialogue, conducted in accordance with certain formal restraints, is the norm. At the same time, the *appearance* of relaxation, of effortless informality, is essential. Hence Maynard's tone of refined colloquialism, studded with ironically deflated "poetic effects": the poet must always be ready to disown the special qualities of the language he uses.

We are at this point not far from Desportes's technique of negation and double negation. Although in Desportes's sonnet the language of court society is not apparent, and although the *impact* of each poem is quite different, both poets compose their discourse in terms of certain fundamental strategies: the play of antithesis and allusiveness, the counterpointing of what is stated with what is not, of poetic effect with its denial. "Originality" consists for them not in the sudden leap out of a predictable series but rather in the discovery, within a limited poetic space, of *feintes* and reversals which overcome—however momentarily—the exhaustion of their material. It is in such conditions, perhaps, that the equilibrium of wit may be observed, and savored, in its purest form.

NOTES

1. Visual, non-linguistic wit is of course also possible. See Paul Barolsky, *Infinite Jest: Wit and Humor in Italian Renaissance Art* (New York: Columbia Univ. Press, 1978).

2. Desportes, *Les Amours d'Hippolyte*, sonnet LXXV, quoted according to the edition by Victor E. Graham (Geneva-Paris, 1960), pp. 130-31 (first published 1573).

3. For a detailed account of variations on this theme from the classical poets to the early seventeenth century, see J.H. Rogers, *Poetry of Change: Etienne Durand (1585-1613) and His Milieu* (unpublished D.Phil. dissertation, Oxford, 1978), chapter 3.

4. In his commentary on the works of Desportes, Malherbe dismisses this mixed metaphor with a typically scathing remark: " 'Un nuage espais de songes volans lave ses pensées des ondes d'oubly': que veut dire cela?"

5. According to an ancient poetic and mythological tradition, Sleep and Death were both children of Night.

6. Quoted according to the edition of Ferdinand Gohin, *Poésies de François Maynard* (Paris, 1927), pp. 223-24 (first published 1607).

7. Contrast the dawn imagery in Du Bellay's *Olive*, sonnets XVI and LXXXIII.

8. For an analogous deflation of myth, see Ronsard's sonnet, "Jaloux Soleil contre Amour envieux" of 1569 in *Oeuvres complètes*, ed. P. Laumonier et al. (Paris, 1914-1975), XV, 199-200; many other examples could be found in the poetry of the late sixteenth and early seventeenth centuries. For a more distant and highly contrasted parallel, see Donne's "The Sunne Rising."

Henri Fluchère

"Beauté, mon beau souci . . .":
Fragment d'un "Malherbe"

Ma déférence pour Malherbe vient de loin. Elle date des jours heureux où, au Collège de Manosque, notre "prof" de français nous faisait apprendre concurremment par cœur le sonnet des "Correspondances" et des passages de l'*Art poétique*, celui, en particulier, que tous les professeurs de littérature française ont dû commenter à leurs élèves: "Enfin Malherbe vint . . ." Mais elle est due surtout à l'insistance que mettait Monsieur Guignard à nous persuader, par quelques exemples bien scandés, que ce Malherbe-là, qui faisait irruption dans la classe, était un grand poète. Un admirateur de Malherbe dans un modeste collège de province en 1913-14, imaginez! Nous n'osions pas nous demander s'il y mettait quelque ironie. Il n'en mettait d'ailleurs aucune. Nous n'admirions pas Malherbe, nous le respections, comme nous respections Corneille, et aimions Racine. "Je le vis, je rougis, je pâlis à sa vue" nous émouvait plus que la "Consolation à du Périer," que nous mettions sur le même pied (si on peut dire) que les stances de *Polyeucte*, où les félicités que procurent les "flatteuses voluptés" du monde ont l'éclat du verre et sa fâcheuse fragilité. Malherbe, comme Corneille, était impressionnant, un poète à vous figer d'admiration, naviguant dans les hautes sphères du devoir, où les épanchements lyriques rendent le son des poèmes religieux.

Un "lyrique," mais tout empreint de gravité classique, un rigoureux modèle de vertu, avec lequel on ne plaisante pas. On ne va pas au-delà de "Et rose elle a vécu ce que vivent les roses." Voilà qui est implacable et définitif. Mais est-ce de la poésie? Comme on a les gouvernements qu'on mérite, on a les poètes qu'on mérite, et à l'époque de notre jeune âge, nous les avions sans recourir à Malherbe. Des poètes plus proches de nous, les romantiques, pourvoyeurs de rêves et d'émotions, les quatre grands, comme on dirait aujourd'hui, Hugo, Lamartine, Musset, Vigny—et leur descendance —qui tissaient en nous la trame séduisante des amours imaginaires, auxquels le récitant, d'une façon ou d'une autre, s'identifiait. Sans nous en rendre compte, nous revivions l'histoire littéraire à partir des lointaines époques où Virgile jouait du pipeau, et Horace de l'ironie. Les classiques, les classiques sacrés, roulaient leurs chariots sur les roues des alexandrins correctement césurés, et cheminaient lourdement, distiques chargés de morale, d'intelligence et d'interdictions. C'était une longue marche vers des vérités éternelles qui traitent de l'amour, de la mort, de Dieu. La nature humaine y est guindée, docile, élégiaque; la nature naturelle y est contrainte et stylisée, encore que dans chaque rocher, derrière l'écorce d'un chêne ou d'un bouleau, sous le ruissellement d'une source vive, un dieu ou une déesse sont tapis.

Mais passe le temps des classiques et des romantiques, et vient celui où la poésie n'est plus affaire d'enseignement ou d'analyses *ex cathedra*, mais de la réflexion et du goût. Je me suis mis à fréquenter Malherbe à petites doses, dans la mince édition Delarue, 3 rue des Grands Augustins (quelle rue, pour y éditer Malherbe!)—que Fromilhague ne mentionne pas. En effet, elle se préoccupe peu de l'histoire littéraire ni de gloses. Sans préface, sans notes, sans cet apparat critique dont les lecteurs sérieux sont friands, elle vous laisse vous débrouiller tout seul. Le texte est là, tout nu. La lecture des poèmes n'est pas des plus faciles. Il faut, pour en comprendre le sens et la portée, d'abord avoir une connaissance exacte des données historiques sur quoi le poème s'articule. Comment savoir qui sont ces grands personnages et ces nobles dames, au nom réel ou travesti, pour qui le poète alignait ces stances bien rimées, impeccables de syntaxe et de scansion? Pourquoi se tourmentait-il à les composer, quels étaient leur sens réel, leur sincérité, leur motivation? Ce sont-là les premières questions que l'on se pose, pour conclure que Malherbe est plongé dans l'histoire de son temps, dans la société de son temps. Il y a là ses protecteurs et ses amis, peut-être les femmes qu'il a aimées, et sans doute aussi l'obscur mépris de la facticité de ses attitudes que seule peut racheter une sincère révérence de la fonction du poète. Cette première difficulté ne peut être vaincue que si les historiens des lettres ont piqueté le terrain pour vous. Chaque poème doit être précédé (ou suivi) d'une documentation ponctuelle qui le situe dans son contexte historique, lequel doit apporter des lumières sur le personnage à qui la pièce appartient, ainsi que sur les rapports intéressés ou affectifs qui unissent le poète au personnage.

La première constatation, c'est que Malherbe est un poète de cour, et de société. Si l'on excepte "Les Larmes de Saint-Pierre," exercice spirituel imité d'un poète italien (Tansille)—et même là, le problème se pose de savoir combien Malherbe y a mis de soi—la majeure partie de ses poèmes sont des épîtres dédicatoires, dont le message est grevé du poids étouffant de la flatterie, qu'une adulation hyperbolique exalte, sans convaincre le lecteur moderne, et dont l'énigmatique historicité laisse bien des ombres floues. Autant dire que la matière du poème est quasiment négligeable, et que seule compte la forme dans laquelle elle est exprimée. Un détenteur de l'édition Delarue doit être un grand savant, ou n'est rien qu'un lecteur torturé.

En effet, compte tenu de la difficulté d'être un lecteur digne de Malherbe sur le plan de l'appropriation mise en exergue, on bute sur celle d'une syntaxe rigoureuse dont il faut opérer le dévoilement. Sa grande pureté exige une lecture attentive, et nous ne sommes comblés que lorsque nous avons réduit la litote, et suivi jusqu'au bout les rapports syntagmatiques des vocables à l'allure inoffensive avec leurs hyperboliques voisins. Le déroulement harmonieux de la phrase, la parfaite retombée du vers, nous entraînent au-delà de la simple appréhension du sens, et c'est cela sans doute qui est un élément de poésie. La strophe entière s'enrichit de la vive clarté de la perfection, et l'adéquation entre ce que nous croyons avoir compris et la façon dont c'est dit est si évidente, que nous n'imaginons pas comment cela pourrait être dit autrement. Ici, peut-être, un exemple serait le bienvenu:

> Le dernier de mes jours est dessus l'Orizon:
> Celle dont mes ennuis avaient leur guérison
> S'en va porter ailleurs ses appas et ses charmes:
> Je fais ce que je puis, l'en pensant divertir:
> Mais tout m'est inutile, et semble que mes larmes
> Excitent sa rigueur à la faire partir.
> (*Stances*, XXVII, éd. Belles-Lettres)

Ce n'est point tant les nuances d'archaïsme ("ennuis" pour "chagrins," "divertir" pour "détourner," ou "rigueur" pour "fermeté de décision") qui donnent à la stance un air étrange de vétusté légèrement énigmatique, c'est, encore que le vers porte son sens jusqu'au bout avec des mots parfaitement clairs, voire familiers, c'est la rigueur que donne au raisonnement le petit pronom "en" qui passe inaperçu, mais dont la modestie grammaticale est grosse de tout le drame de la situation: le fait que celle qui guérissait les chagrins du poète a décidé de "porter ailleurs ses appas et ses charmes." On dira que la difficulté de sens est mineure: c'est exact. Exact pour une lecture superficielle. Mais il faut repenser ce "en" pour saisir toutes ses implications. "En" contient la décision de la dame de partir, de se séparer de son ami—ou son amant. Est-ce lassitude? Poursuite d'autres amours? Ce ne peut être nécessité du voyage: suivre son mari qui a reçu mission de servir ailleurs, par exemple—mais non, car alors le poète ne songerait pas à chercher à dissuader la dame, par ses larmes, et par ses vers. Pur caprice féminin? Le poète insiste sur le fait que la dame emporte avec elle "ses appas et ses charmes": comment pourrait-elle se dispenser de les utiliser ailleurs! Le poète peut bien affirmer d'entrée de jeu (poétique) que son dernier jour s'est levé "dessus l'Orizon," et dans ce vers se déroule la perspective maussade d'une agonie retenue. C'est ici le triomphe de la litote, comme plus loin l'aveu d'une désespérance dans l'échec (ni les larmes ni les vers ne l'empêcheront de partir), suivi à la fin du poème de l'affirmation d'un amour éternel, impliqué dans la promesse faite.

Ce beau poème appelle d'autres remarques. On s'apercevra qu'une lecture attentive délimite raisonnablement le sujet. Au fil des stances le poète se plaint du départ de sa maîtresse, s'efforce de comprendre les raisons qui l'ont poussée à ce départ, constate son impuissance à l'en détourner, déplore qu'elle ne montre aucun signe d'affliction, et conclut par l'affirmation de sa fidélité à lui, seul refuge pour rendre sa solitude supportable, ultime recours contre l'absence, et sauvegarde de sa dignité. Le poème est donc du genre "valédiction," variété de poèmes érotiques (inspirés par l'amour) très cultivés chez les poètes anglais du seizième siècle. Le départ, c'est l'instant d'une rupture, définitive ou momentanée; c'est le point dramatique où se précise et se consomme la réalité de l'absence, où l'on prend conscience de l'unité rompue, où, enfin, peuvent apparaître toutes les modalités des rapports affectifs ou intellectuels d'un être à l'autre. Thème banal, dira-t-on: oui, parce que la chose l'est. Mais c'est un thème infiniment plus riche que la distante froideur de la femme aimée, avec lequel tous les pétrarquisants beaux esprits des Renaissances européennes ont joué de la harpe ou du luth. Malherbe est loin de se prévaloir de ce jeu qu'il lui serait facile d'exploiter. Il ne cherche pas la séduction, ni ne se complaît aux langueurs doucereuses. Il affirme au contraire la souveraineté d'une présence personnelle, fondée sur raison et dignité, qui permettent au poète la calme possession de cette dose de courage et l'orgueil, suprême apanage du poète classique. On pourrait même dire, non sans quelque exagération, que ce poète-là est un roc d'orgueil.

Les "valédictions" expriment la plupart du temps des regrets à voir l'objet aimé s'éloigner, regrets assaisonnés de la tendresse qui enveloppe l'être cher qui s'en va, et qui portent l'espoir des proches retrouvailles. C'est la plus simple attitude du poète envers la situation créée par un départ. A un niveau plus élevé, le poète refuse l'absence et nie, tant son

amour est profond en lui, la dualité des deux êtres qui s'aiment. Ta présence est en moi, où que tu sois. On ne peut résoudre cette impossibilité
que par l'artifice d'une spiritualité qui néglige les contingences en tant que
telles, mais en fait, au contraire, la condition même d'une ascèse qui peut
conduire à la sérénité. Ainsi trouve-t-on chez Scève ou chez Donne des
valédictions si excessives d'adoration et de certitude, au cœur même de
l'incompatibilité des contraires, qu'on les a élevées au niveau de la poésie
métaphysique, qui torture la syntaxe, utilise des métaphores que, faute
d'un terme plus clair, on a appelées baroques, et qui font de la lecture du
poème comme une herméneutique sacrée.

Mais Donne et Scève exigent des efforts d'analyse si poussés que les difficultés que présente Malherbe sont un jeu d'enfant gâté. Chez Donne,
c'est la turbulence des métaphores, les caprices de la syntaxe, et surtout
l'extrême finesse du raisonnement qui cherche toujours la pointe, ce
rapprochement des incompatibles qui fait jaillir l'étincelle de la poésie,
procédé d'élection des esprits tourmentés qui exploitent au suprême degré
le jeu des similitudes et des contradictions. C'est une poésie militante,
agressive, qui explore furieusement les recoins secrets des apparences, et
dont la rhétorique fait fi des règles et de la discrétion. Chez Scève, on
trouve le souci de la contradiction, de la densité, le refus des redondances
et le mépris du bavardage familier si cher à Ronsard. La tension intérieure
des dizains les remplit d'un frémissement proche de l'extase, d'où émane
comme une lumière blanche, incroyable paradoxe d'une poésie malencon-
treusement réputée hermétique, alors que d'elle se dégage la pure clarté de
l'amour.

Comme Malherbe l'est dans la courte période d'écriture qui lui est
impartie (environ trente ans), Donne et Scève sont les sommets de la
poésie de leur âge—et je ne parle ici que de leur poésie "amoureuse," c'est-
à-dire *Songs and Sonnets* et la *Délie*. La grandeur de Malherbe recouvre à
peu près tous ses poèmes, à la fois ses vers officiels, ses poèmes spirituels et
ses poésies galantes. Il est pareil à lui-même partout. Son mode d'expression (pour ne pas dire sa technique) se retrouve dans tous ses vers, quel que
soit le sujet qu'il traite, aussi dissemblable des turbulences de Donne que
des émerveillements secrets de Scève. C'est un miracle assurément que ces
trois poètes, si différents l'un de l'autre, sans avoir été stimulés par l'émula-
tion se retrouvent ainsi au plus haut de la réputation poétique.

Rien n'est plus difficile à définir que la grandeur. On pourra analyser la
perfection de la technique, comme le fait le professeur Fromilhague, dresser
des dénombrements stylistiques—vocabulaire, métaphores, images, figures,

conceits, structure des stances et des pièces, brassage des rimes, inventaire des rythmes: bref tout ce que l'analyse peut isoler et classer—non sans tenir compte des fluctuations de la mode que l'époque et la société infligent au poète qui peut verser du maniérisme dans le baroque, s'élever de la préciosité à la poésie métaphysique; le critique pourra aussi (pour ne pas dire enfin) tirer profit de l'exploitation que lui offre la récente école thématique, ensorceleuse moderne, toute affairée à obéir aux sollicitations romanesques qui créent la matière poétique—sans compter les révélations qu'apporte le pillage, poussé aux limites de la décence, des éléments de la biographie. Il est tant d'autres ruses que la prodigieuse ingéniosité des critiques a mises à leur disposition pour établir cette toujours provisoire échelle des valeurs que les générations successives ne cessent de remanier. Mais on a beau faire, il reste chez tous les poètes un élément d'irréductible qui peut leur conférer la grandeur.

Serait-ce le degré de sincérité qui donne le ton au langage poétique? Mais on a vu des poètes passionnément sincères qui ne jouent que du mirliton. Si l'artiste du mirliton peut souffler avec grâce, et enrober ses émotions du miel de la tendresse, atteindra-t-il les accents de la grandeur? On voit, par contre, Donne écrire un haut texte de la poésie anglaise dont l'incitation repose sur la mort d'une jeune fille qu'il n'a jamais connue, et Malherbe composer des vers enflammés pour un Henri IV, languissant d'amour pour une jeune fille de seize ans, d'une grande beauté, dont il ne put s'assurer la possession. Alexandre, le roi, par plume interposée, soupire en de beaux vers pour Oranthe, la princesse de Condé, et ces stances galantes de commande ont les mêmes résonances malherbiennes que les vers que le sieur de Malherbe composa pour Caliste, la femme qu'il aimait vraiment, la femme dont, comme le roi, il ne souffrait pas d'être séparé.

Serait-ce l'attitude de l'auteur vis-à-vis de son poème? C'est-à-dire le jugement, la plupart du temps implicite, qui se dégage à la façon dont il manipule son instrument d'expression, autant que la matière même qu'il exploite. Ici, la réaction du lecteur se porte garante de l'authenticité du repliement sur soi. La qualité même du poème, révélée par la complexité des rapports engagement-détachement, peut apparaître dérisoire en égard au but poursuivi. Il s'ensuit des fautes de syntaxe, des ruptures de ton, une confusion des genres qui ne peut produire de la grande poésie, celle devant laquelle on passe chapeau bas, disons la poésie irrévocable, qui ne s'embarrasse pas des sentiments de l'auteur. Sans négliger la qualité ni la profondeur de l'émotion déclenchée par les problèmes humains dont il traite, ne faut-il pas, par dessus les thèmes et les personnes, faire appel à la haute vertu d'un langage vivant, perceptible à l'intelligence, et capable d'ébranler la sensibilité?

N'est-ce pas aussi, étrange paradoxe dont T.S. Eliot proclamait la vérité, l'apparent détachement du poète de son objet poétique, cette étrange impersonnalité de l'engagemênt qui transporte le poète au-delà des frontières du divin mensonge. Plus la poésie sera impersonnelle, plus elle pourra s'élever. On en vient au classique "le Moi est haïssable," utilisé à d'autres fins que poétiques; mais la rigueur de l'attitude n'est pas ici étrangère à la grandeur. Elle exclut l'apitoyement sur soi, la dramatisation de soi, constantes du romantisme, on serait porté à dire du bovarysme, qui font si souvent gémir Jules Laforgue, et dont Eliot, déjà mentionné, libère le poète, pour ne garder, avec les ruptures de ton, que la dérision sarcastique, forme amère du détachement. Mais le poète alors s'efface, se cache, s'affuble d'un masque, personnage grotesque et mystérieux qui assume le risque de ses émotions et de ses fantasmes. Ainsi Prufrock, ainsi Sweeney, sont, ou ne sont pas, l'auteur du *Waste Land*; ainsi Phlébas, ainsi Tirésias, sont, ou ne sont pas, le tragiquement noyé, ou de devin-poète crucifié. Affaire de "lecture," drame de l'interprétation. Partout, ou presque, les poètes interposent des *personae*, façon détournée d'être soi, alibi magique, imposture de l'impersonnalité, façon honteuse de battre les cartes de la poésie. Les Tarots surgissent, énigmatiques et menaçants, sur un fond de tableau où se dessine en filigrane le sourire du chat du Cheshire, évanescente antithèse des félins baudelairiens. Et n'oublions pas les symboles, à ce stade de la confusion, auxiliaires fabuleux des transferts d'identité qui peuplent la poésie de leur fantasmagorie.

Malherbe ne se situe pas sur les vagues de ces turbulences poétiques qui font dire à la critique n'importe quoi sur n'importe qui. Depuis longtemps il a été étiqueté le classique par excellence, modèle de cette architecture rigoureuse qui n'a pas subi, ou à peine, les outrages du déséquilibre baroque, propre à charmer les esprits pervers. On a pu sans crainte le soumettre aux analyses de la technique les plus poussées, strophe après strophe, vers après vers, comme lui le faisait pour les poètes imparfaits de son temps. Il a sa place dans l'histoire de la littérature, et les qualifications qu'il mérite. Il est venu à un moment où les exigences du temps n'admettaient plus les effusions élégiaques ni les torrents de l'éloquence ronsardienne, pas plus que la sensualité insolente d'un pétrarquisme pervers—et encore moins les libertés excessives dont s'accommodait la langue qui s'acoquinait avec l'exubérance et l'anarchie. Il fallait donc revigorer l'inspiration, lui rendre une rigueur que les abus de toute sorte avait dévoyée, répudier les afféteries de langage à l'usage des salons, maintenir dans de justes limites les caprices du baroquisme, et, sans méconnaître les aléas de l'expression poétique, établir la souveraineté de la poésie de l'intelligence.

Car la maîtrise de l'expression poétique, dont les ressources sont d'une infinie variété, ne se réalise que grâce à la maîtrise de l'intelligence sur sa matière. C'est ici un problème tant de fois controversé, sans qu'il ait été complètement élucidé. Il ne s'agit pas, dans ma pensée, de l'intelligence analytique qui choisit les sujets, régit les structures, règne sur la métrique, règle la distribution des rythmes, discipline les métaphores, harmonise les traits et les sons, mais de la souveraineté d'une appréhension de la vie intérieure du poème, c'est-à-dire de la sensibilité qui l'anime et lui confère son caractère d'œuvre d'art. Rien n'est plus difficile à définir que cette confusion entre ces éléments contradictoires que sont l'intelligence et la sensibilité. L'une pourvoyeuse d'émotion, l'autre de pensée. Il semble que l'équilibre parfait soit rarement atteint, mais au contraire que les excès, dans l'un et l'autre sens, soient fatals à la poésie. Lorsque la pensée se laisse reléguer au second plan, la poésie s'effiloche et s'affadit; lorsqu'elle domine de haut, la muse devient pédante ou hermétique, ou les deux. Et si, comme le veulent les temps modernes, la poésie se fait voyance, irruption dans le domaine du surréel, de l'irréel et de la prophétie, avec l'ambition de créer de nouvelles formes d'existence des créatures et des objets, elle échappe à toute lecture raisonnable, se fait énigmatique, sollicite une heuristique des images et des symboles, et coiffe le bonnet d'une épistémologie hasardeuse. En vérité il n'y a pas de "poésie scientifique" à proprement parler; l'expression est un abus de terme et un malentendu. Prendre un objet, ou un domaine, scientifique comme incitateur de poésie—le soufre, ou l'astronomie, par exemple—c'est les dépouiller de toute spécificité scientifique, et les métaphoriser, comme ces millions d'étoiles dans le ciel, qui sont ou voie lactée, ou galaxie, ou encore les verts paturages où vont paître les simples d'esprit.

Soucieux d'expliquer l'affadissement de la poésie de son époque (disons celle de la décadence géorgienne et édouardienne) T.S. Eliot utilisait sa formule devenue célèbre: "dissociation de la sensibilité," formule assez imprécise (et d'ailleurs controversée) qui ne prend tout son sens que dans une vue diachronique du développement de la poésie anglaise. Cela signifie, schématiquement, que le poète, ou bien s'est livré complaisamment à la suprématie de la sensibilité, et cela débouche sur le "romantisme," avec sa kyrielle de formes les plus variées de la sensiblerie, ou, au contraire, qu'il s'est délivré de l'emprise de l'émotion pour que règne la raison raisonnante, exploratrice du plan divin, et cela donne le "classicisme," exercice de haute vertu, art suprême de la définition et de l'appropriation du réel. Mais les choses ne sont jamais aussi simples; cependant la fusion des deux tendances ne s'opère que chez des poètes privilégiés, ceux, précisément, qu'on désigne sous le nom de poètes "métaphysiques," chez qui la vigueur de la pensée va de pair avec la profondeur de l'émotion. Ajoutons que, pour ceux-là, il ne s'agit pas de pure spéculation, dogmatisme, ou soumission aux nombres d'or qui divinisent l'architecture du microcosme, mais de l'intervention d'une fulgurance intellectuelle dans l'expression d'une émotion. A son péril extrême, cela peut aboutir au *conceit*, c'est-à-dire, la pointe de la célèbre aiguille sur laquelle une multitude d'anges peuvent s'installer. Le maniériste, par exemple, ne manque pas d'intelligence, tout comme le précieux, dont les pinces intellectuelles captent le futile et le charmant pour les associer à des sentiments fugitifs. Pour le baroque, c'est déjà plus difficile, car le poète ne prend pas toujours juste mesure du déséquilibre souhaité, et la démesure précisément alimente le grotesque. Mais chez les "métaphysiques" dont je m'embarrasse, il en va tout autrement. Leur démarche poétique mène enquête sur l'émotion, tente de l'explorer jusqu'en ses racines, pour lui donner un sens qui la dépasse, l'objective en quelque sorte, dans une réalité perceptible pour l'esprit. C'est ici la vigilance de l'intelligence qui met à profit la moisson de signes de l'expérience vécue.

Lorsque Donne, dans un de ses poèmes les plus fouillés—"Of the progress of the soul"—s'efforce de préciser l'ampleur de l'émotion qui l'envahit à l'évocation de la pure beauté d'une jeune morte dont l'âme n'a pas encore achevé son "progrès" vers le ciel, il fait appel à deux "sciences" initiatiques et divinatoires, la théologie et l'alchimie. Si belle, Elizabeth Drury, que chacun de ses membres aurait pu être doté d'un ange gardien, et si éloquente cette beauté, que, si l'âme déjà avait été transmutée en or, le corps cheminait vers le passage à l'argent, proche de l'or—étrange alchimie de la pureté, comme en un creuset où s'opère la trans-substantialité suprême de la matière en pensée:

> . . . we understood
> Her by her sight; her pure and eloquent blood
> Spoke in her cheeks, and so distinctly wrought
> That one might almost say her body thought.
>   (II. 143-46)

Nous voici parvenu aux limites lointaines du pouvoir de la fonction intellectuelle pour exprimer l'ineffable. C'est là le *conceit* absolu, qui fait fi des impératifs de la causalité, et s'exerce sur les registres d'une logique discordante. La tension conceptuelle tend vers son point de rupture, et toute organisation du réel, perçu, n'est possible que par abandon à une mystique enveloppante. La cohérence du monde éclate, dans le poème de Donne cité en référence, en un hérissement d'images et de métaphores qui sont comme les pétards d'un feu d'artifice éblouissant.

Comme nous sommes loin de l'exercice intellectuel réservé dont la poésie de Malherbe peut se glorifier! Pourquoi aller chercher si loin, dira-t-on, alors que le "classicisme" de Malherbe a été tant de fois décrit? Trouvera-t-on chez lui des *conceits*, rapprochement forcé des incompatibles, jeu capricieux de l'esprit pour qui n'a point d'attraits la facilité de céder à la sensation pure? Oui, s'il s'agit d'une discipline de l'expression, qui consiste à rehausser le prestige de l'écriture au-delà des artifices de la prose, car le langage de la poésie est un langage privilégié, qui ne doit pas toucher le sol. Le poète ne peut, ne doit, en aucune façon, se fier à la facilité—de la langue familière, cela va de soi, mais aussi d'une parole banale, ou affectée systématiquement, ou fautive en quelque manière, c'est-à-dire disproportionnée, en plus ou en moins, à l'objet qu'il s'agit d'attaquer avec des mots. Pour Malherbe, la langue de la poésie ne se contente pas de s'accommoder de la difficulté, il la recherche. Il n'improvise jamais, ne comporte rien de négligé. C'est un art, au vrai sens du terme, proche, peut-être, de l'art oratoire, mais sans la fougue des envolées lyriques de la passion, ni les vulgarités de la controverse. Il y a chez lui une rigueur de raisonnement qui fait de chaque groupe de vers, même sous la forme réduite de la stance ou du quatrain, un enchaînement sans faille, qui se présente à la lecture tout d'une haleinée, un ensemble rythmique auquel on ne saurait rien ajouter ni retrancher, une mélodie intérieure qui distribue ses tonalités en heureuses surprises pour l'oreille: c'est un espace clos, un jardin privé sans fleurs vénéneuses, où règne une noblesse tranquille de la parole, sûre de soi, sans dissonance, qui impose sa fermeté.

Cette maîtrise de l'intelligence s'étend donc sur l'ensemble du poème comme en chacune de ses parties. Elle se soucie du détail pour éliminer des imperfections, autant que pour susciter des trouvailles, images, métaphores, figures, qui donneront de l'éclat à l'élocution. Une logique discrète, et parfois secrète, accompagnera le déroulement de la phrase, si bien que la chute d'un groupe de vers, appuyée et retenue, prendra figure de point d'orgue au dernier mot d'une démonstration amenée à sa conclusion. Les poèmes à forme fixe, les sonnets en particulier, les odes de haut lyrisme, et même les épigrammes de cette période de l'histoire littéraire, en France comme en Angleterre, s'articulaient comme des syllogismes ou des théorèmes. C'est le dernier quatrain, le distique, ou le vers final qui énonce la conclusion devant quoi la raison s'incline. Les sonnets de Sidney, ou de Shakespeare, comme ceux des sonnettistes français de la Renaissance, sont ainsi structurés, et l'on se souviendra que ceux de La Ceppède, de Malherbe très admirés, sont rassemblés, exemple unique, mais significatif, sous le titre de *Théorèmes*.

Ceux-là "démontrent" la robustesse et l'humilité d'une foi qui se donne des raisons de croire et de faire confiance à Dieu et à la mort. D'autres concluent sur des lieux communs profanes, ou des assertions personnelles, que la rigueur de l'énoncé délivre de la banalité. Ainsi les grandes odes de Malherbe, poète de cour, ou qui veut le devenir, dont les stances sont emportées par le souffle oratoire, déjouent la facticité du tribut conventionnel qu'il faut payer aux puissants en place pour obtenir l'estime et la pension auxquelles aspire le poète. Le monarque ou le grand seigneur qui commande à son poète lauréat se voit payé de belle poésie qui chante ses louanges en termes irréfutables. Ne demandons pas au poète la moindre subjectivité. Ce qui compte pour lui c'est sa fonction de poète, c'est l'ordonnance des propositions qui conduisent à la glorification du personnage et de ses actes, c'est la solidité du monument qu'il érige et dont il s'assure qu'il a pour lui l'éternité. Malherbe veut bâtir sur du roc, et ses architectures sont agencées comme des pierres imbriquées qui prennent de la hauteur, sans jamais risquer l'écroulement. Mais en cours d'œuvre, il lui arrive, lassé de la sécheresse apparente d'une matière aride, de placer à l'endroit choisi le rare ornement d'une imagination soucieuse d'ajouter de l'éclat à la construction. Tout à coup le grand poète s'impose, qui n'est pas seulement un architecte, mais aussi un décorateur. Alors, on s'étonne, au sens complet du terme, et on ne peut que retenir la stance par cœur. Ainsi la "Prière pour le Roy allant en Limozin," qui chante les louanges de la prospérité ramenée en France par cet "admirable" roi qu'est Henri IV, béni de Dieu, et qui aime Dieu, s'irradie d'un élan lyrique qui laisse le lecteur pantois:

> Tu nous rendras alors nos douces destinées:
> Nous ne reverrons plus ces fâcheuses années,
> Qui pour les plus heureux n'ont produit que des pleurs;
> Toute sorte de biens comblera nos familles,
> La moisson de nos champs lassera nos faucilles
> Et les fruits passeront les promesses des fleurs.

Tout ici est parfait: le mouvement de la pensée qui procède à pas mesurés, les oppositions de mots, la musique intérieure des assonances et des allitérations, le contenu affectif des épithètes des trois premiers vers, la sensation d'opulence qui se dégage des trois derniers, dont les métaphores éclatantes, soutenues par la répétition des consonnes suaves et la lenteur même du rythme anapestique, prolongent à l'infini la douceur des moments heureux que Dieu dispensera à ce royaume—tout cela procède de l'artiste incomparable que peut être Malherbe à ses moments. En dépit d'un penchant prononcé pour l'hyperbole dans ses poèmes de commande, il sait trouver le ton juste dans la louange, c'est-à-dire celui qui convient aux oreilles d'une aristocratie avide des excès de flatterie—le ton, et la formulation "poétique" qui ne saurait choquer: "Objet divin des âmes et des yeux," pour la Reine: "merveille incomparable en toute qualité," pour la Princesse de Conti: "La voici, la belle Marie / Belle merveille d'Etrurie," pour Marie de Médicis—autant de flatteries qui témoignent d'une attitude et d'une civilisation. Tous les poètes de cette époque, s'adressant à des grands, usaient sans vergogne du même langage: ce rituel fastueux de la politesse était une façon d'embellir les relations humaines bien dans le siècle—c'était une humilité raffinée, émerveillée devant l'appareil somptueux qui enveloppait de bravoure les mines du temps. Et sans doute les parades amoureuses, dans les lettres ou les poésies galantes, procèdent de la même phraséologie distinguée qui permet à Malherbe de se substituer au Roi pour faire, en son nom et lieu, sa cour à la très belle Oranthe, pour qui Henri IV se mourait d'amour.

Précisément, les poésies galantes que Malherbe composa en son nom personnel pour Caliste, la vicomtesse d'Auchy, n'ont, comme ses lettres, d'autres excès que ceux d'une rhétorique de l'adulation qui s'extasie devant une beauté incomparable, comme elle sait aussi affirmer le désir par la fermeté de l'attitude, le badinage qui se permet l'insolence amusé dans les stances "Qu'autres que vous soient désirées," ou même le refus hautain de se plier aux caprices de l'inconstance chez la dame adorée, comme dans le célèbre sonnet "Beauté, mon beau souci . . . ," ou encore cet autre, "C'est fait, belle Caliste . . . ."

Dans ces poèmes galants règne le même souci de perfection, un total déplaisir de se laisser entraîner à la déchéance des larmes affectées—ce n'est pas pleurer qu'on veut, mais mourir—et le même dessein de donner à l'hyperbole banale le prestige de l'exemplarité. Mais toujours et partout on trouve cette fixation du regard sur la beauté, hors d'atteinte des outrages du temps et des hommes, dont les détails se fondent dans l'ensemble, et qui, si on ose dire, se conceptualise dans les profondeurs les plus intimes de la vision du poète. "Beauté, mon beau souci . . . ," la beauté est un "beau souci" (Malherbe avait d'abord écrit "cher," ce qui était tomber dans la tendresse et la mièvrerie), objet d'amour et de désir, inacessible à la possession, et dont l'âme incertaine, intériorisée, indécidée, "fuyante proie," se refuse et s'offre à la fois, comme la mouvance des vagues qui fascine et reste hors de portée. Il y a ici comme une sublimation du désir dépité, face au flux et au reflux des incertitudes de l'âme que traduisent les anapestes. Voyez encore le sonnet "Il n'est rien de si beau comme Caliste est belle"— cette Caliste-ci, dont la beauté fut contesté de vulgaire façon par les ennemis de Malherbe, est, plus encore que la maîtresse rebelle, idéalisée jusqu'au défi. Elle mérite que les gens de son temps ("notre âge") "élève[nt] à sa gloire une marque éternelle," et, sans doute, faut-il ici citer le reste du sonnet sans en retrancher un mot:

> La clarté de son teint n'est pas chose mortelle:
> Le baume est dans sa bouche, et les roses dehors:
> Sa parole et sa voix ressuscitent les morts,
> Et l'art n'égale point sa douceur naturelle.
>
> La blancheur de sa gorge éblouit les regards:
> Amour est dans ses yeux, il y trempe ses dards,
> Et la fait reconnaître un miracle visible.
>
> En ce nombre infini de grâces et d'appas,
> Qu'en dis-tu ma raison? crois-tu qu'il soit possible
> D'avoir du jugement et ne l'adorer pas?

Qu'on relise ces vers admirables. Le pétrarquisme ici est hors de propos. Nous sommes aussi loin de la fadeur que de la préciosité. Rien ne relève de la recherche de la pointe du détail, pour "faire joli." On atteint d'un seul coup l'extrême de l'irréfutable dans la perfection. Du teint émane une clarté surnaturelle, la bouche est embaumée, les joues sont pareilles à des roses qui s'affirment—mais c'est là paraphraser, péché majeur de la critique, toujours vaine à expliciter. Le portrait vaut par la densité de ses traits, l'incroyable surréalité de ses pouvoirs, qui force à la conclusion que ce visage "naturel" surpasse en beauté toute imitation de l'art. Comment, en effet, l'artiste pourrait-il savoir, et surpasser, la "beauté naturelle," le poète ne pas tenter d'exprimer cet ineffable tout en avouant son impuissance, et l'amant ne pas "adorer" ce visage, s'il a du jugement, c'est-à-dire la faculté maîtresse de distinguer les vraies valeurs? C'est la raison, d'où émane le jugement, qui établit son empire sur les troublants territoires de la beauté.

C'est, en effet, la raison qui est souveraine, et guide le choix du poète. Elle est l'inspiratrice des moments heureux où s'est révélée la rare beauté de la femme aimée, dont l'absence frappe les poètes de cécité: "Et moi je ne vois rien quand je ne la vois pas," le jette dans les plus extrêmes tourments: "Où Caliste n'est point, c'est là qu'est mon enfer," et c'est elle qui a contribué à sceller son engagement: "Quant à moi je dispute avant que je m'engage," et qui donne à son amour l'assurance d'une fidélité sans fin: "Et quand je l'ai promis, j'aime éternellement." Comment ne pas croire qu'un amour fondé sur des certitudes pareilles n'ait rien à craindre du temps ni des contingences? La raison a ses rigueurs comme l'amour fondé sur elles; jamais l'impératrice passion n'a trouvé chez un poète d'aussi austères servitudes. Dans un sens, cela mène à Baudelaire, sans les déchirements: "Je suis belle, ô mortels! comme un rêve de pierre," et à Mallarmé, "la fée au chapeau de clarté," sans le "parfum de tristesse," que laisse au cœur la cueillaison d'un rêve. Ces poèmes galants de Malherbe pourraient être intitulés, comme dit si justement Francis Ponge, *Hymnes à la Beauté*. Peu importe que cette Beauté soit insensible ou consentante, elle existe par elle-même, pour elle-même, et on ne saurait ni l'affecter dans son absolu, ni la saisir par des images ou des mots. Elle n'a pas de caractère fugitif, ni d'existence éphémère, elle impose sa dignité au-dessus des bavures sensuelles; il n'est pas possible de la personnaliser, car ce serait la rendre anecdotique, la dépouiller de son austérité, et, oserait-on dire, de robustesse. L'affrontement avec elle ne souffre pas la moindre médiocrité. Il y faut, peut-être, autant de courage que d'orgueil, et le sens très profond que l'on vit une expérience irremplaçable. Ces poèmes méritent plus d'attention qu'on leur en a jamais donnée. Maître de ses mots et de ses sentiments, Malherbe, avec quelques stances et quelques sonnets, domine la cohorte nostalgique des amoureux comblés ou tourmentés de son temps. Il n'y a pas dans ses poèmes un seul vers insignifiant.

Frank J. Warnke

Some Consolations

That the norms of French classicism were not established easily or without competition from opposed aesthetic values is a matter of historical record. The *querelle du Cid*, the persistence of Baroque traits in Corneille's entire *œuvre*,[1] the existence of *poésie libertine* and other pre-classical phenomena have all been studied extensively.[2] It might be instructive to look at a small group of seventeenth-century poems dealing with similar themes and utilizing similar generic conventions, in the hope that the likenesses and contrasts among them will tell us something about the transformations undergone by wit in the process of arriving at its classical equilibrium during the reign of Louis XIV.

The subject will be bereavement, and the genre will be the consolation. François de Malherbe's "Consolation à M. du Périer, Gentilhomme d'Aix-en-Provence, sur la mort de sa fille," composed in 1599, attempts to console the desolated father by reminding him of the healing effects of time, the inevitability of death for all living things, the promise of an after-life, and the wisdom of accepting patiently the will of God. The poet appeals far more to his friend's reason than to his faith in an after-life or a joyous reunion with the lost one. Stanza six has a reference to the "maison céleste" into which the daughter's soul has been received, but the reference is not developed, and, on the whole, the poet stresses more the universality of death and the folly of a grief that exceeds rational limits:

> Ta douleur, du Périer, sera donc éternelle,
> Et les tristes discours
> Que te met en esprit l'amitié paternelle
> L'augmenteront toujours?

Le malheur de ta fille, au tombeau descendue
    Par un commun trépas,
Est-ce quelque dédale, où ta raison perdue
    Ne se retrouve pas?[3]

The questions with which the poem opens are clearly rhetorical, and the answers called for are clearly negative: no, Du Périer's grief will not be eternal; no, his daughter's death does not constitute a maze from which his reason will never emerge. Apart from the conventionally antique "dédale," the diction is abstract and general, the emphasis on reason clearly established.

Reason itself leads Malherbe to allow to the father a *just* degree of grief:

Je sais de quels appas son enfance était pleine
    Et n'ai pas entrepris,
Injurieux ami, de soulager ta peine
    Avecque son mépris.

Mais elle était du monde, où les plus belles choses
    Ont le pire destin,
Et rose elle a vécu ce que vivent les roses,
    L'espace d'un matin.

(p. 48)

With these last two lines, justly the most famous in the poem, a concrete image appears, but it is an altogether decorous, conventional, and unsurprising one. It in no way subverts the common-sense position avowed in the opening stanzas.

At this point, after four stanzas, the poem has pretty much made its statements. The seventeen stanzas that follow reiterate the statements or illustrate their validity through classical, historical, or personal examples: stanzas 3-9 point out that the girl would have had to die sooner or later and that age is irrelevant in the realm of the dead; stanzas 11-12 admit once more that a moderate degree of grief is just and understandable ("Celui qui ne s'émeut a l'âme d'un barbare / Ou n'en a du tout point") but that unmeasured grief is somehow suspect; stanzas 13-18 clinch the previous point with the examples of Priam, François I, and Malherbe himself; the concluding three stanzas recommend submission to the will of God.

In what sense is Malherbe's poem classical, and in what sense is it witty? We may call it classical, I think, only in the more general sense of that term —a conviction of inevitability of limitations, an assumption of universal order, and a humble but firm aspiration toward reflecting that order within those limitations—in life, through the exercise of reason; in art, through decorum, metrical regularity, and a diction purged of any extravagance or subjective novelty. The poem is "witty" only in the most limited sense of that volative term: the poet's wit enables him to re-phrase his common-places with a pithy and memorable elegance, the presumable ideal being "What oft was thought but n'er so well expressed." Only twice in the poem does Malherbe essay wit of a more adventurous sort: "Aime une ombre comme ombre, et de cendres éteintes / Eteins le souvenir" (ll. 35-36), and

> Mais d'être inconsolable, et dedans sa mémoire
> Enfermer un ennui,
> N'est-ce pas se haïr pour acquérir la gloire
> De bien aimer autrui?
>
> (ll. 45-48)

But neither the gentle word play of the first quotation nor the mildly per-verse psychological query of the second really carries us beyond the gates of decorum.

In rhetoric, in diction, in entire manner, this consolation matches its metrical purpose—one of "rhyme-harmony,"[4] in which the well-regulated chimes of rhyme fall always exactly where they are expected, hendecasylla-bic with hendecasyllabic, trisyllable with trisyllable.

In the main, French literature of the sixteenth and seventeenth centuries may be seen as following a course in which classical episodes alternate chronologically with Baroque episodes, classicism being the ultimate win-ner.[5] To put it thus, however, is to imply successive returns of the same manner, and such is not the case. One conception of classicism is followed by—"provokes" is perhaps a better word—its anti-classical reaction, and, when the classical impulse reasserts itself, it is as a significantly different conception. The first of French classicisms was that of Ronsard and his fellows, and what the Pléiade found in classical antiquity was what the English Elizabethans were to find: the sense of lush physical beauty, an abundance of charming images, and a whole storehouse of resonant myths. It was thus a very different classicism from that of Malherbe—or, later, that of La Fontaine.

The first episode of the French Baroque coincides roughly with the Wars of Religion, and it is difficult to define it precisely. (That resistance to definition is, of course, one of the things that make it Baroque.) In poetry, this episode embraces the apocalyptic visions of D'Aubigné, the macabre intensities of Sponde, and the bizarreries and neologisms of Du Bartas, as well as the *pointes* of Bertaut and Motin.[6] Its "wit," in contrast to that of Malherbe, is virtually synonymous with the extravagant, the shocking, the surprising.

It is against this background that Malherbe's reforms are to be seen, and it is remarkable that the reformer found his chief enemy not among the Baroque poets but in Ronsard. His deafness to the earlier poet's charm has often puzzled later critics. Possibly Malherbe recognized that Ronsard was a poet of much greater stature than Du Bartas or D'Aubigné, and for just that reason posed a greater threat to the poetics of limitation and decorum, the new classicism, which he himself was determined to introduce.

Malherbe's first triumph did not outlive him. By the early 1620's, the second episode of the French baroque had announced itself in the libertine poetry of Théophile de Viau, Saint-Amant, and Tristan L'Hermite. Wit as a metaphorical extravagance replaces wit as verbal appropriateness. Not until the 1640's does classicism reassert itself, in yet a third conception, one which, restoring and honoring Malherbe, nevertheless introduces other priorities and norms. With this conception, classicism triumphs in French letters—so completely as to bestow on the phrase "French classicism" a very aura of inevitability.

Théophile's "Ode à M. de L., sur la mort de son père" (ca. 1625) is a consolation, but a rather unusual one—far removed indeed from the conventional pieties of Malherbe's poem. The poet gets into his subject indirectly, devoting the first three stanzas of the poem to an encomium upon the beauties of a natural landscape; with stanza three the theme of death is abruptly announced:

> Mon Dieu, que le soleil est beau!
> Que les froides nuicts du tombeau
> Font d'outrages à la nature!
> La Mort, grosse de desplaisirs,
> De tenebres et de souspirs,
> D'os, de vers et de pourriture,
> Estouffe dans sa sépulture
> Et nos forces et nos desirs.[7]

Like Malherbe, Théophile acknowledges the universal empire of death, like him he expatiates upon it as the common destiny, but, in vivid contrast to the older poet, he dwells upon its horror. Stanza five:

> Tircis, vous y viendrez un jour;
> Alors les Graces et l'Amour
> Vous quitteront sur le passage,
> Et dedans ces royaumes vains,
> Effacé du rang des humains,
> Sans mouvement et sans visage,
> Vous ne trouverez plus l'usage
> Ny de vous yeux ny de vos mains.
> (p. 232)

"Effacé" is perhaps the key word here. Like Sponde, like Gryphius, like Donne—and unlike Malherbe—Théophile is obsessed with the annihilation of the body. We see this even more clearly in the stanza that follows, in which he presents the death of M. de L.'s father—the common destiny already rendered a *fait accompli.*

> Vostre père est ensevely,
> Et, dans les noirs flots de l'oubly
> Où la Parque l'a fait descendre,
> Il ne sçait rien de vostre ennuy,
> Et, ne fût-il mort qu'aujourd'huy,
> Puis qu'il n'est plus qu'os et que cendre,
> Il est aussi mort qu'Alexandre,
> Et vous touche aussi peu que luy.
>
> (p. 232)

Nothing here of eternal life, the "maison céleste," the wisdom of acceding patiently to the will of God (a being conspicuous, in this poem, by His absence). On the contrary, Théophile consoles his friend by pointing out not merely the folly but, in effect, the impossibility of mourning *that which no longer exists.*

A Baroque obsession, the annihilation of the body (as contrasted with its transformation, or even with its decay), and equally Baroque is Théophile's expansion of the motif to embrace the annihilation of the cosmos.[8] The poet moves immediately from the death of the individual to the death of the universe—an ultimate conclusion that his rapid imagination renders immediate. First go the planets, wittily conflated with the classical deities whose names they bear:[9]

> Saturne n'a plus ses maisons,
> Ny ses aisles ni ses saisons:
> Les Destins en ont fait une ombre.
> Ce grand Mars n'est-il pas destruit?
> Ses faits ne sont qu'un peu de bruit.
> Jupiter n'est plus qu'un feu sombre
> Qui se cache parmy le nombre
> Des petits flambeaux de la nuit.
>
> (p. 232)

After two more stanzas evoking universal destruction, the poem concludes with two stanzas insisting upon the cosmic scope of that destruction:

> Les planettes s'arresteront,
> Les elements se mesleront
> En ceste admirable structure
> Dont le ciel nous laisse jouyr.

Ce qu'on voit, ce qu'on peut ouyr,
Passera comme une peinture:
L'impuissance de la Nature
Laissera tout evanouir.

Celuy qui, formant le soleil,
Arracha d'un profond sommeil
L'air et le feu, la terre et l'onde,
Renversera d'un coup de main
La demeure du genre humain
Et la base où le ciel se fonde,
Et ce grand desordre du monde
Peut-estre arrivera demain.

Théophile's anti-classicism consists not so much in either his implied denial of a beneficent deity or his implied disbelief in personal immortality as in his compulsion to give imaginative form to the unimaginable—an aspect of that aspiration toward the boundless and unrestricted which virtually defines all anti-classicisms, whether Baroque, Romantic, or Modernist. His wit, unlike that of the English poets who were his contemporaries, rests not upon the conceit but upon the vivid imagery of a destruction beyond human conception. This imagery is operative not only in the apocalyptic stanzas with which the poem ends but also, equally tellingly, in the stanza on the dead father, in which, paradoxically, a complete and total absence becomes the palpable subject of poetic meditation.

In Malherbe's consolation, a complex but finely ordered metrical scheme orchestrates the poet's classical values. Théophile is too fine a poet —and too much a seventeenth-century artist—to evoke disorder by the simple expedient of writing disorderly verse, but his freely enjambed octo-syllabics allow his images to articulate his vision without implying, inappropriately, a hidden or ultimate harmony.

For whatever reasons, the definitive classicism of the age of Louis XIV did not create an impressive body of lyric poetry. With few exceptions, the titans of the age—Molière, Racine, Pascal, La Rochefoucauld, La Bruyère, Bossuet—dedicated themselves either to drama or to prose, and the two most important non-dramatic poets of the era—La Fontaine and Boileau— pursued, respectively, discursive-narrative and satiric rather than purely lyric paths. With the lyric consigned more or less to *vers de société* status, it becomes difficult to find a full-scale lyric consolation to place in confrontation with those of Malherbe and Théophile de Viau. One might, however, look at one of Molière's infrequent non-dramatic compositions, the sonnet "A Monsieur La Mothe le Vayer" (1664), on the occasion of the death of the latter's son:

Aux larmes, Le Vayer, laisse tes yeux ouverts;
Ton deuil est raisonnable encor qu'il soit extrême.
Et lorsque pour toujours on perd ce que tu perds,
La Sagesse, crois-moi, peut pleurer elle-même.

On se propose à tort cent préceptes divers
Pour vouloir d'un œil sec voir mourir ce qu'on aime:
L'effort en est barbare aux yeux de l'univers,
Et c'est brutalité plus que vertu suprême.

On sait bien que les pleurs ne ramèneront pas
Ce cher fils que t'enlève un imprévu trépas,
Mais la perte par là n'en est pas moins cruelle.

Ses vertus de chacun le faisoient révérer,
Il avoit le cœur grand, l'esprit beau, l'âme belle;
Et ce sont des sujets à toujours le pleurer.[10]

Modest in air and scope, the poem is well-nigh perfect in execution. Rejecting quite specifically all the grounds of Malherbe's consolation, in style, in diction, in rhetoric, it displays, nevertheless, a significant resemblance to the work of the older classicist. And it is clearly the work of an artist to whom both the imaginative flights and the miscalculated excesses of a Théophile would be equally impossible. Worth noting is the poet's designation of his bereaved friend's grief as "raisonnable" at the same time that it is "extrême": for Malherbe, the two terms would have been mutually incompatible; for Molière, psychologically rather than philosophically oriented, extremeness itself is reasonable, given the peculiar decorum imposed by death. Thus, the personified figure of "Sagesse" (a highly effective piece of ornamentation in a poem which, in the classical manner, treats ornamentation with a certain *pudeur*) is seen as herself decorously capable of tears—hyperbole itself is, given the poet's central statement, somehow de-hyperbolized.

Straightforward statement is the general manner of the poem. Like the personification in the fourth line, that of the seventh—"L'effort en est barbare aux yeux de l'univers"—derives special power from the generally unfigurative context in which it appears. The sestet of the sonnet is completely unfigurative, but its quiet rhetoric renders it profoundly moving. The choice of the dignified, poetic term "trépas" operates not as a dishonest evasion (like "passing on" in modern English), but rather as a poignant and sensitive attempt to give dignity to inconsolable loss, the nature of which is admitted by the bald plainness of the rest of the diction. "Il avoit le cœur grand, l'esprit beau, l'âme belle; / Et ce sont des sujets à toujours le pleurer"—the unobtrusive, yet eloquent, ascent from "cœur" to "esprit" to "âme" is accompanied by adjectives that could not possibly be simpler:

"grand," "beau," "belle." We are prepared—as La Mothe le Vayer was pre-pared—for the final line, which, in its refusal to console, offers the only human gesture appropriately consoling.

"Wit" is for Théophile the shocking image that transports us to strange and unimagined worlds of perception: he is Baroque. For Malherbe, "wit" is the appropriate, concise, and memorable couching of the philosophical commonplace. For Molière it is that which is humanly appropriate and psychologically just. The major difference between second-phase classicism (that of Malherbe) and third-phase classicism (that of Molière, Racine, La Fontaine, and Pascal) is the replacement of philosophical truism by psycho-logical perception. Or, more broadly, the replacement of philosophy by psychology. Both Malherbe and Molière are classical, but the latter is a major figure of classicism at its moment of achieved maturity. At that moment, fineness of technique and sharpness of wit were in the service of a full human awareness. That awareness makes Molière's sonnet to La Mothe le Vayer a minor monument of classical perfection and classical wit. It also makes it, one might note, of the three consolations considered here, the only one that would have the ghost of a chance of fulfilling its extra-literary aim.

NOTES

1. See, for example, J. Rousset, *La Littérature de l'âge baroque en France: Circé et le paon* (Paris, 1960).

2. See Rousset, *La Littérature de l'âge baroque en France*; J. Tortel, ed., *Le Préclassicisme français* (Paris, 1952); A. Adam, *Théophile de Viau et la libre pensée française en 1620* (Paris, 1935); O. de Mourgues, *Metaphysical, Baroque and Précieux Poetry* (Oxford, 1953).

3. F. de Malherbe, *Poésies*, ed. L. Becq de Fougières (Paris, 1974), p. 47. Sub-sequent references in the text.

4. The terms "rhyme-harmony" and "rhyme-counterpoint" were coined by Albert McHarg Hayes, "Counterpoint in Herbert," *Studies in Philology*, 35 (1938), 43-60.

5. For a rather similar scheme, see A. Adam, *Grandeur and Illusion: French Literature and Society, 1600-1715* (London, 1972), especially pp. 148-58, 171-81.

6. See De Mourgues, *Metaphysical, Baroque and Précieux Poetry*, and F.J. Warnke, *European Metaphysical Poetry* (New Haven, 1961), especially pp. 30-39.

7. T. de Viau, *Oeuvres complètes*, ed. M. Alleaume, 2 vols. (Paris, 1855), II, 231. Subsequent references in the text.

8. See F.J. Warnke, *Versions of Baroque* (New Haven, 1972), pp. 205-15.

9. Cf. John Donne, "The Second Anniversarie," ll. 195-204 (John Donne, *Poetical Works*, ed. H.J.C. Grierson, 2 vols. [Oxford, 1912], I, 257).

10. J.B.P. Molière, *Oeuvres complètes*, ed. L. Moland, 12 vols. (1863-85; rpt. Nendeln-Liechtenstein: Kraus Reprint, 1976), XII, 223-24.

Gillian Jondorf

Beauty and Coherence in Montchrestien and Corneille

Corneille says in his *Discours de la tragédie* that "le but du poète est de plaire selon les règles de son art" and goes on to mention "des nécessités d'embellissement" and "des choses qui soient de la dernière beauté, et si brillantes qu'elles éblouissent."[1] Beauty for Corneille may lie in heroism, moral excellence, generosity, steadfastness in love, consistency of character (even if evil), or in the wealth of incident, some of it horrific, which his invention has added to his subject. In the preface to *Rodogune* he says:

L'ordre de leur naissance incertain, Rodogune prisonnière, quoiqu'elle ne vînt jamais en Syrie, la haine de Cléopâtre pour elle, la proposition sanglante qu'elle fait à ses fils, celle que cette princesse est obligée de leur faire pour se garantir, l'inclination qu'elle a pour Antiochus, et la jalouse fureur de cette mère qui se résout plutôt à perdre ses fils qu'à se voir sujette de sa rivale, ne sont que des *embellissements* de l'invention . . . . (my italics)

Beauty also lies in language (for example in regularity of verse and in choice of images) and one element of beauty in the language, as well as on the stage, may be the physical and facial beauty of some of the characters.

Beauty of person is usually conveyed in seventeenth-century tragedy in vague and abstract terms. This language allows hyperbolic statement yet does not specify what an actor must look like or how a reader must picture a character. Words such as *charmes, attraits, appas* or *éclat* are used in preference to any more particularizing evocation of beauty.

In sixteenth-century tragedy the acknowledgement of beauty is often already as stylized as in plays of the classical period, but this is not always the case. Sometimes the seductive power of beauty is more emphasized than it would be later, as in the case of Garnier's Cléopâtre, whose "blandices" are associated with her beauty (*Marc-Antoine*, I, l. 11). Sometimes beauty is catalogued in a way which, in the case of Cléopâtre, owes more to conventional love poetry than to Plutarch:

> *Diomède*
> Rien ne vit de si beau; Nature semble avoir
> Par un ouvrage tel surpassé son pouvoir;
> Elle est toute céleste, et ne se voit personne
> La voulant contempler qu'elle ne passionne.
> L'albastre qui blanchist sur son visage saint
> Et le vermeil coral qui ses deux lèvres peint,
> La clairté de ses yeux, deux soleils de ce monde,
> Le fin or rayonnant dessur sa tresse blonde,
> Sa belle taille droitte, et ses frians attraits,
> Ne sont que feux ardans, que cordes, et que traits.
> (*Marc-Antoine*, II, l. 709)

A catalogue of this kind, it may be noted, works differently in a play and in a sonnet. In a sonnet it works on the reader's imagination; in a play the person described may be onstage (as in Garnier's *Hippolyte*, III), or will soon appear (like Racine's Phèdre, described in I, l. 44 as "Une femme mourante"), or has just left the stage (probably the case with Cléopâtre when Diomède makes the speech just quoted). The spectator is thus invited to compare the person with the description. Discrepancy between the two can be used for comic effect, as when Rosalind-Ganymede runs through a check-list of "how to know a man in love" and declares that Orlando does not match the description and cannot therefore be in love (*As You Like It*, III, II. 2, 346). Harmony between the person and the description would presumably "embellir" the play by enhancing *vraisemblance*. Occasionally such harmony would require rather precise "matching" of actor to part if taken seriously—the hair of Thésée-Hippolyte, for instance, in Phèdre's composite description, "comme soye retorce en petits anneletz," where Seneca's Phaedra mentions only "comam" (Garnier, *Hippolyte*, III, l. 1416; Seneca, *Hippolytus*, l. 651).

In all the passages referred to so far, physical beauty is mentioned for its power to evoke love or to seduce. It may however have other "meanings" or connotations, moral or philosophical. Before looking at references to beauty in Corneille, I shall, for contrast, examine the treatment of the theme of beauty in a play by an earlier writer. The *Reine d'Escosse* of Antoine de Montchrestien (published 1601 as *L'Escossoise*; 1604 as *La Reine d'Escosse*) presents the debate preceding the execution of Mary Queen of Scots and the execution itself, described in a *nuntius*-speech and lamented by a chorus. At the time of her execution in 1587, Mary Stuart was in her mid-40's (born 1542) and had endured nineteen years of captivity. Elizabeth Tudor was almost ten years older (born 1533). Mary's supporters and Elizabeth's courtier-poets abundantly praised the beauty of the two women throughout their lives; and we may assume that it is by deliberate literary choice, or for propaganda purposes, that Monchrestien makes only one rather vague and ambiguous reference to Elizabeth's beauty, when she herself says that "un monde de gens me respecte à l'envi, / Me regarde marcher d'œil et d'esprit ravi" (I, l. 11), and a great many to the beauty of the Queen of Scots. Indeed, the beauty of the latter seems to be a kind of leitmotif in the play; what is both interesting and perplexing is that Montchrestien puts this theme to many and conflicting uses.

It is mentioned several times in the context of practical, political problems; it makes the Queen of Scots hard to keep captive and dangerous to release:

> Qu'une beauté royale est de mauvaise garde.
> (I, l. 46)
> Mais vous n'ignorez point que ceste belle Reine,
>
> . . . .
>
> De chercher sa franchise a bien quelque raison;
> Encores que peut estre il nous soit dommageable
> D'eslargir une Dame en beautez admirable.
> (II, ll. 445, 448)

Beauty is also associated with moral qualities. The Queen of England talking to her Conseiller expresses varying degrees of surprise or incredulity at the incongruity between Mary Stuart's beauty and her cruelty.

> O cœur trop inhumain pour si douce beauté,
> (I, l. 75)
> Si ceste volonté barbarement cruelle
> Peut tomber en l'esprit d'une Reine si belle,
>
> . . . .
>
> Je croiray desormais que les Ourses cruelles
> Depoüillent les fureurs qui leur sont naturelles.
> (I, ll. 93, 97)

When the focus shifts, in the last three acts, to the Queen of Scots and her attendants, the use made of the theme of beauty changes. Mary's beauty is now seen as a reflection and indication of her saintly character as well as a charming and lovable aspect of her mortal existence. Even Elizabeth's secretary, Davison, delivering the sentence of death and mentioning sternly and in detail Mary's "forfaits," also speaks straightforwardly of her "beau chef voilé" which is to fall on the scaffold, without any hint of finding her beauty and her morals incompatible.

Praise of Mary's beauty is used in these last three acts in three ways. It is used for pathos, the death of a beautiful woman (especially "A la main d'un Bourreau de carnage entachée," V, l. 1368) being presented as particularly cruel and moving. Thus the Maistre d'Hostel,

> Reine, unique ornement des Dames de nostre âge,
> Que ton malheureux sort afflige mon courage!
> Beau corps, de qui la mort travaille tant d'esprits,
> Dont le plus grand bon-heur en tes yeux fut compris.
> (V, l. 1343)

and the Chœur of Mary's "suivantes":

> Forfait inusité! supplice abominable!
> Cruauté barbaresque! attentat execrable!
> D'un visage si beau les roses et les lis
> Par les doigts de la mort ont donc esté cueillis?
> (V, l. 1407; cf. later in the same
> speech, "cette unique Beauté")

Secondly, Mary's beauty is linked with her mental and moral qualities. The praise and lamentation just quoted move on from physical beauty to intellectual ability: "Cette bouche tantost si pleine d'éloquence / Est close pour jamais d'un eternel silence?" (V, l. 1411). The messenger relating the execution describes how the Queen looked as she walked to the scaffold and links beauty with "mespris de la mort," a virtue in both Stoic and Christian systems:

> Sa face paroist belle encor qu'elle soit palle,
> Non de la mort hastée en sa jeune saison,
> Mais de l'ennuy souffert en si longue prison.
> Lors tous les assistans attendris de courage,
> Et d'ame tous ravis, regardent son visage,
> Lisent sur son beau front le mespris de la mort,
> Admirent ses beaux yeux, considerent son port.
> (V, l. 1453)

Thirdly, Mary's living beauty links her, through a network of images, to the felicity of the blessed souls in heaven. Mary's beauty and her life are described in images of flowers ("les roses et les lis," V, l. 1409; "la fleur de mes jours," V, l. 1437). Heavenly felicity itself is personified as "ceste Belle" (IV, l. 1287), whom the heaven-dwelling soul can "cherir et baiser." The souls in heaven, like Mary, have "beaux yeux": "La musique des Cieux contente vostre oreille, / Et pour en voir le bal vos beaux yeux sont ouvers" (IV, l. 1329, Chœur). Mary speaks of the souls of the blessed as flowers in lines which I quote from the 1601 version of the play, as I think this is one of the passages where Montchrestien in 1604 amended for the worse:

> Si la fleur de mes iours se flestrit en ce temps,
> Elle va refleurir en l'eternel Printemps,
> Où la grace de Dieu, comme vne alme rosée,
> La rendra tousiours gaye & des ames prisée,
> Luy faisant respirer vn air si gratieux,
> Qu'il embasmera tout dans le pourpris des Cieux.
> Les Esprits bien-heureux sont des celestes Roses,
> Au Soleil eternel incessamment escloses;
> Les Roses des iardins ne durent qu'vn matin;
> Mais ces Roses du Ciel n'auront iamais de fin.
> (V, I. 1439, 1601 text)

However, what makes this imagery odd and disjointed is that it is also used, inappropriately, in the earlier part of the play. Act II consists of one scene, between the Queen of England and the "Chœur des Estats." The scene opens with the Chœur des Estats requesting Elizabeth to allow the death sentence, already pronounced "en plein Conseil," to be carried out on the Queen of Scots, for the safety of the realm and for Elizabeth's own safety, on which the well-being of the realm depends. Elizabeth is reluctant and in a long speech applies to herself the beast imagery which has already been associated with Mary and which Mary later uses about Elizabeth. Elizabeth had mentioned "Ourses cruelles" (I, I. 97, quoted above), and her Conseiller had warned her thus of the danger of freeing Mary:

> Le souvenir des fers sa rage augmentera,
> Et sa propre fureur se rendra plus felonne.
> Ainsi voit-on le Tigre ou la rousse Lionne
> Retenus pour un temps dans la cage enfermez,
> S'ils gagnent la campagne estre plus animez,
> Faire plus de degast, de meurtres, de carnages,
> Que ceux qui sont nourris dans les deserts sauvages.
> (I, I. 312)

Now, in Act II, Elizabeth imagines how people will talk about her if she has her royal prisoner killed:

> Elle a pris, diroit-on, naissance de la mer;
> Au bers elle a teté le pis d'une Lionne.
> (II, I. 528)
>
> Cameleon venteux, sujet au changement,
> (II, I. 539)
>
> Que n'establissois-tu ta fiere tyrannie
> Sur les Lions d'Affrique et Tigres d'Hyrcanie,

Puisque ces animaux en leur plus grand courroux
Au prix de toy barbare ont le courage doux.
(II, l. 549)

And Mary's Maistre d'Hostel does indeed speak of Elizabeth in such terms when he says "ce honteux trespas, / Honteux non pas à toy mais à cette Barbare, / Que le visage seul de ses Ourses separe" (V, l. 1362). Elizabeth's use of the beast imagery is not illogical, for she is accurately predicting a certain reaction to the death sentence. However, her speech in Act II ends with her determining to postpone ratification of the death sentence, and the Chœur which had been urging Mary's death then ends the Act, unexpectedly, with a meditation on mortality; here we find the flower imagery which seems so appropriate in the later acts, along with a reference to eyes, which anticipates later references to Mary's beautiful eyes, and a final salute to Mary as a "deesse humaine":

Qu'est-ce ô Dieu que de l'homme! une fleur passagere,
Que la chaleur flestrit ou que le vent fait choir;
Une vaine fumée, une ombre fort legere
Qui se jouë au matin et passe sur le soir.
(II, l. 571)

On ne peut rendre aux fleurs leur couleur printenniere
Lors qu'elles ont senti les chaleurs de l'Esté:
Quand une fois la mort flestrit nostre paupiere,
Yeux, vous pouvez bien dire: adieu, douce clarté.

La vie est sans arrest, et si court à son terme
D'un mouvement si prompt qu'on ne l'apperçoit point,
Là si tost qu'elle arrive elle y demeure ferme;
Le naistre et le mourir est presque un mesme poinct.
Bien certaine est la mort mais la sorte incertaine,
Qui pourroit du matin juger la fin du jour?
L'on veut bien décoler une Deesse humaine
Fille de la vertu et mere de l'amour.
(II, l. 595)

The gentle solemnity and melancholy of these lines, linking classical and biblical commonplaces in delightful harmony, exemplify the sort of writing at which Montchrestien excels; but this graceful elegy is apparently spoken by the very chorus who in the same scene had been urging Mary's death and describing her continued existence as a menace to England, with images of "cruel orage," "tison consommant" and "peste mortelle." We could perhaps assume that the Chœur des Estats has withdrawn at the end of its discussion (II, l. 506), satisfied that Elizabeth has given authority for the execution with the line "Bien, faites mes amis comme vous l'entendez"

(II, l. 491). We can then assume that Elizabeth's next speech is a soliloquy, and this supposition is strengthened by the fact that the choric meditation which follows it, beginning "Qu'est-ce ô Dieu que de l'homme," is in the original edition headed by the word "Chœur" in full and not the abbreviation "Ch" used in the earlier part of the scene. But what Chœur can this be? The Chœur des Estats desires Mary's death, the Chœur des damoiselles has not yet heard the death sentence. Is this a sort of "Chœur à tout faire" for performing meditations on commonplace themes? Or may we imagine it as a combined chorus, able briefly to put aside partisan sympathies in order to lament the fragile human condition? It is tempting to think that by this device Montchrestien has linked the two parts of his play, reconciled the otherwise contradictory use of imagery, and even solved in an imaginative way the problem of place; historically, the events which occupy Acts I and II of the play happened at Richmond, the rest at Fotheringay Castle. Montchrestien may have been unaware of the distance between the two, but plainly a change of scene is entailed between Acts II and III. The last chorus of Act II, if spoken by both choric groups, could be a sort of hinge through which the play swings from one place to another, as well as from one set of sympathies to the opposite one.[2]

The principal weakness of this theory is that there is no real evidence for it; but some such hypothesis is needed if we are to rescue Montchrestien from the charge of incoherence in his deployment of the theme of beauty. The images of flowers and beauty are not the only ones in the play; as well as the wild beast imagery there are also many references to storms and shipwreck, both metaphorical and literal (political storms likely to be provoked by Mary's plotting, storms and threatened shipwreck which she has endured in her travels, and the stormy seas of life from which she will sail into safe harbor after her courageous death), and these images too are used in a random way, although they do briefly and satisfyingly link up with the theme of beauty at a climactic moment, the moment at which Mary approaches the scaffold:

> Son Oraison finie elle esclarcit sa face,
> Par l'air doux et serain d'une riante grace,
> Elle montra ses yeux plus doux qu'auparavant,
> Et son front s'aplanit comme l'onde sans vent.
> (V, l. 1495)

This is a brief moment of harmony and does not resolve Montchrestien's muddle. Montchrestien is a poet who is aware of beauty, sensitive to the pathos of the human condition and able to convey that pathos in tender, sonorous lines: "La vie est comme une ombre ou comme un vent leger, /

Et son cours n'est à rien qu'à un rien comparable" (V, I. 1609). He fails, however, to integrate his poetic images into a satisfying whole and fails to give his reader a coherent pattern of feeling and thought. When we read Montchrestien we are tantalized by an absence of intellectual framework. There is no *doctrina*, he has nothing to tell us about moral or intellectual problems, nor is he showing us that the world is morally dislocated and therefore tragic. He offers us a welter of beautiful lines but the beauty of his verse is undirected, just as the beauty of his heroine is seen from bewilderingly incompatible points of view, as a deceptive mask or as the reflection of a beautiful soul.

Corneille's plays, unlike Montchrestien's, usually have a strong intellectual framework; indeed they can be reproached with making excessive sacrifices to intellectuality, the endings in particular sacrificing pyschological *vraisemblance* to the desire for an almost algebraically tidy solution.

This strong sense of argument in Corneille's plays, his wish to base plays on some motive more "mâle" than love, and the fact that when love is prominent it often has an element of "amour-estime" which is founded on the admiration of another's personal worth, might lead us to expect Corneille to place relatively little emphasis on beauty of face or body. He does however make quite interesting use of it.

The play which I propose to look at from this point of view is *Théodore, vierge et martyre* (performed 1645?; published 1646), a relatively unfamiliar play. Although the title might suggest a parallel with Monchrestien's play about the Virgin Queen and the Martyr Queen, a truer parallel lies in the conflict of values on which each play is built: conflict between expediency and the sanctity of a royal person in *La Reine d'Escosse*, and between pagan and Christian principles in *Théodore*. Corneille's play is about a little-known Christian martyr, Théodore, who is loved both by Didyme, a Christian, and by Placide, son of Valens, Roman governor of Syria, but who refuses all suitors, being determined to die a virgin. Valens's second wife, Marcelle, persecutes Théodore, whom she wishes to destroy so that Placide can be induced to marry Marcelle's daughter, Flavie, who is dying for love of him. Théodore is condemned to public prostitution, escapes unviolated with the help of Didyme, but after the death of the lovelorn Flavie, Didyme and Théodore are both stabbed to death by Marcelle, who then fatally stabs herself. Placide also stabs himself and at the end of the play his death seems likely though not certain.

Compared to the sober historical facts of the condemnation and execution of Mary Queen of Scots, this may sound farfetched and extravagant, although it is allegedly historical. The play has never enjoyed much esteem and Corneille in his *Examen* expresses misgivings about some of the characters, including Théodore, of whom he says caustically, "pour en parler sainement, une vierge et martyre sur une scène n'est autre chose qu'un Terme qui n'a ni jambes ni bras, et par conséquent pas d'action"; he is also uneasy about the "duplicité d'action" or "duplicité de péril" whereby Théodore, having escaped prostitution, offers her life in place of Didyme's (much to Didyme's resentment).

However many faults Corneille can find in the play, it has some qualities and offers an interesting contrast to Montchrestien in terms of coherence, a point which can be illustrated by examining the use made of the theme of beauty.

The person round whom the references to beauty cluster is of course Théodore, but we do not hear immediately about her beauty. We hear first of the impasse in which Placide finds himself—loved by Flavie, whose mother has married his father, offered honors in the expectation that he will marry Flavie, and in love with Théodore, who is unresponsive. This to him reflects cruel and capricious forces shaping human lives:

> Je hais qui m'idolâtre, et j'aime qui me fuit,
> Et je poursuis en vain, ainsi qu'on me poursuit.
> Telle est de mon destin la fatale injustice,
> Telle est la tyrannie ensemble et le caprice
> Du démon aveuglé qui sans discrétion
> Verse l'antipathie et l'inclination.
>
> (I, I. 85)

This pagan view forms a contrast with Théodore's belief in a controlling God who "connaît tout, entend tout" (II, I. 549) and so constitutes an element in the pattern of opposing beliefs and values.

The first time the word "beau" occurs it is with reference to Théodore, but it alludes presumably to her birth and not her beauty (she is of princely rank). Marcelle has told Placide that she will destroy Théodore and he replies defiantly:

> N'épargnez pas mon sang si vous versez le sien;
> Autrement ce beau sang en fera verser d'autre,
> Et ma fureur n'est pas pour se borner au vôtre.
>
> (I, I. 234)

The reference, however, is not only to blood in the sense of rank but also to death by the shedding of blood; and appropriately, in this play which shifts from a potentially comic opening (a chain of lovers, a nasty stepmother, the flash of repartee and word play) to repellent cruelty and violent death, the next reference to beauty is also linked to death, as Marcelle plans to achieve the conquest of Placide by eliminating Théodore and comments:

> Il cessera d'aimer aussi bien que de craindre.
> L'amour va rarement jusque dans un tombeau
> S'unir au reste affreux de l'objet le plus beau.
> (I, l. 260)

This is a pagan view both of love and of death. Another attitude will be displayed later by Théodore and Didyme, who conquer love and the fear of death to seek a deathless love.

We first encounter Théodore in Act II and are struck not only by the "vertu farouche" or "âpre vertu" (so named by her kinsman Cléobule) which makes her treat with particular harshness the suitor (Didyme) to whom she is secretly most drawn, but also by her rapid, intelligent, but erroneous estimate of Placide's share of responsibility for the danger of which Cléobule warns her. Théodore describes love conventionally as "les belles passions" but in fact regards it as a trap set by the senses for the soul. The "coup d'œil fatal" which she fears from Didyme would be "fatal" for her because it would interfere with her resolution and in her view would damage her immortal soul; there is an almost punning overlap between Théodore's special meaning and the conventional or *précieux* force of the words: "Je crains d'en recevoir quelque coup d'œil fatal, / Et chasse un ennemi dont je me défends mal" (II, l. 405). The tired metaphors of conventional love acquire new force because Théodore sees herself as engaged not in a playful battle of amorous resistance but in a fight for the purity of her own soul.

When Théodore first meets Marcelle, events have not yet taken a disastrous turn and the atmosphere can still support wit. When Marcelle utters a Néron-like threat, "Et si vous vous aimez, souffrez que je vous aime," Théodore replies with a cool mockery worthy of Célimène: "Je n'ai point vu, Madame, encor jusqu'à ce jour / Avec tant de menace expliquer tant d'amour" (II, l. 492). But once Théodore has been forced to avow her Christianity, the tone of the play darkens rapidly. In the next scene (sc. 5), Théodore is surrounded by accusers and traducers (Valens, Marcelle, Stéphanie). Two variations are here played on the theme of beauty, both appropriate to the darkening tone. Théodore uses "beau" in one of a string of oxymorons:

> Puisque je suis coupable aux yeux de l'injustice,
> Je fais gloire du crime, et j'aspire au supplice,

> Et d'un crime si beau le supplice est si doux
> Que qui peut le connaître en doit être jaloux.
> (II, I. 595)

There is irony here in that she has not yet heard what the "supplice" will be, but there is irony of another kind in her use of "beau." The crime which Théodore declares "beau" is regarded by us not as a crime but as a virtue (and therefore "beau") and the fact that the forces of "l'injustice" (represented by everyone else onstage) regard Christian faith as a crime reflects ironically the perverse values of the pagan Roman empire.

The second allusion to beauty in this scene is indirect, in that the word "charmes," here used literally, is a frequent dead metaphor for beauty in classical language:

> Je ne recherche plus la damnable origine
> De cette aveugle amour où Placide s'obstine.
> Cette noire magie, ordinaire aux Chrétiens,
> L'arrête indignement dans vos honteux liens;
> Votre charme après lui se répand sur Flavie,
> De l'un il prend le cœur, et de l'autre la vie.
> (II, I. 599)

According to Valens, the speaker here, Placide loves Théodore not because he is enchanted (metaphorically) by her beauty but because he is bewitched (literally) by her spells. We know this to be false, but its silly baseness gives us a measure of the depravity of Valens, a foretaste of his turpitude in choosing for Théodore a "supplice" so repugnant that he will not even tell Marcelle what it is; and the turpitude seems greater, not less, when he then claims a virtuous and even kindly motive for his sentence.

Acts III and IV are occupied by a network of misinterpretations and deceptions surrounding the "supplice" of Théodore in the brothel. Valens at the end of Act II had already announced that his choice of punishment was a ruse to make Théodore renounce Christianity so that he could then promote her marriage to Placide. Now in Act III Théodore accuses Placide of complicity in the choice of sentence, then Marcelle deceives Placide, then at the beginning of Act IV Stéphanie tries to prolong this deception, then Placide misunderstands Paulin, then he misinterprets (as does Paulin) what happened in the brothel, then he falsely accuses both Cléobule and Didyme. Even when he has heard the true story of Didyme's rescue of Théodore, he assumes that Didyme is in league with Valens and Marcelle to deprive him of Théodore. Théodore's beauty is allowed almost to fade from our minds during these two acts, and indeed emphasis on it may have been avoided as part of the tact with which Corneille deals with the brothel episode. But near the end of Act IV the pace of action slows and Placide, contemplating the new state of affairs, expresses confused feelings towards Didyme. Jealousy and gratitude master him by turns until he reconciles them by resolving to maintain an uneasy equilibrium: "Dans une âme jalouse un esprit généreux" (IV, I. 1482). At this moment of introspection (honest although based on the false premise that Didyme and Théodore will wish to marry), Théodore's beauty is alluded to again, and the two references to it in Placide's speech give the theme new significance: "Ta courageuse adresse à ses divins appas / Vient de rendre un secours que leur devait mon bras" (IV, I. 1461). The phrase "divins appas" is conventional but is surely used deliberately here for its appropriateness to the saintly Théodore, who has already stated her intention of preserving "A l'époux sans macule une épouse impollue" (III, I. 780) and who will shortly contend with Didyme for "Et le droit de mourir, et l'honneur du martyre" (V, I. 1628, cf. II. 1624, 1650). Thus a conventional phrase, "divins appas," is used in a context where its conventional meaning remains, but a fuller meaning overlies it. Placide's next reference to Théodore's beauty is also of a superficially conventional kind: "Et que cette beauté qui me tient sous sa loi / Ne saurait plus sans crime être à d'autre qu'à toi?" (IV, I. 1473). Several things nudge this out of its conventional slot. One is our knowledge that Théodore repudiates any idea that she is deliberately subjugating young men "sous sa loi." Cléobule had said to her in Act II, "Je veux bien avec vous que dessous votre empire / Toute notre jeunesse en vain brûle et soupire" (II, I. 359). Théodore's answer showed that she was indifferent to this kind of conquest and only anxious to prevent herself from being "vaincue" in her turn by Didyme. She is not a conventional beauty accepting the worship of her admirers while indifferent to their suffering; she aspires to a higher love, is "sous les lois d'un plus puissant époux" (III, I. 869) and regards human love as a distraction and a danger. The only way she would wish to bring Placide "sous sa loi" would be by his sharing her faith, a possibility he hinted at when urging her to escape to Egypt as his bride: "Et peut-être, suivant ce que vous résoudrez, / Je n'y serai bientôt que ce que vous voudrez" (III, I. 853). Moreover, the second line quoted above from Placide's speech to Didyme—"Ne saurait plus sans crime être à d'autre qu'à toi?"—reminds us of other elements in the predicament of this "beauté," as much by what it does not say as by what it does. The line expresses Placide's view, namely that Didyme has now earned the right to marry Théodore. But Théodore does not recognize any such right and would say rather that she "Ne saurait pas sans crime être à d'autre qu'à Dieu." The "crime" to which Placide refers would be an offense against the code of honor and against a kind of natural justice. But crime, like honor, is defined in terms of values held. Théodore has already pointed out the relativity of such terms as "coupable" and "crime" (II, I. 595, discussed above), and for her marriage to Didyme would be as "criminal" as marriage to Placide, and perhaps more so because more tempting. She is indifferent to the notions of honor that weigh with Placide because she values only "l'honneur du martyre" (see II. 1620, 1624, 1632). The lines in which Placide juxtaposes "beauté" and "crime" recall Théodore's pride in her "crime si beau" and thus remind us of the conflict between rival sets of values.

By Act V, sc. 3, the martyrdom of Didyme and Théodore is imminent but Didyme expects to be the only one to die, and in one of the numerous parallels to Polyeucte he "bequeaths" Théodore to Placide, urging that Théodore save her own life by escaping to Egypt with Placide: "Qu'elle fuie avec lui, c'est tout ce que veut d'elle / Le souvenir mourant d'une flamme si belle" (V, I. 1599). The placing and gender of "mourant" and "belle" and the quasi-personification of "souvenir" as the grammatical subject of "veut," combine to make it easy to transfer the two adjectives to Didyme and Théodore respectively, so that the line suggests a dying man's tribute to his beautiful mistress. But this graceful elegiac tone does not signal the end of the play, for Théodore is not to be disposed of by a gentlemen's agreement of this sort. It is perhaps not surprising that Didyme, desirous of martyrdom as he is, greets Théodore's next entrance (just after his renunciatory lines) with a challenge recalling the use of "charme" in Valens's accusation (II, I. 603, quoted above):

> Pensez-vous m'arracher la palme de la main,
> Madame, et mieux que lui m'expliquant votre envie,
> Par un charme plus fort m'attacher à la vie?
> (V, I. 1602)

(Cléobule had been telling Didyme that Théodore was now in love with him and that Placide would take Théodore and Didyme to Egypt and there allow Didyme to marry Théodore.) When Didyme accuses Théodore of seeking to dissuade him from martyrdom by "un charme," the word might carry only its conventional meaning, but the wickedness, in his eyes, of what she seems to intend ("m'arracher la palme de la main") and the reminiscence of Valens's words in Act II ensure that "charme" also carries its stronger and more sinister meaning. That Didyme should accuse an austerely virtuous fellow-Christian of deliberate "spell-binding" even in the non-literal sense, but particularly in the literal sense (thus repeating a pagan calumny about Christians), is perhaps a measure not only of his fierce desire for martyrdom, but also of the damage done by the atmosphere of deception, both wicked and well-meaning, which has obtained throughout the play, and on both occasions its literal meaning, so forcefully evoked by Valens in Act II, is in the offing. In Act V, sc. 7, Paulin, who is by now rather contemptuous of his pusillanimous master Valens, tells Valens that Placide intends to try to rescue Théodore:

> Placide donc, Seigneur, osera plus que vous.
> Marcelle a fait armer Lycante et sa cohorte,
> Mais sur elle et sur eux il va fondre à main-forte,
> Résolu de forcer pour cet objet charmant
> Jusqu'à votre palais et votre appartement.
>
> (V, l. 1746)

"Charmant" here has its conventional meaning, but it could well convey also the suggestion that a very powerful force must be operating to induce one man to take on the whole praetorian guard (I assume Corneille is using "cohorte" in the sense of *cohors praetoria*, the bodyguard of a governor, rather than in the sense of the tenth part of a legion, which could be over five hundred men). The craven Valens will do nothing to avert the "désordre" and "carnage" predicted by Paulin in this speech, his policy being literally one of "Laisser faire": "N'importe, laissons faire et Marcelle et Placide" (V, l. 1755). The ensuing slaughter is then reported by Stéphanie, and the word "charmant" makes a sinister last appearance in the play, as she describes Marcelle enjoying her vengeance, gloating over the dying martyrs (whom she has stabbed) and over the shocked Placide, who has fainted with horror:

> Cependant, triomphante entre ces deux mourants,
> Marcelle les contemple à ses pieds expirants,
> Jouit de sa vengeance, et d'un regard avide
> En cherche les douceurs jusqu'au cœur de Placide,
> Et tantôt se repaît de leurs derniers soupirs,
> Tantôt goûte à pleins yeux ses mortels déplaisirs,
> Y mesure sa joie, et trouve plus charmante
> La douleur de l'amant que la mort de l'amante,
> Nous témoigne un dépit qu'après ce coup fatal,
> Pour être trop sensible il sent trop peu son mal.
>
> (V, l. 1817)

The horrific effect of this *récit* is created by the active verbs of enjoyment ("jouit," "cherche les douceurs," "se repaît," "goûte," "mesure sa joie") amidst the slaughter, but also by the juxtaposition of death and love vocabulary, including phrases common to both domains ("coup fatal," "douleur," even "mortels déplaisirs"). The couplet in which "charmante" occurs epitomizes this aspect of the speech, with its first line full of the vocabulary of pleasure, and even a refined, critical pleasure ("Y *mesure* sa joie, et trouve *plus* charmante . . .") followed by the rhyming line which reveals what it is that this depraved spectator appreciates so keenly, and what "charmante" means to her. Perversity, the triumph of evil values, has reached a climax, and this is elegantly marked by the application, to Théodore's martyrdom, of a word more appropriate to her living beauty.

In tracing the references to beauty in *Théodore*, we have seen that the idea of beauty is linked to love, to death, to witchcraft, to crime and to sanctity. These links are appropriate and are related to the ideas and conflicts in the play, and the notion of what is beautiful, like the notion of what is just or what is criminal, reflects the values of the speaker.

In neither of the two plays discussed does examination of the theme of beauty give a complete account of the play. It does however seem to give an accurate one. In Montchrestien's case, the theme of beauty is itself one of the sources of beauty in the play, in that it is the subject of some of the loveliest lines of a poet who is very prolific in sumptuously or languourously beautiful lines. But the haphazard way in which it is used is typical of Montchrestien's general intellectual muddle, which extends even to the question of Mary Stuart's guilt or innocence. Most critics have seen this play as faulty in structure because it is "broken-backed" with no proper connections between the first two acts and the last three. Joseph J. Bourque makes an interesting attempt to defend the play from this criticism in an essay accompanying his translation of the play.[3] He suggests that the decision to execute the Queen of Scots seems more and more odious as we hear of her good qualities and see her courage and faith and that the play is "a display of the triumph of the spiritual over the material," so that it has a thematic unity binding the two parts. This is an ingenious way of lending coherence to the play, but I do not think it works, if only because the English Queen is idealized as a monarch (loved by her subjects and enjoying an ideal relationship with them) whereas the Scots are disaffected and described by the Queen of Scots herself as "un peuple agité de felonnie et d'ire, / Qui la mort de sa Reine injustement desire" (III, l. 803), so that we are led to think that her queenship has been destroyed at its very roots, not by the Queen of England but by the failure of trust between monarch and people. There is therefore a sense in which the English Queen is better and more admirable than the Scottish one. It will not do to say that the play shows us first the wrong and then the right way of looking at things, for we cannot tell which is which. In spite of the beguiling beauty of much of its verse, I think the play is severely flawed by its intellectual incoherence, and the random use of the theme of beauty illustrates this.

In the case of Corneille's play, I have pointed out that the theme of beauty is modulated to fit the tone at different moments of the play and to suit different speakers, that is, different perceivers of beauty. It would be absurd to say that this proves that the play is coherent. It can however be argued that this satisfying and intelligent use of the theme of beauty is one manifestation of the control exercised by Corneille, which shows up also in other kinds of patterning. I have pointed out in passing that the play is built on a series of deceptions: Valens/Marcelle; Marcelle/Placide; Stéphanie/Placide; Didyme/soldiers; Cléobule/Didyme, and on a parallel series of misunderstandings or misinterpretations: Cléobule/Théodore; Théodore/Placide (three times); Placide/Paulin; Placide/Cléobule; Placide/Didyme; Didyme/Théodore. It also has a number of recurrent themes, of which I shall mention briefly two of the most prominent. The first is the idea of Egypt as a place of refuge where one can be free and can be what one wishes or what someone else wishes one to be. Egypt seems to offer a possibility of escape, just as heaven does in *La Reine d'Escosse*. But unlike the "sejour eternel" which awaits Mary Stuart (IV, l. 1270), Egypt is a false heaven. It is unattainable, on the factual level because Placide's governorship of Egypt was to be contingent on his marrying Flavie, on the dramatic level because there can be no escape from the scene of a tragedy, and on the moral or spiritual level because true "escape" is that aspired to by Théodore and Didyme. In Judeo-Christian symbolism, Egypt is the land of exile, slavery and darkness, and this too provides a hint that the repeated hopes of a flight to safety and freedom in Egypt are false ones. In any case, for the Christian, true liberty does not consist in being able to live in the kind of freedom imagined by Placide when he dreams of Egypt:

> L'Egypte où l'on m'envoie est un asile ouvert
> Pour mettre notre flamme et notre heur à couvert.
> Là, saisis d'un rayon des puissances suprêmes,
> Nous ne recevrons plus de lois que de nous-mêmes.
> (I, l. 113)

Nor does Christian liberty lie in the freedom offered by Cléobule to Didyme: "entre ses bras / Etre avec sûreté tout ce que tu voudras" (V, l. 1577). For Didyme and Théodore freedom consists in conforming to the will of God and in steadfastly choosing martyrdom rather than flight. They have no need of the "asile ouvert" of Egypt.

Another prominent recurring theme is that of "devoir," in the sense not of duty but of debt. Placide owes gratitude to Marcelle for honors and privileges, but he reckons that once she has demanded gratitude or a service in return she cancels her right to anything of the kind, and therefore he owes her nothing (I, sc. 2). Placide regards Théodore (and himself) as having contracted a debt towards Didyme, and Didyme uses the same vocabulary when he renounces Théodore:

> Si pourtant elle croit me devoir quelque chose,
> Et peut avant ma mort souffrir que j'en dispose,
> Qu'elle paye à Placide . . . .
>
> (V, I. 1595)

Between these two instances, the theme occurs several times, defining the relationships between characters and the responsibility for events.

These patterns and others (imagery of storms; strong symmetry between speeches and scenes; short bursts of stichomythia) assist the reader's consciousness of control in a play which has some of the characteristics of tightrope walking. It treats a shocking subject with dignity, avoiding both lewdness and excessive prudery; it blends comic and tragic tone, with sarcasm forming a transition between them, giving a lively effect yet conveying menace, contempt or defiance (e.g., the deadly badinage between Marcelle and Placide in I, sc. 2). This play succeeds in maintaining a balance between thought and feeling, between intellectual, aesthetic and emotional response, and the theme of beauty illustrates concisely how this is done. The text is less rich in *beaux vers* than *La Reine d'Escosse*, but beauty of various kinds is displayed: Théodore's physical beauty, the moral beauty of faith and steadfastness, the beauty of heroic or self-sacrificing love. At the same time we are also being offered intellectual enjoyment, both in observing the patterns of deception or misunderstanding, and in teasing out the verbal links and pointers connecting and relating various parts of the text. There is a certain playfulness in this aspect of the work, but the somber ending, so unlike the tidy resolutions of many of Corneille's plays, ensures that the impression we are left with is of a dark world, where courageous faith can win its martyr's palm but cannot edify, still less convert, the flawed onlookers.

NOTES

1. The editions used in this essay are: Pierre Corneille, *Oeuvres complètes*, ed. André Stegmann with preface by Raymond Lebègue (Paris, 1963). Robert Garnier, *Oeuvres complètes*, ed. Raymond Lebègue, 4 vols. (Paris, 1949-74). Antoine de Montchrestien, *Two Tragedies: "Hector" and "La Reine d'Escosse,"* ed. C.N. Smith (London, 1972). For the 1601 text of *L'Escossoise*: Antoine de Montchrestien, *La Reine*

d'Escosse, ed. A. Maynor Hardee (Milan, 1975). William Shakespeare, *Complete Works*, ed. Peter Alexander (London-Glasgow, 1951). References to Garnier and Montchrestien are given by act number and line number only.

2. I have suggested elsewhere that the chorus at the end of Act III of Jodelle's *Didon se sacrifiant*, which expresses sympathy for both Enee and Didon, might be spoken by the Trojan and Carthaginian *chœurs* together ("Doctrine and Image in Jodelle's *Didon se sacrifiant*," *French Studies*, 33 [1978], 269).

3. In *Four French Renaissance Plays*, ed. Arthur P. Stabler (Washington, 1978), pp. 315-16.

Ian McFarlane

A Reading of *La Veuve*

In the Letter-preface to *La Suivante*, Corneille quotes from Montaigne (I, 37): "Qu'on me donne l'action la plus excellente et pure, je m'en vais y fournir vraisemblablement cinquante vicieuses intentions." This points to a persistent fascination with the relations between state of mind and outer gesture and with the difficulties that face us when we try to find out what people are really about: one of the factors in play is language, curiously inadequate as a vehicle of communication, concealing as much as it reveals, and working according to some strange principle of refraction. Corneille no doubt found plenty in the *Essais* to confirm him in his views; and his plays often bear on the interplay between intelligence, feeling and language. This is certainly the case with *La Veuve*, though criticism has more often interested itself in its links with *Mélite*, of which it is in part a parodistic variation; in its treatment of the problem of social inequality—a hare too enthusiastically chased; or in a certain realism, a feature which is less obvious to the modern reader accustomed to the text of the later editions. All this is attempting to make the best of a bad job—and unnecessarily so, since *La Veuve* has plenty to catch our eye without appeals to its significance in the development of the dramatist or of contemporary theater. Here we can see the young Corneille on the way to forging a style that can reproduce faithfully the interplay of wit, feeling and the discrepancies between *paraître* and *être*. This is brought about not only by Corneille's growing linguistic maturity but by the way in which certain effects, hitherto left to essentially dramatic effects, are incorporated in the language itself.

As in so many of Corneille's plays, the action is essentially a movement from obscurity towards the manifest, both in the action and in the psychology.[1] Such imagery as occurs often belongs to the domains of darkness and light, as well as of sight. Here, we can detect various sources of obscurity: Alcidon, in his sinister mendacity, and the Nourrice, his agent, who in more coarse-grained fashion muddies the waters and blurs further the margins separating truth and falsehood. Then there is the interference of friendship which is seen to be an obstacle to common sense and decency; it blinds the intelligence of Philiste and Célidan. Moreover, the reticence of the two "personnages sympathiques," Philiste and Clarice, delays the manifestation of true feeling. There are, however, two other factors of a more general nature which complicate the picture: on the one hand, the murkiness of language, with its potential for misunderstanding, manipulation and partial communication; and on the other, the inconsistencies and discontinuities of the human character. The problem of language will engage our attention presently; for the time being, we shall look at the way the characters behave.

I

So far from being simple characters cast in a rigid mold, Corneille's men and women can be highly inconsistent; volte-faces have been defined in terms of dramatic necessity,[2] and there is more than a grain of truth in this explanation; but the reader of Montaigne knew that the contrariness of human nature had deeper roots, that we are patchwork quilts, that virtue and vice are so intermingled that ordinary ethical norms are difficult to apply. And when we are in a world of *feinte* such as is conjured up in *La Veuve*, we can easily lose our way: it seems that everybody is, to a greater or lesser extent, prone to dissimulation. Philiste and Clarice are not exempt, and Célidan outdoes Alcidon on his own ground; useful, indeed good arguments will be found in the mouths of unprincipled persons (as Montaigne had noticed fifty years before), whether it be Alcidon or the Nourrice; Philiste is quite happy "Si d'un mauvais dessein il tire un bon effet" (I. 574), and one would have no trouble in finding other instances. We are in a world of paradox, but the play is not just a *jeu d'esprit*; this is the world as Corneille sees it, the result of human nature with all its warts, twists and obscurities. It cannot be painted in black and white: the characters do not so much divide into convenient ethical camps as illustrate different degrees of dissimulation; but there is a difference in intention and motivation among the characters. Alcidon may be at the other end of the spectrum from Philiste, but one might well ask how it comes about that these two men are bound to each other by ties of friendship.

If there is any looseness in the structure of the action—a point that may be overdone[3]—the conception of human nature gives a unity of its own to the play; and this is reflected in the large space given by Corneille to devices of repetition and echo. Certain traits will be repeated from character to character, a theme developed à propos of one person will reappear in a totally separate context or in the mouth of a character possessed of very different values; major leitmotifs tend to occur in at least two figures: friendship (Philiste and Célidan), money (Chrysante and Géron), family pressures (Chrysante and Doris). One of the features of *La Veuve* is precisely the way in which technical devices are made to harmonize with the values and characters involved.

In fact, the structure of his play is worked out quite satisfactorily; it centers on the theme of feeling, true and false. The "sympathique" couple, Philiste and Clarice, do not contribute actively to the plot: their basic relationship remains unchanged throughout, though the problem of its expression is more difficult to resolve. Philiste's sense of friendship towards Alcidon prevents him from taking any action likely to run counter to his loyalty, which remains unimpaired until the final scene. Clarice is less well defined than Philiste: there are certain inhibitions that prevent her at first from making her feelings explicit, and she is perhaps not much more than the embodiment of love gradually revealed. Philiste has more pronounced features: though at first he appears as rather sly (I, sc. 1) and though one wonders why his reticence has lasted already for two years—the psycho-analytical explanation offered by Verhoeff (hidden fear of women) does not really help here[4]—the rest of his behavior is actuated by feelings very willing to manifest themselves. He is essentially an emotive, perhaps a choleric. His blind friendship for Alcidon, his bouts of *fureur*, his irascibility in his dealings with his mother, or the Nourrice, show him to be related to various dramatic traditions and may give him a slightly comic nuance; but some of this is set off against his silences in his conversations with Clarice. These two have a thematic rather than a dramatic value, for they stand for genuine emotions, and thus provide a backcloth against which the other characters can be assessed.

The action and awareness of the issues involved must therefore come primarily from elsewhere. So far as the action is concerned, the source is Alcidon. He is obviously clever—he is the only character who prides himself on his intelligence and condemns others for their stupidity—and he has an evident pleasure in the sheer mechanics of dissimulation. He has another characteristic which will recur in later plays of Corneille: he works entirely through intermediaries. He tries to use Philiste, Célidan, the Nourrice and Doris to secure his ends; and it is noteworthy that he does not have any dialogue scene with the professed object of his love, Clarice; indeed he sees her for the first time in the unmasking scene at the end of Act V, and even then his reply to Clarice is more in the nature of a private meditation. In the long run, he will be outwitted at his own game, but one must also allow for a certain vanity, which not only makes him look a trifle fatuous, but by clouding his intelligence with an affective element, accounts in some measure for his ultimate downfall. The high-watermark of his success is when Clarice is kidnapped at night; this is a well-known device, but it is symbolic that Alcidon's stratagems should be associated with the dark and that he is unmasked in the fullness of daylight.

His plans are much facilitated by the way in which friendship works to his advantage, though there comes a moment when he is fearful of the con-sequences of overzealous loyalty; it is indeed a principle which seems to override any other ethical consideration. As long as Philiste and Célidan are blinded by ties of loyalty, he can prosper. However, Alcidon's discomfi-ture is initiated by the way he overplays his hand. This is foreshadowed in his dealings with Doris, with whom he is allegedly in love. Doris may be thought to have few distinguishing features: she is fairly passive, she has no strong feelings about marriage, she appears obedient to her mother's wishes, though there are later signs of restiveness on that score. On the other hand, the fact that she is *not* emotionally involved allows her intelli-gence to work unhampered; and right from the outset she has no illusions about Alcidon's professed love: he is simply a "conteur à gages" (l. 178); later she takes over his phrase "le fard de mon langage" at his expense (l. 1715). Admittedly, in view of the psychological "données" of the cast, there is no "reliable witness" among the characters; but Doris is the only one to approximate to this, insofar as she and the audience come to terms. She is the means of puncturing some of the bubbles created by Alcidon, and she is thus the source of comic effect by creating a contrast between Alcidon caught up in his own web of words and deceits, and her own straightforward incisiveness. She helps to reveal the vanity in his make-up, for he continues to imagine fondly that she is in love with him; and more broadly she becomes a source of the dramatic irony which is such a feature of this play. So that, structurally, she is much more important than her character would lead us to think, and this may have been recognized in 1660 by Corneille, who gives her a speech in the final scene of the play which in previous versions was at this point fragmented so that various characters could say their short piece; as a result, her final appearance sticks more in the memory than was previously the case.

However, Doris does not actively take much part in Alcidon's unmask-ing; this role is assigned to Célidan, who first appears in Act III and whose friendship for Alcidon, at first working in his favor, is undermined by a growing awareness of his duplicity. Célidan seems, in a sense, a bit of a *ficelle*; without a further character, there is no reason why Alcidon should not attain his ends, for none of the others has the wit, the vigor or the opportunity to initiate countermeasures. It is also true that Célidan's metamorphosis from the blind, slightly bovine friend to the alert and active schemer is a trifle sudden and schematic. Though there is substance in this, it is fair to point out that Célidan is a man actuated by his feelings: so long as friendship lasts, he preserves a dog-like fidelity which makes him uninteresting and predictable; but when the scales fall from his eyes, his intelligence is fired and sharpened by the injury done to his pride and sense of values, so that the incisiveness and tempo of his language is accordingly quickened. He puts into practice what, in the 1644 text, is placed into the mouth of Chrysante: "Il faut jouer au fin contre un esprit si double" (p. 40); and he wins through by a combination of stratagems borrowed from Alcidon and the play of his own "franchise." He is indeed able to improvise the action of duplicity as he goes along, and he seems to take some slight pleasure in this.

Of Chrysante, there is little to be said: her ancestry in the theater is well known. She stands for the unsympathetic parent, but also for money, something which is not looked on with favor in the play: Clarice after all is not inhibited from marrying Philiste by his own impecunious position. In her volte-face, Chrysante emerges as an example of a woman whose feelings were ignored at the time of her marriage; but her attitudes seem rather forced and improbable, and the cynic might well add that her "conversion" occurs after she becomes aware of Célidan's financial and social position. On the other hand, she is useful as a *repoussoir* for characters (notably Philiste) who can give vent to their feelings.

The structure of the play is thus built round these characters who stand for certain values, but are all capable of dissimulation in varying degree, and whose relationships are further bedevilled by the unreliable nature of language.

II

So far, we have considered the interplay of emotion true and false; but language brings its own problems, since it seems to stand in the way of genuine emotion, and at the same time not only to allow for misunderstanding, but positively to aid and abet the schemes of dissimulation. In this respect, *La Veuve* resembles *Cinna* to the extent that the action marks the progress towards a narrowing of the gap between language and true feeling. That Corneille was fully aware of this emerges from both his comments on various plays and from what the characters themselves have to say in *La Veuve*. In the "Au Lecteur," deleted from 1644 onwards, he draws attention to the "naïveté du stile" to be found in the play (p. 5). What he means is that he wants to avoid linguistic pomp and circumstance or "l'esclat des vers" that would be a superimposed decoration and to ensure that a style commensurate with the action, tone and themes would be brought into play (cf. "La perfection des portraicts consiste en la ressemblance"). He was particularly pleased with the way the characters talked "en équivoques, et en propositions dont ils te laissent les conséquences à tirer," but this equivocity was after all no more than the linguistic correlative of psychological duplicity, so that he was finding his way towards a linguistic instrument that was capable of expressing a more sophisticated text than earlier comedy had provided. For this reason among others, we find him rejecting various stylistic and dramatic elements that had so far found favor. In the *Examen* he pointed to the "aversion naturelle que j'ay tousjours euë pour les *Aparte*" (p. 144). By *aparte* he means the type which is meant to reach the audience, not another character on stage or listening off stage; this latter category is legitimate in his view, and is in fact practiced in *La Veuve*. This is all the more interesting as the action might well, in principle, have called for extensive use of the *aparte* (p. 145). In avoiding it, Corneille was obliged to make much more use of dramatic irony and to sharpen his dialogue in such a way that the audience would obtain the information it needed from conversation of a more natural, but also more sophisticated nature. The elimination of such a dramatic device encourages the development of dialogue of finer precision and art. He also rejects the use of *pointes*, which he regarded as "fausses lumieres": compared with *Mélite*, he considered it "plus net et dégagé des pointes dont l'autre est semée" (p. 146). The reason for this is, as he suggests, that *pointes* are the expression of wit, certainly, but of an external wit, not that which stems from the conversation of characters. Here he may also be reacting against a feature of the Petrarchan idiom to which he was increasingly unsympathetic; but the important thing is that wit must derive from psychology and not remain purely decorative.

Here no doubt is one of the reasons why Corneille indulges in some satire of the Petrarchan idiom. This appears through the off-stage character Florange, ostensibly in love with Doris. He expresses himself in a series of clichés which Doris has little difficulty in deflating.[5] He talks like a book, having little experience of life—he has recently come down from the University; he imagines that to speak like a Petrarchan swain is to give proof of amatory sentiment, and if he goes off on another tack, it is to introduce trivial chitchat into his conversation—a theme incidentally that is echoed in Alcidon's comments on the local "salon." Corneille may be satirizing fashion, but he is also drawing attention to an exaggerated, possibly out-worn idiom that has driven a wedge between the self and the communica-tion of feeling. Such clichés are tantamount to a lack of sentiment, or, in a different context, to the presence of concealment. It may therefore be that Corneille's use of a certain linguistic "realism" is the reverse of this same medal. The dramatist is having to tread a middle path which allows him to remain within a language that certainly had precious features but does not attract caricature, and at the same time remains sufficiently supple and sharp to express sophisticated feeling and intelligence. Corneille is con-centrating his attention on creating a linguistic vehicle that will not only correspond to the psychology of the characters—so that there will be no *pointes*, rhetoric or extraneous sources of comic such as the *aparte*—but will also fill the space left by the absence of elements of farce.

However, this problem is complicated by the fact that language seems to raise barriers between the self and other people; and the problem is doubly compounded when we are dealing with manifestations of hypoc-risy, to which all the characters in greater or lesser degree are prone. The matter is raised by all the main characters: Alcidon, Philiste, Clarice and Célidan. The first scene introduces it as a major theme of the play: Philiste and Alcidon discuss to what extent love should be openly declared. Philiste tells his friend that he is afraid to speak his feelings unambiguously to Clarice, for he believes that such an overt expression would provoke an unwelcome response—of course, this is a theme that gained currency in part through the vogue of Petrarchism. To give verbal shape to a sentiment is possibly to kill it; in I, sc. I, Philiste goes so far as to suggest that signs may be more useful than words. And so he holds his peace (as did Florange on occasion to Doris—once again the echo technique is at work). It may be that Philiste is deeply suspicious of a certain love idiom (such as Petrar-chism), but his critique goes further than this. Alcidon, on the other hand, defends the contrary point of view: frankness in such matters is more wholesome and will lead to a happy outcome. Of course, in the event neither man is being entirely honest: Alcidon, who agrees secretly with part of what Philiste tells him, wants him to declare his love, so that he, Alcidon, will benefit from the lady's expected response. Philiste, for his part, believes that his view, which is really tactical, will lure the lady into a receptive state of mind and thus attain his goal. So here Corneille is linking two questions, the unpredictable, harmful or ineffectual consequences of language, and the various motives that lie behind.

Alcidon marks, one may think, a halfway house between Eraste (*Mélite*) and Dorante (*Le Menteur*). Language is the means whereby he manipulates others—indeed, language more often than not works in the register of *avoir* and not of *être*. He has not reached the stage where language (the form of his duplicity) begins to take on a life of its own so that he is, as it were, carried off into a private world created by the hot air of his rhetoric. He thus does not take on the comic characteristics of Matamore (*Illusion*) or Dorante, but he is not far related: his feelings for Clarice do not seem to be at all that deep, witness his reactions at the end of the play; and his vanity suggests that his self-engrossed cleverness is more important in his eyes. I do not think that he develops such a measure of linguistic dynamism as Dorante and other characters in whom rhetoric is the yardstick of their hypocrisy or mythomania; but he does illustrate the manner in which language can become a means of betrayal, and of removal from the mainsprings of life.

Célidan and Clarice echo in their different ways the themes developed by Alcidon and Philiste: Clarice wishes for a greater outspokenness on the part of her lover, and Célidan duplicates Philiste to the extent that he puts himself at a disadvantage in his relations with Alcidon because he is silent about his love for Doris, though the reasons for his silence are naturally different. Silence is ultimately condemned, for it prevents the beloved from understanding what is going on, and it may create situations which unscrupulous persons can turn to their own advantage.

So, for Corneille, a major dramatic problem is how he is going to bring out into the open the latent feelings of the true lovers. Nor is it simply a technical matter: if the genuine feelings are not given their full ventilation, the gyrations of Alcidon and the Nourrice will seem to be working in a void.

III

One obvious, traditional means is the monologue. At that period, monologues still enjoy considerable popularity; they are an ideal way of communicating to the audience feelings that the characters are unable or unwilling to express to one another. Interestingly, the device is reduced to the bare minimum where Alcidon is concerned: he needs other persons to develop himself. But Philiste and Clarice each have a solo scene couched in lyrical *stances*: this medium of heightened feeling introduces an important tonal quality into the play as a whole, though it may also be exploited for dramatic effect, when Clarice is abducted immediately after her *stances*. It will be recalled that Act I opened in a tone of less than total sincerity, even on the part of Philiste, so that a curtain where genuine emotion has broken through restores a badly needed balance. Philiste's *stances* in the opening scene of Act II (originally addressed to his feelings, whereas in 1660 they are discussed in the third person) rely much on an antithetical presentation for their effect and have more than a trace of preciosity ("Secrets tyrans de ma pensée," "plein de grace et de feu," "mon âme dans cet esclavage," etc.), but he does not come to grips with the difficulties raised by his silence. Clarice, in a metrical scheme that is perhaps more subtle, knows from Philiste's eyes rather than from his language ("propos mystérieux") that his love is real; but she senses that there is no gap between feeling and language ("L'amour est maintenant le maistre de nos bouches / Ainsi que de nos cœurs," II. 1145-46). Philiste's monologue in Act IV, sc. 2, after Clarice's kidnapping, allows him to give vent to his feelings—love, but mingled with despair, *rage*, suffering. Here the more exalted alexandrine is pressed into service. The *fureur* scenes (especially Act IV, sc. I) may belong to a tradition of burlesque, inherited from tragi-comedy or tragedy, and popular enough at the time; but Corneille is using the tradition in its essential spirit, so that the tone of the play is deepened. Once again, consecrated or popular elements that were dramatically effective in their own right are employed only because they reflect the feelings of the characters and are seen as a valid means of their expression.

The most important, and most difficult, manifestation of feeling is to be found in the scenes between Philiste and Clarice; here we see feeling and wit mingling to suggest, often in oblique fashion, the love that exists between Philiste and Clarice. We have seen that Philiste is a man of strong feelings; only in his dealings with Clarice is he tongue-tied.[6] Clarice is a more sedate person but her love is inhibited in its expression of sentiment, perhaps a trace of *amour-propre*. So in the two scenes between Philiste and Clarice (Act I, sc. 5 and Act II, sc. 5) Corneille's problem is to find ways and means of transmitting to the audience (as well as to the two characters) their underlying emotions. Philiste resorts to such oblique reference (by means of the local salon) that Clarice wonders whether he is not in love with one of its denizens. The first scene is mostly an exercise in imperfect communication, and Philiste's expatiating on his theory of love and silence does nothing to help matters. The second scene still shows him on the defensive, though he had previously had doubts about the wisdom of his silent tactics:

> Pourquoy m'imaginer qu'un discours amoureux,
> Par un contraire effet change un amour en haine,
> Et malgré mon bon-heur me rende malheureux?
> (II, sc. I, II. 448-50)

His language verges on the precious; he indulges in *sententiae* which gener-
alize his experience; he sketches, with a flourish of oblique rhetoric, a
theory of love that Dagoucin himself would have rejected. Then when
Clarice is impelled to take the initiative, he is unable to believe his ears,
partly perhaps he is hoist with the petard of his own theories, for he
accuses Clarice of an *accorte feinte* herself. So that the stratagem of the
catcher caught is to be found at a variety of levels in the play. In Act V,
sc. 7, where the two meet on their own before the dénouement, the salon
theme is reintroduced into their dialogue, partly for dramatic symmetry,
partly because their playfulness is an oblique expression of feeling recip-
rocated; and in the final scene, from 1660 Corneille removes the trace of a
dialogue that was exchanged between them; paradoxically, silence is in
order, now that true feelings are uninhibited.

The third device is the juxtaposition of the scenes enacted between
Philiste and Clarice, and those between Alcidon and Doris, so that the
genuine and the bogus are thrown into evident contrast. Corneille pointed
to the link himself when he wrote (in the *Examen*) about painting

un amour reciproque, qui parust dans les entretiens de deux personnes qui ne parlent
point d'amour ensemble, et de mettre des complimens d'amour suivis entre deux gens
qui n'en ont point du tout l'un pour l'autre. (p. 145)

Thus the scenes between Alcidon and Doris form a sort of descant on those
involving the true lovers. Alcidon, as we know, is using Doris as a means of
access to Clarice, and Doris goes through the gestures and language of love
simply because her brother had asked her to do so; but she is more clear-
sighted than Alcidon for all his cleverness. He, ironically, uses the language
of love, because on his own theory love must always be openly expressed,
but also because he fondly imagines that Doris is in love with him. But
Corneille may be using amatory language ironically here: for instance,
braise is used to describe Alcidon's passion; it disappears in 1660, probably
because it was no longer acceptable to good taste. But perhaps it was
already overprecious when the play was performed and therefore telling in
Alcidon's mouth.[7] He even suggests that his incompetent language is due
to the force of his feelings, "En peux tu recevoir de l'entretien d'un
homme / Qui t'explique si mal le feu qui le consomme?" (ll. 671-72), and
he goes on to complain that words fail to correspond to the feelings within.
Later on, he amplifies this in a scene with Philiste (whom he is duping) in
a remark that has wider application:

. . . Qu'à grand peine deux mots se peuvent eschapper
Sans quelque double sens afin de nous tromper,

Et que souvent de bouche un dessein se propose
Ce pendant que l'esprit songe à tout autre chose.
(II. 913-16)

All this allows for a display of contrasted styles between Doris and Alcidon, the latter becoming more and more devious and involved, she more forthright and in a position to use dramatic irony, a device on which the play relies for a great deal of its effect. Interestingly, in Act III, sc. 3, Doris uses monetary imagery to expose Alcidon's linguistic duplicity; and we know from other scenes, notably those where Chrysante appears, exactly what the more sympathetic characters think of money as the measure of all things. But the fun of the scenes lies in the fact, pointed out by Doris, that they resemble one another to the extent that their feelings are not expressed by their language. She also observes that Alcidon knows nothing about love; so that in practice Alcidon confirms, against his own statements, the gap between language and feeling of which Philiste talks so much.

IV

The psychological "données" of the action make it difficult for the lovers to mingle "wit" and feeling in one and the same scene; only occasionally does the combination peep through the veils and filters. But Corneille goes to evident pains to see that true emotion is adequately shown on the stage. The rest of the play should be apprehended with the help of this touchstone. This does not mean that wit is absent from other characters or situations, on the contrary. It arises in the main through two mechanisms: either the contrast of false and genuine sentiment (e.g., Alcidon-Doris), or from an intelligence, usually sharpened by emotion, in conflict with one that is more sluggish through routine, unawareness or vanity. The devices used form a fairly tight cluster and by systematic exploitation they serve to confer a sense of unity of the play: echo techniques, repetition of various kinds, dramatic irony, the working out of themes, situations and stratagems in such a way that they are not confined to one character. All this not only produces a thematic unity, but expresses less cynicism than a Montaignian awareness of the complexity of human nature and its motivation, and of the relations between language and feelings.

This last matter is a major theme, and one may speculate whether the writing of the play, in addition to stemming from Corneille's concern with the problem, did not increase his understanding. Stylistically, this shows in his rejection of effects that were in some measure dissociated from the psychology of the characters: *pointes* (though traces remain, for instance, in the endings of Philiste's *stances*), lines that would impress by literary merit ("vers . . . puissants et majestueux," "Au Lecteur," p. 5), eccentricities of Petrarchan origin and so forth. When figures of traditional rhetoric are pressed into service, they suit situation and pychology. Thus stichomythia occurs more often than not in scenes where different sets of values are contrasted (Philiste and Chrysante) or where a character is being unmasked by another now wise to the situation (Philiste, Nourrice). It does not appear as a means of heightened emotion expressed between major characters at a moment of crisis. *Sententiae* are infrequent: they will be found when the Nourrice is speaking, or when Alcidon tries to reinforce his (bogus) attitude to friendship, or when Philiste converts his personal feelings into generalized experience. Corneille does not as a rule exploit word-play, though the double-entendre, the inevitable concomitant of dramatic irony, naturally comes into play, as for example when Célidan says to Alcidon "Une subtilité si dextrement tissuë / Ne peut jamais avoir qu'une admirable issuë" (II. 1683-84). However, when Corneille makes Célidan, who has pierced Alcidon's devious plans, say "C'est ainsi que tu veux m'obliger doublement" (I. 138), one may think that *doublement* should be taken in two ways.

On the other hand, Corneille is concerned to forge a linguistic instrument which is able, not only to show the duplicity of language, but to take advantage of this state of affairs. What he is in the process of creating in *La Veuve* is an instrument that is shorn of literary cliché and traditions, but is not simply a more "realistic" phenomenon. The realistic elements of language are fairly superficial; what is more important is that Corneille is creating a language that is certainly literary (note over the years his concessions to the evolution of taste) but acquires strength partly because it is closer to the sources of motive and conduct, but also because it carries within itself the seeds of its own comic. By rejecting the registers of farce, of Petrarchism, and certain rhetorical elements, he has narrowed the linguistic range within which he must work, but he has explored in greater depth the possibilities it contained. Of course, it could be said that some of the techniques of farce have become verbalized and incorporated into a higher form of comedy. With the passage of time there comes not only a certain *épuration* of the vocabulary, but a refinement of other elements. Roques and Lièvre in their introduction note that *La Veuve* was less altered in subsequent editions than *Mélite*, but they add "les variantes portent surtout sur la qualité du vocabulaire et du style et la bienséance des manières" (p. xxxvii), an observation that confirms our view of Corneille's linguistic sensitivity in this play, reflecting both his own development and the changes in contemporary taste. Of course, there are minor alterations that show Corneille looking for a more precise epithet or changing its position in the line; sometimes a variant indicates a different attitude to a character, as in l. 1910 where "Ce colere Alcidon" becomes "Ce bizarre Alcidon," Elsewhere, stylistic considerations are in play: in l. 69, "Ses soupirs et les miens" becomes "Mes soupirs et les siens," probably to avoid the repetition of *Ses* at the beginning of the line. But other variants are more fundamental: there is an undoubted reduction of staccato effects and broken lines, in favor of more sustained rhythms. Thus ll. 31-32, "Ouy j'en doute et l'exces de ma beatitude / Est le seul fondement de mon incertitude," become "Ouy, j'en doute, et l'exces du bonheur qui m'accable / Me surprend, me confond, me paroist incroyable," where an increased dynamism is imparted to the lines, brought about by both the triadic movement and the cluster of more active verbs. Elsewhere, rapid exchanges are removed: ll. 1669-73 are a good illustration of this, and in ll. 1910-14, Alcidon's interruption of Philiste is excised in 1660.

Particularly noteworthy is the reduction of a vocabulary that, originally heard as frank and perhaps familiar, may offend the ears of a later generation. Words and phrases such as *lourdaut* or *toucher la grosse corde* (l. 53) make way for more refined language. Even a phrase like *C'est bien le mot pour rire* (l. 202) disappears in later editions; as do such words as *gourmand* (l. 44), *brasser* (ll. 134 and 653), *baiser* (ll. 72, 729, etc.), and *œillade*, which becomes *prunelle* in l. 204. It is perhaps for reasons of decorum that the Nourrice's resemblance to a witch is toned down: thus ll. 528-31

> *Philiste*
>
> . . . Vien ça que je t'estrangle.
>
> *La Nourrice*
>
> Ah, ah.
>
> *Philiste*
>
> Crache, parjure,
> Ton ame abominable, et que l'enfer attend,
>
> *La Nourrice*
>
> De grace quatre mots, et tu seras content.
>
> *Philiste*
>
> Et je seray content! qui te fait si hardie . . .

disappear from 1660 on; the forthrightness of the language may well have jarred by then. But even an image as anodyne as "un ver de jalousie" (l. 947) makes way for the colorless "un peu de jalousie." Alternations are much in evidence in the language of love: here two different considerations are at work. On the other hand, the amatory vocabulary of the 1630's has taken on a shop-soiled air: *feux* disappears, as does *braise*, and ll. 81-83,

> Et que le peu souvent que ce bon-heur arrive
> Picquant nostre appetit tend sa pointe plus vive,
> Nostre flamme irritée en croist de jour en jour,

become

> Et mille autres douceurs aux seuls amants connuës
> Nous font voir chaque jour nos amies toutes nuës,
> Nous sont de bons garands d'un feu qui chaque jour . . . .

These lines are spoken by Philiste and they raise the other problem that was probably in Corneille's mind. Earlier, I mentioned that the dramatist had poked fun at the Petrarchan love idiom through the invisible character Florange. For readers of today the distinction between an outworn Petrarchan idiom and an acceptable precious language may not always be clear cut, and no doubt Corneille had to tread a cautious middle path which kept him clear of obvious pitfalls. However, with the passage of time, the distinctions would be blurred even for the public of 1660, and Corneille would be faced with the problem of Philiste using a language of love that must not be exposed to the irony with which he had treated Petrarchism in his younger days. It is therefore not surprising that Philiste's opening scene with Alcidon contains considerable corrections along these lines. Ll. 21-23,

> Sans te mettre en soucy du feu qui me consomme
> Appren comment l'amour se traicte en honneste homme
> Aussi tost qu'une Dame en ses retz nous a pris,

become in 1660

> Sans te mettre en soucy quelle en sera la suite
> Appren comment l'amour doit regler sa conduite,
> Aussitost qu'une Dame a charmé nos esprits.

The evolution of public taste no doubt deprived Corneille to some extent of one of his linguistic tools intended to ward off the dangers of language; his "realism" in this domain was alas whittled away as the century drew on. But if his sensitivity to developing taste brought some disadvantage in its train, there were compensations, for his language acquired gradually more finesse, it becomes more capable of refined irony, and it is less dependent on dramatic devices that he had earlier used for certain effects. One illustration may be taken from l. 1298. Originally it read "Quoy? ta poltronnerie a changé bien soudain." In 1660 it became "J'admire avec plaisir ce changement soudain," where the interrogative had disappeared and a more elegant balance of the hemistiches has been created.

Obviously, more could be said on this score; but *La Veuve*, probably underestimated these days, is an excellent example of the way Corneille is working towards a solution of the linguistic problems posed, on the one hand, by his view of human nature, and on the other, by his wish to avoid certain well-worn dramatic devices for which he had lost his taste. What is emerging is a linguistic tool that conveys admirably his awareness of the different layers of behavior, the relations between *paraître* and *être*, and the balance between feeling and intelligence. And the variants, over the years, show that though he is highly sensitive to the vagaries of taste, such is his mastery of language that the need to sacrifice something of a relative linguistic "realism" helps him, in the long run, to evolve a more sophisticated style.

NOTES

1. I use the edition prepared by Mario Roques and Marion Liève for the *TLF*: Pierre Corneille, *La Veuve*, comédie, texte de la première édition (1634) publié avec les variantes (Geneva-Lille, 1954).

2. J. Boorsch, "Remarques sur la technique dramatique de Corneille," in *Studies by Members of the French Department of Yale University*, ed. A. Feuillerat, Yale Romance Studies, 18 (1941), pp. 101-62.

3. The older Corneille showed concern about aspects of Act V (*Examen*).

4. Hans Verhoeff, *Les Comédies de Corneille. Une psycholecture* (Paris, 1979).

5. These views are echoed by Géron.

6. Peter Bürger, *Die frühen Komödien Pierre Corneilles und das französische Theater von 1630* (Frankfurt-am-Main), esp. pp. 174-82.

7. On the language of preciosity see Roger Lathuillère, *La Préciosité. Etude historique et linguistique*, I (Geneva, 1966).

W.D. Howarth

Some Thoughts on the Function of Rhyme
in French Classical Tragedy

Nous n'avons aucune tragédie parfaite; et peut-être n'est-il pas possible que l'esprit humain en produise jamais. L'art est trop vaste, les bornes du génie trop étroites, les règles trop gênantes, la langue trop stérile, et les rimes en trop petit nombre.

(*Eloge de M. Crébillon*)

Long before Voltaire wrote these lines in 1762, the French were complaining of the particular constraints imposed by rhyme on the dramatic poet; thus Chapelain, for instance:

En cela notre langue se peut dire plus malheureuse qu'aucune autre, étant obligée, outre les vers, à la tyrannie de la rime, laquelle ôte toute la vraisemblance au théâtre et toute la créance à ceux qui portent quelque étincelle de jugement.[1]

Hugo, in the *Préface de Cromwell*, was able to write of rhyme as "cette esclave reine, cette suprême grâce de notre poésie, ce générateur de notre mètre";[2] but such a perceptive assessment would be difficult to find in seventeenth-century writings on prosody. If rhyme is termed "un des principaux ornements de notre poésie,"[3] if it is allowed that "la rime fait sans doute la plus grande beauté de nos vers,"[4] these are somewhat grudging concessions. The treatises of the period show an unimaginative preoccupation with the technicalities of rhyme, and their authors seem content to follow Malherbe in defending the concept of "la rime difficile"—Malherbe, who as we know from Racan's acccount

s'étudiait fort à chercher des rimes rares et stériles, sur la créance qu'il avait qu'elles lui faisaient produire quelques nouvelles pensées, outre qu'il disait que cela sentait son grand poète de tenter des rimes difficiles qui n'avaient point encore été rimées.[5]

Richelet, it is true, ventures a timid criticism of the master when, taking *montagnes–campagnes* as an example of "rimes communes et faciles à trouver," he comments that "Malherbe ne voulait pas qu'on rimât ces mots; mais quelquefois l'exactitude de Malherbe allait jusques à l'excès."[6] Mourgues, on the other hand, though he is prepared to make an exception for "les grands auteurs . . . une fois dans un ouvrage de grande haleine" (citing Racine's rhymes *peut-être–être, toutefois–fois, désarmée–armée* in this context), still explicitly upholds Malherbe's proscription in general terms:

Quand l'idée que l'usage a attachée à deux termes, c'est-à-dire, la manière de concevoir ce qu'ils signifient, laisse trop apercevoir la dépendance qu'ils ont l'un de l'autre, ils ne doivent pas être joints ensemble; cette vue étant désagréable en ce qu'elle fait comprendre que le poète était travaillé de sécheresse, et que manquant d'expression ou de rimes, il a donné dans une manière de répétition ou de redite.[7]

The view of rhyme expressed by Maucroix in a letter of 1695 to Boileau is a thoroughly orthodox one:

C'est, à mon avis, l'écueil de notre versification. . . . Pour nous, ce n'est rien que faire un vers: il faut en faire deux, et que le second ne paraisse pas fait pour tenir compagnie au premier.[8]

And as is well known, Boileau claimed that it was his own practice, one moreover that he commended to Racine, to compose the second line of a couplet before the first in an attempt to produce this very effect.

What Malherbe had laid down in his uncompromising manner—Fromilhague defines his "exigence fondamentale" as being to "n'admettre une rime que si elle représente la combinaison la plus riche pour chacun des termes qui la constituent"[9]—remained virtually unchallenged in the various "arts poétiques" of the Ancien Régime. What is more, when poetic diction had been emancipated by the Romantic revolution, this merely gave a new impetus to the demand, by Banville and others, for virtuosity in matters of rhyming. If Banville's distinction between the true poet and the versifier is absolutely unexceptionable,

Le poète pense en vers et n'a qu'à transcrire ce qui lui est dicté: l'homme qui n'est pas poète pense en prose, et ne peut que traduire en vers ce qu'il a pensé en prose,[10]

(and if his lampooning of Boileau in this respect is not wholly undeserved), it is nevertheless true that in his call for richness and variety of rhyme he outdoes Malherbe and appears to equate poetic inspiration with technical expertise:

Votre rime sera riche et elle sera variée: implacablement riche et variée. C'est-à-dire que vous ferez rimer ensemble, autant qu'il se pourra, des mots très-semblables entre eux comme son, et très différents entre eux comme sens. Tâchez d'accoupler le moins possible un substantif avec un substantif, un verbe avec un verbe, un adjectif avec un adjectif. (ibid., p. 75)

It is against the background of this traditional insistence on variety and inventiveness in rhyming that the practice of the dramatic poets of the Grand Siècle has commonly been judged. Sainte-Beuve, for instance, was very much of his time in commenting, à propos of rhymes quoted from *Saint-Genest* (*glorieux—cieux, précieux—cieux*): "On voit combien Rotrou se gênait peu pour reproduire à satiété les mêmes rimes."[11] It is difficult to imagine a reader of our own day adopting such a negative approach to this important aspect of versification. In fact, in Rotrou's play no fewer than thirty-two couplets include as rhyming words one or both of the pair *cieux* and *dieux*, which represent respectively the Christian and the pagan worlds whose conflict forms the subject of *Saint-Genest;*[12] the effect is simple, but satisfying; and when he meets similar cases in Corneille (the placing of *Rome, romain* at the rhyming position thirty times in *Horace*, for instance, or twenty-six times in *Sertorius*), I do not think that the responsive reader or spectator is likely to complain of carelessness. On the contrary, the repetition of significant, or "thematic," rhymes is recognized as making a positive contribution to the fabric of seventeenth-century verse drama.

In the case of Racine, there is one category of rhyme-word above all whose function can be (and occasionally has been) assessed in this way. Racine's use of proper names to give topographical, historical or mythological atmosphere to his plays may work in a more diffuse manner than do the insistent *Rome, romain* in Corneille, but the cumulative effect of nominal rhymes is hardly open to doubt. In *Andromaque* there are ninety-one examples, in *Iphigénie* eighty-seven, in *Phèdre* sixty-seven. The relatively low figure for *Phèdre* may cause surprise, since there can be few readers of the play who have not been impressed by this feature; however, while among the main characters the name of Hippolyte occurs twelve times at the rhyme and that of Thésée eleven times, and while there is a substantial number of passing references of an evocative nature, such as the memorable "Depuis que sur ces bords les dieux ont envoyé / La fille de Minos et de Pasiphaé . . ." (ll. 35-36) or "Et les os dispersés du géant d'Epidaure, / Et la Crète fumant du sang du Minotaure" (ll. 81-82), there is not the same overall density here that we find in *Andromaque*, where not only does the name of Hermione occur twelve times at the rhyme, that of Oreste eleven times, those of Hector and Pyrrhus ten and six times respectively, but these are supported by frequent appearances at the rhyme of *Grèce* (nine times), *Troie* (eight times, with the adjective *troyen* a further seven times), and

Epire seven times. Péguy, who seems to have been one of the first to express an opinion on this aspect of Racine's rhyming practice, writes appreciatively of the effect of nominal rhyme:

Il y a aussi *encor* et *Hector* à la rime. Il est extrêmement remarquable, dans tout *Andromaque* déjà, combien Racine met les mots propres à la rime, ce qui est une droite et grande et brave et directe façon de quarrer le vers. *Grèce, Sparte, Hélène, Troie, Ulysse, Achille, Epire, Pyrrhus, Hermione* et même *Etats.* Cela donne au vers une facture délibérée, complète, un achèvement plein carré, une absence d'hésitation, une volonté d'emplir.[13]

It is in *Andromaque*, too, that we find the most memorable case of the repeated association of a character's name with a particular rhyming word. The linking of *Oreste* with *funeste* in itself calls for little comment: its effect is evidently to mark this character out from the beginning of the play onwards—the first of the eight occurrences of this pair of rhymes is at lines 5-6—as the victim of an inescapable fate, and this contributes unmistakably to the tragic mood of the play. There is, however, a subsidiary effect which is not quite so easy to interpret. Not only does *Oreste* appear eight times at the rhyme with *funeste*, but *Oreste* occurs three further times and *funeste* twice, the rhyming word in each case being *reste*. Are we to say that once the close link between the character's name and its attendant epithet has been established, and accepted by the spectator's ear, a subconscious echo attaches to these other rhyming pairs, so that for instance in Act III, where Oreste is seeking to persuade Pylade of Hermione's readiness to return to him, "Ses yeux s'ouvraient, Pylade; elle écoutait Oreste, / Lui parlait, le plaignait. Un mot eût fait le reste" (ll. 945-46), a reminder of the associated rhyme "funeste" serves to underline the irony of his wishful thinking?

This is necessarily speculative, since it depends on very subjective factors and since, if such an effect operates at all, it operates at a subconscious level; however, it is an area in which some interesting work on rhyme in Racine has recently taken place. Unfortunately, it seems also to be an area in which a priori theorizing is all too common, and it must be said that the most substantial publication so far devoted to this particular line of research rests on some very arbitrary assumptions both about the symbolic suggestiveness of which Racine's rhymes are capable and about the phonetic values on which they depend.[14] My own purpose in this essay is less ambitious: to attempt an analysis of the kind of contribution that can be made by rhyme to the dialogue of classical tragedy, the ways in which it may help to establish the dialectical character of certain scenes, and to enhance the emotional impact of others.

To return to *Saint-Genest*: the contrast between Rotrou's tragedy and *Polyeucte* is a commonplace of criticism. The themes of the two plays are similar enough for the differences in treatment to stand out the more clearly: baroque techniques of spectacle and demonstration on the one hand, intellectual appeal and persuasion by argument on the other. Inherent in the two plots, this contrast is reinforced by the dramaturgical manner adopted by each playwright; it is also strongly reflected in the characteristic flavor of their language, tending respectively towards the concrete and the abstract, and in this the choice of rhymes plays a not insignificant part.

An analysis of the rhyme words in the opening scene of *Polyeucte* shows a significant proportion of abstract nouns, of infinitives, and of other verb forms; and the dialectical vigor of the argument between Polyeucte and Néarque is considerably enhanced by this feature:

Avez-vous cependant une pleine assurance
D'avoir assez de vie ou de persévérance?
Et Dieu, qui tient votre âme et vos jours dans sa main,
Promet-il à vos vœux de le pouvoir demain?
Il est toujours tout juste et tout bon; mais sa grâce
Ne descend pas toujours avec même efficace;
Après certains moments que perdent nos longueurs
Elle quitte ces traits qui pénètrent les cœurs;
Le nôtre s'endurcit, la repousse, l'égare:
Le bras qui la versait en devient plus avare,
Et cette sainte ardeur qui doit porter au bien
Tombe plus rarement, ou n'opère plus rien.
Celle qui vous pressait de courir au baptême,
Languissante déjà, cesse d'être la même,
Et, pour quelques soupirs qu'on vous a fait ouïr,
Sa flamme se dissipe, et va s'évanouir.

(II. 25-40)

Only two of these eight couplets conclude with a rhyme that is at all banal (II. 36, 38); for the rest, the rhyme structure articulates Néarque's urgent pleading with obvious effect, and indeed throughout the whole scene hardly a rhyme is wasted.

Rhyme words in *Saint-Genest* show a much greater variety; and if the colorful and the concrete do not exactly predominate, at least they give a distinct flavor to those scenes in which Genest and his colleagues hold the stage (by contrast, in the opening scenes with the Emperor and his courtiers, rhyme words are more conventional and colorless). It is perhaps not so very remarkable that, of the technical vocabulary that the subject matter of the play requires, such words as *rôle, réplique, réciter, scène, comédie* should occasionally gain emphasis by appearing at the rhyming position.

What is surely much more important is the frequency with which thematic-
ally significant words are paired at the rhyme. *Art–fard* (twice); *merveille
–oreille* (five times); *théâtre–idolâtre* (three times); *action–fiction*; *acteur
–spectateur*; *acteur–imitateur*; *structure–peinture*: the prominence of
these, and other similar, rhyming pairs means that the text is suggestively
articulated, or punctuated, for the spectator's ear in the key scenes of the
action. This is particularly the case in Act II, sc. 1, where Genest discusses
with Le Décorateur details of stage design and the technicalities of the perspective set. Again, of the eleven pairs of rhymes composing this scene,
none could be said to be wasted; and the majority of these pairs, *dépense–
magnificence*; *colonnes–couronnes*; *diversité–vivacité*; *paysages–ombrages*;
raccourcissements–refondrements; *cieux–yeux*; *art–fard*, illustrate a fact
that will assume increasing importance as the century progresses. This is,
that the impact of a rhyme is enhanced when it brings together like terms:
when abstract noun is paired with abstract noun, concrete noun with concrete noun, infinitive with infinitive, and so forth.

This effect is by no means negligible in the scene just analyzed from
Saint-Genest, where the playwright's purpose was to demonstrate and illustrate, rather than to persuade; it can be observed more clearly still in a
passage like the following from *Polyeucte*, where Félix is deploying his
characteristically devious persuasive powers:

> Je vous en fais trop voir [de bonté], Pauline, à consentir
> Qu'il évite la mort par un prompt repentir.
> Je devais même peine à des crimes semblables;
> Et mettant différence entre ces deux coupables,
> J'ai trahi la justice à l'amour paternel;
> Je me suis fait pour lui moi-même criminel;
> Et j'attendais de vous, au milieu de vos craintes,
> Plus de remercîments que je n'entends de plaintes.
> (II. 895-902)

The phenomenon may be no easier to account for scientifically than other
aspects of the mechanics of rhyme; but it seems certain that the fuller a
rhyme is (and by "fullness" of rhyme I mean the combination of phonetic
richness and grammatical identity),[15] the more pronounced will be its
capacity to provide the rhythmical "punctuation" on which the texture of
verse drama depends. This must, however, be said with certain reservations.
In the *Eloge* that has already been quoted, Voltaire criticizes Crébillon for
"trop de rimes en épithètes," and it is true that in Crébillon's hands (and
in those of Voltaire himself) the grammatical identity of the pair of rhyming words is a recipe for facile, mechanical versification. On the other
hand, rhymes based on the same part of speech also dominate the verse of

Corneille and Racine to such an extent that it would be difficult not to recognize in this feature an important contribution to the build-up of rhetorical, or emotional, effects typical of the dialogue of these authors.

Rhyme, writes Clive Scott, "contains its own kind of causality" in that it suggests, "more subliminally than otherwise," an inevitable link between two words arbitrarily placed in the rhyming position; and he quotes the seventeenth-century Samuel Daniel: "Whilst seeking to please our ear, we enthrall our judgement."[16] The function of rhyme, with its regular alternation of what Cahen calls "demand" and "response,"[17] is to guide the alert spectator's ear. This may serve the primary purpose of satisfying his curiosity, as in expository scenes:

> Il était aux Romains, et je l'en détachai;
> J'étais à Massinisse, et je m'en arrachai;
> J'en eus de la douleur, j'en sentis de la gêne;
> Mais je servais Carthage, et m'en revoyais reine.
> (Corneille, *Sophonisbe*, II. 45-48)

It may solicit his intellectual support, as in typical passages of Cornelian dialectics:

> Je n'appelle plus Rome un enclos de murailles,
> Que ses proscriptions comblent de funérailles;
> Ces murs, dont le destin fut autrefois si beau,
> N'en sont que la prison, ou plutôt le tombeau:
> Mais, pour revivre ailleurs dans sa première force,
> Avec les faux Romains elle a fait plein divorce;
> Et, comme autour de moi j'ai tous ses vrais appuis,
> Rome n'est plus dans Rome, elle est toute où je suis.
> (*Sertorius*, II. 929-36)

Or it may intensify his emotional sympathy. This is surely the function of rhyme in these poignantly elegiac lines from *Phèdre*:

> Où me cacher? Fuyons dans la nuit infernale.
> Mais que dis-je? Mon père y tient l'urne fatale.
> Le sort, dit-on, l'a mise en ses sévères mains.
> Minos juge aux enfers tous les pâles humains.
> (II. 1277-80)

As it happens, these four lines were selected by Voltaire in order to demonstrate the necessity for rhyme in French verse, a convincing demonstration since the unrhymed version he substitutes becomes not only metrically, but also emotionally, lifeless:

> Où me cacher? Fuyons dans la nuit infernale.
> Mais que dis-je? Mon père y tient l'urne funeste.

Le sort, dit-on, l'a mise en ses sévères mains.
Minos juge aux enfers tous les pâles mortels.[18]

It is no doubt true that, as Scott suggests, such effects are normally sub-conscious; and it may be that rhetorical persuasion works best when this is so. On the other hand, there is a category of rhyme which depends not on surprise, but on predictability: where the demand-response mechanism is not a subliminal process, but one calling for the conscious cooperation of the spectator. Mallarmé, we are told, "avait en horreur les vers que chaque lecteur eût pu terminer, ceux dont le second hémistiche et la rime elle-même sont infailliblement prévisibles,"[19] but there is clearly a vital differ-ence between the solitary reader, bending his mind to the challenge of Mallarmé's hermetic poetry, and the spectator of a tragedy, experiencing as a member of a theater audience the rhetorical or emotional force of a verse text. It would be completely self-defeating if playwrights were to rely more than occasionally on the more extreme forms of what we may call "anticipatory" rhyme—that is the road to parody—but there can be little doubt that the following well-known examples both depend for their impact on the spectator's ability to cooperate in this way, his ear picking up the rhyme quite unambiguously before the speaker has completed the couplet:

De tels désirs, trop bas pour les grands cœurs de Rome . . .
—Ah, pour être Romain, je n'en suis pas moins homme.
(*Sertorius*, II. 1193-94)

Parle-lui tous les jours des vertus de son père;
Et quelquefois aussi parle-lui de sa mère.
(*Andromaque*, II. 1117-18)

The effect produced by these two instances of anticipatory rhyme is not, however, the same. In the example from *Sertorius*, the obviousness of the rhyme (the same pair of words has already appeared together six times before in the play) makes the rhetoric seem very unsubtle, and we may perhaps be forgiven for feeling that it hardly needed Molière's parody to show the heroics in/a somewhat suspect light. On the other hand, in the couplet from *Andromaque*, the simplicity and directness of the rhyme *père—mère* enhances the character's pathetic appeal for us; and there can be no doubt that Racine's consistent preference for the simple, obvious, and frequently predictable rhyme (*père—mère, fille—famille, Oreste—funeste*) in defiance of Malherbe's recommendation of "la rime difficile" reflects a poet's instinctive understanding of the key to the sympathetic involvement of a theater audience.

From the examples discussed so far, it would seem not unreasonable to suppose that Racine's rhyming is not only more varied, but also more sophisticated, than Corneille's in the response it requires from the spectator, and that it is to Racinian tragedy that we should look for the mature handling of rhyme which balances and blends the intellectual and the affective. In order to test this assumption more fully, and to look more closely at similarities and differences of techniques, I propose now to examine together *Bérénice* and *Tite et Bérénice*. The traditional comparison between these two plays, almost always to the disadvantage of the latter, has meant that Corneille's tends to be considered as an example of artificial complication, in contrast to the simplicity of Racine's masterpiece. If, however, we compare it instead with Corneille's own previous manner, *Tite et Bérénice* appears remarkably simple from the point of view of subject matter and theme; indeed, it is its more intimate, domestic quality that justifies the label "comédie héroïque." The dominant vocabulary, especially as articulated by the rhyme structure, is that of intimate personal relations. *Tite* occurs eleven times at the rhyme, *Bérénice* nineteen times, *Domitie* eight times; but *Rome* and *romain* a mere handful of times compared with the other Roman plays, and hardly at all until the final scene, where the rhetorical manner most obviously matches that of the tragedies (note too the high incidence of grammatical identity of the rhyming words at this point in the play):

> Ne me renvoyez pas, mais laissez-moi partir.
> Ma gloire ne peut croître, et peut se démentir.
> Elle passe aujourd'hui celle du plus grand homme,
> Puisqu'enfin je triomphe et dans Rome et de Rome:
> J'y vois à mes genoux le peuple et le sénat;
> Plus j'y craignais de honte, et plus j'y prends d'éclat;
> J'y tremblais sous sa haine, et la laisse impuissante;
> J'y rentrais exilée, et j'en sors triomphante.
> (II. 1717-24)

For the rest, the group recurring most frequently at the rhyme is *moi—foi* (fourteen times), supported by *moi—loi, foi—roi*, and other pairs, giving a total of 24 couplets; while *vous*, paired with *doux* (ten times), *jaloux* (six times), as well as with *époux, courroux*, and a variety of other rhymes, appears thirty times at the end of the line. Add to this the groups based on *père* and *frère*, on *aimer/amour/amant*, on *haine/haïr*; an interesting group involving the semantically related *contraindre/contrainte/gêner/gêne/supplice*; and such rhymes as *âme—flamme, infidèle—belle, rival—égal*, as well as a large number of more neutral, functional rhymes (for instance the groups *vôtre—autre* or *mien—tien—sien*), and one might well suppose that Corneille has here reverted to the manner of the early comedies. However, whatever observations one may make about dominant rhyme from a strictly lexical point of view, it must be remembered that the quality, and the dramatic impact, of a rhyme will depend on its relation to the structure of the alexandrines as a whole. Even where Corneille is using a relatively domesticated vocabulary, his characters remain unmistakable because of the attitudes they strike; the rhetorical quality of his rhymes plays its part in this, but so too do the emphatic caesura and the almost invariably end-stopped line. Domitie in particular, although she is a latter-day *glorieuse* rather than a true exponent of "l'éthique de la gloire," speaks with the confident authority that typifies the Cornelian hero. In her sparring matches with Domitian she constantly gains the upper hand, as can be seen by comparing the dramatic effect of the following couplets, in both of which the rhyme is shared between these characters:

> Telle que je puis être, obtenez-moi d'un frère.
> —Hélas! si je n'ai pu vous obtenir d'un père,
> Si même je ne puis vous obtenir de vous,
> Qu'obtiendrai-je d'un frère amoureux et jaloux?
> (II. 175-78)

> Je dirai que le ciel doit à votre mérite . . .
> —Non, seigneur; faites mieux, et quittez qui vous quitte.
> (II. 247-48)

In the first case we have a hesitant rejoinder in the shape of a line whose sense remains incomplete, the weak *père* referring the listener's ear forward to the stronger *vous* and *jaloux*. In the second example, Domitie interrupts her lover with the self-confidence that befits the true Cornelian hero. Such devices do not, it is true, invariably give the advantage to Domitie; but a close analysis of rhyming practice in the scenes between the two lovers will show that the predominance of strong, emphatic rhymes, on the one hand, and of more tentative, colorless rhymes, on the other, gives a clear pointer, if not to the spectator's sympathy, at least to the admiration that Corneille aims to arouse for his heroes. At this stage in his career it is almost always his women characters whom the playwright endows with heroic qualities; and in the following passage, the rhetorical abstraction of rhymes is one of the tangible means by which Domitie asserts her moral authority over both her suitors:

> Je ne sais de vous deux, seigneur, à ne rien feindre,
> Duquel je dois le plus me louer ou me plaindre.
> C'est aimer assez mal, que remettre tous deux
> Au choix de mes désirs le succès de vos vœux;
> Et cette liberté, par tous les deux offerte,
> Montre que tous les deux peuvent souffrir ma perte,
> Et que tout leur amour est prêt à consentir
> Que mon cœur ou ma foi veuillent se démentir.
> Je me plains de tous deux, et vous plains l'un et l'autre,

Si pour voir tout ce cœur vous m'ouvrez tout le vôtre.
Le prince n'agit point en amant fort discret;
S'il ne m'impose rien, il trahit mon secret:
Tout ce qu'il vous en dit m'offense ou vous abuse.
Mais ce que fait l'amour, l'amour aussi l'excuse.
Vous, seigneur, je croyais que vous m'aimiez assez
Pour m'épargner le trouble où vous m'embarrassez,
Et laisser pour couleur à mon peu de constance
La gloire d'obéir à la toute-puissance:
Vous m'ôtez cette excuse, et me voulez charger
De ce qu'a d'odieux la honte de changer.
Si le prince en mon cœur garde encor même place,
C'est manquer de respect que vous le dire en face;
Et si mon choix pour vous n'est point violenté,
C'est trop d'ambition et d'infidélité.
Ainsi des deux côtés tout sert à me confondre.
J'ai cent choses à dire, et rien à vous répondre;
Et ne voulant déplaire à pas un de vous deux,
Je veux, ainsi que vous, douter où vont mes vœux.
Ce qui le plus m'étonne en cette déférence
Qui veut du cœur entier une entière assurance,
C'est que dans ce haut rang vous ne vouliez pas voir
Qu'il n'importe du cœur quand on sait son devoir,
Et que de vos pareils les hautes destinées
Ne le consultent point sur les grands hyménées.

(II. 579-612)

Some time before he wrote *Tite et Bérénice*, Corneille had complained of the changing taste of Paris audiences:

A force de vieillir un auteur perd son rang;
On croit ses vers glacés par la froideur du sang.
Leur dureté rebute, et leur poids incommode,
Et la seule tendresse est toujours à la mode.[20]

If *Tite et Bérénice* makes some concession to current taste in modifying the "dureté" and the "froideur" of plays like *Othon* and *Attila*, there is little that could pass for "tendresse" in Corneille's play: like the "tragédies matrimoniales," this *comédie héroïque* is motivated almost entirely by ambition:

... Je n'ai point une âme à se laisser charmer
Du ridicule honneur de savoir bien aimer.
La passion du trône est seule toujours belle,
Seule à qui l'âme doive une ardeur immortelle,

(II. 221-24)

says Domitie; and, although Tite affects to believe that "Bérénice aime Tite, et non pas l'empereur; / Elle en veut à mon cœur, et non pas à l'empire" (II. 1526-27), this is not always borne out by the Queen's behavior. To turn from Corneille's play to Racine's is indeed to move from psychological skirmishing and logic-chopping to a display of genuine emotion, spontaneously expressed. How does Racine's use of rhyme contribute to the impression?

A major difficulty in analyzing *Bérénice* from this point of view is that Racine's use of rhyme here, in keeping with the nature of tragedy in this play, is extremely discreet and unobtrusive. Rhyme is not used in *Bérénice*, as it is in *Andromaque, Iphigénie* or *Phèdre*, to help build up the mythological atmosphere on which these tragedies so largely depend; it does not, as it does in *Britannicus, Bajazet* and *Mithridate*, help to establish the State as a sinister power that will be used by the strong to tyrannize and oppress the weak. *Bérénice* is the most simply human of Racine's tragedies, the only one in which the affairs of the great are scaled down to the proportions of a domestic drama; and *mutatis mutandis*—for there is a world of difference between the tone of the *comédie héroïque* and the "tristesse majestueuse" that informs Racine's play—the vocabulary here too, as in *Tite et Bérénice*, is above all that of personal relationships. Of course, the protagonists in these relationships are an Emperor, a Queen and a King, and their names are resonant with the destiny of the great. *Bérénice* appears fourteen times as the rhyme (paired with *impératrice, justice, injustice, sacrifice*, but also with a cluster of tentative or hypothetical subjunctive forms from *avertir, obéir, finir, haïr* and *éclaircir*), *Titus* four times, and *Antiochus* twice (with *Comagène* a further three times). *Rome*, which occurs 52 times in the text, appears rarely at the rhyme; *romain* slightly more often, but *Empire* and *reine* respectively eleven and thirteen times: together with *Etat(s), Césars* and *Empereur*, frequently enough to remind the spectator's ear, by means of this irregular but insistent articulation, of the importance of the imperial setting in which the personal drama is being acted out.

But if rhyme can be seen to serve the poet's purpose in reminding us discreetly of the "majesté" he claims as one component of his tragedy, it is much more clearly brought into service to express the other component: the "tristesse," that elegiac quality that is this play's most distinctive feature. It is in this respect that the pairing of grammatically identical terms is particularly important: the cumulative effect of a succession of pairs of (usually abstract) nouns, of verbs dealing with the emotions, and of epithets denoting a psychological state, is something which, if it cannot be accounted for precisely, it is nevertheless impossible to deny; and here again, the fact that Racine plays on our expectations by repeating over and over again what are virtual clichés (*alarmes—larmes, douleur—malheur*, *gloire—victoire*) is of considerable significance. However obvious these pairs have become—perhaps, indeed, because of their very predictability—such rhymes play an essential part in establishing the mood of the play; and in this connection "le triste Antiochus" has a particularly important role in introducing the theme of past happiness and present suffering:

> Hé bien! Antiochus, es-tu toujours le même?
> Pourrais-je, sans trembler, lui dire 'Je vous aime'?
> Mais quoi! déjà je tremble, et mon cœur agité
> Craint autant ce moment que je l'ai souhaité.
> Bérénice autrefois m'ôta toute espérance;
> Elle m'imposa même un éternel silence.
> Je me suis tu cinq ans. Et jusques à ce jour
> D'un voile d'amitié j'ai couvert mon amour.
> Dois-je croire qu'au rang où Titus la destine
> Elle m'écoute mieux que dans la Palestine?
> Il l'épouse. Ai-je donc attendu ce moment
> Pour me venir encor déclarer son amant?
> Quel fruit me reviendra d'un aveu téméraire?
> Ah! puisqu'il faut partir, partons sans lui déplaire.
> Retirons-nous, sortons, et, sans nous découvrir,
> Allons loin de ses yeux l'oublier, ou mourir.
>   (II. 19-34)

In one striking exceptional case, where the material trappings of Court life are evoked—not the concentration of rhymes *hommages—images, splendeur —grandeur, enflammée—armée, sénat—éclat, gloire—victoire* in Bérénice's speech at the end of Act I—this serves to establish a temporary and precarious illusion of hope, soon to be dispelled by the realities expressed by the dominant psychological abstractions:

> J'espérais que du moins mon trouble et ma douleur
> Lui ferait pressentir notre commun malheur;
> Mais sans me soupçonner, sensible à mes alarmes,
> Elle m'offre sa main pour essuyer ses larmes,
> Et ne prévoit rien moins, dans cette obscurité,
> Que la fin d'un amour qu'elle a trop mérité.
> Enfin j'ai ce matin rappelé ma constance.
> Il faut la voir, Paulin, et rompre le silence.
> J'attends Antiochus pour lui recommander
> Ce dépôt précieux que je ne puis garder.
> Jusque dans l'Orient je veux qu'il la remeine.
> Demain Rome avec lui verra partir la Reine.
> Elle en sera bientôt instruite par ma voix,
> Et je vais lui parler pour la dernière fois.
>   (II. 477-90)[21]

The play contains little in the way of dramatic confrontation, though the scene in Act III between Antiochus and Bérénice does provide a rare example of the couplet being used for a sharp exchange, the shared rhyme denoting the domination of one character by the other: "Quoi? vous pourriez ici me regarder . . . / —Vous le souhaitez trop pour me persuader" (ll. 913-14). Even the "scène à faire," the confrontation in Act IV in which Titus declares to Bérénice that they must separate, maintains the mood of elegiac lament. Note how the rhymes in Act IV, sc. 5 make their contributions not by any rhetorical emphasis, but in a muted manner, by the maintaining of the dominant tone; note too, at the climax of this scene, how completely conventional nearly all the rhymes are and how, even in the marvellously evocative line 1116, the placing of *Bérénice* in the rhyming position produces a striking example of "anticipatory" rhyme:

> Hé bien, régnez, cruel; contentez votre gloire:
> Je ne dispute plus. J'attendais, pour vous croire,
> Que cette même bouche, après mille serments
> D'un amour qui devait unir tous nos moments,
> Cette bouche, à mes yeux s'avouant infidèle,
> M'ordonnât elle-même une absence éternelle.
> Moi-même, j'ai voulu vous entendre en ce lieu.
> Je n'écoute plus rien; et pour jamais, adieu.
> Pour jamais! Ah! Seigneur, songez-vous en vous-même
> Combien ce mot cruel est affreux quand on aime?
> Dans un mois, dans un an, comment souffrirons-nous,
> Seigneur, que tant de mers me séparent de vous?
> Que le jour recommence, et que le jour finisse,
> Sans que jamais Titus puisse voir Bérénice,
> Sans que de tout le jour je puisse voir Titus?
> Mais quelle est mon erreur, et que de soins perdus!
> L'ingrat, de mon départ consolé par avance,
> Daignera-t-il compter les jours de mon absence?
> Ces jours si longs pour moi lui sembleront trop courts.
> —Je n'aurai pas, Madame, à compter tant de jours.
> (ll. 1103-22)

Rhyme used in this way, to give a rhythmical punctuation to the familiar language of the emotions, is suggestive rather than coercive. The vocabulary of *Bérénice* is confined to fewer than 1200 words,[22] and the range of Racine's rhymes is proportionately restricted. The manner in which the three protagonists express their repeated variations on the theme of suffering, renunciation and resignation can be compared to that of the three instrumentalists in a string trio. The musical analogy is an obvious one and has impressed several commentators,[23] but it cannot be pressed too closely. Marcelle Blum's investigation of rhyme in Racine is based on her concept of "le thème symbolique": that is, the attribution to each character of a leitmotif possessing a combination of semantic and phonetic characteristics.

For instance, in *Bérénice*, in the case of the heroine, the key to the leit-motif is the word *silence*, which we are invited to associate with the Queen not only in those couplets which contain this word itself at the rhyme, but wherever the [ãis] rhyme occurs, and whoever the speaker may be. Thus, we are told, "la reine se chante, pour ainsi dire, par ses rimes dès son cin-quième vers; soulignant ainsi son entrée selon la technique du symbole rimé que nous étudions: 'Il ne faut point mentir, ma juste impatience / Vous accusait déjà de quelque négligence [II. 139-40],'"[24] while in the following example Bérénice's thematic rhyme is "borrowed," to use Blum's terminol-ogy, by Paulin when he says "Hé quoi! Seigneur! hé quoi, cette magnifi-cence / Qui va jusqu'à l'Euphrate étendre sa puissance" (II. 523-24) (ibid., p. 76). Interesting though this postulate is, it is far too schematic in its application and is surely based on a misconception of the suggestive power of the phonetic group (in this case the final [ã:s], wherever it occurs). For the primary appeal that rhyme makes to our ear is through the lexical value and semantic associations of the rhyming word; its phonetic quality plays a secondary, supporting role and seldom possesses the autonomy that Blum and others would see in it. P. Delbouille's enlightened comment on the association of sense and sound—"La sonorité n'agit sur notre sensibilité que par l'intermédiaire de la signification des mots. Par elle-même, elle n'est rien: elle met simplement en valeur un complexe de significations"[25] — is certainly no less true of rhyme in dramatic verse than in other forms of poetry; for in verse drama we are concerned not with Bremond's "poésie pure," but with what Vinaver called "la poésie tragique."

Compared with Marcelle Blum's pursuit of "thèmes symboliques," it may seem excessively prosaic and positivistic to study rhyme within the narrow limits I have set myself. On the one hand, I have tried to focus on rhyme as a feature of *dramatic* verse and to be guided by the effect it can reasonably be expected to have on the spectator in the theater. When the spectator is allowed, or compelled, to enter the dramatist's "univers imagi-naire," this is not the private, personal world of Racine the poet that some "nouveaux critiques" would have us explore, but the created other world of his theater, peopled by characters who for two hours are permitted to lead an existence independent of their creator. We may all too often take for granted the medium through which these characters address each other and speak to us, but the protagonists of seventeenth-century tragedy are inseparable from the alexandrine couplet, and from its rhyme structure, which defines them. If Corneille's heroes are constantly striking attitudes in front of each other and of us, this is no doubt partly because the desire to create characters of a heroic stamp led to the choice of an emphatic verse medium, while equally, no doubt, habits of poetic composition led in turn to the perpetuation of such characters. In the case of Racine, we may presume that cause and effect were similarly interrelated: on the one hand, the imaginative conception of characters in the grip of extreme emotion dictated the choice of a simpler and more spontaneous form of expression, while, on the other hand, it was the poet's characteristic handling of vocabulary, metre and rhyme that endowed his heroes with their unique emotional power.

NOTES

1. Quoted in C. Arnaud, *Les Théories dramatiques au XVIIe siècle* (Paris, 1888), p. 346.

2. Ed. M. Souriau, 8th edition (Paris, n.d.), p. 279.

3. Vaugelas, *Remarques sur la langue française*, ed. Streicher (Paris, 1934), p. 235.

4. Lancelot, *Quatre Traités de poésies* (Paris, 1663), p. 61.

5. Malherbe, *Les Poésies*, ed. Martinon (Paris, n.d.), p. 277.

6. *La Versification française* [1671] (Paris, 1672), p. 208.

7. *Traité de la poésie française* [1684] (Paris, 1724), pp. 15-16.

8. Quoted in Y. Le Hir, *Esthétique et structure du vers français* (Paris, 1956), p. 64.

9. *Malherbe: Technique et création poétique* (Paris, 1954), p. 540.

10. *Petit Traité de poésie française* [1872] (Paris, 1909), p. 53.

11. *Port-Royal* [1840-1859] (Paris, n.d.), I, 45.

12. In addition, the singular form *Dieu* occurs a further four times.

13. *Oeuvres en prose, 1909-1914* (Paris, 1961), p. 717.

14. Marcelle Blum, *Le Thème symbolique dans le théâtre de Racine*, 2 vols. (Paris, 1962-1965).

15. J.-C. Cahen, *Le Vocabulaire de Racine* (Paris, 1946), makes excellent use of the concept of "isometry," relating rhyme, and the grammatical identity of the rhyming word, to the overall structure of the complete line.

16. *French Verse-Art: A Study* (Cambridge, 1980), pp. 113, 114.

17. *Le Vocabulaire de Racine*, p. 171.

18. *Nouvelle Préface d'Œdipe* (1729).

19. H. Mondor, quoted in Cahen, p. 171.

20. *Au Roi sur son retour de Flandre* (1667).

21. The hemistich "pour la dernière fois," which occurs a score of times in Racine's tragedies, appears five times in *Bérénice*: three times as the first half and twice as the second half of a line. These latter cases illustrate the close dependence of the rhyming word on the hemistich, if not the whole line, to which it belongs.

22. Cf. *Bérénice*, ed. C.L. Walton (London, 1965), p. 49.

23. Cf. ibid., p. 50.

24. *Le Thème symbolique dans le théâtre de Racine*, p. 66.

25. *Poésie et sonorités* (Paris, 1961), p. 221. See also Cahen, *Le Vocabulaire de Racine*, p. 233.

Michael Black

Myth, Folklore and Character in Shakespeare and Racine

We all see the play *Macbeth* as preoccupied with a supernatural of a particular sort: a Northern folk supernatural seized at the level of popular superstition, so that the modern reader is not sure that he can take it seriously
(the witches, for instance, stick in the modern reader's throat). But I think
Shakespeare does take it seriously: at any rate he writes as a near inheritor
of the tradition, as naturally inherited as the language he speaks. *Phèdre*,
on the other hand, is not just a classical play in that it alludes to a Greek
mythology which, as twentieth-century readers, we do not share and which
was not even shared by seventeenth-century hearers. The myth is actually
the substance of the play, providing not only plot and dramatis personae,
but, once again, the language.

It is at the level of language that I want to try to grasp this relationship
between the plays, for my third term, "character," is also a matter of
language.

"Character" is a problematic concept, in English studies at least. This is
partly because we use the word to point to different things. I do not mean
character in the sense of the Theophrastic amalgam of externally observed
"traits," still less "quirks," of character. I mean our sense that the person
in the play, especially the chief role, is always, in poetic drama, expressing
an inner life and nature. The convention of soliloquy aside, tirades were
developed by Renaissance dramatists as ways of letting the persona reveal
what is passing within. In this respect Shakespeare and Racine are alike.
The central characters Macbeth and Phèdre are engaged in an enormous
effort of self-expression—not conscious self-analysis, since they are often

self-deceived: they are living from an imagined center which cannot see and hear itself as we hear and see it.

The verse is the instrument of this convention of self-revelation, as it is the instrument of all the other conventions of the drama. The element of the verse which conveys the subtler constituents is its metaphoric power. Metaphor is what is most personal and immediate in language. It is the natural vehicle, we know, of any attempt to surprise the movements of the mind. These movements are themselves often analogically expressive, in that the analogies may conceal or reveal a personal mental set. I suggest that in both plays the metaphors derive, to a large extent, from folklore or myth. It is a further resource for the dramatist that these metaphors, started as original perceptions by a single mind, also become thematic in the play and link the main character with others. In the same way, an original perception expressed as a metaphor can become a shared possession and in the end move down the social scale to become proverb (a respected form) or cliché (a despised one).

I attempt to illustrate this with some example. For instance, in Act III, sc. 4, Macbeth has just seen Banquo's ghost. Deeply shaken, he begins to fear that he is lost. This comes out as a peasant's gloomy certainties: "It will have blood; they say blood will have blood." At a structural level, the references to blood are deeply thematic; the play swarms with them. But the reference to what "they say" takes us into a world of references to common sayings and beliefs: folklore, superstition and proverb. Macbeth begins to turn over in his mind what "they say": "Stones have been known to move, and trees to speak." This is not an Orpheus allusion, though the Arden editor tells us that there may be a reference to the tree which reveals the murder of Polydorus in *Aeneid*, 3. I do not think that is the world we are in at this moment. Macbeth goes on:

> Augures and understood relations have
> By maggot-pies and choughs and rooks brought forth
> The secret'st man of blood.

"Augures and understood relations" means the initiate's power of understanding occult signs, but not in a classical world, despite the latinate term. One thinks "maggot-pies" are a fearful dish, then realizes it is an old and horribly expressive form of magpies. Choughs are still seen on inn signs in Cornwall: they were coastal birds, black with a red bill and red shanks.

These ominous birds—magpies, choughs and rooks—are also thematic. We remember Lady Macbeth's "The raven himself is hoarse / That croaks the fatal entrance of Duncan / Under my battlements." It is she too who says "It was the owl that shrieked, the fatal bellman." Someone else points out that "The obscure bird / Clamoured the livelong night." There is a rather too allegorical falcon, hawked at and killed by "the mousing owl." Macbeth sees the crow "making wing to the rooky wood." This flock of harbingers is epitomized when Macbeth himself is described by Macduff as the "hell kite" who killed all Macduff's "pretty chickens and their dam / At one fell swoop." The only birds of good omen in the play are the "temple-haunting martlets," and they fatally mislead Duncan.

Here is one way into the world of feeling of the play *Macbeth*: a world of strange vernacular country lore, in which birds, crossing man's path, speak to him of occult powers, mostly powers for harm, and become part of his expressive vocabulary.

I have suggested that it is really a peasant's world, and I was skeptical of an allusion to the *Aeneid*. Yet there are also numerous classical allusions, made by the highborn. "Bellona's bridegroom" comes in the first few lines, "Tarquin's ravishing stride," "all great Neptune's ocean," "destroy your sight with a new Gorgon," the word "augure" itself. These references are apt enough, but come from another world, about which the educated learn in books, not the one in which they live. They are taken into that living world and transformed or naturalized, as in Macbeth's

> Nature seems dead, and wicked dreams abuse
> The curtained sleep; witchcraft celebrates
> Pale Hecate's offerings; and withered murder,
> Alarumed by his sentinel, the wolf
> Whose howl's his wrath, thus with his stealthy pace,
> With Tarquin's ravishing strides, towards his design
> Moves like a ghost.

Wonderful lines! The word "curtained," in "curtained sleep," has manifold effects. It suggests the closed eye (remember Prospero in *The Tempest* saying to Miranda "The fringéd curtain of thine eye advance . . ."). It suggests a hanging behind which witchcraft is going to celebrate its horrid rite. It partly suppresses the thought that the unnamed Duncan is lying behind bedcurtains and so cannot see or hear his murderer. "Withered Murder" is a cinematic shift to Macbeth, who here speaks of himself with a horrified dissociation, amazed to see how he can prowl across the room, almost without his own consent. Tarquin is taken into this process by another cinematic shift and is instantly transformed into a ghost, a third shift in the kaleidoscopic movement.

This tells something about Macbeth's part-horrified, part-consenting sense of himself. In his self-disclosure he reveals a mind which is in and of this very unclassical, peasant Northern world, for all the reference to Hecate and Tarquin. His eloquence comes from a deeply credulous being and expresses itself as this fund of rapidly shifting illustrations, which are a whole element of his metaphorical language, and an immediate access to his consciousness.

The passage which gives us the crow making wing to the rooky wood shows it is not just a folk ornament, but a part of his whole apprehension of himself and his situation. It occurs in the exchange in Act III, sc. 2, which begins with Lady Macbeth's grim joke:

> *Macbeth*
> Thou know'st that Banquo and his Fleance lives.
>
> *Lady Macbeth*
> But in them nature's copy's not eterne.
>
> *Macbeth*
> There's comfort yet. They are assailable.

"Nature's copy" is the copy-holder's lease, or tenure. So Lady Macbeth is grimly joking: saying simultaneously that the lease can be revoked and that the momentary single identity produced from the universal mold—the "copy" in the other sense—can be destroyed. Macbeth then takes off into this extraordinary flight:

> Then be thou jocund; ere the bat hath flown
> His cloistered flight, ere to black Hecate's summons
> The shard-borne beetle with his drowsy hums
> Hath rung night's yawning peal, there shall be done
> A deed of dreadful note.

This is a summoning up of propitious things, an invocation of the agents of night. The bat, with its "cloistered flight," is the inhabitant of churchyards: there is a hint of sacrilege. The "shard-borne beetle" blundering by at night-fall is a countryman's perception, but its drone is turned to something ominous. "Night's yawning peal" is a complex perception linking the drone, the yawn, and the curfew: hence "dreadful note." After an interjection by Lady Macbeth, he returns to this invocation, with "Come seeling night / Scarf up the tender eye of pitiful day." I interrupt to ask what is this "eye"? I think it is evoked by the sinking sun itself, going down like a great blood-shot eye. There are reasons for saying this. First of all, Macbeth sees it as looking at him, and he wants *not* to be looked at. This too is thematic; Lady Macbeth wanted Heaven not to peep "through the blanket of the dark." There is a link back to "curtained sleep." Second, and more complex, there is a link with the phrase "nature's copy," which would be a document with a seal. Hence, partly, "seeling night." "Seeling" is another pun: one stage of a hawk's training is to sew up its eyelids, and this is called seeling. It would of course produce a tender eye, perhaps some blood. This

idea is meshed with the perception of the sun as a great red disc, like hot
wax awaiting the seal. And he goes on:

> And with thy bloody and invisible hand
> Cancel and tear to pieces that great bond
> Which keeps me pale!

The "great bond," suggested by the copy holder's lease and the sun's accus-
ing red disc, is the canon against murder. The web of association is drawn
out further. The sun is dropping below the horizon in a great effusion of
red light, like blood. Shed blood darkens and congeals: this gives us his
next perception:

> Light *thickens*, and the crow
> Makes wing to the rooky wood.
> Good things of day begin to droop and drowse
> And night's black agents to their preys do rouse.

"Droop and drowse" are a response to the "yawning peal." "Night's black
agents" would include himself, if he envisaged himself clearly.

I sum up this argument. The mind or center of consciousness that we
are in touch with here and through the play is mediated to us by the language. A distinctive characteristic of the poetry of *Macbeth* is this strong
element of the folkloric, the popular superstition. The elements of this
lore might be called a mythology, but they are like a broken-down or poor
man's mythology, diffused into a myriad animist omens and associations
linked with everyday country life, mostly very simple and homespun. This
is quite distinct in its effect, I have implied, from the classical allusions in
the play. An allusion is to something that we have all read about and is an
appeal to the solidarity of the educated. The folklore is an appeal to an
involuntary response that we do not grasp in that way, since it is not intellectual; it is taken in from the atmosphere, not from books; and it is characteristically earthy and vernacular. Macbeth's superstitions, if I can use
the word, come out of him unbidden, like an instinctive response. They
are, therefore, part of the deeper level of the psyche, where unfocused
beliefs and fears are directly at the service of the movements of the personality. They are part of him, his nature, what I call his character: also by
definition his language.

If we return to Racine's *Phèdre*, we find some striking similarities, but
also basic differences. At a simple level, we can see that the word *sang*
recurs as obsessively as the word "blood" in *Macbeth*. There is, however,
the fundamental difference that the play escapes being merely allusive by
being a direct enactment of one of the high classical myths. What would be
allusions in Shakespeare are organic here. Yet the plays are similar in the
respect that the myth is for Racine the source of his themes and his meta-

phors, and this language in the mouth of his central character is our way into the enormous self-disclosure which Phèdre, like Macbeth, unwittingly makes.

The one line of *Phèdre* that everybody knows is "C'est Vénus tout entière à sa proie attachée." The goddess of love is seen as a predatory wild beast which leaps on to a chosen victim and drags it down. Already that is a new and surprising aspect of Vénus. But we should look at the two previous lines as well. Phèdre is saying that, stricken with love for her stepson Hippolyte, she had attempted to avoid him. But returning to Troezen, she had seen him once more, and "Ma blessure trop vive aussitôt a saigné."

This is a reference to the conventional stricken-deer image which goes back to Petrarch, but it is being given a real force by being taken as felt, not as cliché. Blood which is shed is scented by predators, which close in for the kill. Phèdre goes on: "Ce n'est plus une ardeur dans mes veines cachée, / C'est Vénus tout entière à sa proie attachée." Here a number of themes coincide in a chordal passage. The *ardeur*, the fire in her blood, is a disease, that of love. Throughout the play, love is seen as a *mal*, a disease and an evil. It is a disease specifically *of* the blood, and this is given the same extended senses as in English. One's blood is also one's race, one's degree of nobility, and one's heredity, therefore a kind of fate.

The theme of race is important. Phèdre's Greek name, Phaedra, means "light-bringer," and that is an irony. She was one of the daughters of Minos, King of Crete, the island where the Minotaur, at the center of the labyrinth, received every nine years a blood-tribute of male and female virgins, until Thésée, guided through the labyrinth by holding a thread unwound from a bobbin held by Ariane, Phèdre's sister, killed the monster. So Phèdre's ancestry is charged with strange elements. Her father Minos had divine ancestry and was associated with the kingdom of the dead. Her mother was a daughter of the sun-god, was impregnated by a god-sent bull, and so was the mother of the Minotaur, who was, therefore, Phèdre's half-brother. Thésée killed the monster, and she thereafter married Thésée. Throughout the play she invokes her father as a witnessing light cast on her pollution, and a potential judge in the other world. Her mother and sister are examples of the degradation caused by love.

So the old legend begins to set up relationships in which tainted heredity, bloodshed and monstrosity are dominant elements. So is the idea of the labyrinth: a winding recess in which there lurks a monster who will kill you, or who must be killed. You are its prey, in a preordained sacrifice, if you are a virgin or youth.

Hippolyte is a virgin and he is at the end of the play sacrificed to another monster, sent by Neptune because Thésée has cursed his son and invoked the god's aid. Hippolyte is a hunter and horseman, associated persistently with Diana images: the free wild young beasts of the forest, who are the prey of various predators, including man, and may become stricken deer. One central image, blood, links these themes of tainted ancestry, sacrifice, hunting, virginity. There is also established a link between the darkness of the forest in which hunters and hunted move freely, and the darkness of the labyrinth, where a narrow, twisting corridor leads to a fatal encounter. These two darknesses contrast with the other master image of the whole play, light. Ancestrally, light is shed by the sun-god; morally, it is the light of justice and goodness which falls on things polluted. It does not penetrate the forest (which can be a cool retreat from detection) or the labyrinth (which is a place where one is lost, kills, or is killed).

There are other elements. While the blood may be tainted by an ancestral fate or curse, it may also be fired with disease. A perverse or guilty love is naturally figured as a disease of the blood. A virgin young man whom you love in a guilty way is quickly associated with the free young animals he hunts; therefore, a dominating love would tame him, break him in. A disastrously guilty love would turn him into a sacrificial victim, if his blood were shed. This not only happens: it is commented on at some length.

These resonances in the play are not merely announced, or merely exchanged. They have an active interplay with each other which builds up into a network of motifs which are mutually modified and enriched. It is a peculiar property of language that words have, as we now say, "semantic fields," areas of overlapping meanings where one word calls up, naturally enough, another which is a near synonym. But that is a very simple operation: words also call up their opposites, by a natural reversal process. They also call up words which are associated in much more complex associative ways.

Racine sets up associations within this play which operate for the play alone. So the word "forest" acquires the sense of coolness and retreat and darkness, naturally enough. And this associates, by reversal, with "light." But in the play there are added overtones about guilt and innocence, which are enforced by the context. The inhabitants of the forest, hunters and hunted, are linked in a natural association. The qualification of virginity is perhaps a natural mythological association with Diana as huntress. The idea that the animals may be caught and tamed, or sacrificed, is a natural extension. The idea that Hippolyte, the hunter, is himself such an animal is, so to speak, "induced" by the context. So is the idea that the stricken deer, hit by the huntsman's arrow, trails a scent of shed blood, that this attracts a ravenous beast of prey which leaps onto its back and drags it down. But the play induces the idea that this beast attracted by blood is the goddess of love ("Vénus tout entière à sa proie attachée").

Though the predator is here seen as the goddess, this can shift cinemati-
cally into the loved one. Both Aricie and Phèdre speak of Hippolyte as a
fierce or proud young animal who must be tamed. The implication is that
if he is not tamed, he may attack. Early in the play Aricie lets slip the word
dompter in talking of Hippolyte. Phèdre brings that notion out into the
open, when having learned at last that Hippolyte loves Aricie, she abandons
herself to rage and jealousy in which values and facts are madly inverted:

> Ce farouche ennemi qu'on ne pouvait dompter,
> Qu'offensait le respect, qu'importunait la plainte,
> Ce tigre que jamais je n'abordai sans crainte;
> Soumis, apprivoisé, reconnait un vainqueur!
> Aricie a trouvé le chemin de son cœur.

The *chemin* is of course the way through the labyrinth. Why do I say that?
It might be said that "chemin" is a merely neutral word, operating at cliché
level. It is my argument that the system of cross-references in the play
gives the language a constant extra charge, which, so to speak, lights up
otherwise neutral words and gives them a specific local sense. In the same
way Oenone says to Phèdre "Et quel affreux dessein avez-vous enfanté?" I
would argue that in the total context of the play *affreux* and *enfanté* combine to make an allusion to the dynastic theme of monstrosity: this is the
Minotaur of Phèdre's guilty thought.

We need to realize that these correspondences are not neat equivalences.
In Racine, as in Shakespeare, this is not an algebra of motifs in which figure
1 always equals meaning 1. I am suggesting instead that the figures move in
and out of relationship with each other, producing something like harmonic
mutations of each other. There are large domains of conceptual force, gov-
erned by the key words *sang, lumière, monstre* and so on. But they are not
unchanging and neatly mapped.

So when Phèdre in her agony envisages Hippolyte and Aricie enjoying a
love which is all that hers is not—innocent, mutual, self-approved—she
launches into a music which is ostensibly simple but enriched with the
meanings Racine has been building up:

> Les a-t-on vus souvent se parler, se chercher?
> Dans le fond des forêts allaient-ils se cacher?
> Hélas! Ils se voyaient avec pleine licence!
> Le ciel de leurs soupirs approuvait l'innocence;
> Ils suivaient sans remords leur penchant amoureux,
> Tous les jours se levaient clairs et sereins pour eux.

The forest brings its thoughts of retreat from the light, healing calm, the
innocence of the young people, perhaps a sexuality which is itself innocent.

Phèdre is almost free from envy, and a strange thing happens: for once the light floods into the forest and is approving. So a master image of the play is given a momentary kindliness; for once the list is warm and clear rather than pitiless or sullied. But she goes on: "Et moi, triste rebut de la nature entière; / Je me cachais au jour, je fuyais la lumière." She herself is like Cain or a scapegoat; like the monster in the labyrinth.

The imagination of the state of grace enjoyed by the young lovers but denied to her links with her very last words:

> Déjà je ne vois plus qu'à travers un nuage
> Et le ciel et l'époux que ma présence outrage;
> Et la mort à mes yeux dérobant la clarté
> Rend au jour qu'ils souillaient toute sa pureté.

The clouded vision is an obvious and striking irony; hers had been clouded all through life. But the simple figure is marvellously enriched in the last two lines. The film over her eye is transferred to the eye of day itself; it was she who polluted the light, and her death vindicates her ancestor and restores to his light its purity. With that word, the impossible deal, on her lips, she dies.

One might point out that at some moment in the play everyone is called a "monster": Phèdre sees even Hippolyte as a monster. The monster in us which bursts out and does things which amaze even us, since we had not known what we are capable of, this is I believe the largest theme of the play, enforced by the reiterated pattern of the action in which the main characters are consistently unable to stop themselves doing something disastrous. The monster in the labyrinth, one might too neatly but not inappropriately say, is the irreducible self at the end of the recesses of personality. Since it turns out that we prey on the people we love, the Minotaur also figures the loved one whom in the end we destroy or are destroyed by.

Pressing for "meanings" of the play, we come out with these equations. They are not exactly false: something like that is strongly implied. But Racine is not using his mythology to provide him with flat allegorical equivalences, obvious morals, or even psychological theories. He is producing what one can hardly avoid calling a music of themes, which develop, harmonize, clash, build up or dissolve. They are carrying a meaning which is meant to be felt, not paraphrased; and, in this respect too, dramatic poetry is like music.

I do find myself saying however that the texture of this verse, much subtler than is generally allowed, is nonetheless distinctly less dense, rich and full than Shakespeare's. This is a matter of the local metaphoric life, which has in Shakespeare both a remarkable directness and vernacular earthiness and a constantly surprising inventiveness: which does not, paradoxically, strike us as Shakespeare's inventiveness, but as the character's self, in an immediacy which has a living texture laid bare in more layers than Racine's. It is not a question of a self-advertising "medium," still less of poetic "ornamentation." The language is inseparable from the revelation it mediates. A part of the authenticity of Shakespeare's insight is the actual element of gratuitousness, unpredictability, refusal to be schematically systematic. Racine's motivic structure in *Phèdre* is more grand and symmetrical in outline than anything in Shakespeare: looks more planned, is in detail more neat. This has something to do with its being derived from a mythology—which is not, in the end, Racine's own system of beliefs, however marvellously he has given it life. It has a good deal also to do with a language which is ceasing to be popular—losing contact with the vigor of spontaneous utterance by the generality of human beings speaking their life and their nature directly, so that the heart moves into the mouth.[1]

NOTES

1. This article is considerably adapted from a talk originally given to the Cambridge Modern Language Society and borrows some paragraphs from the Appendix to my book *Poetic Drama as Mirror of the Will*. It is offered to Odette de Mourgues as the critic who more than any other taught me to see how much Racine's language is systematically functional, and poetic largely by being those things.

Jean-Pierre Collinet

Racine et ses personnages invisibles: Le cas d'*Iphigénie*

Par personnage invisible, je n'entends pas ici, l'on s'en doute, quelqu'un qui posséderait le pouvoir de disparaître à volonté grâce à l'anneau de Gygès ou bien au chapeau de Fortunatus, et qui deviendrait transparent comme le héros de Wells. Je veux parler de ces personnages de théâtre qui n'existent que dans les coulisses ou dans les marges de la pièce et dont Alphonse Daudet a donné l'exemple le plus célèbre avec son Arlésienne. On pourrait croire qu'il s'agit là d'une exception. Mais quelle œuvre dramatique ne laisse pas plus ou moins deviner l'obscure présence de quelqu'un derrière la porte? La toile de fond invite l'imagination du spectateur à se demander ce qui se passe dans cet ailleurs fictif, dans cet au-delà que le décor nous masque et dont il nous sépare. Chez Molière, il est presque aussi peuplé que le devant de la scène. Mais la comédie favorise un tel foisonnement. Voyons comment le problème se pose pour la tragédie racinienne. Il va sans dire que la réponse varie d'une œuvre à l'autre, en fonction du sujet. *Iphigénie* présente à cet égard un cas privilégié.

Etroitement circonscrite dans l'espace comme dans le temps, la tragédie classique rejette les guerres interminables, les longues navigations, les batailles et les naufrages qui fournissent à l'épopée sa matière. Elle n'admet pas davantage les complications et les rebondissements où les romanciers trouvent leur pâture. Rien de plus éloigné d'autre part, en apparence, de son esthétique dépouillée et harmonieuse que le tumulte du drame shakespearien. On sait enfin quelle concurrence oppose, à l'époque d'*Iphigénie*, le genre tragique à celui, tout nouveau, de l'opéra. Le retour au modèle d'Euripide marque pour le poète, en ce débat, un choix délibéré. Son idéal de simplicité noble et touchante atteint ici, semble-t-il, à l'une de ses expressions les plus pures. Cependant je me propose de montrer que, par le biais des personnages invisibles, il a su condenser dans sa tragédie la matière épique du cycle troyen; qu'Eriphile qui, par son origine inconnue, s'apparente à des héroïnes telles que la Marianne de Marivaux introduit dans la pièce un romanesque inattendu; que l'action se déroule sur fond de drame shakespearien; qu'enfin le dénouement s'organise comme un finale d'opéra. La couleur épique domine surtout à l'acte I. Le romanesque se glisse à la faveur de la seconde exposition, au début de l'acte II. Les scènes de violence populaire se développent essentiellement à l'acte IV, tandis que la mise en scène à grand spectacle dont bénéficient les événements contés à la fin par Ulysse permet à la pièce de s'achever en apothéose. L'unité d'ensemble n'en sort pas compromise, tant Racine a su parfaitement amalgamer ces apports divers.

Racine a réussi le tour de force d'inclure dans sa tragédie une *Iliade*, une *Odyssée*, une *Enéide*, dans une sorte de tapisserie composite qui donne à la pièce une riche toile de fond. Il en rappelle indirectement certains épisodes, leur emprunte quelques-uns de leurs personnages les plus connus, les résume en l'espace de quelques vers.

Examinons d'abord ce qui vient de l'*Iliade*. Le catalogue achéen, au chant II du poème homérique, et le dénombrement des nefs, sont suggérés par ces quatre vers de l'exposition:

> Quelle gloire, Seigneur, quels triomphes égalent
> Le spectacle pompeux que ces bords vous étalent,
> Tous ces mille vaisseaux, qui chargés de vingt rois,
> N'attendent que les vents pour partir sous vos lois?
>
> (vv. 25-28)

Racine, plus loin, développant une brève indication d'Euripide, évoque la consultation de l'oracle sur le prodige qui tient la flotte arrêtée; cinq personnages seulement assistent à la scène: Agamemnon, Calchas et trois héros de l'*Iliade*. L'un (Ménélas), visible dans la tragédie grecque, régresse dans l'adaptation française au rang de personnage invisible;[1] le troisième (Ulysse), au contraire, a suivi l'évolution inverse. Nestor, au centre de l'énumération, vient tout droit d'Homère:

> Ce miracle inouï me fit tourner les yeux
> Vers la divinité qu'on adore en ces lieux.
> Suivi de Ménélas, de Nestor, et d'Ulysse,
> J'offris sur ses autels un secret sacrifice.
> Quelle fut sa réponse! Et que devins-je, Arcas,
> Quand j'entendis ces mots prononcés par Calchas!
>
> (vv. 51-56)

On sait comment plus tard, chez Homère, le vieux Nestor tentera de fléchir
la colère d'Achille. Ici déjà, le voici qui parlemente avec le héros, dans une
de ces scènes qui ne sont pas mises sous les yeux du spectateur:

> Que dis-je? en ce moment Calchas, Nestor, Ulysse,
> De leur vaine éloquence employant l'artifice,
> Combattaient mon amour et semblaient m'annoncer
> Que si j'en crois ma gloire, il y faut renoncer.
>   (vv. 749-52)

Patrocle ne saurait manquer non plus à l'appel. L'étroite union des deux
célèbres amis est rappelée avec vigueur: "Et quand moi seul enfin il faudrait l'assiéger, / Patrocle et moi, Seigneur, nous irons vous venger" (vv.
267-68). Comme les deux amis de La Fontaine, l'un ne possède rien qui
n'appartienne à l'autre: ils partagent la gloire et le danger. Patrocle se
montre pour Achille un auxiliaire efficace quand il s'agit de protéger
Iphigénie: "Patrocle, et quelques chefs qui marchent à ma suite, / De mes
Thessaliens vous amènent l'élite" (vv. 1521-22).

De l'*Odyssée* vient Télémaque. Agamemnon évoque les affres de son
père s'il devait au lieu d'Iphigénie servir de victime au sacrifice; scène imagi-
naire, mais pathétique, où semble frémir par avance la sensibilité fénélo-
nienne:

> Mais que si vous voyiez ceint du bandeau mortel
> Votre fils Télémaque approcher de l'autel,
> Nous vous verrions, troublé de cette affreuse image,
> Changer bientôt en pleurs ce superbe langage,
> Eprouver la douleur que j'éprouve aujourd'hui,
> Et courir vous jeter entre Calchas et lui!
>   (vv. 323-28)

Pénélope, un peu plus haut, restait plus discrètement alléguée: "Vous seul,
nous arrachant à de nouvelles flammes, / Nous avez fait laisser nos enfants
et nos femmes" (vv. 309-10). Le souffle du large passe au début puis à la
fin sur la tragédie. Racine sait peindre l'allégresse des embarquements:

> Tu te souviens du jour qu'en Aulide assemblés
> Nos vaisseaux par les vents semblaient être appelés.
> Nous partions; et déjà par mille cris de joie
> Nous menacions de loin les rivages de Troie.
>   (vv. 43-46)

Comme aussi bien la décourageante tranquillité du calme plat:

> Un prodige étonnant fit taire ce transport:
> Le vent qui nous flattait nous laissa dans le port.

Il fallut s'arrêter, et la rame inutile
Fatigua vainement une mer immobile.
(vv. 47-50)

Il n'élude pas même la tempête, motif obligé de l'épopée. Clytemnestre l'appelle sur la flotte achéenne dans ses imprécations:

Quoi! pour noyer les Grecs et leurs mille vaisseaux,
Mer, tu n'ouvriras pas des abîmes nouveaux?
Quoi! lorsque les chassant du port qui les recèle,
L'Aulide aura vomi leur flotte criminelle,
Les vents, les mêmes vents, si longtemps accusés,
Ne te couvriront pas de ses vaisseaux brisés?
(vv. 1683-88)

Grâce à ces échappées, *Iphigénie* contient quelques-unes des marines les plus sobrement réussies de toute notre littérature classique. Sans compter ce vers chargé de musique mélodieuse, de suggestive poésie, de lumière et de couleur: "La rive au loin gémit, blanchissante d'écume" (v. 1781), réalisation en train de s'accomplir de sa grandiose vision évoquée par Ulysse au premier acte pour stimuler le courage d'Agamemnon, lui donner la force de consentir au sacrifice: "Voyez tout l'Hellespont blanchissant sous nos rames" (v. 381); se répondant à distance, les deux vers servent à mettre comme entre parenthèses toute la tragédie qui se déroule dans l'intervalle.[2]

Lorsque Eriphile imagine la joie des Troyens si la discorde se mettait dans le camp de leurs adversaires,

Que d'encens brûlerait dans les temples de Troie,
Si troublant tous les Grecs, et vengeant ma prison,
Je pouvais contre Achille armer Agamemnon;
Si leur haine, de Troie oubliant la querelle,
Tournait contre eux le fer qu'ils aiguisent contre elle,
Et si de tout le camp mes avis dangereux
Faisaient à ma patrie un sacrifice heureux!
(vv. 1134-40)

et quand au contraire Iphigénie s'exalte, allant au bûcher, sur leur défaite future,

Déjà Priam pâlit; déjà Troie en alarmes
Redoute mon bûcher et frémit de vos larmes.
Allez; et dans ses murs vides de citoyens,
Faites pleurer ma mort aux veuves des Troyens.
(vv. 1553-56)

on songe évidemment aux alternatives de victoires et de revers qui rythmaient l'*Iliade*. Mais l'incendie de Lesbos préfigure la prison de Troie telle que la raconte Enée au deuxième livre du poème virgilien: "Jam ardet Ucalegon . . . ." Impossible à voir depuis Ilion, distante d'une cinquantaine de kilomètres à vol d'oiseau, le reflet des flammes prend valeur de sinistre avertissement. Le grandissement épique donne à l'évocation une force saisissante:

> Les malheurs de Lesbos, par vos mains ravagée,
> Epouvantent encor toute la mer Egée.
> Troie en a vu la flamme; et jusque dans ses ports,
> Les flots en ont poussé le débris et les morts.
>
> (vv. 233-36)

On constate combien l'épopée affleure, surtout au début, dans *Iphigénie*. L'acte I s'achève sur une vision prophétique d'Ulysse qui prend avec exaltation tout l'avenir en enfilade. Après un nouvel écho de Virgile, voici, fugitive, une allusion à la belle scène de Priam aux pieds d'Achille, venu redemander le cadavre d'Hector, les retrouvailles d'Hélène et de son époux, les *nostoi* qui se termineront pour certains, et pour Agamemnon tout le premier, si tragiquement:

> Voyez tout l'Hellespont blanchissant sous nos rames,
> Et la perfide Troie abandonnée aux flammes,
> Ses peuples dans vos fers, Priam à vos genoux,
> Hélène par vos mains rendue à son époux.
> Voyez de vos vaisseaux les poupes couronnées
> Dans cette même Aulide avec vous retournées,
> Et ce triomphe heureux qui s'en va devenir
> L'éternel entretien des siècles à venir.
>
> (vv. 381-88)

Iphigénie ou *La Guerre de Troie aura-t-elle lieu*? Racine montre en son héroïne une adolescente giralducienne avant la lettre, qui s'instruit en géographie par les nouvelles de son père et se prépare longtemps d'avance pour le jour où reviendront, couverts de gloire, les anciens combattants:

> Hélas! avec plaisir je me faisais conter
> Tous les noms des pays que vous allez dompter;
> Et déjà d'Ilion présageant la conquête,
> D'un triomphe si beau je préparais la fête.
>
> (vv. 1199-1202)

Naturellement aucun des passages qui viennent d'être cités n'existait dans la pièce d'Euripide. Ils représentent une greffe de l'épopée sur la tragédie de Racine. Le poète paraît même bien avoir tiré l'expédition contre Lesbos qu'il prête à son Achille, et d'où le héros emmène Eriphile captive, d'une indication qui se trouve quelque part comme perdue dans le chant IX de l'*Iliade*. De même, l'idée de cette campagne-éclair en Thessalie, pour secourir Pélée contre un voisin hostile pourrait bien avoir été suggérée au dramaturge par la célèbre adjuration du vieux Priam, au dernier chant du poème: "Souviens-toi de ton père, Achille égal aux Dieux! Du même âge que moi, voici qu'il est au seuil maudit de la vieillesse. Peut-être de cruels voisins l'entourent-ils, et personne n'est là pour écarter de lui le péril, la détresse."[3] Racine, on le voit, est imprégné d'Homère: sa tragédie est toute baignée par des réminiscences de l'antique épopée. Il en vient tout un peuple d'ombres qui hantent les coulisses immédiates de la pièce ou plus lointainement son arrière-pays et que ressuscite avec une remarquable économie dans les moyens la magie du texte.

Je m'attarderai moins longuement sur la veine romanesque. Elle apparaît à la faveur d'une modification significative apportée au modèle fourni par Euripide. Le poète grec montrait l'arrivée de Clytemnestre. On la voyait descendre de son char avec le petit Oreste, être reçue non sans gêne par Agamemnon. Au lieu de mettre cette scène sous les yeux des spectateurs, Racine, comme s'il disposait d'un plateau tournant, l'escamote, la relègue dans la coulisse. A la place des protagonistes surgit en revanche de l'ombre la princesse captive, malheureuse et jalouse qui vient ruminer sa tristesse:

> Ne les contraignons point, Doris, retirons-nous;
> Laissons-les dans les bras d'un père et d'un époux,
> Et tandis qu'à l'envi leur amour se déploie,
> Mettons en liberté ma tristesse et leur joie.
>
> (vv. 395-98)

Ce renversement de la perspective, qui laisse pour un moment dans l'éloignement les personnages principaux marque une sorte de pause, permet le changement de l'éclairage et le passage de la couleur épique à la tonalité du roman.

Cette composante romanesque se concentre toute, au début de l'acte II, dans un bref passage, où, non sans amertume, Eriphile se penche sur son passé. La Marianne de Marivaux, héroïne de roman par excellence, pourrait prendre à son compte, sans y rien changer, ce qu'elle dit de son enfance:

> Et moi, toujours en butte à de nouveaux dangers,
> Remise dès l'enfance en des bras étrangers,
> Je reçus et je vois le jour que je respire,
> Sans que mère ni père ait daigné me sourire.
> J'ignore qui je suis . . . .
>
> (vv. 423-27)

L'oracle effrayant qui l'attache à son erreur et qui lui dit, quand elle veut chercher ses parents, que sans périr elle ne se peut connaître évoque en plus tragique, mais en non moins sibyllin ceux de l'*Astrée*. Elle s'apparente, en particulier, par sa situation, au personnage de Silvandre. Mais le passé dont la dote Racine pourrait bien venir surtout du *Grand Cyrus*. Un des épisodes les plus attachants, au tome II, montrait en effet Policrite, la fille de Solon élevée clandestinement à Chypre par le sage Cléanthe, père de la jeune Doride. Eriphile, de même, a vécu, jusqu'à ce qu'elle soit enlevée par Achille, inconnue à Lesbos, et le père de sa confidente Doris connaissait lui seul sa véritable identité. Ces multiples analogies laissent ici pressentir l'affleurement d'une source inattendue que personne encore, semble-t-il, n'a signalée. Simplement, le romanesque, dans *Iphigénie*, s'infléchit vers le tragique par la disparition, au moment même où la jeune fille allait apprendre le secret de sa naissance, de celui-là même qui se disposait à le lui révéler:

> *Doris*
> Songez que votre nom fut changé dès l'enfance.
>
> *Eriphile*
> Je n'ai de tout mon sort que cette connaissance,
> Et ton père, du reste infortuné témoin,
> Ne me permit jamais de pénétrer plus loin.
> Hélas! dans cette Troie où j'étais attendue,
> Ma gloire, disait-il, m'allait être rendue;
> J'allais, en reprenant et mon nom et mon rang,
> Des plus grand rois en moi reconnaître le sang.
> Déjà je découvrais cette fameuse ville;
> Le ciel mène à Lesbos l'impitoyable Achille:
> Tout cède, tout ressent ses funestes efforts;
> Ton père, enseveli dans la foule des morts,
> Me laisse dans les fers à moi-même inconnue.
>   (vv. 437-49)

La cohorte des personnages invisibles, grâce aux parents nourriciers d'Eriphile, se grossit, on le voit, d'un couple qui sort en droite ligne du roman.

Le théâtre classique n'aime pas en général les figurations nombreuses. Il rejette par conséquent dans l'ombre des coulisses les masses qui compromettraient la belle ordonnance de la tragédie et nuiraient à sa simplicité dépouillée. Mais, ici, la tente du général en chef est entourée du camp. L'armée, que Racine désigne aussi par "les Grecs" lorsqu'il faut mettre l'accent sur le sentiment patriotique, et par "le peuple" ou "la foule" quand elle se montre indisciplinée et turbulente, constitue un personnage invisible anonyme et collectif, composé des soldats, des matelots et de leurs chefs, qui non seulement exerce du dehors sur les décisions des protagonistes une pression de plus en plus forte, mais devient lui-même un des

acteurs principaux dans le drame. Le poète sait rendre en quelques vers,
comme plus tard un Schiller dans *La Mort de Wallenstein*, mais avec une
tout autre sobriété de moyens, le climat des bivouacs, la brutale rudesse de
cette vie militaire que le badaud parisien aime aller contempler de près lors
des revues d'Achères, d'Ouilles, ou de Compiègne, ainsi qu'on peut le voir
chez La Bruyère ou chez Dancourt:

> Vous voyez en quels lieux vous l'avez amenée:
> Tout y ressent la guerre, et non point l'hyménée.
> Le tumulte d'un camp, soldats et matelots,
> Un autel hérissé de dards, de javelots,
> Tout ce spectacle enfin, pompe digne d'Achille,
> Pour attirer vos yeux n'est point assez tranquille,
> Et les Grecs y verraient l'épouse de leur roi
> Dans un état indigne et de vous et de moi.
>
> (vv. 785-92)

On assiste à la montée progressive de la violence, dans une troupe que
le fanatisme et la passion aveugle incitent à perdre tout respect pour la
majesté souveraine. Clytemnestre est presque insultée:

> Pour ce sang malheureux qu'on leur veut dérober,
> Regarde quel orage est tout prêt à tomber.
> Considère l'état où la reine est réduite.
> Vois comme tout le camp s'oppose à notre fuite;
> Avec quelle insolence ils ont de toutes parts
> Fait briller à nos yeux la pointe de leurs dards.
> Nos gardes repoussés, la reine évanouie . . . .
>
> (vv. 1495-1501)

Cette reine prisonnière de son peuple rappelle ce qui s'est passé lors de
la Fronde. Et le sang-froid d'Achille, son plan de bataille pour protéger
Iphigénie contre la soldatesque déchaînée ne vont pas sans évoquer l'habi-
leté stratégique d'un Condé pendant les troubles et son mépris tout aristo-
cratique pour une vaine populace:

> Ne craignez ni les cris ni la foule impuissante
> D'un peuple qui se presse autour de cette tente.
> Paraissez; et bientôt, sans attendre mes coups,
> Ces flots tumultueux s'ouvriront devant vous.
> Patrocle, et quelques chefs qui marchent à ma suite,
> De mes Thessaliens vous amènent l'élite.
> Tout le reste, assemblé près de mon étendard,
> Vous offre de ses rangs l'invincible rempart.
> A vos persécuteurs opposons cet asile.
> Qu'ils viennent vous chercher sous les tentes d'Achille.
>
> (vv. 1517-26)

Le héros assure ici le maintien de l'ordre. Mais il ne laissera pas lui-même celle qu'il aime affronter le bûcher sans venger sa mort par un affreux carnage qui menace de terminer la tragédie comme dans l'*Hamlet* de Shakespeare, par un massacre et une tuerie générale:

> Le prêtre deviendra la première victime;
> Le bûcher, par mes mains détruit et renversé,
> Dans le sang des bourreaux nagera dispersé;
> Et si dans les horreurs de ce désordre extrême
> Votre père frappé tombe et périt lui-même,
> Alors de vos respects voyant les tristes fruits,
> Reconnaissez les coups que vous aurez conduits.
>
> (vv. 1606-12)

Il ne sera pas forcé d'en arriver là. Mais la situation devient si tendue qu'on se trouve au bord de la guerre civile:

> Achille en ce moment exauce vos prières;
> Il a brisé des Grecs les trop faibles barrières.
> Achille est à l'autel. Calchas est éperdu.
> Le fatal sacrifice est encor suspendu.
> On se menace, on court, l'air gémit, le fer brille.
> Achille fait ranger autour de votre fille
> Tous ses amis, pour lui prêts à se dévouer.
> Le triste Agamemnon, qui n'ose l'avouer,
> Pour détourner ses yeux des meurtres qu'il présage,
> Ou pour cacher ses pleurs, s'est voilé le visage.
>
> (vv. 1701-10)

Le poète, pour évoquer ce climat, retrouve les accents de Lucain dans la *Pharsale*:

> De ce spectacle affreux votre fille alarmée
> Voyait pour elle Achille, et contre elle l'armée.
> Mais, quoique seul pour elle, Achille furieux
> Epouvantait l'armée, et partageait les Dieux.
>
> (vv. 1737-40)

Le drame élisabéthain aurait montré ces scènes de révolte, en aurait tiré la matière d'une fresque historique. La tragédie classique s'y refuse, par principe esthétique et souci des convenances. De tels spectacles eussent détonné dans ce Versailles qui servit de cadre à la création d'*Iphigénie*. Mais l'émeute, refoulée et comme conjurée, n'en gronde qu'avec plus de force. Elle semble même, étrangement, annoncer plus d'un siècle à l'avance les violences révolutionnaires de 1789. Agamemnon complote l'évasion de sa fille dans une atmosphère de fuite à Varennes:

> Mes gardes vous suivront, commandés par Arcas:
> Je veux bien excuser son heureuse imprudence.
> Tout dépend du secret et de la diligence.
> Ulysse ni Calchas n'ont point encor parlé;
> Gardez que ce départ ne leur soit révélé.
> Cachez bien votre fille, et que tout le camp croie
> Que je la retiens seule, et que je vous renvoie.
>
> (vv. 1472-78)

Il recommande à la princesse de monter à l'échafaud avec la résignation et dignité courageuse que montreront les victimes de la Terreur:

> Ne vous assurez point sur ma faible puissance.
> Quel frein pourrait d'un peuple arrêter la licence,
> Quand les Dieux, nous livrant à son zèle indiscret,
> L'affranchissent d'un joug qu'il portait à regret?
> Ma fille, il faut céder. Votre heure est arrivée.
> Songez bien dans quel rang vous êtes élevée.
>
> (vv. 1237-42)

Racine développe la métaphore de la tempête pour peindre l'irrésistible déchaînement de la puissance populaire, avec le fougueux lyrisme qu'au cinéma l'on retrouvera dans le *Napoléon* d'Abel Gance:

> Le Roi de son pouvoir se voit déposséder,
> Et lui-même au torrent nous contraint de céder.
> Achille à qui tout cède, Achille à cet orage
> Voudrait lui-même en vain opposer son courage.
> Que fera-t-il, Madame? et qui peut dissiper
> Tous les flots d'ennemis prêts à l'envelopper?
>
> (vv. 1627-32)

Iphigénie imagine sa mère outragée, livrée aux brutalités de la soldatesque, comme le sera plus tard l'Autrichienne:

> N'allez point, dans un camp rebelle à votre époux,
> Seule à me retenir vainement obstinée,
> Par des soldats peut-être indignement traînée,
> Présenter, pour tout fruit d'un déplorable effort,
> Un spectacle à mes yeux plus cruel que la mort.
>
> (vv. 1644-48)

Eriphile, à la fin, se voit à l'unanimité condamnée à mort par un jury populaire qui ne rend pas une justice moins expéditive que les tribunaux de la Convention:

> Ainsi parle Calchas. Tout le camp immobile
> L'écoute avec frayeur et regarde Eriphile.

Elle était à l'autel, et peut-être en son cœur
Du fatal sacrifice accusait la lenteur.
Elle-même tantôt, d'une course subite,
Etait venue aux Grecs annoncer votre fuite.
On admire en secret sa naissance et son sort.
Mais puisque Troie enfin est le prix de sa mort,
L'armée à haute voix se déclare contre elle,
Et prononce à Calchas sa sentence mortelle.

(vv. 1761-69)

Combien, comme elle, n'échapperont que par le suicide au couperet de la guillotine? Quelle étrange résonance prend, par un beau soir d'été, quand Louis XIV touche à l'apogée de sa puissance, dans cette Orangerie de Versailles, toute proche de l'endroit où sera bâti le Hameau de la Reine, un vers tel que celui-ci: "D'un peuple impatient vous entendez la voix" (v. 1663)! On dirait que la Révolution, déjà, frappe à la porte. Peut-être même envahissait-elle un instant la scène de son irruption lorsque Clytemnestre veut se jeter sur les pas de sa fille et qu'on lui barre le passage: l'incident se situe dans cette zone indécise, laissée à la liberté du metteur en scène, où la face cachée de la pièce confine immédiatement à sa partie visible: "Mais on se jette en foule au-devant de mes pas. / Perfides, contentez votre soif sanguinaire" (vv. 1668-69). Ces masses invisibles assiègent de si près la scène qu'elles se prêtent à se transformer en une figuration houleuse et même hurlante.

Une révolution se joue donc dans la coulisse et s'y réfugie parce qu'on ne saurait guère, au XVIIᵉ siècle, la mettre sous les yeux du spectateur sans paraître porter atteinte à l'ordre monarchique. Mais la peinture, pour n'être pas montrée, ne perd ni sa force, ni sa vérité. Un empereur contraint d'abdiquer devant l'autorité morale d'un chef religieux bientôt menacé d'être débordé par ses propres partisans; un passé récent pourrait offrir l'exemple de pareils bouleversements:

Ce n'est plus un vain peuple en désordre assemblé;
C'est d'un zèle fatal tout le camp aveuglé.
Plus de pitié. Calchas seul règne, seul commande:
La piété sévère exige son offrande.
Le Roi de son pouvoir se voit déposséder,
Et lui-même au torrent est contraint de céder.

(vv. 1623-28)

Certes, n'assimilons pas Racine à Shakespeare, bien que Stendhal ait pu le considérer comme romantique en son temps, et moins encore à Bertolt Brecht. Mais constatons qu'*Iphigénie*, grâce à ses foules invisibles, contient un drame historique en puissance.

Il reste à montrer qu'elle renferme aussi, dans sa partie finale, tous les ingrédients de l'opéra. Déjà l'entrée de la reine, à l'acte premier, donnait l'impression d'être organisée comme une scène à grand spectacle avec des évolutions réglées comme dans un ballet et des chœurs qui tantôt se divisent en deux, tantôt réunissent leurs voix. "Gloire, gloire à Didon." Les Grecs entonnent ici un hymne à la reine comparable à celui que Berlioz mettra plus tard en musique pour ses *Troyens*:

> Déjà de leur abord la nouvelle est semée,
> Et déjà de soldats une foule charmée,
> Surtout d'Iphigénie admirant la beauté,
> Pousse au ciel mille vœux pour sa félicité.
> Les uns avec respect environnaient la Reine,
> D'autres me demandaient le sujet qui l'amène.
> Mais tous ils confessaient que si jamais les Dieux
> Ne mirent sur le trône un roi plus glorieux,
> Egalement comblé de leurs faveurs secrètes,
> Jamais père ne fut plus heureux que vous l'êtes.
>
> (vv. 349-58)

La fête finie, n'en resteront que de mélancoliques vestiges: "Je verrai les chemins encor tout parfumés / Des fleurs dont sous ses pas on les avait semés?" (vv. 1307-08). Souvenirs des fastes évanouis semblables à ceux qui subsistaient encore dans le parc de Versailles quand le Poliphile de La Fontaine vient y lire à ses trois amis l'histoire de Psyché.

Calchas ne paraît jamais. Il représente cependant de loin le plus souvent évoqué des personnages invisibles, et le seul d'entre eux dont les paroles nous soient, à deux reprises, directement rapportées. Au début lors de la consultation de l'oracle:

> Vous armez contre Troie une puissance vaine,
> Si dans un sacrifice auguste et solonnel
>   Une fille du sang d'Hélène
> De Diane en ces lieux n'ensanglante l'autel.
> Pour obtenir les vents que le ciel vous dénie,
>   Sacrifiez Iphigénie.
>
> (vv. 57-62)

A la fin, lorsqu'il ramène la concorde dans l'armée:

> Vous, Achille, a-t-il dit, et vous, Grecs, qu'on m'écoute.
> Le Dieu qui maintenant vous parle par ma voix
> M'explique son oracle, et m'instruit de son choix.
> Un autre sang d'Hélène, une autre Iphigénie
> Sur ce bord immolée y doit laisser sa vie.
> Thésée avec Hélène uni secrètement

> Fit succéder l'hymen à son enlèvement.
> Une fille en sortit, que sa mère a celée;
> Du nom d'Iphigénie elle fut appelée.
> Je vis moi-même alors ce fruit de leurs amours.
> D'un sinistre avenir je menaçai ses jours.
> Sous un nom emprunté sa noire destinée
> Et ses propres fureurs l'ont ici amenée.
> Elle me voit, m'entend, elle est devant vos yeux,
> Et c'est elle, en un mot, que demandent les Dieux.
> (vv. 1746-60)

Entre temps, il nous est montré haranguant les Grecs, mais l'impétueux Achille se contente de résumer son discours:

> Les Dieux vont s'apaiser. Du moins Calchas publie
> Qu'avec eux, dans une heure, il nous réconcilie;
> Que Neptune et les vents, prêts à nous exaucer,
> N'attendent que le sang que sa main va verser.
> (vv. 837-40)

Son rôle, dans les trois cas, apparaît comme celui d'une basse ou d'un baryton, capable de descendre au plus profond des notes graves et de débiter largement un ample récitatif chanté.

La tragédie, grâce à lui, présente deux pôles, ou, comme on dirait en géométrie pour une ellipse, deux foyers (car dès qu'un cercle s'étire, son centre se divise en deux): l'un, visible, est constitué par Agamemnon; la pièce est construite tout entière autour de lui. L'autre foyer, invisible, est représenté par le grand-prêtre. Toute l'action repose sur l'affrontement de la puissance royale et de l'autorité religieuse. Il suffirait de prendre Calchas pour centre visible, au lieu du roi, de retourner la pièce comme un vêtement, d'intervertir en quelque sorte son endroit et son envers, pour qu'apparaisse une autre tragédie qu'*Iphigénie* contient en creux. Supposons que Racine ait choisi de suivre moins fidèlement Euripide, de laisser Agamemnon dans l'ombre et de mettre sur la scène à sa place le devin. Le conflit tragique de l'ambition et de l'amour paternel, relégué à l'arrière-plan, s'estomperait au profit d'un drame religieux comparable, dans le registre du paganisme, à l'histoire d'*Athalie* telle que Racine l'évoquera dans sa tragédie biblique. Calchas apparaît en effet comme un premier crayon, une préfiguration païenne de Joad. Aux révélations de l'un répondront les prophéties de l'autre. Tous deux possèdent la stature de personnages sacrés qui communiquent avec le divin, entrent dans le secret des dieux, ou de Dieu. *Iphigénie* contient, comme à l'état latent, la promesse et le germe de l'œuvre ultime. Mais Racine y laisse pour le moment dans l'ombre les éléments spectaculaires que sa pièce sacrée lui permettra plus tard de produire au grand jour. L'opéra, dans le récit final d'Ulysse, reste pour ainsi dire virtuel, mais il existe et Racine prouve qu'il pourrait sans difficulté, comme librettiste, battre Quinault sur son propre terrain: prolongement inattendu de la Querelle qui met alors aux prises, avant celle de 1687, les Anciens et les Modernes.

La scène qu'il vient de voir a produit sur Ulysse une impression à la fois forte et mêlée: "Vous m'en voyez moi-même en cet heureux moment / Saisi d'horreur, de joie et de ravissement" (vv. 1731-32). Cette émotion violente correspond précisément à celle que veut provoquer la tragédie en musique. Le poète sait mettre en œuvre les allégories décoratives et les abstractions personnifiées, telles que la Discorde, dont La Fontaine avait précédemment tiré le sujet d'une fable (VI, 20) et que Boileau, parodiquement, n'avait pas manqué d'introduire dans son *Lutrin* (I, vv. 25 ss.):

> Jamais jour n'a paru si mortel à la Grèce.
> Déjà de tout le camp la Discorde maîtresse
> Avait sur tous les yeux mis son bandeau fatal,
> Et donné du combat le funeste signal.
> (vv. 1733-36)

L'opéra qui plaît à Louis XIV se présente comme un spectacle belliqueux: La Fontaine l'a naguère appris à ses dépens, quand il s'est vu reprocher d'avoir mis trop de pastorale dans son livret de *Daphné*. Aussi, l'année même d'*Iphigénie*, dans son épître à M. de Nyert, ironise-t-il sur cette musique trop guerrière où domine le fifre et le tambour plus que la flûte champêtre, la viole et le téorbe. Le récit d'Ulysse débute dans cette tonalité martiale: "Déjà de traits en l'air s'élevait un nuage. / Déjà coulait le sang, prémices du carnage" (vv. 1741-42). Vient ensuite le long récitatif du grand-prêtre, monodie qui s'achève sur un coup de théâtre. Puis le chœur, après un temps de silence, prononce à l'unisson le verdict qui condamne à mort Eriphile. La notation des gestes, des paroles, des mouvements, l'indication du décor, de l'accessoire, accentuent le caractère théâtral d'un suicide auquel Ulysse, rhéteur consommé, nous donne l'illusion d'assister nous-mêmes:

> Déjà pour la saisir Calchas lève le bras:
> Arrête, a-t-elle dit, et ne m'approche pas.
> Le sang de ces héros dont tu me fais descendre
> Sans tes profanes mains saura bien se répandre.
> Furieuse elle vole, et sur l'autel prochain
> Prend le sacré couteau, le plonge dans son sein.
> (vv. 1771-76)

La tragédie emprunte à l'opéra son merveilleux: la participation cosmique des éléments au drame qui se joue relève de l'esthétique baroque dont le genre nouveau dérive, tandis que celui de la tragédie marque l'aboutissement d'un goût classique tout opposé. Cette mise en scène à grand spectacle, qui nous est donnée, non à voir, mais à imaginer, est soutenue par une symphonie richement orchestrée, avec de violents contrastes de fortissimo et de pianissimo, une série de doubles croches pour la ligne mélodique du dessus, le grondement de la basse continue, des effets de fugue et d'écho: rarement on aura plus subtilement traduit la musique par l'équivalent des mots. Longtemps avant Baudelaire, ici, par une délicate correspondance, les couleurs et les sons se répondent. Un paysage à la fois visuel et sonore se construit dont s'impose à nous l'invisible présence:

> A peine son sang coule et fait rougir la terre,
> Les Dieux font sur l'autel entendre le tonnerre,
> Les vents agitent l'air d'heureux frémissements,
> Et la mer leur répond par ses mugissements.
> La rive au loin gémit, blanchissante d'écume.
> La flamme du bûcher d'elle-même s'allume.
> Le ciel brille d'éclairs, s'entr'ouvre, et parmi nous
> Jette une sainte horreur qui nous rassure tous.
>
> (vv. 1777-84)

Il ne manque même pas les machines et les vols auxquels l'opéra doit la meilleure partie de son succès. Autosuggestion? Réalité? Qu'importe! Le ciel semble mis en communication avec la terre. La déesse en vient puis y remonte dans cette nacelle qu'on appelle une gloire:

> Le soldat étonné dit que dans une nue
> Jusque sur le bûcher Diane est descendue,
> Et croit que s'élevant au travers de ses feux
> Elle portait au ciel notre encens et nos vœux.
>
> (vv. 1785-88)

Le récit d'Ulysse pouvait se terminer plus brillamment que sur cette apothéose. La tragédie pourtant reprend ses droits quand il nous montre l'héroïne s'appitoyant sur Eriphile: "La seule Iphigénie / Dans ce commun bonheur pleure son ennemie" (vv. 1789-90).

L'examen des personnages invisibles permet, on le voit, une analyse spectrale de la pièce, dont elle met en lumière les diverses composantes et les richesses cachées. L'œuvre, à travers son modèle grec, renoue avec ses origines épiques, remonte, par-delà Euripide, jusqu'à Homère. Mais elle rejoint d'un autre côté l'opéra naissant, témoigne qu'elle peut le concurrencer. Elle ouvre ainsi tout le champ culturel qui conduit de la plus lointaine antiquité jusqu'à la modernité la plus récente. Sur son chemin elle rencontre incidemment le romanesque et regarde à d'autres moments vers le drame, dont elle semble pressentir les fécondes possibilités. Elle doit à cette confluence son originalité la plus profonde. On y retrouve le personnel de l'épopée (Nestor, Patrocle, Priam, Pâris, Hélène), du roman (les parents adoptifs d'Eriphile), du théâtre historique et politique (la foule des soldats), de la tragédie en musique (le grand-prêtre, la déesse qui se manifeste à la fin par son apparition), harmonieusement fondus les uns avec les autres. Le soin de Racine, ici, n'a pas moins porté sur l'envers de la tapisserie que sur son endroit. Les scènes pathétiques et les tableaux touchants que la pièce nous met sous les yeux n'en épuisent pas plus le contenu que le nombre des personnages impliqués dans son intrigue ne se limite à la liste des acteurs. Certes, elle montre au spectateur Agamemnon et sa famille, de même que *Britannicus* peignait Néron dans son domestique. Mais l'action se prolonge au dehors dans cet espace imaginaire qui constitue l'au-delà de la scène. Nulle part ailleurs, sans doute, dans le théâtre racinien, les personnages invisibles, individualisés, comme Calchas, ou collectifs, comme l'armée, ne présentent autant d'importance et d'intérêt. Cas privilégié pour la question qui nous occupe, *Iphigénie* n'apparaît cependant pas comme une exception. *Andromaque*, qui se rattachait de même au cycle troyen, emprunte également à l'épopée sa toile de fond, et l'on pourrait montrer qu'il se mêle à cette trame des éléments romanesques ou dramatiques. *Britannicus*, *Bérénice*, comme on sait, se déroulent sur fond d'histoire romaine. *Bajazet* laisse deviner le sérail, Byzance, le Bosphore, beaucoup plus loin Bagdad, sous le nom de Babylone, qu'assiège avec ses janissaires l'invisible et tout-puissant Amurat. Mithridate rêve de porter la guerre depuis le Pont-Euxin jusqu'à Rome. Dans *Phèdre*, voici le monde grec, à peine purgé de ses brigands et de ses monstres par Hercule: Athènes, où l'absence de Thésée crée un vide politique, mais aussi la Crète et son labyrinthe, le Péloponnèse, contourné par Théramène dans son périple, la lointaine et sauvage Epire, qui confine au royaume des ombres: zones concentriques, toutes chargées de sens, autour de l'étouffante Trézène. Le monde biblique, enfin, passera de même dans *Esther* et *Athalie*. Partout s'ouvrent et se multiplient ces échappées sur un univers extérieur à l'aire de jeu, sans lesquelles Racine se sentirait assurément moins à l'aise et plus à l'étroit dans les limites contraignantes imposées à la tragédie classique par la règle des unités, et qui donnent à son théâtre une si poétique résonance. Mais *Iphigénie*, mieux qu'aucune autre de ses pièces, montre quelles ressources le dramaturge a su tirer de ces personnages, les uns tout proches, les autres absents ou morts, dont le texte parle, mais qui, voués par l'économie de l'intrigue à demeurer dans les limbes de la tragédie, n'ont pas reçu le privilège de paraître aux feux de la rampe.

NOTES

1. Il en va de même pour Oreste, encore au berceau: le théâtre classique sauf exception, comme l'Eliacin d'*Athalie*, bannit les enfants.

2. On retrouvera dans *Phèdre* des marines exquises: "Déjà de ses vaisseaux la pointe était tournée, / Et la voile flottait aux vents abandonnée" (vv. 797-98).

3. Traduction de Robert Flacelière, dans Homère, *Iliade, Odyssée* (Paris, 1955), p. 526.

Michael Edwards

La Fontaine and the Subversion of Poetry

There is a line in La Fontaine's *Fables*—"L'onde était transparente ainsi qu'aux plus beaux jours"—which has often been commented on (notably by Odette de Mourgues) for its beauty. It is also a bit of a joke. For us, sensitive readers of poetry that we are, and delicate appreciators of nature, the water attains that limpidity which we associate with the clearest, most perfect weathers. For the heron in the scene, the transparency of the water allows him to see the fish and promises him another substantial catch like those he remembers from his best days' angling. The bird's prosaic gaze subverts the line throughout its length, reading into it another, gastronomic, meaning and altering most completely, and perhaps pointedly, the word "beaux."

A similar line occurs in "Le Chêne et le roseau," when the oak describes reeds as growing "Sur les humides bords des royaumes du vent." Again, the muted magniloquence of the writing is prosaically troubled: behind the solemnity of the "humides bords" (La Fontaine elsewhere calls the sea "l'humide séjour," as Ronsard had called it the "plus humide espace") is the oak's pitying distaste for the "dampness," the "dankness," of rivers and marshes.

From one point of view, the writing is recreative; it delivers a world still recognizable, but also unforeseeably transformed. One might argue, in fact, that to recreate is a property of all language. Even outside poetry, water travels some way to reach the word "water," or the word "eau," crossing into a mental space and acquiring breath, body movement, sound. Yet the change is so familiar, and so apparently unimportant, that we have to be nudged into noticing it. "Onde" is a very powerful nudge, a word that by its variability plays the river in the fable against all waters from wave to ocean, and that by its overtly poetic nature poises the water somewhere between a river bed and artifice. Much the same happens to our recollections of favorite weathers, of fine "days" and "daylights," when they too are named and yet also not named in "les plus beaux jours." The world has become "transparent" and weightless; it has been renamed not only by words, but by the language where they interact, and lifted (the metaphor seems appropriate) into a new condition, which is both physical—the body of the world and the human body are somehow present—and strangely not physical.

In the line spoken by the oak tree, the transforming and lifting are progressive. "Humides," which is our world, becomes "les humides bords," which is no longer quite the world as we know it, since "bords" is another expressively inexpressive word, capable of subsuming any number of edges, margins and shores. The shores also become those not of fens or streams, but of "kingdoms." In entering language the place has been eased of its habitual names; and the final touch—the king is the "vent"—produces a wind which is neither a personification nor the wind of every day, and which blows in a realm of its own, that of the world re-imagined.

The writing in the *Fables* is, in fact, continually recreative. Of course, La Fontaine does not describe it in quite those terms: his vocabulary is actually more striking. He notes from the beginning, in the dedication of the first book, and repeatedly throughout, that he has re-conceived the world by granting to everything within it the possibility of language: "Tout parle en mon ouvrage, et même les poissons." That language, moreover, is itself transformed, since it has taken on syllable count and, deepest of mysteries, rhyme: "Sire loup, sire corbeau, / Chez moi se parlent en rime." There really is nothing trivial about this rhyming, as if it were merely the consequence of the animals occurring in poetry rather than prose; for verse, according to a suggestive commonplace of the time, is the language of the gods. The animals in conversation with each other achieve not only a superhuman elegance (our conversations being conducted without benefit of rhyme), but a "divine" one. The distance covered is vast, though La Fontaine states it with his usual blandness: "Le loup, en langue des dieux, / Parle au chien dans mes ouvrages."

He has wrought on the world what he describes as a "spell," or rather, to adopt his defter way of suggesting the idea, what could be taken for a spell: "Qui ne prendrait ceci pour un enchantement?" The world trembles, clears, and is different. It has become the territory of "feinte," or fiction, which one enters by "conte," "récit," "histoire." It may also be reached by "exagérations," is hyperbolic without necessarily employing hyperbole, and is the domain, according to another and particularly strong way of designating it, of "mensonge." It possesses its own language, which is, quite simply, a "langage nouveau."

At the same time, however, the writing reasserts a world and a language untransformed. It homes to a reality both quotidian and common. I don't mean low as opposed to elevated; it is not only when he considers such dignities as "l'onde . . . transparente" or the "royaume du vent" that La Fontaine uses his arts, or when, in the line "Damoiselle belette, au corps long et flouet," he clothes the young weazel of quality in a fashionable sequence of l's. The craft is also at work, though with different effects, when he deals with the existential and verbal populace, as in "Le Chat et le Renard":

> C'était deux vrais tartufs, deux archipatelins,
> Deux francs patte-pelus qui, des frais du voyage,
> Croquant mainte volaille, escroquant maint fromage,
> S'indemnisaient à qui mieux mieux.

The two animals, as well as becoming literary twice over, are gathered into a rhetoric of accumulation and into an unfailing succession of cram-full syllables, of energetic and varied mouth movements. (Rabelais's French, as it were, after Racine's.) The verse also appears to be engendering itself: from "vrais" and "francs" it derives "frais," from "archipatelins" "patte-pelus," and from "croquant" "escroquant." (Here one may think of Queneau.) The passage mimes extravagantly and at high speed the way in which, in creation, words continually give rise to other words, through the mind's, mostly unobserved, pleasure in repeating sounds. It happens at every literary "level"; once Enobarbus has spoken of the "burnish'd throne" of Cleopatra, for example, he is led on to say that it "burn'd" on the water. The process, as "croquant" and "escroquant" show, is linked to the pun; rhyme, by which "voyage" supplies "fromage," is its formulation.

No: what I am thinking of are certain moments when he suddenly refocuses on (what seems) a plain world and a plain language, as in this incident concerning a fox: "Un soir il aperçut / La lune au fond d'un puits: l'orbiculaire image / Lui parut un ample fromage." Having gone one better, or several better, than "image ronde" by calling the moon's reflection "orbiculaire," La Fontaine replaces the silvery refinement with a cheese. On this occasion, it's true, "ample" maintains the more stylish approach; and the next two lines, "Deux seaux alternativement / Puisaient le liquide élément," sublimate the willing and acting of the potential users of the buckets, along with the water, and they fetch, into a kind of near-abstract geometry, circumlocution and polysyllabic elegance.

The procedure is more pointed when the drop to the ordinary involves repetition. After saying of two well-born she-goats who decline to yield on a narrow bridge "Faute de reculer, leur chute fut commune," he says it again without the distingué phrasing and without the u's: "Toutes deux tombèrent dans l'eau." He may even point to the fact that he is repeating, as in "Le Cierge":

> Quand on eut des palais de ces filles du ciel
> Enlevé l'ambroisie en leurs chambres enclose,
> Ou, pour dire en français la chose,
> Après que les ruches sans miel
> N'eurent plus que la cire . . . .

That shift into "French" is, I take it, extremely important, despite the unconcerned gaiety with which, when poetry is in question, La Fontaine generally conceals what matters to him. His writing renews the world as it renews language; in these few lines, "filles du ciel" is doubly transfigurative, since it names the bees both as daughters of heaven—they come from the "séjour des dieux"—and as daughters of the sky. (A fly in another poem is "la fille de l'air." An English poet might envy the way in which gender peoples the world.) Yet the world which La Fontaine desires is not another world but his own, changed, and the language he desires is not a foreign language but his own become different. If he is drawn in imagination, he also delights in perception; if he glimpses language in a new condition, he also takes purchase on the splendor that already exists in mere French. The dialectic, I believe, is exemplary. Though because of the nature of writing, even what he advances as honest French has been arranged, and when it passes through the mouth and ear—"Après que les ruches sans miel / N'eurent plus que la cire, on fit mainte bougie"—it too renders the reader astonishingly eloquent.

Strictly speaking, reality and language (if they can be separated) are not to be found in an objective state independent of ourselves that we may choose either to observe or to alter, since what we know is what we "half-create." Yet we do feel the pull of what is beyond us, and we sense that experience comes to us day by day and is shared with others. We realize too that a certain high-handed processing of the real can produce an intransitive poetry, an autonomous, though maybe dazzling, nowhere and no-speech, powerless to reach back into that daily communion. A writer, therefore, may well feel a tension at the very heart of writing, between the possibility and need of working the material of the world, in keeping with the nature of consciousness and of language, and the summons to be faithful to "what is there," to defer to an otherness. In the epilogue to Book II,

La Fontaine defers—profoundly and, for a writer, most movingly. After a further claim to have translated "en langue des dieux / Tout ce que disent sous les cieux / Tant d'êtres empruntant la voix de la nature," he continues, as a first step: "Car tout parle dans l'univers; / Il n'est rien qui n'ait son langage." The context here is really quite heavy, since allusion is presumably being made to 1 Corinthians 14:10 as rendered (and seemingly misrendered) in the Vulgate: "Tam multa, ut puta, genera linguarum sunt in hoc mundo : et nihil sine voce est." Then, having acknowledged in this way that, prior to his poetry, languages are already in the world, among non-human creatures as well as men, he wonders, only half-humorously and in a line that arrives out of the blue, whether the "peoples" that he introduces into that poetry may not be "Plus éloquents chez eux qu'ils ne sont dans mes vers."

To see La Fontaine's poetry as recreative may allow one to understand him rather better when, along with his contemporaries, he writes of poetry as an addition. He presents the fables as "mises en vers par M. de La Fontaine," tells the Dauphin that to Aesop's Fables he has "ajouté les ornements de la poésie," and mentions in the preface that Socrates also thought it appropriate to "les habiller des livrées des Muses." We have inherited such a long and sustained rejection of this language and of the way of thinking which it implies that we not only find it impossible, I fancy, to conceive that our own way of thinking could be wrong, but we also can not really get into the mind of someone who thinks like La Fontaine. I am not suggesting, in fact, that La Fontaine is "right," but that when he adopts what were then the commonplaces of literary theory he means by them something precise and pertinent. He sees poetry, in my terms, as transforming or renewing language and the world, or in his terms as putting them into verse, as ornamenting them, as attiring them in the livery of the Muses. His metaphors (which derive, as it happens, from what has been by far the most common view of the matter throughout the history of writing about writing) are perfectly adequate to a recreative theory, and even suggest such a theory: they quite pointedly indicate that things are going to be better apparelled inside verse than outside.

The actual elaboration of the verse, moreover, tends towards the additional, the extra—indeed, towards the superfluous. That would seem paradoxical, given one's sense of the poems' pace and coherence. Consider again, however, the oak's line about the kingdoms of the wind: it is irrelevant to the oak's approach to the reed, and its eloquence emerges from a sudden and "unnecessary" forgetting of self. Similarly, this is how a frog begins to complain to another frog that the loser in a contest between two bulls will come to their waters and create havoc:

—Eh! ne voyez-vous pas, dit-elle,
Que la fin de cette querelle
Sera l'exil de l'un; que l'autre, le chassant,
Le fera renoncer aux campagnes fleuries?
Il ne régnera plus sur l'herbe des prairies.

Not only is there the same unnecessary and eccentric lyricism, and the same spacious pause in the narrative, but the last line quoted contains almost a paraphrase of the previous line. There is again a pause, this time by the narrator—again an absorbed, unhurried contemplation—when in a later fable some other poetical frogs are disturbed by a hare: "Grenouilles aussitôt de sauter dans les ondes; / Grenouilles de rentrer en leurs grottes profondes."

Naturally, none of these passages is merely incidental decoration: they serve a creative necessity of their own, collaborating in the total poem by providing it with a further dimension. They are generated, nevertheless, by an aesthetic of superfluity, which also gives rise to periphrasis. It is by periphrasis that La Fontaine calls expanses of water the "royaumes du vent," water in general "le liquide élément," the sea "l'humide séjour" or bees "les filles du ciel." One thinks, inevitably, of preciosity, and might reflect that preciosity too, however ultimately uninteresting, saw poetry as recreative, if only, where periphrasis was concerned, by a kind of fixed nomination ("le conseiller des grâces" and so on) which displaces the world, or certain of its commodities, into an artifice pure but inert. La Fontaine's artifice, on the contrary, is always changing, is continually suggestive and teems with reality. He names and renames, slowing for momentary intensities of concentration and transmutation, dressing the world in the unnecessary, and using more syllables than he need to designate the simplest things:

Les reines des étangs, grenouilles veux-je dire
(Car que coûte-t-il d'appeler
Les choses par noms honorables?)

What indeed? To call frogs by an honorable name is merely to invest them with poetry, that is, language become redundant, circumlocutory, or gratuitous.

On the other hand, a frog is, as they say, a frog, and it also needs protecting from poetry. Hence the importance of the two alexandrines with which we began. They reaffirm the common—specifically, the positive and negative spontaneities of the body—through burlesque. Beneath the transparency of the day is the heron's hunger; beneath the realms of the wind is the oak's disgust.

This relates partly to the underlying mock-heroic project of the *Fables*, which eventually became a work beginning "Je chante les héros . . ." and having, although they were not numbered in that way by La Fontaine himself, twelve books like the *Aeneid*. Not, parenthetically, that mock-heroic is always simple in the *Fables*. In "Le Chêne et le roseau," the oak is mocked for seeing itself at the heroic level and for adopting a suitable idiom; yet it is allowed the line about the kingdoms of the wind which, in its "serious" reading, is genuinely epic and even represents a moment of self-effacement, in which, furthermore, the oak is disinterestedly contemplating what belongs to its enemy. Above all, the ending decisively reverses what we have assumed by then to be the relation between the oak and the reed. The reed may be right (though no moral, interestingly, is extracted from the fable), but the poem is about the oak. The concluding quotation from Virgil, describing the oak, for once without derision, as "Celui de qui la tête au ciel était voisine, / Et dont les pieds touchaient à l'empire des morts," removes the poem's mock epic, which has been at the tree's expense, and establishes, in its favor, the epic *tout court*. One might notice in passing that epic hyperbole (the oak's head is "near heaven"), devised when the imagination is attentive to truth, is not less, but more extravagant than the hyperbole of mock epic (the oak had only considered its forehead to be "like the Caucasus")—which is, after all, how it should be. The oak at the moment of death, therefore, is not a mock hero, but a hero, and he is even associated with Aeneas, since it is to Aeneas that Virgil's original lines on the oak tree refer by way of comparison. Indeed, the oak which resists—silently now, and, on La Fontaine's part, laconically: "L'arbre tient bon"—and which is destroyed as well as being an epic hero and a certain type of tragic hero, seems to be man himself, spanning the worlds, rising by godlike intelligence and aspiration, yet drawn downward by his involvement with death. Even the anthropomorphisms are more insisted on here than in La Fontaine's sources. Whatever the manner in which most of the fable is told, its approach to values is devious and complex, and its theme remarkably weighty. It is a powerful instance, though a small one, in keeping with La Fontaine's way of doing things, of that difficult, disturbing kind of text which is both mock-heroic and heroic, large-scale examples of which would be *The Dunciad* and *The Waste Land*.

From another perspective, the two alexandrines are also a mockery of the reader. La Fontaine offers them and, when we have abandoned ourselves, withdraws them, to reveal other lines in their place. They are even unreadable, not simply, as is often if not usually the case with poetry, because of a wealth of moves that no single reading could track, but because, each line consisting of two contradictory lines inhabiting the same words, the reader is obliged to exclude one of the appropriate tones of voice.

They are above all a mockery of poetry, where the mockery works from inside. The poetry is not delivered and then, in subsequent lines, subverted: the poetry and the subversion accompany each other syllable by syllable.

What is even more arresting, however, is the fact that La Fontaine takes liberties with his writing at the moment of its greatest achievement. These are not merely good lines. Their diction, the relating and modifying of their words, the world they rouse, the sounds they place and vary—this is La Fontaine at his most consummate, and the qualities here are those we associate with the very best poetry of the period. It is when writing at the utmost edge of his demands for his poetry that he also wants to joke. Having reached perfection, he puns.

La Fontaine transfigures the world and mocks the transfiguration with indecorous appetite or clammy fens, raises language above itself and puts it down by returning it to a common expressiveness; and he does so while using the one set of words. It is, clearly, a form of wit, of the wit that Eliot, in the course of his Marvell essay, indicated in "Lafontaine," and that La Fontaine may, reciprocally, have helped Eliot to define ("un certain charme, un air agréable qu'on peut donner à toutes sortes de sujets, même les plus sérieux" could well prompt an "alliance of levity and seriousness," while "grâces légères," "ces badineries . . . dans le fond . . . portent un sens très solide" are not far from the "tough reasonableness" which lies "beneath the slight lyric grace"). Here, however, the wit has become more radical. It engages with the fundamental possibility of poetry, with the recreation, or not, of language and the world. Yet the disturbing of the poetry does not leave it with the *fêlure*, the *faille*, that a poet might intend now: the "beautiful" version of each line remains intact and may still be read. There seems no disquiet about poetry, no pulling back from a writing seen as too ordered for our disorder, too good to be true. On the contrary, when the joking intervenes, at the moment of maximum power, it does not damage the perfection, it passes beyond it. The writing achieves itself and then self-delightedly over-achieves.

To mock perfection while accomplishing it is, after all, the final enactment of mastery. It also denotes a particularly desirable kind of freedom, beyond the disciplines that creativity wills: a freedom which is irregular, or, in Freudian terms, uncensored, and which, therefore, naturally expresses itself in play. So La Fontaine, with a last flourish, subverts the subversion. His burlesque vindicates our world and our speech, prior to writing; but at the same time, in mocking poetry it produces more poetry, and as it derides it celebrates.

David Lee Rubin

Four Modes of Double Irony in La Fontaine's *Fables*[1]

I

Infinite variation, infinite artfulness: these are the traits of La Fontaine's
irony that Odette de Mourgues disclosed in *O Muse, fuyante proie* . . . .[2]
And of all its kinds, the most fascinating—and perplexing—is that to which
one might apply (somewhat cavalierly, perhaps) her own description of "un
équilibre très savant des éléments fondamentalement discordants."[3] It is
this species of statement and covert counterstatement which invites readers to the very brink of misconstruction, where—like the personages of the
Fables—they, too, may fall victim to the poet's wit.

While this essay cannot resolve the hermeneutic problem on a theoreti-
cal level, it will suggest ways—both negative and positive—by which readers
may do less injustice to La Fontaine's richness and finesse. Avoided here,
first of all, are concepts which predetermine the *general* interpretation of
"équilibre savant"—either by reducing it to a neutral display of opposed
attitudes, or by assimilating it to a world view of perpetually expanding,
absolute negativity. At the same time, neither of the general alternatives is
automatically excluded as the reading of a *particular* poem (or group of
poems), provided that the interpretation arises from inductive textual analysis. For its part, inductive analysis, as practiced here, has no empirical
pretension: indeed, it posits a framework of independent variables in whose
terms the shaping principle and the sense of a work may be recognized,
described, and related to one another without foreordained results.[4]

A key variable in the framework for this essay is D.C. Muecke's differ-
ential account of "équilibre savant":

The more familiar kind of irony is Simple Irony, in which an apparently or ostensibly
true statement, serious question, valid assumption, or legitimate expectation is corrected, invalidated, or frustrated by the ironist's real meaning, by the true state of
affairs, or by what actually happens. . . . *The less familiar kind of irony is Double
Irony . . . in which two equally invalid points of view cancel each other out . . .
[or] there is a single victim to whom both terms, though contradictory, seem equally
valid . . . [or] the ironist or ironic observer feels the paradox or dilemma as a real one.*[5]

To discover the double ironist's meaning can be a tortuous process, especially without two distinctions furnished by Wayne C. Booth. The first of
these opposes stable and unstable ironies. The former "[is] fixed, in the
sense that once a reconstruction has been made, the reader is not then invited to undermine it."[6] For its part, unstable irony solicits further norma-
tive interpretation. Booth also discriminates between local and infinite
irony: whereas local irony applies only to the immediate subject matter,
the scope of its counterpart implicitly expands.[7] This expansion may be
vertical—to ever higher levels of generality—or horizontal—to an even more
inclusive range of topics on the same level of abstraction.

Seen from the perspective made possible by these terms and distinctions,
"équilibre savant" varies widely in La Fontaine's *Fables*. At the very least
it encompasses not only a blend of stability and circumscription that may
be called "classic," but its polar opposite as well and two points that lie
between.

II. A False Dilemma

Book II of the *Fables* opens with a lyric as extraordinary in form as in
the problem it addresses. Commonly—and, I believe, mistakenly—seen as
one of La Fontaine's many *arts poétiques*, "Contre ceux qui ont le goût
difficile" is in the main concerned with a narrower, but no less important
issue: the poet's choice of audience. Moreover, this is one of the few fables
in which the author appears to speak in his own voice to completely dis-
junct sets of addressees.

Nothing could be clearer, first of all, than the subject of the dispute
that furnishes a pretext for the poem. To La Fontaine, the selection of a
literary genre is a function of temperament first and then of talent:

> Quand j'aurais, en naissant, reçu de Calliope
> Les dons qu'à ses amants cette Muse a promis,
> Je les consacrerais aux mensonges d'Esope.
> (II. 1-3)[8]

The happy conjunction of both forces has resulted in his own great success:

> Cependant jusqu'ici d'un langage nouveau
> J'ai fait parler le Loup et répondre l'Agneau;
> J'ai passé plus avant: les arbres et les plantes
> Sont devenus chez moi créatures parlantes.
> Qui ne prendrait ceci pour un enchantement?
> (ll. 10-13)

In the dialogue to follow, it becomes evident that the only possible reply is not "Personne!" Here La Fontaine dramatizes the antagonism between his beliefs and those of certain *critiques* (l. 14) *censeurs* (l. 17) and an *auteur* (l. 32). Narrow, rigid, and closed to all but a preordained hierarchy of poetic forms and formulas, these detractors would force the poet to choose between equally unacceptable alternatives. To them, fables are a priori frivolous and trivial: *contes d'enfant* (l. 16). Implicitly, the epic and pastoral are vastly preferable. Hence, the adamant poet "demonstrates" that he cannot rise above ineptitude in either mode. His exercise in the epic, beginning

> *Les Troyens,*
> *Après dix ans de guerre autour de leurs murailles,*
> *Avaient lassé les Grecs qui, par mille moyens,*
> *Par mille assauts, par cent batailles,*
> *N'avaient pu mettre à bout cette fière cité.*
> (ll. 18-22, italics mine)

is justly reproached for its breathlessness and the oddity of its circumlocutions (ll. 33-36).[9] The *adversarius* concludes, as the poet wishes him to, "il vous sied mal d'écrire en si haut style" (l. 38). Understanding, however, that by elimination only the pastoral remains, the poet indites a banal and insipid passage verging on the bathetic:

> *La jalouse Amarylle*
> *Songeait à son Alcippe, et croyait de ses soins*
> *N'avoir que ses moutons et son chien pour témoins.*
> *Tircis, qui l'aperçut, se glisse entre des saules;*
> *Il entend la bergère adressant ces paroles*
> *Au doux Zéphire, et le priant*
> *De les porter à son amant.*
> (ll. 39-45, italics mine)

Instead of recognizing the inferiority of this confection (and granting the poet's point on the relationship between talent, temperament, and genre), the *critique* merely interrupts with a complaint about the *rime pauvre* in the last two lines (ll. 46-49) and implies that with revision, the idyll will do: "Remettez, pour le mieux, ces deux vers à la fonte" (l. 50). To please his interlocutors, then, the poet must cultivate a genre for which he has no inclination and (if his specimen text is taken seriously) even less talent. His alternatives are equally unwelcome: to continue accepting his adversaries' *censure* for writing *contes d'enfant,* or to fall silent. Authorial reaction is violent:

> —Maudi censeur! te tairas-tu?
> Ne saurais-je achever mon conte?
> C'est un dessein très dangereux
> Que d'entreprendre de te plaire.
>
> Les délicats sont malheureux:
> Rien ne saurait les satisfaire.
>   (II. 51-56)[10]

Though dramatic and closural, such a finale is suspiciously out of keeping with La Fontaine's customary equipoise and leaves the impression that the issue has not been resolved in an intellectually satisfying manner.[11] Specifically, La Fontaine appears to end the fable merely by "disqualifying the recalcitrant"[12] readers and commentators of his work. Throughout the text however—even as he develops grounds for this disqualification—he assiduously constructs an implied foil to the *critiques*: an elite audience,[13] a set of ideal readers.

As though to underscore the opposition between model and antimodel,[14] La Fontaine plays subtly on the term *délicat* (l. 55). In its primary sense, and its explicit application here, *délicat* accurately characterizes the critics, who are punctilious in their adherence to literary laws and hence not only demanding but easily put off as well. It is no wonder that to the unorthodox poet, they seem *malheureux*: both misguided and contemptible. The implied elite—who are none other than the poet's silent addressee from the very beginning of the fable—are also a species of *délicat*, but one altogether right-minded and estimable. To judge from the poet's tone, arguments, and ellipses, these *délicats* are sympathetic to sound principles, however playfully put, and sensitive to the enchantments of successful poetry, whatever its mode or provenance. Moreover, the poet presupposes their ability to discern the nature and limits of his adversaries' thought and their approval of his efforts to manipulate that thought. (The ideal audience even serves as the poet's confidant in a moment of rage.) It is for this audience,[15] then, that the poet may continue to practice his non-conformist art; their existence—real or only hoped for—dispels the false dilemma created by the *malheureux délicats.*[16]

Thus in II, 1, La Fontaine's double irony is both stable and local; that is, the conflict of attitudes is resolved on recovery of a covert counterstatement from the poem's rhetorical structure and style. Moreover, the scope of the irony does not transcend the ostensible problem of poet and audience. Though the fable is doctrinally perverse, its irony is decidedly classic.

III. The Unseen Dilemma

Many—perhaps the majority—of La Fontaine's fables are assertional lyrics consisting of one or more subjects and predicates (the primary structural parts) along with illustrative materials (the secondary structural parts).[17] The latter usually take the form of concrete or abstract allegory or analogy.[18] The poet of course gave pride of place to the illustrative materials and even at times omitted the subject(s) or predicate(s), either wholly or in part.[19]

In "Le Loup et le chien" (I, 5), all subjects and predicates are omitted; only the illustration, a concrete allegory with animal personages, subsists. *Grosso modo*, the subjects of I, 5, are easily inferred from the illustration: freedom and constraint. Traditionally understood, the fable predicates that freedom, even when accompanied by privation and uncertainty, is preferable to constraint, however great the prosperity it entails. The basis for this reading is the case La Fontaine's illustrative material presents for the wolf and against the dog. Though lean with hunger, the former seems free and in full possession of his dignity, while the latter seems confined, regimented, and hence degraded, despite his *embonpoint* and shiny coat. But is the anecdote so uncomplicated in structure or meaning? The wolf, after all, is *not* perfectly free: owing to circumstances and prudence, for instance, he cannot behave exactly as he wishes and must resort to an hypocrisy which is far from ennobling:

> L'attaquer, le mettre en quartiers,
> Sire Loup l'eût fait volontiers;
> Mais il fallait livrer bataille,
> Et le mâtin était de taille
> A se défendre hardiment.
> Le Loup donc l'aborde humblement . . . .
> (II. 5-10)

Similarly, the dog is not quite as restricted as he appears to be. When the wolf asks, "Vous ne courez donc pas / Où vous voulez?" (II. 36-37), the dog's reply, "Pas toujours" (I. 37) is *not* an example of litotes, to be reconstructed "Jamais." After all, the dog is uncollared (II. 32-35), he has encountered the wolf after "s'[être] fourvoyé par mégarde" (I. 4), and apparently feels no uneasiness about passing his time in idle conversation with an avowed enemy of the household. Like the dog in La Fontaine's model, he is at times perfectly free to wander wherever he likes: *crepusculo solutus qua visum vagor.*[20]

This undercutting of the ostensibly correct interpretation suggests that there may even be grounds for a paradoxical case—*against* the wolf and *for* the dog. Eager to persuade the wolf to join him in a "meilleur destin" (l. 21), the dog's benevolent intention is supported by genuine pride (ll. 39-40) and contentment (ll. 26-29), as well as the half-spoken conviction that when the totality of circumstances are considered, absolutes, including absolute freedom, are immaterial and irrelevant (l. 37). Within this contractual arrangement, the dog has achieved a *modus vivendi* where relatively little labor and ceremony (ll. 23-25) are exchanged for material and psychological well-being. By contrast, the wolf is a wretch. The idea of sharing in the dog's life moves him deeply: "Le Loup déjà se forge une félicité / Qui le fait pleurer de tendresse" (ll. 30-31). Despite his forced hypocrisies, however, he is so possessed by a priori notions concerning absolute freedom that he cannot act in his own best interest and refuses to trade his cheerless liberty even for "un trésor" (l. 40). That the wolf is no exemplar should be plain; indeed, he seems to be an anti-model: myopic, incoherent, and bigoted. Still, La Fontaine furnishes further grounds for undercutting. If the dog has his pride, for example, he certainly manifests it pompously, e.g.,

> Il ne tiendra qu'à vous, beau sire,
> D'être aussi gras que moi, lui repartit le chien.
> Quittez les bois, vous ferez bien:
> Cancres, haires, et pauvres diables,
> Dont la condition est de mourir de faim.
> Car quoi? rien d'assuré, point de franche lippée;
> Tout à la pointe de l'épée.
>
> (II. 13-20)

And though degraded by circumstances and his own moral conflicts, the wolf is, nevertheless, a touching, even romanesque figure, especially at the moment of formal closure: "Cela dit, maître Loup s'enfuit, et court encor" (l. 41).[21]

Indeed, the only closure or sense of finality that the fable possesses *is* formal. Ideologically, I, 5 is unresolved: the predicates are never clearly implied, the conflict between viewpoints never satisfactorily resolved. Interpretation after undercutting interpretation can and surely will be made without end. However unstable the irony of the fable is, there is no wandering away from the ostensible subject matter, the problematic of freedom and constraint. In the end, it may well be this problematic, nothing more nor less, that La Fontaine seeks to disclose to the reader in a text which makes a major deviation from "classic" irony.

IV. The Problem of Locus

Like "Le Loup et le chien," "La Cigale et la fourmi" (I, 1) is an ellipti-
cal lyric, but the effects of ellipsis are not identical in the two poems.
While omission of subject and predicate contributes to a destabilization of
local irony in I, 5, the same device vastly extends the scope of stable irony
in I, 1.

To the narrator, even-handed judgment is necessary in this case. Both
the grasshopper and the ant have qualities and defects that balance each
other out, almost point by point. The grasshopper's languorous charm and
estheticism, as well as the touching *badinage* of its sollicitation, are generally summarized and represented with sympathy. There is, however, an
unmistakable suggestion of parody or gentle mockery in the opening lines,
and of dismay, joined with mild disapproval in the verses to follow, where
panic precedes the worst imaginable choice of creditors. For its part, the
ant is certainly an exemplar of planning, labor, and thrift, although La
Fontaine treats it with sarcasm, when the subject turns to social impulses.[22]
And in what follows, *le fruit dépasse la promesse des fleurs*. The fable,
therefore, presents an equilibrium where each embodiment of clashing attitudes appears partially validated but partially contradicted at the same
time. But what is the "field of observation," the domain of correctness
and error?

There can be no doubt that the *interprétation scolaire* is altogether
plausible: La Fontaine has, on one level, at least, dramatized the conflict
between an improvident sensualism and a prudentialism as insensitive
socially as it is esthetically. The absence of a formal assertion, however,
invites the extension of this reading in several complementary directions.
Both personages, for example, may represent epicureanism in its principal
modes. The ant, subscribing to classical tenets, seeks to avoid pain and has
thus desensitized itself not only to the blandishments of art (which would
distract it from productivity and preservation) but also to the pleas of the
needy (who would consume its good without a credible promise of repay-
ment). A hedonist, the grasshopper enjoys and incidentally offers others
the pleasures of music, as well as theatricality, but never considering the
potentially adverse effects of its unproductivity it becomes a social burden,
then an outcast, and finally, a statistic. Alternatively, both grasshopper and
ant may be seen as tenants of extreme positions on certain of Aristotle's
ethical *continua*: whereas the grasshopper is prodigal, self-indulgent, and a
buffoon, the ant is niggardly, insensible, and boorish. Neither even remotely
approaches *aurea mediocritas*. Finally, it is possible to shift from ethical to

esthetic categories and see the ant as the embodiment of the *utile* and the grasshopper as a symbol of the *dulce*: though largely divergent and potentially antagonistic, each one without the other is insufficient and incomplete.[23] Thus, "La Cigale et la fourmi" represents a second kind of deviation from classic irony, a step in the direction of the open-ended, not to say, the modern.

V. Homeric Smile

Fable XII, 1, "Les Compagnons d'Ulysse," presents no apparent problem of interpretation. The narrator wishes to assert that "le sens et la raison" should prevail, dominating all instincts and emotions (ll. 22 ff., l. 105). To illustrate—and equally important, to provide the immediate addressee, the duc de Bourgogne, opportunity to exercise his *sens* and *raison*—the narrator recounts

> un fait, où les Grecs,
> Imprudents et peu circonspects,
> S'abandonnèrent à des charmes
> Qui métamorphosaient en bêtes les humains.
> (ll. 23-26)

The *abandon* is indeed a permanent abnegation, for when offered the chance to resume their human forms,

> Chacun d'eux fit même réponse,
> Autant le grand que le petit,
> La liberté, les bois, suivre leur appétit,
> C'étaient leurs délices suprêmes;
> Tous renonçaient au lot des belles actions.
> Ils croyaient s'affranchir, suivant leurs passions;
> Ils étaient esclaves d'eux-mêmes.
> (ll. 100-06)

In case of doubt about the appropriate response to all this, the narrator explicitly prescribes for the young duke: the companions of Ulysses

> . . . ont force pareils en ce bas univers,
> Gens à qui j'impose pour peine
> Votre censure et votre haine.
> (ll. 112-15)

Like the convoluted and unctuous overture in praise of the duke, this harsh and mean-spirited finale is so uncharacteristic of La Fontaine's tone and thought that it suggests a great gulf between the implied author and the narrator.

And indeed the narrator *is* unreliable. As my *argumentum* shows, he asserts the primacy of reason, but prescribes hatred as the fitting response to Ulysses' crew and to their similars here and now. This incoherence is aggravated and complemented by a lack of correspondence between the narrator's comments (including his basic assertion) and the very structure of the illustrative anecdote. Ulysses, for instance, is far from being a model of rationality. Darting frenetically from one beast to another, he never reasons, but rather exclaims, issues commands, puts questions, and expresses profound discomfiture—to all: "Chers amis, voulez-vous hommes redevenir?" (l. 56); to the bear: "Eh! mon frère, / Comme te voilà fait! je t'ai vu si joli!" (ll. 65-66); to the wolf:

> Camarade, je suis confus
> Qu'une jeune et belle bergère
> Conte aux échos les appétits gloutons
> Qui t'ont fait manger ses moutons
> Autrefois on t'eût vu sauver sa bergerie:
> Tu menais une honnête vie.
> Quitte ces bois et redeviens
> Au lieu de loup, homme de bien.
> (ll. 79-86)

By contrast, when the beasts defend their refusal to assume their former shapes, it is with at least a semblance of logic. The lion cites his improved status—"Je suis roi" (l. 62)—as reason for renouncing "aux dons que je viens d'acquérir" (l. 60); the bear answers Ulysses with an indirect assertion of esthetic relativity: "Qui t'a dit qu'une forme est plus belle qu'une autre?" (l. 70); and the wolf argues that Ulysses is nothing more nor less than a pot calling a kettle black: "Tu t'en viens me traiter de bête carnassière; / Toi qui parles, qu'es-tu?" (ll. 88-89). By the narrator's own standard, the duc de Bourgogne should hate Ulysses and admire his companions!

The real issue, however, is not the relative merit of reason or passion, but the conflict between different hierarchies of value. For Ulysses, the privileged quality is human dignity, which is absolutely inseparable from the form that distinguishes man in appearance from what our hero might call "the lower orders." Abandonment of that form entails forfeiture of rank, purely and simply. For the *compagnons*, however, human dignity is either a sham or an irrelevancy, especially when compared with the merits of their current condition. The lion, for instance, cherishes his invulnerability: "J'ai griffe et dent, et mets en pièces, qui m'attaque" (l. 61) and would never trade this for the apparently empty perquisites of "un citoyen d'Ithaque" or a "simple soldat" (ll. 62 and 63). The bear prizes his creature comforts above all else and his autonomy: "Je vis libre, content, sans nul soin qui me presse" (l. 74); to the moral dogmatist who decries his choice he replies, "Te déplais-je? va-t'en; suis ta route et me laisse" (l. 73). The wolf, finally, believes that appearance and essence should always be one; for him, disparity is disguise and hence morally reprehensible. Since men are wolves to one another (l. 94), it is only proper that a man should assume a wolf's outer form.

Whereas the narrator sees no dilemma here, the implied author surely does, but offers no solution, directly or indirectly. In XII, 1, as in "Le Loup et le chien," cases for and against both parties in the debate can be made, undercut, and constructed anew—virtually *ad infinitum*. If the spokesman for the ostensible norm is a mediocrity, his adversaries, though brighter than he, are from his point of view grotesques. Equally problematic is the scope of the disagreement; on this the text itself places no limit. Indeed, beyond the immediate issue, many others are suggested, most pertinently, perhaps, the proper relationship between self-knowledge and moral choice. Should one, for instance, follow the line of least resistance (however well rationalized) or that of highest apparent merit? Are the two alternatives neatly distinguishable in every instance? Another problem is the conflict between relativistic and dogmatic standards of personal worth, happiness, and conduct—a major issue throughout the French seventeenth century and, of course, throughout the *Fables* of La Fontaine.[24]

With XII, 1, this survey of modes is complete, ending with a fable whose double irony deviates as fully as possible from "classic" stability and circumspection. Anticlosural because unresolved and unlimited in scope, it most nearly approaches what readers expect in the literature of our time.

Much, of course, remains to be discovered about double irony in the *Fables—all* its types, for instance, and its subtypes, as well as the relations and correlations that hold between it and the variants of La Fontaine's lyric forms, his themes and theses, his narrative voices and implied audiences, his devices of language, and even his prosodic techniques. Closer and more extensive study[25] will, I feel sure, disclose the fact that double irony ranks with concision, allusion, and paranomasia among the chief devices La Fontaine exploited to meet the difficult standard that he set himself in the "Discours à M. le duc de La Rochefoucauld" (X, 14): "qu'il faut laisser / Dans les plus beaux sujets quelque chose à penser" (ll. 55-56).

NOTES

1. I am indebted to the John Simon Guggenheim Memorial Foundation and the University of Virginia Center for Advanced Studies, under whose auspices this essay was completed as part of a larger project. I also wish to thank G. Richard Danner and members of the Folger Institute Colloquium for their astute and helpful comments on an early draft of the study.

2. (Paris, 1962), pp. 131-55.

3. *O Muse, fuyante proie* . . . , p. 140.

4. For a detailed account of this framework, see the foreword to my study, *The Knot of Artifice: A Poetic of the French Lyric in the Early Seventeenth Century* (Columbus, Ohio, 1981).

5. *The Compass of Irony* (London, 1969), pp. 23-25, emphasis mine.

6. *The Rhetoric of Irony* (Chicago, 1974), p. 6.

7. Ibid.

8. All quotations from La Fontaine refer to *Fables*, ed. Georges Couton (Paris, 1962). I have occasionally normalized the text.

9. For a penetrating comment on this passage, see Margaret Guiton, *La Fontaine: Poet and Counterpoet* (New Brunswick, N.J., 1961), pp. 66-68.

10. Fable II, 1, invites comparison with Horace's ode I, 6 ("Scriberis Vario fortis et hostium"). Both are *recusationes*, lyrics in which the poets profess inability to write in a genre requested or required by another. In each, both talent *and* temperament are cited as reasons for working in lesser modes. But Horace's pastiche of epic style—in the first, second and fourth stanzas—is meant to suggest that had he wished to do so, he could have written heroic poetry of value, whereas La Fontaine strives through his stylistic exercise to leave an unmistakable impression of incompetence. Furthermore, while La Fontaine explicitly—and heretically—asserts his superiority as poet on the strength of the *Fables*, Horace merely implies his and ascribes it not only to his proven range, but above all to his steadfast insistence on working in the form of his choice, regardless of external pressures.

11. Indeed, as subsequent analyses will show, La Fontaine tends to proceed in precisely the opposite manner, by creating the semblance of resolution where in fact none exists.

12. Chaim Perelman and L. Olbrechts-Tyteca, *The New Rhetoric: A Treatise on Argumentation*, trans. John Wilkinson and Purcell Smith (Notre Dame, Ind., and London, 1969), p. 33.

13. Ibid., p. 34.

14. Ibid., pp. 363-67.

15. For incisive comments on La Fontaine's authorial voices and the various audiences addressed in the *Fables*, see Roseann Runte, "Reconstruction and Deconstruction: La Fontaine, Aesop, and the Eighteenth-Century Fabulist," *Papers on French Seventeenth-Century Literature*, 11 (1979), 29-46.

16. In this sense, La Fontaine and Molière were in complete agreement. See my articles "Image, Argument and Esthetics in *La Critique de l'Ecole des Femmes*," in *Molière Studies*, ed. G.B. Daniel, Supplement 1 of *Romance Notes*, 15 (1973), 98-107, and "In All Line of Order: The Structure of *L'Impromptu de Versailles*," *Romance Notes*, 16 (1975), 653-61.

17. See Norman Friedman and Norman McLaughlin, *Poetry: An Introduction to Its Form and Art* (New York, 1961), pp. 44-46, 76-78, 121-22. This little-known work is the most complete exposition of the "Chicago" theory of the lyric.

18. For useful discriminations between the various modes of didactic literature, see David Richter, *Fable's End* (Chicago, 1974), esp. pp. 1-21.

19. From this point of view, "Contre ceux qui ont le goût difficile" contains two assertions, one about *malheureux délicats*, the other about their foils. The first assertion is complete; the second, incomplete, being without subject or predicate and illustrated only indirectly through the poem's rhetorical structure and crucial pun.

20. Phaedrus, *Fabulae Aesopicae*, III, 7, v. 20. See Phèdre, *Fables*, ed. Alice Brenot (Paris, 1924), p. 40 (normalization mine).

21. For a contrasting view, see G. Richard Danner, "Individualism in 'Le Loup et le chien,'" *Kentucky Romance Quarterly*, 24 (1977), 185-90.

22. J.D. Biard, *The Style of La Fontaine's Fables* (New York, 1966), p. 135.

23. I am indebted to Terence Cave for this interpretation, which gains in plausibility when the fable's location—at the beginning of Book I—is considered. See also VI, 9, II. 21-22.

24. For a corroborating analysis of XII, 1, see G. Richard Danner, "La Fontaine's 'Compagnons d'Ulysse': The Merits of Metamorphosis," *French Review*, 53 (1980), 239-47.

25. Incorporating such approaches as that of Susan W. Tiefenbrun in her brilliant treatment of conflicting yet overlapping codes, "Signs of Irony in La Fontaine's *Fables*," *Papers on French Seventeenth-Century Literature*, 11 (1979), 51-76. See as well Jules Brody's commentary in the same number, pp. 77-90.

Alain Seznec

Connaissance philosophique-création poétique: "Discours à Mme de la Sablière"

"Le Rat et l'huître"[1] rapproche deux mondes qui n'ont, en principe, rien de commun. La campagne et la mer, le petit rustre qui sort (comme le dit La Fontaine jouant sur les mots) de son "trou," et la quasi-divine créature qui se prélasse à l'intérieur de sa coquille, comme une odalisque au bain; plus simplement l'animal champêtre et souterrain et l'animal marin; autant de rencontres surprenantes. Le monde réaliste et le monde mythique s'enchevêtrent parfois comme, ailleurs, le monde troublant des grands fauves semble côtoyer celui de la basse-cour. Par moment, l'univers dans lequel se situe une fable particulière semble homogène et reconnaissable, parfois, au contraire, les détails du monde ne se correspondent plus. L'effet n'est pas toujours celui que l'on escompte. Dans "Le Cerf malade" (XII, 6, p. 326), par exemple, nous sommes, si l'on peut dire, "entre cerfs": "En pays de Cerfs, un Cerf tomba malade," nous dit le premier vers, et de fait, aucune autre créature, humaine ou animale, ne paraît dans le récit. Ni lion grand seigneur, ni personnage exotique, dragon, dieu, allégorie, ni créature incongrue, singe, tortue, aigle qui se serait fourvoyée par mégarde. L'effet n'en est pas pour cela plus réaliste. Au contraire, dans ce monde homogène, mais où le poète se préoccupe à peine de la réalité concrète, les cerfs cessent assez vite de ressembler à des animaux. Nous oublions à qui nous avons affaire. Le dernier masque est humain et, pour une fois, l'illustrateur Grandville, qui insiste presque toujours sur l'anthropomorphisme, est dans le ton de la fable. De même, dans "Le Fermier, le chien et le renard" (XI, 3, p. 300), si la première situation paraît tout à fait réaliste (il s'agit pour un fermier de protéger sa basse-cour des incursions d'un renard), et chargée de détails descriptifs, nous découvrons vers le milieu de la fable que c'était en vue de produire un effet bouffon. La fable va, tout d'un coup, tourner au poème héroï-comique où paraissent Apollon et Ajax. Les détails et l'échelle de la vie quotidienne n'ont servi qu'à établir le contraste. Là encore, le contenu concret s'évapore.

Par un mouvement contraire, La Fontaine parfois nous désoriente en juxtaposant des éléments qui proviennent de systèmes différents. Dans "La Génisse, la chèvre et la brebis en société avec le lion" (I, 6, p. 39), les quatre personnages font cause commune. La chèvre capture un cerf, qui est alors dépecé, mais au moment du partage, le lion insiste pour garder les quatre quarts. La fable d'Esope qui semble la source la plus lointaine de La Fontaine, met en scène un lion et un âne sauvage, ce qui est moins déroutant. Le fabuliste ancien explique que l'un a la force, l'autre la rapidité, ce qui fait de ces deux animaux disparates une équipe plausible. La conclusion est la même que chez La Fontaine, et le lion garde sa part . . . proverbiale. L'autre source, et beaucoup plus proche de La Fontaine, nous la trouvons chez Phèdre: "Vacca, et capella, ouis et leo."[2] Le groupe hétéroclite n'est pas, par conséquent, de l'invention du fabuliste français, mais, lorsque l'on compare les deux textes, c'est le soin de Phèdre à éviter tout effet réaliste qui fait qu'après la lecture du titre, nous oublions l'incongru. En fait, la fable de Phèdre pourrait s'appeler "Le Lion et les créatures faibles no. 1, no. 2 et no. 3." Phèdre, de plus, nous fait sentir que la constitution de cette équipe est fortuite et imposée d'avance. La Fontaine, lui, prend plaisir à insister sur le côté réaliste. Mélangeant les détails anthropomorphiques (il parle de "Seigneur du voisinage," de "faire société," de "gain et dommage") avec des détails "vrais" (le cerf va bel et bien être dépecé), il situe à mi-chemin des éléments saugrenus: les trois herbivores se prennent apparemment pour des carnassiers et, qui mieux est, c'est la chèvre qui va se montrer le meilleur chasseur et prendre le cerf dans ses lacs. A chaque instant, La Fontaine change les règles du jeu. Le monde des bovins et des ovins n'est pas le monde habité par les lions; ce ne sont pas non plus ceux de la vénerie. Nous ne pouvons pourtant pas (comme dans la fable de Phèdre) ignorer entièrement de la réalité animale de chacun des personnages. L'incongru finit donc par produire un effet menaçant. Dans la mesure où le littéral signale, même légèrement, sa présence nous nous sentons troublés. Cette génisse ou cette chèvre seraient-elles vraiment prêtes à prendre leur part de ce cerf écartelé et sanglant? Ne serait-ce qu'un instant, les règles habituelles de l'univers semblent suspendues; dans la mesure où nous ne pouvons pas retransformer ces personnages en allégories, en faire des abstractions, des symboles, nous ressentons un certain malaise. Il suffirait de peu pour que surgisse le cauchemar.

Pour mieux saisir le procédé par lequel chaque fable acquiert sa densité et sa richesse intérieure, examinons un certain nombre de textes, choisis parmi ceux dans lesquels les mélanges de mondes ou de personnages, les juxtapositions surprenantes, les rencontres inattendues jouent un rôle primordial. Voyons d'abord un texte où la transition porte sur le genre de la fable lui-même: il s'agit de la fable XIII du huitième livre, "Tircis et Amarante" (pour Mademoiselle de Sillery). Le titre fait penser au conte plutôt qu'à la fable, et nous prépare même à pénétrer dans le monde de la pastorale. Or, justement, après la parution des six premiers livres de fables (1668) La Fontaine avait presque abandonné ce genre (huit fables seulement en trois ans) et s'était remis (plus ou moins sous le manteau) à écrire des contes. Cette fable marque donc une rentrée, comme l'indiquent les deux premiers vers. Il abandonne le monde du conte licencieux pour ne pas effaroucher la jeune Mademoiselle de Sillery (nièce de La Rochefoucauld), mais malgré l'appel qui l'encourage à revenir au monde de la fable, le poète ne se sent pas encore prêt à refaire parler "Sire Loup et Sire Corbeau." La pastorale sera donc la transition parfaite entre la fable et le conte. Il va y "amener des bergers," tout d'abord, et qui ne parleront que d'amour, comme il se doit. Mais qui dit "bergers" dit aussi "moutons," et là où se trouve le troupeau, le loup n'est pas loin. Insensiblement les ébats des bergers amoureux dans un site pastoral ramènent au monde de la fable. Nous n'entendrons plus les soupirs des bergers et des bergères, désormais figés et devenus de simples décorations. En revanche, les moutons qui n'étaient dans la pastorale que des objets silencieux et indistincts vont devenir, à leur tour, des personnages. Les loups et les moutons vont se mettre à parler. Voici la première partie de ce conte-pastorale-fable:

> J'avais Esope quitté
> Pour être tout à Boccace:
> Mais une Divinité
> Veut revoir sur le Parnasse
> Des Fables de ma façon;
> Or d'aller lui dire, Non,
> Sans quelque valable excuse,
> Ce n'est pas comme on en use
> Avec des Divinités,
> Surtout quand ce sont de celles
> Que la qualité de belles
> Fait Reines des volontés.
> Car afin que l'on le sache,
> C'est Sillery qui s'attache
> A vouloir que, de nouveau,
> Sire Loup, Sire Corbeau
> Chez moi se parlent en rime.

Qui dit Sillery, dit tout;
Peu de gens en leur estime
Lui refusent de haut bout;
Comment le pourrait-on faire?
Pour venir à notre affaire,
Mes contes à son avis
Sont obscurs; les beaux esprits
N'entendent pas toute chose;
Faisons donc quelques récits
Qu'elle déchiffre sans glose.
Amenons des Bergers et puis nous rimerons
Ce que disent entre eux les Loups et les Moutons.

Si l'on regarde la liste complète des fables de La Fontaine, on note que le groupe le plus large met en scène uniquement des animaux, et ceci de manière à peu près égale tout au long de l'œuvre. Toutefois les fables aux personnages uniquement humains (y compris des fables qui se rapprochent des *Contes* et passent même pour en être: "Daphnis et Alcimadure," "Philémon et Baucis," "La Matrone d'Ephèse," "Belphégor," "Les Filles de Minée") se font en général plus nombreuses au fil des livres. Par un mouvement parallèle, les sources qui prédominent dans les premiers livres (Esope et Phèdre) tendent à disparaître complètement.[3] L'exotisme ne tient pas une place importante. Ici et là paraissent un éléphant, une gazelle, un chameau, un léopard, mais nous sommes le plus souvent dans un milieu familier où, à part la présence relativement fréquente du lion, prédominent la basse-cour, les troupeaux, les animaux de la ferme et les animaux des bois.[4]

Une troisième catégorie moins nombreuse, de fables, mêle des hommes et des animaux. La rencontre en général est fâcheuse, rarement favorable aux quadrupèdes, et l'homme se révèle être un animal plus retors, plus brutal et plus insensible. Sans doute quelque rapide renard sait-il parfois saccager le poulailler d'un fermier par trop naïf, ou, à l'occasion, tel ours ou tel lion met-il en fuite un chasseur par trop téméraire, mais la plupart du temps, nous avons plutôt le spectacle affligeant de la cruauté humaine envers les animaux. L'exemple le plus frappant est la première fable du deuxième livre, "L'Homme et la couleuvre" (X, 1, pp. 275-77):

Un Homme vit une Couleuvre:
Ah! méchante, dit-il, je m'en vais faire une œuvre
Agréable à tout l'univers!
A ces mots, l'animal pervers
(C'est le Serpent que je veux dire,
Et non l'Homme: on pourrait aisément s'y tromper),
A ces mots le Serpent, se laissant attraper,
Est pris, mis en un sac; et, ce qui fut le pire,
On résolut sa mort, fût-il coupable ou non.

Afin de le payer toutefois de raison,
  L'autre lui fit cette harangue:
Symbole des ingrats! être bon aux méchants,
C'est être sot; meurs donc: ta colère et tes dents
Ne me nuiront jamais. Le Serpent, en sa langue,
Reprit du mieux qu'il put: S'il fallait condamner
  Tous les ingrats qui sont au monde,
  A qui pourrait-on pardonner?
Toi-même, tu te fais ton procès: je me fonde
Sur tes propres leçons; jette les yeux sur toi.
Mes jours sont en tes mains, tranche-les; ta justice,
C'est ton utilité, ton plaisir, ton caprice:
  Selon ces lois, condamne-moi;
  Mais trouve bon qu'avec franchise
  En mourant au moins je te dise
  Que le symbole des ingrats
Ce n'est point le Serpent, c'est l'Homme. Ces paroles
Firent arrêter l'autre; il recula d'un pas.
Enfin il repartit: Tes raisons sont frivoles.
Je pourrais décider, car ce droit m'appartient;
Mais rapportons-nous-en. —Soit fait, dit le Reptile.

Viendront alors témoigner une vache, un bœuf, un arbre fruitier—chacun condamnera l'ingratitude de l'homme et celui-ci ne pourra plus recourir qu'à la mauvaise foi et à la violence:

L'Homme, trouvant mauvais que l'on l'eût convaincu,
Voulut à toute force avoir cause gagnée.
Je suis bien bon, dit-il, d'écouter ces gens-là!
Du sac et du Serpent aussitôt il donna
  Contre les murs, tant qu'il tua la bête.

  On en use ainsi chez les grands:
La raison les offense; ils se mettent en tête
Que tout est né pour eux, quadrupèdes et gens,
  Et serpents.
  Si quelqu'un desserre les dents,
C'est un sot. —J'en conviens: mais que faut-il donc faire?
  Parler de loin, ou bien se taire.

Par une astucieuse trouvaille, La Fontaine choisit d'abord un être "symbolique," et pourtant familier, le serpent. Cet animal qui tend à inspirer une peur superstitieuse est en effet souvent la victime d'une réaction hystérique de la part des humains même les plus raisonnables. Ce qui est vrai dans la pratique courante, l'est aussi dans le domaine mythique, car le serpent c'est le "malin," le traître, le responsable du malheur humain, c'est, par sa forme, la représentation du mal personnifié qu'il s'agit d'écraser. Dans cette fable, justement, La Fontaine va changer la perspective traditionnelle. Il écrit dans les premiers vers du "Discours à Monsieur le duc de la Rochefoucauld" (X, 14, p. 291):

> Je me suis souvent dit, voyant de quelle sorte
> L'homme agit et qu'il se comporte
> En mille occasions, comme les animaux:. . . .

Il y a plusieurs ambiguïtés dans un tel jugement: s'agit-il d'observation objective et neutre, ou de comparaison satirique; le mot "animal" sera-t-il pris dans un sens plus ou moins abstrait et symbolique ou, au contraire, réaliste et "behavioriste"? La perspective traditionnelle (celle de La Rochefoucauld, par exemple) pose comme axiome l'infériorité des animaux, ainsi la comparaison sera toujours péjorative; l'animal ne sera qu'un miroir déformant, une pauvre caricature de l'homme; les faiblesses humaines, en revanche, seront qualifiées d' "animales." La perspective de cette fable renverse ses conventions. Ainsi l'inoffensive couleuvre va payer pour tous les malheurs des hommes. Notons en passant que La Fontaine n'a pas dit "serpent," encore moins "vipère," il a choisi délibérément un serpent non vénimeux. Notons surtout que La Fontaine insiste sur un défaut particulièrement humain, la volonté de moraliser et de rationaliser. Comme le loup du "Loup et l'agneau," l'homme est celui qui forge un raisonnement, et feint de suivre une procédure judiciaire. Il veut à tous prix "avoir raison," et voilà bien le terrible paradoxe de sa nature. Cet être considère que le monde lui appartient, que la création terrestre est une sorte de compensation pour sa perte de Paradis. Tout "lui semble né pour lui." Qu'a-t-il fait pourtant depuis qu'il est sur terre? Du témoignage des autres personnages ressort un portrait peu favorable: la vache et le bœuf tour à tour rappellent son ingratitude, sa brutalité, son égoïsme. Bien pis, l'arbre fruitier (décidément l'image de paradis persiste tout le long de la fable) va aussi dire son mot. Parlant, pourrait-on dire, au nom de la nature tout entière, il va révéler ce que représente la présence de l'homme dans le monde: il saccage et détruit.[5] Aucune harmonie entre cette créature rationnelle mais déraisonnable et la nature.

Ce qui donne à cette fable sa pleine force, c'est une perspective inhabituelle, soudain découverte. Si les animaux, et à plus forte raison les plantes, ne sont pour l'homme que des objets dont il peut user et abuser, pour le lecteur qui voit par les yeux du poète et ceux de la couleuvre, c'est l'homme qui ressemble au fléau sans visage et sans individualité. Au vers neuf, La Fontaine écrit: "On résolut sa mort, fût-il coupable ou non." Les vrais personnages, pour nous, ceux qui vivent et palpitent, ce sont justement les victimes, ces animaux que l'homme se plaît à appeler "brutes" et dont il veut croire qu'elles sont "insensibles."

La partie essentielle du "Discours à Mme de la Sablière" se réduit à cette question: quel est le rapport de la "nature humaine" et de la "nature animale"? Les deux mondes sont-ils séparés par des frontières infranchissables? Où s'arrête la définition de ce qui est "en vie"? Que veulent dire "sentir," "ressentir," "agir instinctivement," "réfléchir"? Ces questions qui expriment une préoccupation majeure des *Fables*, font du "Discours" une œuvre capitale. De nombreuses études ont situé ce document par rapport aux discussions intellectuelles de l'époque, et rappelé plus particulièrement l'influence de Descartes à côté d'autres courants philosophiques, le Gassendisme, par exemple.[6] Il est certain que les fréquentations de La Fontaine (surtout dans le salon de Mme de la Sablière), ses amitiés (celle de Saint-Evremond en particulier) et sa propre curiosité intellectuelle, n'ont pu le laisser indifférent à ces débats; mais il nous semble que sa pensée (même dans cette fable "philosophique" par excellence) est à la fois souple et trop subtile pour le mener à des considérations doctrinaires. La fable tout entière, avec ses raisonnements sous forme de dialogues philosophiques, interrompus par de nombreux exemples—dont chacun est comme une petite fable individuelle—semble organisée autour de principes ambigus, d'hésitations, et même de contradictions.

Dès les premiers vers, la fable se situe sous le signe du multiple et du changeant. Félicitant Mme de la Sablière (sous le nom d'Iris) de la variété de ses talents et des richesses de son esprit, il évoque son salon où l'on goûte les plaisirs sans cesse différents de la conversation: "Propos, agréables commerces, / Où le hasard fournit cent matières diverses."[7] Il rapproche comiquement ce qu'il appelle "la bagatelle," c'est-à-dire, on le suppose, tout ce qui est propos léger (et d'art et d'amour), de la "science" (dont il va être sérieusement question dans le reste de la fable); il leur adjoint le rêve, la vision, la spéculation plus ou moins vaporeuse, qu'il appelle "les chimères." "Tout est bon," conclut-il, tout par conséquent finit par contribuer à notre connaissance du monde et à notre plaisir. "Tout parle dans l'Univers," eût-il pu dire en se paraphrasant lui-même. Il abolit les distinctions entre différentes formes de savoir et de sagesse, comme il semble abolir les catégories des sujets d'étude. Il ne s'agit ici que "d'entretiens," de pures conversations, et non de débats scolaires ou d'écrits savants; mais cette attitude modeste qui voudrait cacher le poète et son amie sous un masque frivole, n'en laisse pas moins paraître l'ambition du créateur. Les vers qui le décrivent sont comme le sigle de l'œuvre entière de La Fontaine:

> ... je soutiens
> Qu'il faut de tout aux entretiens:
> C'est un parterre où Flore épand ses biens;
> Sur différentes fleurs l'abeille s'y repose,

> Et fait du miel de toute chose.
>
> (vv. 19-23)

Ainsi, connaissance philosophique et création poétique vont s'entremêler, tout comme la fable va faire alterner dialogue, ou monologue spéculatif, et illustration. Ce "Discours" est lui-même le parfait exemple de la fable et de l'emblême. Ce schéma idéal comporte pourtant un paradoxe; en effet, l'illustration va se trouver plus d'une fois contredire la proposition philosophique. Dès le début l'attitude de La Fontaine est ambiguë. Il commence par chanter les louanges "de certaine Philosophie / Subtile, engageante et hardie / qu'on appelle nouvelle" (vv. 26-28), mais bien vite il prend ses distances vis-à-vis de celle-ci: "ils disent donc," "au dire de ces gens," "selon eux," ces formules donnent l'impression que La Fontaine, par ironie, présente la doctrine cartésienne en raccourcis vraiment excessifs:

> Mais ce n'est point cela: ne vous y trompez pas.
> Qu'est-ce donc? —Une montre. —Et nous? —C'est autre chose.
> Voici de la façon que Descartes l'expose.
>
> (vv. 51-53)

Changeant de direction, La Fontaine fait, en suite, l'éloge du grand philosophe:

> Descartes, ce mortel dont on eût fait un dieu
> Chez les païens, et qui tient le milieu
> Entre l'homme et l'esprit, comme entre l'huître et l'homme
> Le tient tel de nos gens, franche bête de somme.
>
> (vv. 54-57)

Ne se glisse-t-il pas un léger sourire dans ce dithyrambe? De même, lorsqu'il insiste sur la vérité absolue de la doctrine: "Vous savez, Iris, de certaine science,"[8] et conclut:

> Descartes va plus loin, et soutient nettement
> Qu'elle ne pense nullement.
> Vous n'êtes point embarrassée
> De le croire; ni moi.
>
> (vv. 65-68)

Echo moqueur pour tant de certitude frisant la suffisance. Le fuyant et changeant La Fontaine nous semble ici plus circonspect, voire cynique.

Quoi qu'il en soit, les illustrations qu'il propose (vv. 69-81, 82-91, 91-113) tendent à mettre en doute la doctrine; elles présentent, justement, des exemples de comportement animal que ne peut expliquer la théorie des "animaux-machines." Qui plus est, il se dresse lui-même en face du grand philosophe et, non sans verve, s'écrie: "Que ces castors ne soient

qu'un corps vide d'esprit, / Jamais on ne pourra m'obliger à le croire" (vv.
114-15). Et, tout de suite, comme pour défaire une fois pour toutes la
"subtile philosophie" des cartésiens, il se lance dans une nouvelle anecdote,
un dernier exemple qu'il veut définitif (vv. 116-39). Après ce quatrième
récit, La Fontaine reprend le débat. Il commence par atténuer la distance
qui le sépare de Descartes, et même par accepter certaines notions fonda-
mentales portant sur la mémoire, l'instinct et la volonté, et il souligne la
différence entre les hommes et les animaux (vv. 140 ss.). Peu à peu, le ton
est moins affirmatif, les distinctions se font moins certaines; alors apparaissent non plus des phrases déclaratives, mais des interrogatives. Les questions
resteront sans réponse:

> Mais comment le corps l'entend-il?
> C'est là le point. Je vois l'outil
> Obéir à la main; mais la main, qui la guide?
> Eh! qui guide les cieux et leur course rapide?
> (vv. 161-64)

Dans ce dernier vers s'est glissé une considération nouvelle. Le mystère s'est
fait plus épais, et la "certitude" scientifique va faire place à l'incertitude
métaphysique. Si l'on mesure à l'échelle cosmique les connaissances humaines, même celles qui nous sont fournies par la doctrine moderne, et "nouvelle" par excellence, on est forcé de sourire. Même Descartes, "qui tient
le milieu / entre l'homme et l'esprit," n'en sait sur ce chapitre pas plus
qu'un autre:

> Quelque ange est attaché peut-être à ces grands corps.
> Un esprit vit en nous, et meut tous nos ressorts;
> L'impression se fait: le moyen, je l'ignore:
> On ne l'apprend qu'au sein de la Divinité;
> Et, s'il faut en parler avec sincérité,
> Descartes l'ignorait encore.
> Nous et lui là-dessus nous sommes tous égaux.
> (vv. 165-71)

Attaquer la doctrine cartésienne amène La Fontaine à une position qui
pourrait être suspecte. En effet, mettre en doute l'explication purement
mécaniste de Descartes, c'est peut-être laisser la place à une théorie animiste
et même, qui sait, à une doctrine panthéiste. L'orthodoxie de Descartes,
sur ce point au moins, le met à l'abri de tout soupçon de paganisme. La
Fontaine n'est-il pas en danger? Il conclut rapidement et revient à l'orthodoxie (scientifique et, surtout, religieuse). Pourtant ces quelques vers
laissent percer ses hésitations:

> Ce que je sais, Iris, c'est qu'en ces animaux
> Dont je viens de citer l'exemple,

> Cet esprit n'agit pas: l'homme seul est son temple.
> Aussi faut-il donner à l'animal un point,
> Que la plante, après tout, n'a point:
> Cependant la plante respire.
>
> (vv. 171-76)

Et il ajoute, comme pour lui-même: "Mais que répondra-t-on à ce que je vais dire?" "Ce que je vais dire," c'est la fable que nous connaissons sous le nom des "Deux Rats, le renard et l'œuf." Or, dans cette fable, il ne va pas seulement être question d'intelligence, mais de véritable "ingéniosité," c'est-à-dire d' "invention."[9] L'invention se situe hors de la mémoire et donc hors de l'habitude, elle ne peut s'expliquer que par le raisonnement. Les rats vont créer un moyen de transport, ils vont ainsi improviser un *outil*. Or, les recherches les plus récentes du "behaviorisme" animal étudient la création d'outils chez les animaux dans la mesure où ce phénomène vient tout de suite après celui du langage articulé et complexe, dans l'évaluation de l'intelligence animale. L'exemple choisi par La Fontaine nous semble ainsi troublant. Malgré la forme un peu comique du récit (c'est celui qui se rapproche le plus d'une fable traditionnelle), il pose la question la plus sérieuse, amène la conclusion catégorique: "Qu'on m'aille soutenir après un tel récit, / Que les bêtes n'ont point d'esprit" (vv. 198-99).

Dans la deuxième partie du "Discours" (vv. 199-237), La Fontaine reprend directement la parole et va proposer (mais au conditionnel) l'esquisse d'une théorie explicative. Il entre beaucoup de convention et même d'orthodoxie dans cette théorie. Mais le langage est nuancé et subtil. Là où le début du "Discours" semblait résolument prosaïque (dialogue, langage familier, idées simplifiées), cette fin est tout en images. La langue en est souvent élevée, et la syntaxe recherchée. Le dialogue du début s'exprimait dans une versification volontairement disloquée et parfois chaotique; le monologue de la fin utilise toutes les ressources du vers libre. Ce qui reste constant, ce sont les thèmes: multiplicité et mouvement; quintessence et nuance, degrés, et niveaux. Par exemple:

> J'attribuerais à l'animal,
> Non point une raison selon notre manière,
> Mais beaucoup plus aussi qu'un aveugle ressort:
> Je subtiliserais un morceau de matière,
> Que l'on ne pourrait plus concevoir sans effort,
> Quintessence d'atome, extrait de la lumière,
> Je ne sais quoi plus vif et plus mobile encor
> Que le feu.
>
> (vv. 204-11)

Plus loin, il s'agit de dédoublement:

Nous aurions un double trésor:
L'un, cette âme, pareille en tous tant que nous sommes,
Sages, fous, enfants, idiots,
Hôtes de l'univers sous le nom d'animaux;
L'autre, encore une autre âme, entre nous et les anges
Commune en un certain degré.

(vv. 220-25)

Les catégories cartésiennes disparaissent, ou tout au moins deviennent moins rigides, les notions de temps et d'espace se font moins nettes:

Et ce trésor à part créé
Suivrait parmi les airs les célestes phalanges,
Entrerait dans un point sans en être pressé,
Ne finirait jamais, quoique ayant commencé.

(vv. 226-69)

L'avant dernière image du poème évoque "une tendre et faible lumière" qui "percerait" (nous sommes toujours au conditionnel) "les ténèbres de la matière." Mais la dernière impression est moins lumineuse; elle rappelle les ténèbres qui enveloppent "L'autre âme imparfaite et grossière." Le premier mot du poème était "Iris," par conséquent feu, flamme, lumière, intelligence, raison; le dernier mot du poème résonne comme un sombre écho.

Quant aux illustrations qui viennent s'insérer dans le débat philosophique, il s'agit de cinq textes; les quatre premiers se suivent de près, le cinquième est séparé et forme comme une articulation entre la deuxième partie de l'argument et la dernière. Dans le cas des quatre premiers textes on ne peut parler de "fable"; il n'y a ni titres, ni personnages à proprement parler, ni intrigue dramatique. Il s'agit d'exemples, tirés de la nature, présentés comme vrais, et nous y voyons agir les animaux en tant qu'animaux. Le paradoxe est que ces véritables animaux (tels que nous pouvons les observer autour de nous) n'ont aucune des caractéristiques anthropomorphiques que l'on retrouve dans la plupart des fables, et pourtant la vérité implicite est qu'ils agissent (nous les voyons de loin, sans les entendre, ce ne sont pas des "personnages") de manière rationnelle et par conséquent humaine. Une progression ironique ordonne ces récits.

Dans le premier exemple, La Fontaine explique que parfois, quand un vieux cerf, plein d'expérience, est pourchassé par les chasseurs, il emprunte le sentier d'un cerf plus jeune que lui, brouillant ainsi les traces en les multipliant. Le monde où se situe le récit est celui de la forêt, le "personnage" est le vieux cerf, alors que l'homme est un envahisseur anonyme et brutal; on n'entend que ses bruits lointains jusqu'au moment où il vient porter la violence et la mort au cœur même du monde naturel. L'homme est ici un mécanisme implacable et insensible qui détruit tout sans même comprendre la portée de son geste. C'est le cerf qui, devant l'animal vicieux qu'est le chasseur, est obligé de trouver "cent stratagèmes." C'est lui, donc, dont la seule intelligence et le seul raisonnement peuvent le protéger de la bestialité humaine:

Cependant, quand aux bois
Le bruit des cors, celui des voix,
N'a donné nul relâche à la fuyante proie,
Qu'en vain elle a mis ses efforts
A confondre et brouiller la voie,
L'animal chargé d'ans, vieux cerf, et de dix cors,
En suppose un plus jeune, et l'oblige par force
A présenter aux chiens une nouvelle amorce.
Que de raisonnements pour conserver ses jours!
Le retour sur ses pas, les malices, les tours,
     Et le change, et cent stratagèmes
Dignes des plus grands chefs, dignes d'un meilleur sort!
On le déchire après sa mort:
Ce sont tous ses honneurs suprêmes.

(vv. 68-81)

Dans le deuxième exemple, il s'agit encore de chasse, et les forces sont encore plus inégales. D'un côté chasseur et chien, de l'autre une perdrix et ses petits. Nous sommes en terrain découvert où la perdrix est vulnérable, d'autant plus qu'elle doit s'occuper de ses petits. Encore une fois c'est l'homme qui représente la force brute, et l'animal dont la seule ressource est l'intelligence. La perdrix feint d'être blessée (détournant ainsi le danger de ses petits); à la dernière minute elle "prend sa volée" et s'échappe. Ultime ironie, c'est l'homme qui est "confus" (parce que sa fameuse supériorité intellectuelle a été mise en question) et c'est la perdrix qui se donne le luxe, purement psychologique et spirituel, de rire:

Quand la Perdrix
Voit ses petits
En danger, et n'ayant qu'une plume nouvelle
Qui ne peut fuir encor par les airs le trépas,
Elle fait la blessée, et va, traînant de l'aile,
Attirant le Chasseur et le Chien sur ses pas,
Détourne le danger, sauve ainsi sa famille;
Et puis quand le Chasseur croit que son Chien la pille,
Elle lui dit adieu, prend sa volée et rit
De l'Homme, qui, confus, des yeux en vain la suit.

(vv. 83-91)

Nous avons pu observer chez la perdrix, outre l'esprit d'invention qui va jusqu'au théâtral, un instinct protecteur et familial. Comme pour le cerf, dont l'intelligence se double de noblesse, l'intelligence de la perdrix est

rehaussée par un sentiment de devoir et d'abnégation. Le récit suivant met
en scène des castors, et nous fait faire un pas de plus dans la conception
du monde animal. La leçon commence par une ironie cinglante envers les
hommes:

> Non loin du Nord, il est un monde
> Où l'on sait que les habitants
> Vivent, ainsi qu'aux premiers temps,
> Dans une ignorance profonde:
> Je parle des humains; car, quant aux animaux,
> Ils y construisent des travaux
> Qui des torrents grossis arrêtent le ravage
> Et font communiquer l'un et l'autre rivage.
>
> (vv. 92-99)

Les animaux ont développé une technique précise et rationnelle pour construire digues et ponts. Cette technique est hors de portée pour les hommes
de ces mêmes contrées. Non seulement sont-ils incapables d'inventer, mais
ils n'ont pas même le don d'observation qui leur permettrait de *copier* la
réussite des animaux!

> Ils savent en hiver élever leurs maisons,
> Passent les étangs sur des ponts,
> Fruit de leur art, savant ouvrage;
> Et nos pareils ont beau le voir,
> Jusqu'à présent tout leur savoir
> Est de passer l'onde à la nage.
>
> (vv. 108-13)

Le monde est à l'envers; les animaux raisonnent, et les hommes en sont
réduits à compter uniquement sur leur instinct et leur force physique.
Entre les deux passages que nous venons de citer, où l'industrie et le savoir
des castors sont mis en relief, se situe un passage où La Fontaine pousse
encore plus avant le paradoxe:

> Chaque castor agit: commune en est la tâche;
> Le vieux y fait marcher le jeune sans relâche;
> Maint maître d'œuvre y court, et tient haut le bâton.
> La république de Platon
> Ne serait rien que l'apprentie
> De cette famille amphibie.
>
> (vv. 102-07)

Organisation, travail, ordre, discipline, voilà ce qui distingue les castors.
Fort bien. Mais ne percevons-nous pas ici quelque ironie? Quel est ce monde
idéal dans lequel "chaque castor agit" et où il règne une certaine fébrilité?
Est-ce vraiment un idéal pour le paresseux La Fontaine que cette société
dans laquelle "le vieux fait marcher le jeune," et ceci "sans relâche"? Vaut-il

la peine de vivre en pleine nature si l'on doit y retrouver les contraintes humaines: "Maint maître d'œuvre y court, et tient haut le bâton"? La république idéale pour La Fontaine est-elle, enfin, celle de Platon? Les poètes n'y avaient guère le beau rôle. Par un renversement vraiment comique, il semble que ces animaux soient devenus *trop* humains.

Si nous doutions de l'intention ironique, il suffit de considérer la progression des quatre exemples. Dans le premier nous trouvons le vieux cerf l'être solitaire et indépendent par excellence, dans le second nous apercevons un embryon de groupe social, la famille de la perdrix, dans le troisième c'est toute une société dont il s'agit, dont le moins que l'on puisse dire c'est qu'elle est organisée. Dans la dernière illustration, les "bobaques" entrent en scène. Tout ce que nous saurons de ces animaux c'est que ce sont

> Des animaux [qui] entre eux ont guerre de tout temps:
> Le sang qui se transmet des pères aux enfants
> En renouvelle la matière.
> Ces animaux, dit-il, sont germains du renard.
> Jamais la guerre avec tant d'art
> Ne s'est faite parmi les hommes,
> Non pas même au siècle où nous sommes.
> Corps de garde avancé, vedettes, espions,
> Embuscades, partis, et mille inventions
> D'une pernicieuse et maudite science,
> Fille du Styx, et mère des héros,
> Exercent de ces animaux
> Le bon sens et l'expérience.
>
> (vv. 123-35)

Voilà bien la suprême ironie de la nature. Le "bon sens et l'expérience" de ces animaux sont si extraordinaires, leur ressemblance avec les humains est si grande, qu'ils ont adopté et perfectionné l'ultime création du génie humain: l'art de la guerre. L'exemple est empoisonné. Nous aurions voulu applaudir à l'ingéniosité et à l'esprit de raisonnement de ces animaux, mais décidément ils sont allés trop loin; les voilà par trop "du siècle où nous sommes." Le cercle est fermé, l'homme que nous voyions dans le premier exemple, brutal et cruel, nous retrouvons sa navrante caricature chez les animaux qui ont fini le plus par lui ressembler. La *raison* de l'homme est ainsi doublement mise en doute.

La cinquième et dernière illustration ressemble davantage à une fable. Elle comporte un titre, des personnages—muets, il est vrai—et un développement dramatique. Il s'agit du stratagème inventé par les deux rats pour rapporter chez eux, sain et sauf, un œuf, et ceci en dépit du renard qui rôde. Pas plus de moralité ici que dans les autres exemples, sauf la conclusion qui suggère que les animaux "ont de l'esprit." En attendant, nous pouvons noter une nouvelle ironie de plus, celle-ci à l'égard du lecteur. On ne sait jamais, disons-nous, ce qui dans une fable va s'animer et devenir personnage. Revoyons le titre "Les Deux Rats, le renard et l'œuf." Peut-on imaginer un personnage plus "en puissance" qu'un œuf? Ultime caricature de l'homme, les rats, ces animaux si inventifs et intelligents, vont commettre la même erreur que les humains auxquels ils semblent avoir emprunté la raison. Ceux-ci ne voient, quand ils regardent les animaux, que des "machines"; les deux rats ne voient dans l'œuf fragile qu'ils transportent qu'un objet.

Le "Discours à Mme de la Sablière" fournit ainsi matière à réflexion. L'intelligence, l'instinct, les procédés de l'invention et de la création, les rapports infiniment complexes entre la matière et l'esprit, tout y trouve sa place. Cette vision nuancée semble plus large et plus flexible que la doctrine précise et mathématique de Descartes, aussi bien que les théories de Gassendi et même de son disciple Bernier. Les sens et l'intelligence, l'intuition et le raisonnement s'y mêlent et s'y correspondent, non pas comme des éléments séparés, et encore moins contradictoires, mais comme des aspects complémentaires de la connaissance humaine. Tout le long de cette œuvre, deux mondes se côtoyent et se superposent, celui de la connaissance scientifique et celui de la connaissance poétique. Comme chez Lucrèce, argument et vision se juxtaposent. Dans la mesure où La Fontaine est poète, c'est en définitive cette dernière voix qui va l'emporter. Ainsi, comme s'il voulait mieux marquer le passage d'une forme à l'autre, La Fontaine choisit au milieu de son œuvre de placer côte à côte deux échantillons des deux formes du discours humain, la prose et la poésie, et articule le poème autour de cette rencontre. La première partie (qui se présente sous forme d'apostrophe, puis de dialogue) se termine ainsi:

> Or vous savez, Iris, de certaine science,
> Que, quand la bête penserait,
> La bête ne réfléchirait
> Sur l'objet ni sur la pensée.
> Descartes va plus loin, et soutient nettement
> Qu'elle ne pense nullement.
> Vous n'êtes point embarrassée
> De la croire; ni moi.
>   (vv. 61-68)

A part la rime un peu forcée de "nettement" et "nullement," rien ici ne nous rappelle la prosodie. Aucun rythme, ou presque, ne sous-tend les vers; aucune harmonie (voyez "que/quand"). La syntaxe n'est pas des plus limpides, comme l'indique la ponctuation, elle disloque et aplatit la phrase comme le fait souvent la prose. Chaque vers comporte quelque lourdeur. Dans le premier, par exemple, "Or" et "Iris" sentent un peu la cheville. De même, le rythme du deuxième hémistiche est incertain dans la mesure où nous avons un accent secondaire, suivi d'une syllabe dans laquelle le e muet ne peut s'élider, suivi à son tour du compte double qu'il faut donner à "science" pour avoir douze syllabes. Autre exemple d'indifférence stylistique: au sixième vers, l'accumulation d'e muets qui doivent pourtant chacun constituer un pied: Qu'el / le / ne / pen / se / nul / le / ment.

L'enjambement de la fin (sans parler de la formule particulièrement parlée "ni moi") achève l'effet d'une conversation naturelle où la recherche élégante est absente. Voici le texte qui suit immédiatement:

> Cependant, quand au bois
> Le bruit des cors, celui des voix,
> N'a donné nul relâche à la fuyante proie,
> Qu'en vain elle a mis ses efforts
> A confondre et brouiller la voie,
> L'animal chargé d'ans, vieux cerf, et de dix cors,
> En suppose un plus jeune, et l'oblige par force
> A présenter aux chiens une nouvelle amorce.
> Que de raisonnements pour conserver ses jours!
> Le retour sur ses pas, les malices, les tours,
> Et le change, et cent stratagèmes
> Dignes des plus grands chefs, dignes d'un meilleur sort!
> On le déchire après sa mort:
> Ce sont tous ses honneurs suprêmes.
>
> (vv. 68-81)

Dès les premiers vers, la voix a changé. L'on sait à peine où commencer l'analyse tant les effets sont nombreux. Le rythme d'abord: le léger martèlement de "cependant quand au bois," hémistiche régulier (3/3), renforcé par la triade nasale, en, ant, and, et la série impressionnante de consonnes momentanées (occlusives) où les sourdes dominent, et labiales et dentales alternent (p, d, K, t, b); puis l'octosyllabe régulier rendu encore plus symétrique par la syntaxe ("le bruit des," "celui des") et l'écho sonore qui s'y retrouve (e, ui, é/e, ui, é); enfin, l'alexandrin qui prolonge le rythme régulier (3/3) dans le premier hémistiche ("n'a donné nul relâche"), mais change et accélère (4/2, "à la fuyante proie"). Elargissement progressif et régulier, donc (six pieds, huit pieds, douze pieds), avec un rythme essentiellement égal, sauf dans l'effet d'accélération de la fin. Cet effet est d'ailleurs renforcé par l'effacement presque total de toute coupure à l'hémistiche ("relâche à") où la syntaxe, aussi bien que l'élision, empêchent la moindre pause.

L'effet des occlusives du premier vers se prolonge dans le second, mais se transforme, car des consonnes continues (constrictives), spirantes et liquides, viennent s'intercaler dans la série des occlusives: l, b, d, k, S, l, d, v. Dans l'alexandrin le procédé de transformation est presque complet, il ne reste que deux occlusives stratégiquement situées (d et p) qui reprennent une dernière fois, comme amorti, le son principal du premier vers; par contre le premier hémistiche est dominé par les nasales (n, n, n), les liquides augmentent ("nu/ re/âche à /a . . . proie"), et, surtout, nous percevons pour la première fois les sons les plus continus (chuintantes et fricatives) de "relâche" et "fuyante." Le rythme bref et martelé du premier vers se transforme ainsi en un mouvement plus ample et plus rapide, comme la démarche régulière de la course du cerf se transforme en fuite effrénée.

Les nasales du premier vers et la répétition vocalique e, ui, é/e, ui, é, ces triades de voyelles claires (où dominent les aiguës i et u) se terminent toutes deux par de forts contrastes avec des voyelles graves (cors, proie). Ces deux sons annoncent l'alternance principale des rimes et allitérations qui vont dominer le reste du récit: "bois," "voix," "proie," "efforts," "voie," "cors," "force," "amorce," "sort," "mort." Une autre construction vocalique, au milieu de l'alexandrin, est particulièrement harmonieuse: "nul relâche à la fuyante." Quelle insistance, aussi, dans le retour des rimes. D'abord, "bois," qui fait écho au "moi" du vers précédent et relie les deux parties,[10] et "voix" et leurs équivalents féminins "proie," "voie." La série dramatique de "cors" (au milieu de l'octosyllabe), puis "efforts," "cors" (à nouveau), "sort" et "mort." Un même son établit l'unité dramatique puisque ces cors que nous entendons au début vont justement être un signal de mort. La structure dramatique, chasse, fuite, efforts, stratagèmes, mort, ressemble à un schéma tragique, d'autant plus que les lieux (bois mystérieux), la menace qui y règne (voix et cors à distance et, d'abord, invisibles) ont un pouvoir de suggestion tel qu'on retrouve ces mêmes éléments de La Chanson de Roland à Hugo et de Vigny à Verlaine et Apollinaire, à travers toute l'histoire de la poésie française.

Deux derniers éléments: l'articulation entre la fin du dialogue philosophique et prosaïque et le début de l'illustration, est assurée par le mot "cependant." Ce mot a une double valeur dans l'usage courant. Mot de logique et de discussion ("pourtant"), il annonce qu'il s'agit d'un argument et va opposer une vision révélatrice aux conclusions dogmatiques de Descartes. Mais c'est aussi une expression temporelle ("pendant ce temps"), et nous ne pouvons éviter l'impression qu'au cours de la discussion philosophique, ailleurs, au fond des bois, un drame est en train de se dérouler. Continuant notre lecture nous nous apercevrons qu'il s'agit en fait d'un exemple a-temporel, d'une observation répétée, mais l'ambiguïté entre le présent qui exprime une vérité éternelle et le présent dramatique qui décrit une action unique et immédiate, n'est pas complètement dissipée.

De même, la fermeté du raisonnement logique qui précède l'illustration fait place à une description plus incertaine (sons distants, présences invisibles, bois profonds, détours sans fin, récit tronqué). Cette chasse à travers bois d'une créature à peine entrevue et qui semble insaisissable, cette "fuyante proie," nous rappelle le "O Muse, fuyante proie . . . ," qui est, comme l'a si bien montré Odette de Mourgues, le cri d'extase et de désespoir du poète.[11] De fait, lorsqu'on relit les derniers vers du dialogue, puis, sans s'arrêter, les premiers vers de l'illustration, l'on peut croire assister à la naissance même de la poésie:

> Or vous savez, Iris, de certaine science,
> Que, quand la bête penserait,
> La bête ne réfléchirait
> Sur l'objet ni sur la pensée.
> Descartes va plus loin, et soutient nettement
> Qu'elle ne pense nullement.
> Vous n'êtes point embarrassée
> De le croire; ni moi.

> Cependant, quand au bois
> Le bruit des cors, celui des voix,
> N'a donné nul relâche à la fuyante proie,
> Qu'en vain elle a mis ses efforts
> A confondre et brouiller la voie,
> L'animal chargé d'ans, vieux cerf, et de dix cors,
> En suppose un plus jeune, et l'oblige par force
> A présenter aux chiens une nouvelle amorce.

NOTES

1. *Fables*, ed. G. Couton (Paris, 1962), VIII, 9, p. 215. Toutes nos références dans le texte se rapportent à cette édition.

2. En voici la version française tirée de Léon Herrmann, *Phèdre et ses fables* (Leiden, 1950), p. 241: "Jamais l'association avec un puissant n'est loyale. Cette fable atteste la vérité de ma proposition. La vache, la chèvre, et la brebis résignée à l'injustice furent les associées du lion dans les clairières. Après la capture d'un cerf au corps gigantesque, voici ce que dit le lion, une fois les parts faites: 'Moi je prends la première, parce que je me nomme le lion, la seconde me sera dévolue par vous à cause de ma force; puis, parce que j'ai plus de valeur, la troisième sera mienne; le mal accablera quiconque touchera à la quatrième.' Ainsi la proie tout entière fut emportée par la malhonnêteté d'un seul."

3. Esope est la source première de plus de la moitié des fables du premier volume (Livres I-VI), Phèdre serait à citer pour près d'un quart; par contre, à partir du Livre VII, Esope n'apparaît qu'épisodiquement comme source, et Phèdre disparaît presque complètement (moins d'une dizaine de fables des livres VII à XII).

4. Voici une liste approximative des animaux par importance et catégorie: renard (22), rat et souris (21), lion (15), âne (15), loup (15), chien (13), chat/chatte (12), singe (8). Viennent ensuite les ovins (11), la basse-cour (9), chevaux et mulets (7), les bovins (4). Plus de 25 oiseaux familiers (pie, alouette, corbeau, pigeon, etc.),

13 oiseaux de proie, quelques oiseaux exotiques (cygne, perroquet, paon, etc.). Toutes sortes d'animaux des bois (ours, belette, cerf, lapin, lièvre, écureuil, etc.). Un assez grand nombre d'insectes (araignée, cigale, fourmi, mouche, frelon, etc.), quelques créatures aquatiques (poisson, grenouille, tortue, écrevisse, huître). Enfin un dauphin, un léopard, deux éléphants, une gazelle et un chameau. Un livre fort utile aux fins de comparaison est celui d'Hélène Naïs, *Les Animaux dans la poésie française de la Renaissance* (Paris, 1961). En ce qui concerne les trois catégories que nous mentionnons, notons que 114 fables ne comportent que des personnages animaux, 78 ne mettent en scène que des humains, 44 portent sur la rencontre des hommes et des animaux. Quelques fables n'ont ni de personnages animaux ni de personnages humains. Le nombre de fables dans lesquelles ne paraissent que des humains augmente proportionnellement à partir du Livre VII.

5. Voir aussi "L'Ecolier, le pédant et le maître d'un jardin" (IX, 5, pp. 250-51).

6. De nombreux critiques ont traité la question des influences philosophiques qui pourraient éclairer ce "Discours." Ces opinions varient grandement et ont même donné lieu, à certaines époques, à des discussions suivies. Nous ne citerons que quelques auteurs: Henri Busson, "La Fontaine et l'âme des bêtes," *Revue d'Histoire Littéraire de la France*, 42 (1935) et 43 (1936); Ferdinand Gohin, *La Fontaine: Etudes et recherches* (Paris, 1937); René Jasinski, "Sur la philosophie de La Fontaine dans les Livres VII à XII des *Fables*," *Revue d'Histoire de la Philosophie*, 1 (1933) et 2 (1934).

7. IX, la fable, non numérotée, se situe après la fable 19, p. 266, vv. 13-14.

8. "De science certaine." La Fontaine insiste sur la notion de la certitude absolue et l'on flaire l'ironie. Plus haut il avait déjà dit "certaine philosophie" dans le sens anodin de "quelque": y avait-il déjà jeu de mot?

9. C'est ce que fait, fort justement, remarquer Georges Couton dans la n. 58 (p. 516) de son édition des fables.

10. Selon les éditions, on retrouve deux dispositions légèrement différentes: soit une séparation entre "De le croire; ni moi" et "Cependant, quand au bois," qui fait de chacun un vers de six pieds et insiste sur le changement de sujet (il paraît même un espace blanc entre ces deux vers), soit, au contraire, le texte reste ininterrompu, et "De le croire; ni moi. Cependant, quand au bois" forme un seul alexandrin.

11. Odette de Mourgues, *O Muse, fuyante proie . . . Essai sur la poésie de La Fontaine* (Paris, 1962).

Michel Jeanneret

Psyché de La Fontaine: La recherche d'un équilibre romanesque

1. Le roman, un genre littéraire?

Soit la définition suivante du genre littéraire: "classe de textes soumis à un ensemble de constantes structurales, stylistiques et thématiques." Le roman, on le sait, est une catégorie trop générale, trop peu formalisée, pour s'accommoder de telles déterminations. Parmi les différentes propriétés qui, en lui, échappent à la réduction du genre, je voudrais (pour préparer la suite de l'exposé) en retenir deux.

Lorsque, dans leur tableau des genres, les arts poétiques classiques[1] attribuent une case distincte à la tragédie et à la comédie, à l'épopée et à la satire, ils postulent que certains paramètres interdépendants—la condition des personnages, la nature de l'action, le niveau du style, tous plus ou moins "élevés"—fonctionnent comme des critères absolus. Sur ce point déjà, le roman apparaît irréductible. Il est bien sûr possible, pour satisfaire ces normes, de construire un modèle abstrait, en adoptant, par exemple, le canon qui est aujourd'hui le plus courant: le roman de type balzacien. On disposerait alors, par induction, de données suffisamment précises pour délimiter un genre: j'en retiens ici quelques-unes. Orientée vers l'analyse psychologique et sociale, l'intrigue obéit à une alternance de description et d'action. Elle se déroule, avec quelques écarts possibles, selon les lois ordinaires de la chronologie et de la logique, de manière à garantir la vraisemblance de l'histoire. Convié à pénétrer dans un monde qui lui est familier, le lecteur se prête au plaisir de l'illusion, d'autant plus que les indices de fabrication du récit ont été soigneusement gommés. Une seule voix, celle du narrateur omniscient, traverse le texte; elle camoufle la fiction, se porte garante de l'authenticité des événements et assure enfin, par la cohésion de son discours le maintien d'un niveau stylistique égal: style moyen, plus soucieux de précision que d'élégance, en conformité avec une vision du monde, elle aussi équilibrée, réaliste et pragmatique.

Ce paradigme, qui correspond à peu près à l'image du roman reçu aujourd'hui dans le public moyen, est assez différencié, c'est vrai, pour définir un genre. Mais le problème surgit dès lors que d'autres "romans" obéissent à des procédés radicalement différents. La continuité psychologique, temporelle ou stylistique peut se fissurer jusqu'à compromettre l'unité du récit. Les voix et les modes narratifs peuvent se multiplier, se télescoper, et la fiction, à force d'étaler ses ruses, interdire au lecteur toute velléité d'identification. C'est dire que le roman, oscillant entre deux pôles, est loin d'être homogène. Chacune des propriétés du modèle posé tout à l'heure peut s'inverser ou présenter une version plus ou moins altérée, de sorte que le jeu des variables, aux différents niveaux du récit, se déploie en une combinatoire virtuellement infinie. Depuis que le monde est monde et qu'on y raconte des histoires, le roman, bi-face, implique sa propre parodie, sa propre subversion. Le dispositif du récit réaliste peut bien nous paraître aujourd'hui revêtu d'une légitimité naturelle ou originelle; c'est un effet de culture que le passé plus lointain infirme. Il n'y a pas de modèle premier du roman, dont les variantes ne seraient que des avatars logiques ou des succédanés historiques. Le corpus de la littérature narrative amassé au cours des siècles ressemble à une nébuleuse dont le foyer central nous échappe et où toutes les mutations, tous les renversements, paraissent possibles. On ne fonde pas un genre sur un matériel en perpétuelle fusion.

A côté de l'*Iliade*, la *Batrachomyomachie*; d'*Amadis*, *Don Quichotte*; de *La Nouvelle Héloïse*, *Jacques le fataliste*: dans le sillage du roman affleure toujours un anti-roman, qui exploite toute la latitude qu'autorise, justement, l'absence de lois génériques. Après avoir établi la polarité de ces textes, je voudrais en souligner maintenant la radicale hétérogénéité, latente dans le roman "sérieux," patente dans le roman "comique," afin de dégager une seconde raison, complémentaire, de l'incompatibilité entre les restrictions inhérentes au genre, d'une part, et la liberté du roman, d'autre part. Le guide le plus sûr est ici Mikhaïl Bakhtine, dont l'étude sur la polyphonie dans le discours romanesque[2] apporte des arguments décisifs; je voudrais en rappeler l'essentiel.

L'idée que nous nous faisons d'une langue—un système unitaire et clos, dont les usagers respectent tous le même code—est une abstraction que dément la réalité vivante. Une situation linguistique concrète n'est jamais simple ni pure: elle procède de l'équilibre instable de toute espèce de langues particulières—jargons professionnels, maniérismes de classe, d'âge ou de monde, dialectes, idiotismes personnels, etc.—qui, dans chaque énoncé, se combinent et se stratifient selon un dosage imprévisible. La définition de la langue comme une structure homogène, fermée, ne correspond qu'à une vue de l'esprit, officielle et académique. Dans la pratique, le locuteur est confronté à une pluralité de langues possibles auxquelles sa parole, nécessairement hétérogène, s'alimente. La façade unie de l'institution dissimule à peine le multilinguisme effectif où nous sommes plongés. Or le roman, selon Bakhtine, se distingue des autres discours littéraires dans la mesure où justement il reproduit, sans chercher à le neutraliser, le foisonnement propre à la langue. Ouvert aux voix de la place publique, il reflète, dans son architecture, dans son style, l'épaisseur verbale, les tensions idiomatiques qui sous-tendent naturellement l'acte d'énonciation. Morcelé, composite, polyglotte, il se présente comme l'assemblage, plus ou moins stable, plus ou moins intégré, d'unités autonomes, prélevées sans restriction dans les multiples secteurs où s'étage ordinairement la langue.

Le contraste avec les autres types de discours littéraire est significatif. La poésie, prise dans des formes et un lexique stylisés, use d'un parler beaucoup plus homogène, où les forces centrifuges ont été canalisées vers un centre commun. Autant le roman, engagé dans le plurilinguisme de la vie quotidienne, cherche son équilibre entre la déconstruction et la reconstruction d'une cohésion problématique, autant la poésie relève d'un système unitaire et factice, où elle fonde la stabilité de ses structures et la régularité de son style. Contre les facteurs spontanés de diversification au travail dans la langue, les tentatives d'intégration, de nivellement, en effet, ne manquent pas. Bakhtine les attribue aux instances officielles (cour, salons, académies, etc.) qui, aux périodes de forte centralisation politique, édifient artificiellement un parler uniforme, socialement épuré, afin de l'imposer comme véhicule exclusif de la culture nationale. Intervention violente de l'idéologie dans le champ mobile et disparate de la langue: c'est là, dans la vulgate d'une société réduite au soliloque en vase clos, que s'alimenterait la littérature traditionnelle et monolingue—la poésie, par exemple —à laquelle le roman opposerait précisément sa vocation à la pluralité.

Encore joue-t-il sur d'autres registres que celui de la langue lorsqu'il déploie, parallèlement, la pluralité des références propres au discours littéraire. Qu'un texte soit toujours dans une relation d'échange ou de dialogue avec d'autres textes, implicitement présente en lui, c'est une loi générale sur laquelle il n'est pas nécessaire d'insister. Sauf pour souligner que le roman, contrairement aux genres qui camouflent leur dépendance intertextuelle, exhibe volontiers la diversité de ses matériaux scripturaires. Citations, paraphrase, allusions, plagiat, parodie, etc.: il répète, imite, transforme, juxtapose ostensiblement des morceaux empruntés, qu'il récrit et intègre tant bien que mal au contexte nouveau. Son bricolage ne se limite d'ailleurs pas à des échantillons de littérature narrative. Il opère des prélèvements dans d'autres types de discours, quelle que soit leur formalisation spécifique: genre épistolaire, traité savant, fragments poétiques, chronique historique, éloquence, dialogue théâtral, échange parlé, etc. Il n'y a pas de style spécialisé que le roman, dans sa structure protéiforme, ne puisse absorber. A la stratification naturelle de la langue se superpose ainsi l'apport de styles hétérogènes, déjà codés, sans renier leur différence, introduisent dans le récit autant d'idiomes insolites.

Le roman serait donc ce carrefour où toutes les voix en puissance dans la langue, dans la parole, dans le texte s'actualisent librement. Dans la bouche des personnages, sous la plume des narrateurs, partout où résonne, dans le texte, un autre texte, se déploie, sonore ou tamisée, une polyphonie sans limite. On l'a compris: l'auteur ne parle pas une langue propre; il orchestre, sans toujours voiler les dissonances, des tonalités particulières, il combine des fragments verbaux venus d'ailleurs. Il s'exprime indirectement, à travers les mots et les formes d'autrui, de sorte que tout énoncé renvoie à la fois à une instance externe et à son usager actuel, réduit à communiquer son message par voix interposées. L'acte du locuteur ressemble ici à une opération de greffe: il se superpose à un autre discours, il est, comme dit Bakhtine, dialogique et bivocal. Lire le texte du roman, ça n'est donc pas suivre le monologue personnel et continue d'un auteur qui en garantirait l'unité; c'est se livrer à une opération bien plus complexe, qui consiste à reconnaître, véhiculée par toute sorte de discours étrangers et sous-jacents, une parole qui se cherche dans le concert des voix ambiantes. Pas de texte sans un hors-texte virtuellement infini; pas d'auteur qui ne soit aussi un écho sonore.

Le roman comme discours polyglotte et composite? *La Princesse de Clèves*, multiforme? *Le Père Goriot*, dissonant? La thèse risque de paraître forcée. Les propositions qui précèdent exigent assurément une mise au point.

Parce qu'il a (presque) toujours échappé à la normalisation des arts poétiques, le roman dispose, dans la sélection et l'agencement de ses matériaux, d'une latitude énorme. Encore cette virtuelle disparité peut-elle être soit exhibée, soit au contraire neutralisée et masquée. Toute une tradition narrative, la veine comique, parodique, grotesque (qui n'a rien de second ni d'inférieur), se nourrit en parasite de langues et de styles hétérogènes: elle étale joyeusement son impureté. Une autre, en revanche, travaille à styliser, uniformiser, intégrer les éléments centrifuges, qui ne font plus qu'affleurer ou sont définitivement censurés. Contrairement à tout à l'heure, un auteur impose alors sa voix propre, égalise ses matériaux, ramène la bigarrure du concret à la continuité d'un discours abstrait et personnel. Roman monodique, plus noble, plus maîtrisé, qui s'efforce de ressembler à un genre littéraire canonique—et pourrait, à la limite, s'y laisser réduire.

Tel serait donc l'espace, vaste entre ses deux pôles, où s'inscrirait l'histoire du roman. Mais je voudrais maintenant vérifier ces thèses générales et limiter, en deux temps, le domaine de l'observation. Montrer d'abord (sans m'y attarder, tant cela est évident) que la littérature narrative, dans le XVIIe siècle français, obéit effectivement à la double vocation que nous avons définie. Etablir ensuite que *Psyché* de La Fontaine cherche à couvrir le champ du roman d'alpha à oméga, en réalisant, sans rien sacrifier, la synthèse de toutes ses possibilités, du multilingue au monologique.

2. Le roman au XVIIe siècle

Pour observer, dans toute son extension, l'éventail des variétés narratives en germe dans le roman, pas de meilleur terrain que le XVIIe siècle: la didactique littéraire y trouve un matériel aussi pédagogique que possible. Je n'ai pas ici l'ambition d'innover, mais de rappeler seulement les grandes orientations,[3] afin de prouver la pertinence des catégories générales qui précèdent et de poser le cadre où situer, plus tard, l'intervention de La Fontaine.

C'est bien connu: la tendance, jusque vers 1660, est aux structures composites et polyphoniques. Par gain de simplification, on distinguera deux écoles, où la libération des forces excentriques connaît une amplitude variable. Dans un premier ensemble, les romans comiques ou burlesques d'un Sorel, d'un Scarron, d'un Furetière, la diversité des matériaux et des styles se déploie avec ostentation. Le *Roman comique*, à cet égard, est exemplaire: les narrateurs se multiplient et déversent dans le récit, à des niveaux de langue très contrastés, toute sorte de voix singulières, du jargon provincial à la préciosité de salon, de la vulgarité du parler populaire au raffinement de la bienséance. Comme dans Rabelais et *Don Quichotte*, le roman est un microcosme où se croisent toutes les langues en suspension dans la langue et, réverbérés par la parodie, tous les styles ailleurs confinés à des genres particuliers. Faute d'une voix unificatrice, pas de structure close: prise en charge par différents locuteurs, l'histoire s'attarde à des digressions ou s'abandonne à la prolifération d'épisodes disproportionnés.

Le foisonnement des péripéties, le mouvement hasardeux d'une intrigue qui s'engage, et parfois s'égare, dans des voies latérales: c'est par là qu'un deuxième groupe, le roman sentimental (pastoral avec *L'Astrée*, héroïque chez Mlle de Scudéry), marque encore sa solidarité avec les formes ouvertes du récit polyphonique. Le mouvement fluvial, la libre circulation des matériaux sont plus sensibles que jamais. Reste pourtant que le style, ici, s'est considérablement nivelé. Le texte n'enregistre plus la diversité de la langue concrète: monopolisé par une voix soucieuse d'unité et d'élégance, il échappe aux décalages et à la fragmentation de la veine burlesque. Le dialogisme de la parodie, l'ambiguïté de l'intertexte sont neutralisés. A la place, un discours orné, délicat ou emphatique, se concentre sur l'analyse des sentiments; le lexique abstrait s'affine, la vraisemblance psychologique se conquiert dans les nuances d'une langue sélectionnée et sophistiquée.

La tendance monodique s'accuse, on le sait, dès 1660 et détermine, dans les techniques narratives, une radicale épuration. La coïncidence avec l'évolution socio-politique est frappante: le roman bannit le désordre et la pluralité tandis qu'un régime absolutiste et centralisé s'installe: il cultive l'homogénéité de la structure et du style au moment où la littérature, plus que jamais, s'écrit et se consomme dans un milieu clos, attentif au respect d'un code exclusif. Comment le roman suivrait-il sa pente polymorphe, lorsque la culture noble prétend parler une langue universelle et découvre dans la sobriété le comble du beau? Naguère stratifiée ou morcelée, la littérature s'étale désormais sur une ligne plane et sans surprise. Aux romans à tiroir succèdent des textes brefs, qui réduisent l'intrigue à une aventure simple, entre un petit nombre de personnages, sans digressions ni coups du théâtre. Surtout, l'action s'intériorise et, témoin *La Princesse de Clèves*, se répercute dans la pensée, dans la sensibilité; une même voix, calme, grave, presque anonyme, couvre le récit; la parole des personnages, les histoires que parfois ils se hasardent encore à raconter sont soigneusement intégrées: aucune dissonance n'altère l'harmonie d'une langue parfaitement uniforme.

Dans la mesure (étroite) où ils daignent s'intéresser à la littérature narrative, les théoriciens de l'âge classique renchérissent sur l'exigence d'unité. Ce qu'ils demandent au théâtre—une action dont toutes les parties soient nécessaires et organiquement liées en une structure close—ils l'attendent aussi du roman:

S'il est vray . . . que le Roman doit ressembler à un corps parfait, et estre composé de plusieurs parties différentes et proportionnées sous un seul chef, il s'ensuit que l'action principale, qui est comme le chef du Roman, doit estre unique et illustre en comparaison des autres; et que les actions subordonnées, qui sont comme les membres, doivent se rapporter à ce chef, luy céder en beauté et en dignité, l'orner, le soustenir, et l'accompagner avec dépendance: autrement ce sera un corps à plusieurs testes, monstrueux, et difforme.[4]

L'abus des digressions a conduit le roman héroïque à de telles excentricités que chaque épisode doit désormais remplir une fonction indispensable dans la logique de l'intrigue. Les fameux récits insérés de *La Princesse de Clèves*, pourtant conformes à la tonalité ambiante, apparaissent inutiles et sont condamnés.[5] L'exigence de continuité est si grande qu'une critique sans appel frappe les ruptures de style et les écarts dans la composition. L'espace de quelques décennies, le roman aura fait taire les voix qui l'animent et résorbé les tensions d'une forme en équilibre instable. Cette belle consistance, le XVIIIe siècle ne tardera pas à l'ébranler. Et La Fontaine, déjà, la jugeait trop artificielle pour lui sacrifier les jeux de la polyphonie.

3. "Un juste tempérament"

Les *Amours de Psyché et de Cupidon* s'ouvrent sur une Préface dont le début est pour nous d'une grande portée. "J'ai trouvé de plus grandes difficultés dans cet ouvrage qu'en aucun autre qui soit sorti de ma plume" (p. 123).[6] C'est que la prose narrative n'a pas de statut littéraire déterminé; elle peut prendre la forme de différents genres et exige une mise au point extrêmement délicate. Entre plusieurs styles possibles, comment trouver le plus convenable?

Je ne savais quel caractère choisir: celui de l'histoire est trop simple; celui du roman n'est pas encore assez orné; et celui du poème l'est plus qu'il ne faut. (p. 123)

Certaines matières occupent dans l'échelle des styles une position fixe—adéquation mécanique et bien commode: l'histoire, "narration des choses comme elles sont,"[7] cultive une langue sobre et s'en tient à l'expression littérale; le roman (entendez: le roman héroïque et galant d'avant 1660) adopte les compromis du style moyen; la poésie enfin se charge de figures et multiplie les ornements. Mais il est d'autres sujets, plus divers, qui ne se coulent pas automatiquement dans un moule préfabriqué:

Mes personnages me demandaient quelque chose de galant; leurs aventures, étant pleines de merveilleux en beaucoup d'endroits, me demandaient quelque chose d'héroïque et de relevé. (p. 123)

Situation inconfortable: La Fontaine trouve dans Apulée une matière toute faite, mais qui ne cadre pas avec les compartiments usuels du discours littéraire. Contre la taxinomie simpliste des théoriciens, il s'avise que son roman à lui est trop hétérogène pour coïncider avec un genre quelconque. Il faudra donc composer, tâtonner, trouver une formule mixte. Serait-il, sans le savoir, en train de raviver, en plein âge classique, la vocation polyphonique du roman? Pas vraiment, car il s'interdit de juxtaposer brutalement des styles étrangers l'un à l'autre: "l'uniformité de style est la règle la plus étroite que nous ayons" (p. 123). Conserver plusieurs voix, certes, mais à condition qu'elles soient soigneusement orchestrées:

> J'avais donc besoin d'un caractère nouveau, et qui fût mêlé de tous ceux-là: il me le fallait réduire dans un juste tempérament. J'ai cherché ce tempérament avec un grand soin. (p. 123)

Tempérament: le mot est d'autant plus intéressant que son emploi dans le champ de la théorie littéraire semble alors nouveau.[8] Il relève surtout du lexique médical: "Le meslange et l'harmonie des quatre simples qualités élémentaires," mais peut revêtir aussi une acception morale: "Adoucissement, voye moyenne qu'on trouve dans les affaires pour accorder des parties. . . . Quand nos passions sont trop violentes, il faut que la raison y apporte du tempérament."[9] L'analogie est claire: de même qu'en physiologie et en psychologie, la nature, spontanément multiple, appelle l'équilibrage de forces adverses, ainsi en littérature, un sujet normalement varié demande un style composite, dont les parties soient pondérées et fusionnées.

Encore le récit lui-même étend-il le projet de tempérament à bien autre chose que la simple intégration des styles. Pour en expérimenter l'alliage. La Fontaine convoque dans *Psyché* un matériel extrêmement varié, comme s'il voulait à la fois réveiller toutes les forces centrifuges latentes dans le roman et s'en assurer la maîtrise dans une structure homogène.[10] Ecrire un roman qui ne soit ni polyphonique ni monodique, ni baroque ni classique, mais les deux à la fois;[11] tel est le programme, qu'il nous faut maintenant parcourir.

4. Le brassage des voix

Loin de se concentrer seulement sur l'axe référentiel, *Psyché* tient simultanément un discours sur soi-même, se donne à voir dans son propre fonctionnement. Deux voix dialoguent dans le récit, l'une transitive, l'autre réflexive, déterminant une structure romanesque double et mobile: voilà La Fontaine qui s'oriente déjà vers la polyphonie. L'ambivalence est d'ailleurs multiforme. Par exemple: un narrateur raconte. Raconte l'histoire de Psyché, bien sûr, mais qui est elle-même une histoire déjà racontée, dans le roman d'Apulée, dans le discours du folklore et du mythe, dans la peinture, etc. Elle n'appartient pas en propre au récitant, mais relève d'origines collectives et s'inscrit dans la mémoire culturelle.[12] Sous-jacent au message du narrateur, nous lisons donc un autre texte, nous percevons d'autres voix; elles se superposent, s'écartent ou se confondent et, dans leur concert à multiples parties, brouillent l'univocité du récit, problématisent l'identité de l'auteur.

Le burlesque, dont la mode, parmi les écrivains comiques des générations antérieures, n'est pas un hasard, joue également sur la duplicité du discours et fournit à l'intertexte une de ses ruses les plus voyantes: deux enoncés dialoguent, l'un patent et caricatural, mais qui n'a de sens qu'en fonction d'un autre, latent et sérieux, nécessairement présent à la conscience du lecteur. La Fontaine ne manque pas cet effet, si nettement typé, de double registre: en faisant de Vénus une pimbêche et de l'Olympe, un salon de province, il exhibe l'ambiguïté de son texte, affranchi du modèle antique et pourtant enraciné en lui. Par delà cet exemple, on pourrait dresser un inventaire, virtuellement sans fin, des jeux de la parodie; les allusions littéraires nous mettent en porte-à-faux, des échos de lecture, plus ou moins dissimulés, nous donnent l'impression de lire plusieurs textes à la fois.

L'ironie, largement distribuée, produit le même type d'équivoque. Ici encore, deux voix s'impliquent mutuellement: l'une, explicite et trompeuse, qui en postule une autre, la bonne, laquelle pourtant n'existerait pas sans la première. Nous ne sommes plus transportés ici d'un texte à un autre: l'écho est à l'intérieur du même énoncé, qui se dédouble et altère ainsi l'uniformité du message.

Un autre procédé qui, à son tour, confirme l'affinité de *Psyché* avec le roman polyphonique, repose sur une ambiguïté du même genre. Lorsque le récit à la fois raconte et se raconte, parle du monde tout en analysant ses propres mécanismes, la lecture, comme tout à l'heure, perçoit deux discours simultanés. Elle suit le fil d'aventures merveilleuses, s'abandonne à la séduction du conteur, mais capte en même temps, du moins par endroits, une autre voix, plus secrète, qui s'interroge sur la production du texte et sa réception, s'exprime sur des questions d'esthétique et définit, sous le voile de l'histoire, le statut littéraire du récit lui-même. Le thème de la curiosité s'applique bien sûr à Psyché, mais pas moins au lecteur, dans sa relation à l'œuvre; les développements sur la beauté et la grâce ont bien sûr une fonction dans l'intrigue, mais se prêtent aussi à une projection en abîme, pour mieux saisir les choix stylistiques de l'auteur. Bref: que le texte comprenne en soi la référence à d'autres textes, avec lesquels il dialogue (comme je l'ai suggéré d'abord), ou qu'il s'étage lui-même sur plus d'un plan (comme je viens de le montrer), il reste que différentes voix se croisent, dans une structure polymorphe, dynamique et composite.

En optant pour un dispositif narratif à double niveaux, La Fontaine poursuit une expérience analogue. On le sait: deux narrateurs se succèdent, et confèrent à *Psyché* son architecture de récit emboîté. A un premier plan, une voix anonyme raconte la promenade de quatre amis à Versailles et décrit les merveilles récemment érigées dans le parc: strate supérieure, qui resurgira par intermittence et fonctionne comme cadre porteur. Car un second récit vient bientôt s'insérer dans le premier: c'est l'histoire de Psyché, telle que Poliphile, qui détient maintenant la parole, va la lire à ses camarades. Deux voix se relaient donc pour raconter. Mais elles ne resteront pas seules. Car les trois auditeurs interrompent çà et là le récitant pour exprimer leurs commentaires: eux aussi parlent, dans une terminologie bien sûr différente. Si l'on tient compte, enfin, du dialogue des personnages, autour de Psyché, on reconnaîtra que La Fontaine se plaît manifestement à multiplier les foyers linguistiques. Mettre en scène l'émission et la réception du récit, comme il choisit de le faire, c'est accroître le nombre des locuteurs et des langues: on ne s'étonne pas que le roman polyphonique fasse du procédé un large usage.

Deux mondes, ainsi, se côtoient: quatre beaux esprits, amateurs cultivés des années 1660, d'une part; la Grèce primitive ou plutôt le milieu sans âge du mythe et du merveilleux, d'autre part. Nous tenons là un nouveau facteur de diversité, puisqu'à chacune des sphères correspondent bien sûr des thèmes nettement contrastés. Au niveau des quatre amis, un débat sur l'esthétique littéraire, la description d'œuvres d'art, l'éloge du Souverain et des travaux de Versailles. Autour de Psyché, toutes les variations qu'on voudra sur la psychologie et la morale, un large éventail de passions, les deux pôles de l'amour, du narcissisme à la volupté partagée, le parcours initiatique de l'âme, de la damnation au salut, etc. Le récit a beau être bref, il multiplie les perspectives sémantiques. Comme pour jouer, il tâte d'un peu toutes les grandes idées alors dans l'air. Il ne vise pas à l'efficacité d'un message exclusif, mais témoigne plutôt, avec désinvolture, de la curiosité d'un esprit éclectique, qui prend son bien où il le trouve. Le profane et le sacré, l'immédiat et le merveilleux, le sérieux et le gratuit: La Fontaine prodigue les contrastes et ne se soucie guère d'unifier ses thèmes. Odette de Mourgues l'a déjà dit: il "brouille si bien les pistes que nous ne savons plus si cette œuvre ambiguë est un conte de fées, un roman psychologique ou un poème philosophique."[13]

Nous ne savons pas, au juste, ce que *Psyché* veut dire, parce que trop de choses, sans doute, y sont dites. Nous ne savons pas à quel genre l'assigner, parce que plusieurs genres s'y trouvent contaminés.[14] Et nous ne saurions décrire non plus le style de l'ensemble, parce que différentes voix s'y mêlent. Aux mutations thématiques correspondent des variations d'écriture, que le "tempérament" assourdit, sans pourtant les réduire au silence.

Sur la volonté de diversification stylistique, un indice, en tout cas, ne trompe pas: ce sont les poèmes qui, nombreux, rompent la continuité graphique et rythmique de la prose, pour y introduire une langue plus recherchée, plus découpée. Des poèmes qui d'ailleurs ne se ressemblent pas entre eux: des longues pièces en alexandrins à rimes plates jusqu'aux morceaux brefs, hétérométriques et irréguliers, le récit s'essaie à toute sorte de formules prosodiques, lesquelles, à leur tour, postulent des niveaux de style différents.[15] En choisissant, après bien d'autres, de faire alterner le vers et la prose, La Fontaine, par un signe fort, démontre l'aptitude du roman à se transformer et se réinventer à l'infini.

Sur un autre axe, les variations du pathétique et du badin, l'infiltration de la galanterie dans les épisodes les plus graves, le voisinage du sérieux et du ludique, tout cela entraîne de sensibles fluctuations de ton, comme si, une fois de plus, nous passions sans crier gare, d'un genre à l'autre, du tragique au comique. A cet égard aussi, La Fontaine explicite son intention avec netteté. Parmi les trois auditeurs à qui, dans la mise-en-scène du récit, Poliphile destine sa lecture, deux expriment des goûts contraires: Ariste plaide pour le plaisir des larmes et la noblesse de la compassion, tandis que Gélaste préfère le rire. Ils s'opposent, dans le grand débat central, en pesant les mérites respectifs de la tragédie et de la comédie. Pas de doute: ils représentent, inscrites en abîme, deux puissances du récit. Ils réduiraient volontiers la littérature à un genre spécifique, alors que Poliphile alias La Fontaine revendique justement pour son roman le droit d'être triste et gai, sublime et familier, c'est-à-dire impur et polyphonique.

5. Vers la monodie

Toute la différence est là: celui qui raconte, c'est Poliphile, qui "aimait toutes choses" (p. 127). Supposons un instant qu'il partage la narration avec ses camarades: des blocs de style disparate, l'un comique, l'autre pathétique, un troisième élégiaque, avec Acante, se heurteraient alors en une bigarrure discordante: comme dans la tradition comique, des voix centrifuges démembreraient le récit. Or La Fontaine, au contraire, instaure la parole totalisante de Poliphile; il délègue son pouvoir à un artiste du mixage, un équilibriste consommé, qui rassemble les forces adverses et en réalise la synthèse. Eclectique, disponible, il ne cherche pas à gommer l'hétérogénéité de ses matériaux; il ne renie pas la vocation polyphonique du roman. Mais, au nom des vertus modératrices du "tempérament," qu'il incarne, il travaille à réduire les écarts et à définir pour son récit une ligne continue. Il joue une partition à multiples portées, et en garantit l'harmonie.

Virtuose de l'intégration et de la fusion, Poliphile dispose, pour uniformiser son discours, de différentes méthodes. Je me contenterai de deux exemples. Psyché connaît des aventures palpitantes, des sentiments intenses, si bien que le récit aurait tôt fait de verser dans le pathétique ou le tragique. Pour inverser cette tendance, Poliphile n'économise ni galanteries ni badinages. Que l'héroïne soit livrée à la violence des passions, aux tourments de l'incertitude, cela n'est légitime qu'à condition que le lecteur, lui, rassuré par les clins d'œil du narrateur, garde sa sérénité. Du coup, un ton léger alterne avec la gravité de passages plus sombres. Dans le même but, Poliphile fait souvent usage de la prétérition ou de la réticence: il amorce un développement poignant ou sublime, mobilise l'arsenal des hyperboles, sollicite notre participation affective, pour s'interrompre soudain, capituler, dit-il, devant la difficulté du sujet et le laisser à moitié tu. D'une pirouette, il neutralise les excès et coupe court à la terreur. Rieurs et pleureurs, spécialistes de toute obédience, sont renvoyés dos à dos.

Mon deuxième exemple porte sur l'usage des vers, dont Poliphile, on l'a dit, parsème son récit. Signe de son ralliement à la polyphonie? Sans doute. Encore faudrait-il examiner de près la forme et le style des poèmes. Faute de pouvoir livrer ici le détail, j'indique la tendance. Quelques morceaux, c'est vrai, par la régularité de la prosodie et la densité des figures, assument entièrement la différence du langage poétique. D'autres, au contraire, s'ingénient à atténuer les indices de poéticité, de manière à poursuivre sans cassure le mouvement de la prose: l'asymétrie des mètres et la liberté des coupes intérieures perturbent la distribution harmonieuse du rythme; la rime, autre signe spécifique, est souvent disposée inégalement, et relativement pauvre; le style n'atteste pas toujours de recherche particulière; les thèmes sont parfois communs. Poliphile a beau dire qu'il recourt aux vers pour des causes exceptionnelles, il travaille manifestement à réduire l'écart. Il apporte d'ailleurs aux transitions un soin jaloux: si les poèmes vont à la rencontre de la prose en la mimant, la prose s'achemine vers eux en se poétisant. Des idiomes bien distincts se font face, mais quelque peu dégénérés!

A côté de Poliphile et de son discours uniforme, une autre voix parle: celle du narrateur premier. Nouvelle occasion, escamotée, de jouer sur le contraste des langues. D'un niveau à l'autre, le style n'accuse en effet aucun décalage sensible. Le ton que La Fontaine a adopté dès le début s'étend à toute la suite du récit. Un auteur unique, réduisant le bariolage multilingue de son matériel, assume la responsabilité de l'ensemble de son texte et en garantit l'homogénéité. Il feint de déléguer son pouvoir de narrateur à un personnage de la fiction, mais garde lui-même la parole. Le dispositif par excellence du roman polyphonique est resté en place, mais vidé de son contenu. Une ligne égale nivelle les dissonances: le "tempérament" a fait son travail.

Des divertissements de Versailles à l'initiation de Psyché, la continuité n'est pas seulement d'ordre stylistique. D'autres enchaînements contribuent à unifier le dissemblable, ménageant d'un palier à l'autre d'imperceptibles glissements.[16] Ainsi pour les lieux: du cadre de la narration au décor de l'histoire narrée, le dépaysement paraît total. A y regarder de près pourtant, les espaces communiquent. Pour entendre raconter la première moitié du récit, les amis s'installent dans la Grotte de Thétys; il leur suffira de regarder autour d'eux—et à nous d'imaginer le spectacle—pour entrer de plein-pied dans l'univers de Psyché. La grotte de Versailles est sombre et vouée aux voluptés nocturnes, comme celle où l'héroïne rencontre son amant; c'est un chef-d'œuvre de l'art, comme le palais merveilleux du dieu Amour; elle évoque les profondeurs sous-marines et annonce ainsi le cortège nautique de Vénus. Même liaison pour amorcer la deuxième partie: le palais enchanté vient de s'évanouir et Psyché va s'égarer dans une nature désolée—histoire d'errance que Poliphile lira dans un pavillon éphémère, destiné à être remplacé par "de plus durables" (p. 187).[17] Du coup la fiction, si lointaine et fantastique puisse-t-elle paraître, s'inscrit sans heurt dans le décor quotidien, comme un reflet de plus dans les bassins du parc.

Par delà les correspondances ponctuelles, Versailles et l'univers du mythe participent d'une même vision du monde. Sur les pas des quatre amis, pendant leur promenade, surgissent des dieux et des prodiges; par la grâce des statuaires, Apollon et toutes les merveilles de l'Olympe sont là, vivants, intégrés à l'espace familier. Il suffit d'une sortie à la campagne pour pénétrer, naturellement, dans le monde semi-divin du Roi-Soleil; Psyché et Cupidon pourraient se cacher au détour d'un bosquet. Du réel au surnaturel, par la médiation de l'art, le passage est donc imperceptible, d'autant plus que, par un mouvement inverse, l'univers du mythe se dégrade jusqu'à s'identifier à la sphère de tous les jours: avec ses dieux en goguette, ses paysages domestiques, sa féérie édulcorée, le merveilleux s'est mis à la portée du commun des mortels. Tandis que Versailles est devenu le séjour des dieux, la légende héroïque est descendue parmi les hommes: une même géographie homogène couvre l'ensemble du récit, tous règnes confondus.

Immergés dans l'espace ambigu du parc, les quatre amis subissent encore un autre conditionnement: c'est à leur rôle littéraire, comme producteur et récepteurs du récit, qu'ils s'initient sans le savoir. Les monuments de Versailles se donnent à lire comme une vaste allégorie, puisque le mythe d'Apollon, qu'ils représentent, renvoie en fait, par un système de parallèles flatteurs, au Roi-Soleil et à sa gloire. Les statues, les édifices et leur savante disposition forment un réseau de signes à double entente, avec des correspondances assez claires, cependant, pour autoriser la traduction du message chiffré, à la louange du Souverain. L'apparence dissimule des significations plus secrètes: cette méthode d'écriture ou de lecture, qu'ils acquièrent dans leur promenade, les amis pourront bientôt s'en servir, lorsqu'il s'agira pour eux d'extraire des aventures de Psyché le sens caché. Du texte allégorique inscrit dans le parc aux symboles de la destinée de l'âme dont Poliphile jalonne son discours, le même code parcourt l'ensemble du récit et assure, d'un plan à l'autre, une profonde continuité. Deux genres aussi opposés que possible—un reportage, un conte de fées—auraient pu se heurter avec éclat; ils fusionnent en fait dans une zone tempérée, où la circulation est fluide et les distances, à peine sensibles.

Il reste enfin, dans le matériel polyphonique que brasse La Fontaine, un dernier télescope possible, et soigneusement amorti. On l'a dit: Poliphile aurait pu exhiber le texte d'Apulée, ou tels témoignages de la tradition, du folklore, pour instaurer avec eux un dialogue et jouer de la différence des langues. Toute une documentation latente gît entre les lignes, mais si bien absorbée qu'elle est imperceptible. Pensons un instant au parti qu'auraient tiré un Rabelais, un Scarron, de ce bariolage intertextuel; La Fontaine, lui, a si bien digéré ses sources qu'il n'y paraît plus. Le triomphe de la monodie se répète d'ailleurs dans le dialogue du texte avec lui-même: il se dédouble entre un discours référentiel et un discours réflexif, nous le savons, et il y avait, ici encore, de quoi faire entendre maintes dissonances. Mais l'intégration, au contraire, est parfaite. Les images et les motifs dans lesquels le roman thématise son propre fonctionnement ne se détachent jamais de la cohérence de l'histoire. Les descriptions d'œuvres d'art, où se miroite le problème du style; le leitmotiv de la curiosité, qui renvoie aux silences du texte; l'épisode de Myrtis et Mégano, qui justifie une esthétique de la surprise et de l'agrément contre les canons d'une beauté trop régulière, tout cela introduit dans le récit une théorie du récit, mais si discrète, si solidaire de la fiction, que les deux voix se confondent.

6. "Tous vergers sont faits parcs" (p. 187)

Comme Psyché, qui s'entoure de miroirs où elle s'admire, le récit se penche sur soi et se regarde fonctionner. Discours sur l'art autant qu'allégorie de l'âme, il interroge, à travers ses propres structures, le statut et les mécanismes du roman. Les matériaux hétérogènes qu'il met en œuvre ne sont pas gratuits: il en éprouve la puissance centrifuge, et tente simultanément de les clôturer. Psyché est un texte réflexif et expérimental, qui transgresse les cloisons génériques, échappe aux fluctuations des modes littéraires—le baroque, le classique—afin d'assumer l'indétermination propre au roman: une forme vacante où les langues, les styles et les plans narratifs, plus ou moins émancipés, plus ou moins unifiés, se combinent en une série virtuellement infinie de modèles.

Et pourtant, rien de moins pédant, rien de plus gracieux et facile d'accès. Parmi les différentes manœuvres d'équilibrage auxquelles s'essaie

La Fontaine, la symbiose du discours théorique et du pur plaisir de l'histoire n'est pas la moindre. La dernière page du récit, à cet égard, est chargée de sens. Au terme de sa lecture, Poliphile a prononcé un hymne à la Volupté, ce qui est déjà tout un programme. Mais le mot de la fin revient à Acante, l'ami de la Nature. Il coupe court à un nouveau débat littéraire:

"Mais je vous prie de considérer ce gris de lin, ce couleur d'aurore, cet organé, et surtout ce pourpre, qui environnent le roi des astres." En effet, il y avait très longtemps que le soir ne s'était trouvé si beau. (p. 259)

Puis il complète de quelques vers l'évocation du soleil couchant:

Dans un nuage bigarré
Il se coucha cette soirée.
L'air était peint de cent couleurs:
Jamais parterre plein de fleurs
N'eut tant de sortes de nuances.
(p. 259)

Cet épilogue permet de situer dans sa juste lumière l'expérience narrative de *Psyché*. La bigarrure n'est pas une invention des romanciers: elle est inscrite dans la Nature. Le foisonnement des couleurs, la circulation dynamique des forces et des formes participent de l'épanouissement normal des énergies vitales. Le roman qui, affranchi de l'artificielle pureté des genres, conserve les vestiges de cette luxuriance ne fait que se ranger à la consigne des arts poétiques: imiter la Nature. Au nom de l'irréductible variété du soleil couchant, par fidélité au jaillissement et aux mutations de la vie, il est légitime que l'écriture mobilise et anime l'ensemble des possibles. Encore la Nature que le texte se donne pour modèle est-elle spontanément harmonieuse: le bariolage du ciel s'adoucit en délicates nuances, les fragments du paysage s'accordent au gré de justes proportions. Pour avoir tenté de capter, dans le champ de l'art, les traces de la Nature agissante et créatrice, *Natura naturans*, La Fontaine ne cherche pas moins à maîtriser les énergies qu'il a libérées, *Natura naturata*. Il dévoile à vif les puissances au travail dans le roman, mais leur impose une stabilité qui est la condition du plaisir; il exploite l'absence de lois génériques, mais définit sa propre règle, le "tempérament," pour conjurer l'anarchie des voix en liberté.

Cet équilibre de la vie et de l'art, de la force et de la forme, c'est précisément l'idéal que La Fontaine désigne dans le parc de Versailles: des figures saisies dans l'instant d'une métamorphose, mais qui sont de pierre; des jets d'eau qui fusent et ruissellent, mais contrôlés par la technique; des jardins qui se déploient, mais assujettis au discours de l'idéologie et de la culture. Musée végétal, nature artificielle où le récit, en un autre miroir, reproduit sa formule. Peut-être même, au-delà de *Psyché*, l'esthétique classique tout entière est-elle ici en jeu: non le triomphe unilatéral de l'art et de l'ordre sur le jaillissement de la Nature, mais l'intégration du multiple dans l'un, la conquête du spontané, de l'hétérogène, dans l'harmonie d'une œuvre totalisante. Equilibre suprême, que je n'aurais pas la sotte prétention d'expliquer aux lecteurs d'Odette de Mourgues!

NOTES

1. J'entends par là les traités du XVIe et du XVIIe siècles. Sur l'histoire de la notion de genre, voir G. Genette, *Introduction à l'architexte* (Paris, 1979).

2. "Du discours romanesque," dans Mikhaïl Bakhtine, *Esthétique et théorie du roman*, trad. D. Olivier (Paris, 1978).

3. Sur l'histoire du roman au XVIIe siècle, voir Henri Coulet, *Le Roman jusqu'à la Révolution*, 2 vols. (Paris, 1968). Sur la théorie, voir A. Pizzorusso, *La Poetica del Romanzo in Francia (1660-1685)* (Rome, 1962).

4. Huet, *Traité de l'origine du roman*, cité par A. Pizzorusso, pp. 27-28.

5. Parmi les pièces du débat de 1678, qu'on trouvera dans M. Laugaa, *Lectures de Mme de La Fayette* (Paris, 1971), voir surtout Valincour, *Lettres à Madame la Marquise * * * sur le sujet de "La Princesse de Clèves."*

6. La pagination, pour *Les Amours de Psyché et de Cupidon*, renvoie au t. II des *Oeuvres complètes*, Bibliothèque de la Pléiade (Paris, 1968).

7. Furetière, *Dictionnaire universel . . .* (La Haye et Rotterdam, 1690).

8. A ma connaissance, le premier dictionnaire qui l'atteste est celui de l'Académie, en 1798: *Tempéré* "est aussi un terme de Rhétorique. . . . Il désigne un certain degré mitoyen entre le genre simple et le genre sublime, et qui admet plus d'ornemens que le premier, et moins de mouvement que le second." En revanche, l'acception musicale est déjà enregistrée par Furetière.

9. Furetière, *Dictionaire universel.*

10. L'analyse interne de *Psyché* suffirait à établir que La Fontaine ne rejette pas complètement le modèle du grand roman héroïque ou pastoral. Selon la *Ballade* "Hier je mis, chez Chloris . . ." (Pléiade, II, pp. 585-86), il lit *L'Astrée, Polexandre, Le Grand Cyrus, Perceval le Gallois, Don Quichotte*, et bien d'autres.

11. P. Clarac, *La Fontaine* (Paris, 1959), note que "*Psyché* n'eut aucun succès" (p. 93). Serait-ce que le récit était alors anachronique et qu'il décevait à la fois les tenants du roman polyphonique et les avocats du récit classique?

12. Jean Rousset le dit bien: "Cette littérature ouvre sur une enfilade de littératures, elle fait de l'art avec de l'art et de la poésie avec de la poétique. Que de lectures et de souvenirs de lectures dans ces pages limpides . . ." ("*Psyché* ou le plaisir des larmes," dans *L'Intérieur et l'extérieur* [Paris, 1968], p. 115). Voir aussi "*Psyché* ou le génie de l'artifice," dans *Renaissance, maniérisme, baroque. Actes du XIe stage international de Tours* (Paris, 1972), pp. 179-86.

13. *O Muse, fuyante proie . . . Essai sur la poésie de la Fontaine* (Paris, 1962), p. 64.

14. K. Kupisz, "*Les Amours de Psyché et de Cupidon* de La Fontaine. Essai d'une étude générique," *Romanica Wratislaviensia*, 10 (1975), 5-35, consacre un

article intéressant à la diversité des genres dans *Psyché*: il diagnostique, au niveau de la forme, un "roman à tiroirs" (p. 18) et, au niveau du contenu, note le concours de "roman mythique, roman psychologique, roman d'amour, roman réaliste, roman philosophique, roman pédagogique" (p. 32), pour conclure que le récit se situe "à mi-chemin entre les trois genres littéraires distincts: le conte, le poème et le roman" (p. 34). Il opte pour le terme de "poème en prose" (p. 34).

15. "Poèmes épiques descriptifs, poèmes épiques narratifs proches de l'épopée, chanson, chanson-madrigal, sonnet, préface poétique, portrait en vers, élégie, ode, incantation poétique, temple, avis officiel, oracle, hymne, harangue en vers, rimes plates et rimes croisées, stances et strophe saphique, quatrain, huitains et distiques— que de genres littéraires et que de formes de vers, intercalés dans le texte de La Fontaine!" K. Kupisz, p. 17.

16. Leo Spitzer signale la même technique dans les *Fables*: "L'art de la transition chez La Fontaine," dans *Etudes de style*, trad. fr. (Paris, 1970), pp. 166-207.

17. Bâtiment provisoire, érigé pour une fête, qu'il s'agisse des *Plaisirs de l'île enchantée*, 1664 ou de la célébration de la Paix d'Aix-la-Chapelle, 1668.

Peter France

Equilibrium and Excess

Lov is infinitly Delightfull to its Object, and the more Violent the more glorious. It is infinitly High, Nothing can hurt it. And infinitly Great in all Extremes: of Beauty and Excellency. Excess is its true Moderation.[1]

So Traherne, writing of divine love. A far remove from Philinte's all too famous advice for human life, "La parfaite raison fuit toute extrémité, / Et veut que l'on soit sage avec sobriété," or its echo in Father Dominique Bouhours's *La Manière de bien penser*: "Tout ce qui est excessif est vicieux, jusqu'à la vertu, qui cesse d'estre vertu dés qu'elle va aux extrémitez."[2] The maxims of the *raisonneurs* may be good for ordinary living, but Traherne's praise of excess seems to me more true to the impulse which gives us not only religion but literature. For all the praise of balance and moderation which are so familiar to readers of French classical criticism, the reading of the great (and the not-so-great) works of classical literature bears out the central importance of extravagance in the poetry, drama and fiction of the time. Extravagant behavior, extravagant feeling and extravagant language may be subjected to irony or held in a stabilizing formal order, but it is they that provide the motive force. Fascination with the excessive is more potent than the pleasures of normality. It is the "salt of life" of which Erasmus had written in his great (and ambiguous) "praise" of extravagance—to be echoed two centuries later in that emblematic figure of folly and excess, *Rameau le neveu*.

This is perhaps a familiar notion—with its echoes of Nietzsche's model of tragedy or indeed of Gide's idea of classicism as "un romantisme dompté." It seems to me, however, that in discussions of classical French writing equilibrium and reason often overshadow excess and folly. The purpose of this essay is to look at two of the more obvious forms of extravagance and to ask how far they were accepted, tamed or moderated and what their place was in the practice of some French writers of the late seventeenth century.

I shall concentrate on verbal extravagance, but let me begin with extravagance of subject matter in its simplest and perhaps most vulnerable form: giants and ogres. It is not really possible to tell how widely people in seventeenth-century France believed in the existence, past or present, of such monstrous beings. Descriptions of the inhabitants of distant lands ("here be giants") may have encouraged such beliefs, and certainly there were plenty of respected written records of giants in former days. Alongside the long-lived patriarchs, the Old Testament spoke of "large-limbed Og" (in Milton's phrase) and of the great Goliath, "whose height was six cubits and a span." Much larger was Homer's Cyclops, and for all the current mockeries of Homer's fabulous matter (in Perrault's *Parallèles*, for instance), the Cyclops is seriously discussed by Bouhours in the *Manière de bien penser*. The discussion concerns not so much the probability of the giant's existence as the way in which Homer leads the listener or reader to accept such a figure. Bouhours is critical of a really extravagant writer "qui en parlant de la roche que le Cyclope lança contre le navire d'Ulysse, disoit que les chévres y paissoient" (p. 359). This strains credibility. By contrast Homer makes it relatively easy for us to go along with his improbable fiction:

Il ne dit pas tout d'un coup que Polyphême arracha le sommet d'une montagne: cela auroit paru peu digne de foy. Il dispose le lecteur par la description du Cyclope qu'il dépeint d'une taille énorme, et auquel il donne des forces égales à sa taille, en luy faisant porter le tronc d'un grand arbre pour massuë et fermer l'entrée de sa caverne avec une grosse roche . . . et enfin il ajoute que Néptune estoit son pere. Aprés toutes ces préparations, quand le Poéte vient à dire que Polyphême arracha le sommet d'une montagne, on ne trouve point son action trop étrange. Rien n'est ce semble impossible à un homme qui est fils du Dieu de la mer, et qui n'est pas fait comme les hommes ordinaires. (pp. 32-33)

Presumably Bouhours did not believe in the literal existence of Polyphemus any more than the rationalist critics of Homer. Neither, one imagines, did Turner when he painted Ulysses deriding Polyphemus and wreathed the gigantic figure of the Cyclops in mists which both aggrandize him and attenuate the plain, "factual" presentation that we find in the *Odyssey*. Bouhours knew as Racine (and indeed Perrault) did that the "ornements de la Fable . . . ajoutent extrêmement à la poésie" (Preface to *Phèdre*). "La Fable"—mythology, a tarnished accessory from the store cupboards of

classical culture, but also, still, a potent source of excitement.[3] The giant
is one figure from that land of the *merveilleux*, the larger-than-life, which
was mocked in such writings as Fontenelle's *De l'origine des fables*, but
continued to cast its spell over this society where opera and fairy tale,
metamorphosis and apotheosis were as strong an element as the literature
of good sense.

Literal belief in giants, in the late seventeenth century as today, was
probably left to children, but also perhaps to the common people, who
are so often assimilated to children or savages in the writings of the upper
classes. Whatever people actually believed, the stories of Gargantua (taken
from Rabelais or from the original *Cronicques*) continued to be published
in the *Bibliothèque bleue*, together with stories from the Charlemagne
cycle, where pagan giants such as Fierabras, the modern equivalent of
Goliath, defied the crusading armies.[4] Probably more important was the
oral tradition, including the popular stories which were to make with Perrault their decisive move into childrens' literature, though a children's literature meant for adults too.[5]

As a Modern, Perrault had mocked the silly fables of the Ancients
("quand on a douze ans passez peut-on prendre plaisir à de tels contes?"
he asks of the Polyphemus story),[6] but kept a modest place for the *merveilleux* in literature. Fable is admissible, but not necessarily ancient fable;
for instance, the popular notion of giants with seven-league boots is better
(because more easily conceivable) than the winged horses of the pagan
gods.[7] Certainly seven-league boots and ogres have their place in the *Contes
de ma mère loye*, and I do not think that their impact is destroyed by the
irony with which Perrault habitually surrounds them. Sometimes, it is true,
the ogre motif is simply a source of amusement, except for very small children. Thus in "Le Chat botté": "l'Ogre le reçut aussi civilement que le peut
un Ogre, et le fit reposer."[8]

In "Le Chat botté" the ogre has no particular ogre-like characteristics
and could easily be replaced by a normal human being. This is less true of
the ogress of "La Belle au bois dormant," who is eaten by her own collection of toads and snakes (like the tyrant whose death is reported by Thésée
in *Phèdre*, III, sc. 5). It is even less true of the ogre family in "Le Petit Pou-
cet." Here we are very close to the Cyclops, for the children in their wandering have strayed unwittingly into the den of an ogre "qui mange les
petits enfants." As in the *Odyssey*, there is some uncertainty about the size
of this creature; he seems to fit easily into a normal house, but he has his
seven-league boots and he eats a whole sheep for supper. (The same fluctu-
ation is visible in Gustave Doré's illustrations for the *Contes*, where the ogre
is about five times as tall as the children in one picture and much closer to

their size in the next.) In any case, he is a truly fearful ogre and the night scene in which he is tricked into killing his own daughters inspired one of Doré's most horrific drawings. But while laying on the horror with one hand, Perrault does all he can with the other to mitigate its effect with ironical asides, comic juxtapositions and a verse moral from which the superhuman is entirely excluded. The clash of excessive brutality and deflating humor is well seen in this brief passage:

Elle [l'ogresse] monta en haut, où elle fut bien surprise lorsqu'elle aperçut ses sept filles égorgées et nageant dans leur sang.
    Elle commença par s'évanouir (car c'est le premier expédient que trouvent presque toutes les femmes en pareilles rencontres).

Throughout the story there is this to-and-fro between the hyperbolic image which momentarily catches the imagination and the ironic remark which reassures the child and winks knowingly to the adult. At one moment we catch a striking glimpse of the ogre in action ("Ils virent l'Ogre qui allait de montagne en montagne, et qui traversait des rivières aussi aisément qu'il aurait fait le moindre ruisseau") and then we are brought back to a more ordinary reality ("car les bottes de sept lieues fatiguent fort leur homme").

Some critics (for instance, Bruno Bettelheim in *The Uses of Enchantment*) have objected to the sophisticated play which adulterates the original force of the old stories in Perrault's *Contes*. I should be more inclined to put the argument the other way round. Perrault knew that, as Bouhours puts it, "dès qu'on raille ou qu'on badine, on est en droit de tout dire" (*Manière de bien penser*, p. 36). By giving them a protective garb of irony, he was able to keep his fabulous figures alive and hand them on to subsequent readers, including Gustave Doré.

There is a great deal more to be said about the fabulous in classical culture, more than can be said here. Perrault's ogres are extreme examples of the exceptional, the larger-than-life, of which Thomas Hardy wrote, "The real, if unavowed, purpose of fiction is to give pleasure by gratifying the love of the uncommon in human experience."[9] More frequently in classical literature this taste was gratified by astonishing actions, excessive passions and outstanding heroes and heroines. It is true, of course, that critics of the time were ready enough to mock writers who made fools of themselves in their attempt to transcend the ordinary, and that there was a strong impulse to bring the apparently superhuman hero down to earth. As Pradon's Hippolyte puts it, "Quoiqu'au-dessus de nous, ils sont ce que nous sommes, / Et comme nous enfin les Héros sont des Hommes" (*Phèdre et Hippolyte*, I, sc. 1). These lines, coming in the context of a discussion of Thésée's improbable descent into the underworld, are an implied criticism of the "sublimity" of Racine (who allows his audience to believe in such extravagant fables if they wish). They are thus a reminder that Racine, like other "classical" writers, continues to deal in extremes, extreme greatness (Alexandre), extreme unhappiness (Tite and Bérénice), extreme passion (Phèdre). Excess is the chosen subject of tragedy and comedy alike.

The ogre, like the hero, may be thought of as a hyperbolic figure; Bouhours, in the *Manière de bien penser*, does not make any clear distinction between extravagance of material and extravagance of writing. Properly speaking, however, hyperbole is a figure of speech, technically a trope. It is often thought that in this sense it is uncharacteristic of classical French literature; indeed Gide picked out the opposite figure, litotes, as the essential feature of classical writing. This is misleading. Just as the *merveilleux* pulls against the probable, hyperbole expands the limits of plain speaking.

To many readers today, the very word is probably pejorative, and even the rhetorical theory of classical France was often somewhat reticent about this figure; a snobbish distaste for it is seen in Nicole's dictum in his short treatise on the epigram: "Cette figure est la ressource des petits esprits qui écrivent pour le bas peuple."[10] Quintilian defines it as "an elegant straining of the truth" (*decens veri superiectio*), which can consist either in saying more than is literally true, or in exaggerating through comparison and metaphor. He makes the expected proviso: "Although every hyperbole involves the incredible, it must not go too far in this direction, which provides the easiest road to extravagant affectation." Otherwise, however, hyperbole is welcomed; it is "a virtue, when the subject on which we have to speak is abnormal. For we are allowed to amplify, when the magnitude of the facts passes all words, and in such circumstances our language will be more effective if it goes beyond the truth than if it falls short of it."[11] This is a good account of one of the basic functions of hyperbole; the other one, mentioned by many theoreticians, is that it is the natural way of expressing and communicating strong feeling. And indeed, if one reflects a little, one realizes that hyperbole is one of the most indispensible figures of speech. To deny it would be to deny rhetoric.

To many rhetoricians hyperbole seemed particularly appropriate to poetry. Thus Bernard Lamy:

Les Poëtes veulent plaire, et surprendre par des choses extraordinaires et merveilleuses: ils ne peuvent arriver à ce but qu'ils se proposent, s'ils ne soûtiennent la grandeur des choses par la grandeur des paroles. Tout ce qu'ils disent étant extraordinaire, les expressions qui doivent égaler la dignité de la matiere, doivent être extraordinaires, et éloignées des expressions communes. Les Hyperboles et les Metaphores sont absolument necessaires dans la Poësie, l'usage ne fournissant point de termes assez forts.[12]

Boileau too, although he might create for himself the image of the plain speaker, knew—and was confirmed in his knowledge by Longinus—that hyperbole is essential in poetry and in the "sublime." He was conscious of the perils of grandiloquence and rarely ventured into hyperbole without putting up a guard of irony, but in theory at least he maintained the value of high poetic language against his opponents in the camp of the Moderns.[13] In his tenth *Epître* he writes of the belittling criticism which the true poet will have to meet:

> Et bientost vous verrés mille Auteurs pointilleux
> Piece à piece épluchant vos sons, et vos paroles,
> Interdire chez vous l'entrée aux hyperboles . . . .[14]

In the face of such opposition, hyperbole becomes almost the mark of a noble spirit.

Bouhours is particularly interesting on this subject. He is of his age in rejecting what is felt as the extravagance of former times, especially when it is also the extravagance of other nations. Exaggeration is the characteristic vice of the Spanish language; as against this and Italian "puerility," French is the language of unaffected adult discourse. Perhaps, as Charles V is reputed to have said, Spanish is the language for talking to God; Bouhours replies: "Accordons à l'Empereur . . . que leur langage est le langage des Dieux . . . le nôtre est le langage des hommes raisonnables."[15]

This remark comes from Bouhours's *Entretiens d'Ariste et d'Eugène*; his later work, *La Manière de bien penser*, is a more extended discussion of what the English would have called true and false wit. The book is a dialogue between Philanthe (Mr. Loveflower) and Eudoxe (Mr. Goodsense). The latter is of course Bouhours's mouthpiece and he finally convinces his interlocutor that the kinds of wit he admires are really false diamonds, all glitter and no solidity. In the course of this demonstration hyperbole is critically scrutinized. The first part of the third dialogue considers the vice of "excès de grandeur." Eudoxe's typical move is to say that a given expression may seem striking at first, but that when you look more closely you see that it has no firm base in truth. Thus with Brébeuf's translation of a passage where Lucan writes that Pompey

> Ou n'a point de sépulcre, ou gît dans l'univers:
> Tout ce qu'a mis son bras sous le pouvoir de Rome
> Est à peine un cercueil digne d'un si grand homme.

Bouhours comments: "Ces pensées ont un éclat qui frappe d'abord, et semblent mesme convainquantes à la première veuë: car c'est quelque chose de plus noble en apparence d'estre couvert du ciel que d'un marbre, et d'avoir le monde entier pour tombeau, qu'un petit espace de terre: mais ce n'est au fonds qu'une noblesse chimérique" (p. 339).

Since excess is never worthy of praise, "les pensées qui roulent sur l'hyperbole sont toutes fausses d'elles-mesmes, et ne méritent pas d'avoir place dans un ouvrage raisonnable." However, Bouhours immediately qualifies this: "à moins que l'hyperbole ne soit d'une espece particuliere, ou qu'on y mette des adoucissemens qui en temperent l'excès" (pp. 30-31). The first variety is like the lexicalized metaphor; there is nothing shocking about such familiar expressions as "C'est la vertu même," or even "Il va plus vite que le vent." But as soon as the hyperbole becomes noticeable it must be attenuated, either by some qualification such as "si j'ose parler ainsi" or better still by an ironical tone which makes it plain that it is to be taken as a figure. Thus the Italian Tesauro's qualifying "par che" ("it seems that") is not enough when he writes of fireworks: "Par che sagliano ad infiammar la sfera del fuoco; a fulminare i fulmini ed a gridar allarme contra le stelle." He should have put his tongue more obviously in his cheek: "S'il badinoit comme Voiture, on luy passeroit ses pensées toutes hardies, toutes fausses qu'elles sont" (p. 39). The urbane Voiture is Bouhours's ideal.

Nevertheless, for all their timidity, these are ways of letting hyperbole through the mesh of rational criticism. Bouhours is aware that hyperbole is sometimes necessary and quotes Quintilian to that effect. When the subject is great enough, "l'hyperbole la plus hardie est une perfection du discours" (p. 357). Although *La Manière de bien penser* tries to trace the limits beyond which hyperbole seems excessive, the sensible Eudoxe is not always censorious. He declares that "outre la solidité, on veut de la grandeur, de l'agrément et même de la délicatesse." "Le vrai" is not enough, one must also have "quelque chose d'extraordinaire qui frappe l'esprit" (p. 105). Moreover, the very use of dialogue allows Philanthe to express his love of the showy. He can be thought of as the representative of youthful taste, since at this time a love of verbal extravagance was thought of as the prerogative of the young,[16] a childish toy to be put away by those who want to be serious adults. Bouhours's book is a paradoxical showcase of false diamonds, which glitter briefly before being exposed for what they are.

What is more, many of the diamonds, which might seem false to a modern taste, turn out to be solid after all. This is particularly noticeable when he is discussing ways of praising great men, above all the King. The place in seventeenth-century French literature of eulogy (*laus*) is perhaps not sufficiently recognized today. It belonged to *epideictic* (or demonstrative) rhetoric, which was the subject of innumerable schoolroom exercises before occupying a great deal of space in adult poetry, prose and public speaking. In harangues of all kinds, in funeral orations, in history, in court poetry, in much religious poetry and love poetry, indeed in many of the long speeches of tragedy, there is the same impulse to praise and magnify. Among the set objects of praise, the Monarch occupied a privileged place. The problems of flattery were very familiar to Bouhours and his contemporaries. As he says, "c'est un grand art que de sçavoir bien loûër" (p. 266). This was a generation of writers who liked to think of themselves as returning to good sense after the excesses of the previous generation, but their society revolved around a king who had to be virtually deified and who probably did produce in many of his subjects the dazzlement of the *merveilleux*. In writing about Louis, if anywhere, hyperbole was surely in order, but how could this be reconciled with the demands of truth? I have discussed elsewhere the case of Boileau, whose attempts to resolve this dilemma are particularly fascinating.[17] In *La Manière de bien penser*, several interesting pages are devoted to the same problem; they show their author treading a tricky narrow path just this side of excess.

The tone is set by Eudoxe in the second dialogue, in a discussion of the "grandeur" which is one of the characteristics of a "pensée ingénieuse": "Mais c'est sur le Prince qui nous gouverne . . . que nos meilleurs Ecrivains ont pensé peut-être le plus noblement; comme si la hauteur du sujet avoit élévé leur génie" (p. 145). This "hauteur" is such that the panegyrist is freed from the bonds of moderation. Bouhours cites a series of "pensées" about the King, of which the following may serve as an example:

> Ton esprit que rien ne limite,
> Fait honneur à la Royauté:
> Et l'on ne voit que ton mérite
> Audessus de ta dignité.
>
> (p. 146)

This is "une pensée également juste et sublime" and Bouhours does not remark specifically on the hyperbole of the first line.

Later in his book, he returns to this question when he comes to discuss the vice of "enfleure." Many examples are given of hyperbolic eulogies which go beyond the limits of acceptability. One of the worst offenders is the Spaniard Gracián, whose praise of Alexander contains these words already mocked in the *Entretiens d'Ariste et d'Eugène*: "Grande fue el de Alexandro y el archicoraçón, pues cupo en un rincón del todo este mundo holgadamente, dexando lugar para otros seis." Eudoxe's comment is: "Avez-vous rien veû de plus recherché et de plus enflé!" Philanthe attempts a defense: although the "pensée" is "un peu hardie" and "un peu fanfaronne" it "marque bien un grand cœur que le monde entier ne pouvait remplir." But Eudoxe takes no pleasure in Gracián's exuberance and puts it down firmly: "Croyez-moy, cela est énorme, et ne sied point bien" (p. 328).

It is usually Spaniards or Italians who are condemned in this way. Bouhours is ingenious in defending French authors who have praised Louis XIV. Thus the idea that "nostre sage Monarque . . . dit en ses réponses plus de choses que de paroles" is justified (reasonably enough) on the grounds that "d'une parole on peut faire entendre plus d'une chose" (p. 251). The apparently paradoxical hyperbole is thus resolved into a sound thought, and this very resolution of apparent falsity into underlying truth is a potent source of pleasure, akin to the pleasures of metaphor and allegory as Bouhours understands them.

A slightly trickier case is provided by four lines on the crossing of the Rhine (that great source of panegyrics), which might remind an English reader of the story of King Canute:

> De tant de coups affreux la tempeste orageuse
> Tient un temps sur les eaux la fortune douteuse:
> Mais LOUIS d'un regard sçait bientost la fixer;
> Le destin à ses yeux n'oseroit balancer.

Philanthe says that these lines are quite as "hardis" as those of an Italian poet who has just been censured, but Eudoxe protests: "Ils ne sont point fanfarons; ils ne sont que forts, et ils ont une vraye noblesse qui les autorise." His argument is that the poet is not claiming that "les destins en général dépendent du Roy," but only the "destin de la guerre." He continues:

Comme le système de sa pensée est tout poétique, il a droit de mettre la Fortune en jeu; et comme la présence d'un Prince aussi magnanime que le nostre rend les soldats invincibles, il a pu dire poétiquement:

> Mais LOUIS d'un regard sçait bientost la fixer;
> Le destin à ses yeux n'oseroit balancer.

C'est comme s'il disoit: Dés-que LOUIS paroist, on est asseûré de la victoire. Y a-t-il quelque chose d'outré, et toute l'Europe n'a-t-elle pas esté témoin d'une vérité si surprenante? (pp. 368-70)

Of course, Bouhours, like his poet, is doing his bit of flattery here (notice his hyperbolic "invincibles"), but the essential point for our purposes is that, while doing his best to meet the demands of basic truthfulness, he is well aware of the virtues of exaggeration. Perhaps excessive moderation is a vice too.

Praising great men was one important field in which hyperbole retained its place in the age of Boileau. Another was religious writing, since here, in Traherne's words, to the believer "excess is . . . true moderation." And a third area, which accounts for a large part of what we now call literature, was the poetry and prose of love. Hyperbole is justified here not so much because the object of speech is (as they say) beyond praise, but because extravagant language seems the natural expression of strong passion. Bacon writes in his essay "Of Love" that "the speaking in perpetual hyperbole is comely in nothing but love,"[18] and in Renaissance love poetry there is a powerful tradition of exaggeration ("En sa beauté gît ma mort et ma vie"), and as a natural concomitant to it an apparently down-to-earth counter-tradition ("My mistress' eyes are nothing like the sun"), which may in its turn serve as a springboard for new flights of eloquence.

A great deal of classical French literature is devoted to excessive love of many different kinds. "A quel excès d'amour m'avez-vous amenée?" cries Bérénice, and her cry is taken up and repeated a hundred times over in the *Lettres portugaises*. This short and immensely successful work is almost entirely made up of a recital of mad, hopeless love, expressed throughout in vehement language which is frequently that of hyperbole. It may be an unusual production, but its success demonstrates the continuing appeal of excess to the seventeenth-century reader.

In love letters such as those of the supposed nun it is difficult to isolate particular examples of hyperbole, since the whole context is one of extravagant passion. This is clear from the very first sentence: "Considère, mon amour, jusqu'à quel excès tu as manqué de prévoyance"[19] (the word "excès" will recur like a leitmotif in each of the five letters). A few lines further on, there is what is unmistakeably a "straining of the truth":

Hélas! les miens [yeux] sont privés de la seule lumière qui les animait, il ne leur reste que des larmes, et je ne les ai employés à aucun usage qu'à pleurer sans cesse . . . .
(p. 39)

And even before this there is an inverted hyperbole (of a sort which can easily be matched in the eulogies of Louis XIV by Boileau and others), whereby the speaker proclaims that his subject beggars all description: "cette absence, à laquelle ma douleur, toute ingénieuse qu'elle est, ne peut donner un nom assez funeste" (p. 39). The words "toute ingénieuse qu'elle est" suggest the relationship between this passionate writing and the essential movement of epideictic eloquence; one might compare it with similar turns of phrase in a very different piece of writing, a "lettre pointue" of Cyrano de Bergerac: "Mais que diray-je de ce miroir fluide . . . et puis, quel autre chose pourrois-je ajouter à la description de cette Image enluminée . . .?"[20] In both cases there is a striving after the most striking formulation possible.

So even if it is difficult to say that this or that expression in the *Lettres portugaises* is a hyperbole, the writing works constantly to magnify the experience of unhappy love. This can be seen first of all in the concentration of strong words and phrases which are at the borders of hyperbole, words and phrases which are the staple of Racinian tragedy: "excès," "insupportable," "aveuglement," "insensé," "fureur," "violence," "tyranniser," "accabler," "déchirer," and constant references to death. Then there are the declarations of extravagant feeling: "Je vous ai destiné ma vie aussitôt que je vous ai vu," "je me flattais de sentir que je mourais d'amour," "je suis résolue à vous adorer toute ma vie," "je suis jalouse avec fureur de tout ce qui vous donne de la joie." Such extremity of emotion is preferred to everything else: "Pourriez-vous être content d'une passion moins ardente que la mienne? Vous trouverez, peut-être plus de beauté . . . mais vous ne trouverez jamais tant d'amour, et tout le reste n'est rien" (p. 41). "Tout le reste n'est rien"—the world well lost; throughout the letters there is the lack of "measure" of which the nun speaks: "j'irais, sans garder aucune mesure, vous chercher, vous suivre, et vous aimer par tout le monde" (ibid.).

It is true that the five letters are like the five acts of a tragedy, and the work is shaped to lead the final movement of repentance and apparent detachment, as in *Phèdre*:

> J'ai vécu longtemps dans un abandonnement et dans une idolâtrie qui me donne de l'horreur, et mon remords me persécute avec une rigueur insupportable, je sens vivement la honte des crimes que vous m'avez fait commettre. (p. 67)

But here too the language shows the same vehemence, and the very last sentence of the *Lettres* contains the revealing words: "je suis une folle de redire les mêmes choses si souvent." The interest of the work lies in this obsessive repetition which exceeds all measure. Indeed the excess is visible not only in the sentiments and the vocabulary, but in the rhetoric and the rhythm of the letters, the accumulation of questions and exclamations, the endless repetition of "je," the piling of clause on clause in what elsewhere would seem ill-formed sentences such as this one:

> Quoi! cette absence, à laquelle ma douleur, toute ingénieuse qu'elle est, ne peut donner un nom assez funeste, me privera donc pour toujours de regarder ces yeux dans lesquels je voyais tant d'amour, et qui me faisaient connaître des mouvements qui me comblaient de joie, qui me tenaient lieu de toutes choses, et qui enfin me suffisaient?

Such writing shocked the taste of at least one contemporary: Gabriel Guéret, in his *Promenade de Saint-Cloud* published in the same year as the *Lettres*, makes one of his interlocutors observe: "D'ailleurs, il n'y a pas même de style; la plupart des périodes y sont sans mesure; et ce que j'y trouve de plus ennuyeux, ce sont les continuelles répétitions, qui rebattent ce qui méritait à peine d'être dit une seule fois" (*Lettres portugaises*, p. xiii).

If, as seems almost certain, the *Lettres* were not the work of a Portuguese nun, but of Guilleragues, then we must take this hyperbolic style, with all its excesses, to be a successful imitation of the language of real emotion (successful, that is, in that it convinced innumerable readers of its authenticity). It is all the more remarkable to think of this book as the creation of the man whom Boileau addressed as an "esprit né pour la cour et maître en l'art de plaire," the ambassador who wrote elegant *Valentins*. Just as Perrault the rationalist let ogres and fairies loose upon the polite society of his time, so the composed Guilleragues found satisfaction in imagining himself in the skin of an unbalanced Portuguese nun—Portuguese, one presumes, because as Bouhours repeatedly says, the inhabitants of the Iberian peninsula are given to an extravagance which French good sense repudiates.

I have written here mainly of hyperbole and exaggeration. Extravagance takes other forms; it would be possible for instance to show the persistence of exuberant verbal display in such feasts of unreason as *Le Bourgeois Gentilhomme* and *Monsieur de Pourceaugnac*. My aim has not of course been to suggest an image of French classical literature as a surrealism before its time. Perrault and Guilleragues, Bouhours and Boileau, Racine and Molière did not see salvation in the excess of unreason. Characteristically, these are finally put in their place. Thésée says in the last speech of *Phèdre* "D'une action si noire / Que ne peut avec elle expirer la mémoire!" The impulse is to suppress the monstrous love of the queen, but this love (rather than the cautionary tale of Racine's preface) is what the play is all about. Similarly, in tales of giants, praise of the King or the depiction of love, the writers of Louis XIV's France knew the power of excess. Hyperbole was as essential to their art as litotes.

NOTES

1. Thomas Traherne, Century II, 52. I owe this quotation and many other insights to the excellent essay by Brian Vickers, "The *Songs and Sonnets* and the Rhetoric of Hyperbole," in *John Donne: Essays in Celebration*, ed. A.J. Smith (London, 1972).

2. D. Bouhours, *La Manière de bien penser dans les ouvrages d'esprit*, nouvelle édition (1715; rpt. Brighton: Sussex Reprints, 1971), p. 30. The first edition of this work dates from 1687.

3. See B. Beugnot, "Pour une poétique de l'allégorie classique" in *Critique et création littéraires en France au XVIIe siècle* (Paris, 1977), pp. 409-19.

4. See for instance R. Mandrou, *De la culture populaire en France aux 17e et 18e siècles* (Paris, 1964), pp. 216-20, and G. Bollème, *La Bibliothèque bleue* (Paris, 1971), pp. 189-98. For a perhaps extreme view of Rabelais's hyperbolic fiction see P. Nicole, *Traité de la vraie et de la fausse beauté dans les ouvrages d'esprit* (Paris, 1698), translated from the Latin original of 1659: "Comment donc se trouve-t-il des gens qui peuvent non seulement lire, mais qui ont encore assez de hardiesse pour approuver et pour louer même à l'excès les contes de Rabelais, remplis de tant d'hyperboles extravagants?" (p. 38).

5. On this subject see M. Soriano, *Les Contes de Perrault, culture savante et traditions populaires* (Paris, 1968).

6. Charles Perrault, *Parallèle des anciens et des modernes* (Paris, 1688-1697), III, 85.

7. *Parallèle*, III, 119-20. See also Boileau, *Réflexions critiques*, IV.

8. Perrault's *Contes* are quoted in the edition of G. Rouger (Paris, 1967).

9. Quoted in M. Allott, *Novelists on the Novel* (London-New York, 1959), p. 58.

10. Nicole, *Traité de la vraie et de la fausse beauté dans les ouvrages d'esprit*, p. 38.

11. Quintilian, *Institutio oratoria*, ed. H.E. Butler (London, 1920-22), III, 338-45.

12. B. Lamy, *La Rhétorique ou l'art de parler*, 4th ed. (1699; rpt. Brighton: Sussex Reprints, 1969), pp. 284-85.

13. See P. France, *Rhetoric and Truth in France: Descartes to Diderot* (Oxford, 1972), pp. 151-63.

14. Boileau, *Epitres*, ed. C.H. Boudhors, 3rd ed. (Paris, 1967), p. 58.

15. *Entretiens d'Ariste et d'Eugène* (1671), reprint ed. F. Brunot (Paris, 1962), p. 42.

16. See for instance Du Marsais, *Des tropes*, 3rd ed. (Paris, 1775): "L'hyperbole est ordinaire aux Orientaux. Les jeunes gens en font plus souvent usage que les personnes avancées en âge" (p. 149). Hyperbole is thus connected with foreigners, young people and, as we saw in the remarks of Nicole quoted above (p. 253), with the plebs.

17. France, *Rhetoric and Truth*, pp. 163-72.

18. See Vickers, "The *Songs and Sonnets* and Rhetoric of Hyperbole," p. 148.

19. *Lettres portugaises, Valentins et autres œuvres de Guilleragues*, eds. F. Deloffre and J. Rougeot (Paris, 1962), p. 39.

20. Cyrano de Bergerac, *Oeuvres complètes* ed. J. Prévot (Paris, 1977), p. 47.

Peter Bayley

The Art of the "pointe" in Bossuet

To come across the name of Bossuet, or of any preacher for that matter, in the company of poets and playwrights, will nowadays be less surprising for those who are familiar with the English Metaphysical tradition. If the efforts made by readers over the last eighty years to train their sensibilities and sharpen their minds to grapple with "wit," "the conceit," or "passionate ratiocination" were initially directed towards Donne's or Herbert's or Crashaw's poetry, it was not long before they were extended to embrace prose as well, and hence, inevitably, the metaphysical sermon. It is as a preacher that Lancelot Andrewes lays his primary claim to our consideration, and there are those for whom Donne's artistry in the pulpit is not less, though of a different kind, than in his verse. It is not so in France; nor was it once possible to appreciate Scève, or Sponde, or La Ceppède; and yet the belief that a comparison between the French and English traditions may illuminate both is one aspect of the achievement it is the purpose of this volume to celebrate. It may be as well, therefore, to begin with a direct parallel.

Donne and Bossuet both wrote sermons on death.[1] Donne's has acquired a romantic notoriety that perhaps derives less from its substance than from the circumstances in which it was preached, "stiled the Authors owne funeral Sermon" since he preached it only days before he died. Bossuet's, by contrast, is admired as a high point of French classicism. It is, says the preface to its latest popular edition, "le plus connu de Bossuet. Il le mérite par sa vigueur, ainsi que par sa parfaite unité."[2] The difference between the two texts is, at first sight, considerable: the stylistic difference between

Senecan and Ciceronian, Asiatic and Attic, between—to use the vogue-words of the seventeenth-century English pulpit—"witty" and "golden." Donne's first paragraph plunges into a general statement of a fact that everyone knows but that no one assumes to have connection with his subject or with his biblical text, "And unto God the Lord belong the issues of death," i.e. from death (Psalm 68, 2):

> Buildings stand by the benefit of their *foundations* that susteine and *support* them, and of their *butteresses* that comprehend and *embrace* them, and of their *contignations* that knit and *unite* them: the *foundations* suffer them not to *sinke*, the *butteresses* suffer them not to *swerve*, and the *contignation* and knitting suffers them not to *cleave*. The body of our building is in the former part of this verse . . . . (p. 230)

Only after the initial surprise of the solemn, precise, almost scholastic explanation of why buildings stand up does he make it clear that this is going to be a comparison and that we may expect it to be pressed and squeezed in ever more unlikely ways until it yields its message. We soon see, though, that the message is not entirely to be contained in the similitude. Donne quite quickly introduces a further notion, that the "issues of death" are in natural life often "entrances into life," and instances birth from the womb ("The *wombe* which should be the *house of life*, becomes *death* it selfe, if *God* leave us there," p. 232). In fact, the theme of house building announced in the bold beginning grows progressively fainter as the sermon develops, until its place in the argument becomes largely one of allusive decoration: "*In domo Patris*, says our blessed *Saviour*, speaking of *heaven*, *multae mansiones*, there are *many mansions*, divers and durable, so that if a man cannot possess a *martyrs* house . . . yet hee may have a Confessors" (p. 233); "yet he hath the *keys of death*, and hee can let me out at that dore" (p. 235); "Even those bodies that were *the temples of the holy Ghost*, come to this *dilapidation*, to ruin, to rubbidge, to dust" (p. 239). Eventually Donne dismisses it with a pun as he ends the first "point," or section, of his sermon and begins the second: "And so we pass unto our *second accommodation* of *these words* . . ." (p. 240). What stuns and gives the impression of wit in this first section is not, after the opening paragraph, the image of the building but the constant use of other images ("the worme is spread *under thee*, and the worme *covers thee*; There's the *Mats* and the *Carpets* that *lye under*, and there's the *State* and the *Canopye*, that *hangs over* the greatest of the sons of men," pp. 238-39), of alliteration ("bee mingled in his dust, with the dust of every high way, and of every dunghill, and swallowed in every puddle and pond," p. 239), or of erudite wordplay ("Mansions, the *word* [the word is *Nasang*] signifies but a *journey*, but a preparation," p. 234).

Beneath the brilliant surface texture of this part of "Death's Duell" there lies in fact a much more straightforward application of classical rhetorical techniques. The initial statement about buildings acts as a *captatio benevolentiae* because it appeals to and confirms the common experience, the common sense even, of the hearers. And before they are tempted to grow bored with it, the preacher has nimbly moved on to a second source of analogies—the cycle of human life from womb to grave—which is equally confirmed by common experience. This constant *confirmatio* is part of the forensic orator's armory; but Donne is careful to include a central element of tough theological argumentation. In the first part, it is about the hypostatic union of the divine and human natures in Christ and the parallel union of body and soul which make a man alive ("for the union of the *body* and *soule* makes the man, and he whose soule and body are separated by death, [as long as that state lasts] is properly no man," p. 236). One must beware of being blinded by Donne's verbal fireworks from seeing the solid architecture of his reasoning. He cheerfully upsets our sense of literary decorum (Evelyn Simpson speaks of the way in which, for him, "anything in heaven or earth could be used to illustrate anything else"),[3] but he never strays far from the paths of strict logical and theological rigor.

Bossuet's *avant-propos* seems, by contrast, the epitome of literary decorum and tact:

Me sera-t-il permis aujourd'hui d'ouvrir un tombeau devant la cour, et des yeux si délicats ne seront-ils point offensés par un objet si funèbre? Je ne pense pas, Messieurs, que des chrétiens doivent refuser d'assister à ce spectacle avec Jésus-Christ. (p. 262)

But this too is the classical *captatio benevolentiae*. Whereas Donne appeals to his hearers' experience of the physical world, Bossuet deals with their experience of the very medium he is working in: the sermon on death. There is no need, in 1662, to tell the Court what one finds inside a tomb; they have heard hundreds of sermons on the subject, and Bossuet knows it. A discreet reference will suffice.[4] Bossuet goes beyond a mere allusion to a tradition, however. He indulges his audience's understandable familiarity with the theme and thereby shows that he shares it; then he teases them about the refinement ("des yeux si délicats"); then he tells them outright that their reluctance is uncharitable and unchristian ("Je ne pense pas, Messieurs . . ."). Only when we have reached the end of the sermon, though, do we see the real twist in the tail: he has never actually intended to open a tomb before our eyes at all. What he proposes is a discussion of man's nature.

This, the real theme of the sermon, is introduced in the exordium and, once again, with an interesting direct address to the audience: "Vous serez peut-être étonnés que je vous adresse à la mort pour être instruits de ce que vous êtes" (p. 264), in which the word "étonnés" is less a reasonable representation of what might be going through our minds (he concedes that with "peut-être") than an exaggeration of it in order to highlight his paradox. The continuation of the sentence, apparently a merely routine oratorical repetition of the previous phrase, in fact sharpens it and defines it further as a paradox. It is the first example of what I mean by the *pointe* in Bossuet: "et vous croirez que ce n'est pas bien représenter l'homme, que de le montrer où il n'est plus" (ibid.). The remark could come, not from a sermon itself, but from a clever and worldly dismissal of the sermon by a critic in the audience.[5] Bossuet has anticipated the flippant witticism and used it to heighten curiosity as to what he may say next. (It turns out to be a rather dry piece of theorizing about "la nature d'un composé" never being so clearly manifest as "dans la dissolution de ses parties.") We may call this a *pointe*, but we should also note that it is the classical rhetorical figure of *concessio*.

A remark of this kind on Bossuet's part betrays a considerable consciousness of his genre, his audience, and the uses of language. More interesting still is to observe the way this consciousness itself is later to be incorporated into his argument. The chief idea around which he eventually organizes these reflections on death turns out, of course, to be that dual notion of time, based on Psalm 38, 6 (*Ecce mensurabiles posuisti dies meos, et substantia mea tanquam nihilum ante te*), which he had already explored in the *Oraison funèbre d'Yolande de Monterby* of 1655. Time can determine eternity and therefore contain acts of lasting value; time can also come to a stop with death and thereby reveal its apparent achievements to be wholly insubstantial or *vains*. There is no need to repeat here how Bossuet exploits the traditional perceptions of the *néant* which lies behind *paraître*, that life's a dream, the world's a stage, that outwardly stable human individuality is but a river flowing fast towards the anonymous ocean of dispersed atoms.

Donne, we might suppose, pushes these commonplaces to their limit in "Death's Duell." He, too, tries to go beyond a banal visualization of what happens in the grave, and he does it by choosing an accumulation of abstract nouns to probe beyond experience, to seize and clutch and penetrate the mystery of bodily decay and resurrection:

But for us that dye now and sleep in the state of the dead, we must al passe this *posthume* death, this *death* after *death*, nay this death after buriall, this *dissolution* after *dissolution*, this *death* of *corruption* and *putrifaction*, of *vermiculation* and *incinera-tion*, of *dissolution* and *dispersion* in and *from* the grave. (p. 238)

It is instructive to set beside this the central passage from Bossuet's sermon which, transposed into an interestingly different key,[6] he will use again in 1670 for the funeral oration of Henriette d'Angleterre:

Qu'est-ce que cent ans, qu'est-ce que mille ans, puisqu'un seul moment les efface? Multipliez vos jours, comme les cerfs, que la Fable ou l'histoire de la nature fait vivre durant tant de siècles; durez autant que ces grands chênes sous lesquels nos ancêtres se sont reposés, et qui donneront encore de l'ombre à notre postérité; entassez dans cet espace, qui paraît immense, honneurs, richesses, plaisirs: que vous profitera cet amas, puisque le dernier souffle de la mort, tout faible, tout languissant, abattra tout à coup cette vaine pompe avec la même facilité qu'un château de cartes, vain amuse-ment des enfants? Que vous servira d'avoir tant écrit dans ce livre, d'en avoir rempli toutes les pages de beaux caractères, puisque enfin une seule rature doit tout effacer? Encore une rature laisserait-elle quelques traces du moins d'elle-même; au lieu que ce dernier moment, qui effacera d'un seul trait toute votre vie, s'ira perdre lui-même, avec tout le reste, dans ce grand gouffre du néant. Il n'y aura plus sur la terre aucuns vestiges de ce que nous sommes: la chair changera de nature; le corps prendra un autre nom; *même celui de cadavre ne lui demeurera pas longtemps: il deviendra*, dit Tertullien, *un je ne sais quoi qui n'a plus de nom dans aucune langue*: tant il est vrai que tout meurt en lui, jusqu'à ces termes funèbres par lesquels on exprime ses mal-heureux restes. (pp. 267-68)

There is the same probing, but Donne's odd, latinate, Abstract Entities are here replaced by a different Latin tradition—the urgent rhetorical questions addressed directly to the audience, the inexorable tidal onrush of their swelling and falling Ciceronian periods. Bossuet proceeds, in the approved manner for disposing the *loci* of *inventio*, from the general to the particu-lar, beginning logically with the notion of time taken up from the psalm he has just quoted. The tradition of the analogy drawn from Pliny and hal-lowed by the preachers' reference books is duly given its place ("les cerfs"), as is the reassuringly trite image of the age-old oaks; the transition to the playthings with which mankind foolishly amuses its allotted span is accom-panied by the warning signal of the parenthesis "qui paraît immense"; then comes the actual experience of hearing people die, with their last faint whisper; and finally the whole illusion is swept aside with an arrest-ingly original image which seems extraordinarily inappropriate to the solemnity of its context until we see, with a shock of recognition, that men have been speaking as a child, understanding as a child, thinking as a child: "For now we see through a glass darkly, but then face to face" (1 Corinthians xiii, 11-12). Bossuet does not, however, stop there. The image of the logbook of our worldly achievements simultaneously conveys, of course, an allusion to the book of life in which our real worth is recorded, but it also irresistibly conjures up the picture of the writer himself, striving to improve the very message he is intent on by the painstaking process of revision and correction, finally and impatiently striking out whole passages.[7] With that consciousness of the medium he himself is using which I noted earlier, Bossuet now turns his meditation in upon itself at the very moment he extends its range to the furthest physical limits ("la terre," "ce que nous sommes"). The quotation from Tertullian encompasses not only the utter dissolution of our bodies, but the very language which the preacher is using to impress that dissolution upon us. To what Donne calls "this peremptory nullification of Man" (p. 239) Bossuet adds the even more radical nullification of language.

The "château de cartes" in this passage is not the first appearance in the sermon of the imagery of buildings we met at the start of Donne's. A few lines earlier we are told that "l'accident ne peut pas être plus noble que la substance; ni l'accessoire plus considérable que le principal; ni le bâtiment plus solide que le fonds sur lequel il est élevé" (p. 267). Donne, we saw, concentrates chiefly on the leaving of a house, the ways of entry and departure which are the doors of life and death. Both preachers talk of the way buildings, as analogues of the body, crumble and decay into dust. If we look at how each ends his sermon, however, we find a curious reversal of what we might expect. Donne, having not pushed, extended or explored his simile as much as we are initially led to suppose he would, has by the time he reaches his peroration long since discarded it. He opts for a classical ending, classical in the sense that the peroration is distinguished from the body of the text by the use of a different register of style. Like many preachers in contemporary Europe, he does not effect this by the straightforward application of schemes and tropes proper to the *genus sublime*, but by the appeal and pathos of a meditative colloquy. The result, however, is much the same:

There wee leave you in that *blessed dependancy*, to *hang* upon *him* that *hangs* upon the *Crosse*, there *bath* in his *teares*, there *suck* at his *woundes*, and *lye down in peace in his grave*, till hee vouchsafe you a *resurrection*, and an *ascension* into that *Kingdome*, which hee *hath purchas'd for you*, with the *inestimable price* of his *incorruptible blood*. Amen. (p. 248)

The hallmarks of Donne's style are still present, of course: the pun in "*dependancy*," the devotional extravagance of "*bath* in his *teares*" and "*suck* at his *woundes*," the final reference to the sermon's whole theme (our grave) being continued and yet transmuted into "his *grave*." But the strong and direct emotional tone contrasts sharply with the questing intellectuality of the earlier passages. In the dialogue between passion and ratiocination, it is passion that provides the concluding note.

Given the classical tradition in which we usually place Bossuet, it is

strange to turn to his peroration. He does, it is true, provide in his penulti-
mate paragraph a satisfying circularity to the sermon by returning to the
raising of Lazarus which was his opening text. He does use the classical rhetorical figure of direct address in the singular form and characteristically
combines that perorational technique with the first person plural of the
affective meditational tone. He is careful to support his remarks with the
authority of St. Paul and St. John Chrysostom and with the claims of
rationality. But he is far from having discreetly dropped his secular imagery:

> Que crains-tu donc, âme chrétienne, dans les approches de la mort? Peut-être qu'en
> voyant tomber ta maison, tu appréhendes d'être sans retraite? Mais écoute le divin
> Apôtre: *Nous savons*, nous savons, dit-il, nous ne sommes pas induits à le croire par
> des conjectures douteuses, mais nous le savons très assurément et avec une entière
> certitude, *que si cette maison de terre et de boue, dans laquelle nous habitons, est
> détruite, nous avons une autre maison qui nous est préparée au ciel.* O conduite misé-
> ricordieuse de celui qui pourvoit à nos besoins! Il a dessein, dit excellemment saint
> Jean Chrysostome, de réparer la maison qu'il nous a donnée: pendant qu'il la détruit
> et qu'il la renverse pour la refaire toute neuve, il est nécessaire que nous délogions. Et
> lui-même nous offre son palais; il nous donne un appartement, pour nous faire atten-
> dre en repos l'entière réparation de notre ancien édifice. (p. 281)

To end a sermon on death with the familiar vocabulary of moving house,
of repairs and construction work, as if God were a kindly landlord lending
us a wing of his own residence while the builders are in, is an extraordinary
thing to have done. It is shocking, this conceit in which the conjunction of
the two elements, domestic upheaval and the repose of the soul while it
awaits the resurrection of the body, is extravagantly inappropriate. It is a
jeu d'esprit, cultivatedly amusing to the same courtly hearers whose sensibilities were teased in the sermon's opening words, and yet it is authenti-
cated and redeemed from triviality by what has gone before. It is a blend
of levity and seriousness by which the seriousness is intensified.

These aspects of Bossuet's sermon are obviously related to a particular
conception of his art and notably to his sense of an audience. A great deal
here depends upon *knowingness*. It is not simply that Bossuet is familiar
with the rather tarnished armory of conceits and quotations and authorities
that characterize the preaching tradition he inherits; he is also aware of his
audience's familiarity with these things, and so of their consequent need
for novelty, even though they might profess to be shocked by novel far-
fetchedness. The parallel has a rather different dilemma, since he is simultaneously bound to respect the continuity of his tradition and to go beyond
it. The *jeu d'esprit* in the peroration is perceived as disclosing a kind of new
vision of an age-old theme: the meaning of Christian death. This maintaining of balance between tradition and renewal can be effective only when
the conceit is surrounded by an elaborate apparatus of controls.

Control, appropriateness and so forth seem to be the chief preoccupations of the literary and social theorists of later seventeenth-century France who discuss this subject—Méré, for instance, or Bouhours. Even the lexicographers, from whom we might expect more explicit definitions, play a cautious crossword game of self-authenticating references around the word *esprit*. Thus Richelet[8] defines a *pointe* as "Rencontre spirituelle. Bon mot" and a *rencontre* as "Jeu de mots. Jeu d'esprit qui se trouve agréablement dans l'arrangement et la liaison des mots les uns avec les autres." "L'Epigramme," he says, "doit finir par une pointe ingénieuse," and we turn to *ingénieux* only to find "Qui a de l'esprit." The very ambiguity of the word *esprit* lies at the root of this. Furetière[9] gives the example of a socially approving comment ("Ce jeune homme a beaucoup de vivacité, de *pointe* d'esprit") which bespeaks a natural impatience with the dull and slow-witted, but not necessarily a fondness for certain turns of phrase. In his next line, on the other hand, he simply plunders Richelet: "Les Epigrammes doivent finir par quelque agréable *pointe*. Les *pointes* sont des équivoques, et des jeux d'esprit." And then comes the inevitable warning about a lack of control: "Il faut se donner de garde des fausses *pointes*, des turlupinades." Similarly, one has to pass through his negative entry under *jeux de paroles* ("les allusions, les équivoques, et les pointes, qui ne consistent que dans les mots, sans aucune subtilité pour le sens") in order to discern beyond it a possible good type of *pointe*, the sort which does have a certain "subtilité pour le sens." The ambivalence of this relatively impoverished lexical group emerges more clearly, *s.v. Allusion*:

Terme de Rhetorique. C'est une figure qui se fait par un petit jeu de mots qui sont presque semblables. L'affectation des allusions est extremement vicieuse en France. Mais on peut élegamment faire *allusion* à quelque apophthegme, à quelque histoire, à quelque coutume, lors qu'on dit quelque chose qui y a du rapport, et qu'on veut faire entendre au lecteur ou à l'auditeur, qu'on y a pensé en l'escrivant.

Is it fanciful to see here not only the difference between "witty" "Senecan" surface styles of the early seventeenth century and the taste of the later period which condemns them, but also the deep, self-renovating continuity of temper which unites them? Bossuet does not use the "Marie mère de Dieu et mer des grâces" sort of *allusion* we find in the sermons of Jean Boucher, Jean-Pierre Camus, even François de Sales, any more than we could find in Jeremy Taylor Lancelot Andrewes' remark that Mary Magdalene at the resurrection "saw *Him*, and was her selfe made an Angel by *Him*, a good Angel, to cary the Evangel."[10] We shall shortly see that he does make telling use of the figure in its second sense.

The restraints that "classicism" places on the "metaphysical" temper have a social dimension, an awareness of what is tolerable in polite discourse

—the very quality we find in La Fontaine's preface to the *Fables* or, indeed, in the exordium of Bossuet we have just been reading. For clearer notions of what is involved in the substance of that temper we may have to go outside France. Two famous European theorists of wit, whom Bossuet may never have read (though many of his contemporaries had, including Bouhours, as Peter France notes), actually discuss the use of conceits in sermons, and they do so in a way that illuminates Bossuet's practice.

In Italian or Spanish there is a more immediately manifest link between the words for *ingénieux* and the *ingegno* or *ingenio* which the theologians place, as understanding, among the gifts of the Spirit. The very first chapter of Gracián's *Agudeza y arte de ingenio* of 1642 balances the two human faculties: "Understanding without subtlety or conceits is a sun without light or sunbeams; and the rays which shine in the heavens are consubstantial with those of wit."[11] Gracián immediately goes on to substantiate this with a reference not only to antiquity, but also to the Fathers and to the duty which must be uppermost in every preacher's mind ("esta urgencia de lo conceptuoso," he calls it): "This persuasiveness of witty material is the same in prose and verse. What would Augustine be without his subtleties or Ambrose without his intellectual explorations (*ponderaciones*), Martial without his Attic salt, or Horace without his *sententiae*?"[12] So wit, not defined in a narrow stylistic sense, conforms to the aims of religious writing, firstly because it continues the style of the Fathers and secondly because it involves the exploration of mysteries with the light of a God-given intelligence. The rather difficult expression *ponderación misteriosa* is more fully explained in Gracián's sixth chapter. "The artifice here," he says, "consists in creating a mystery about the connection between two extremes or the correlatives of the subject—causes, effects, circumstances, contingencies; and having pondered the coincidence that unites them, one provides a subtle and appropriate reason that makes the parallel clear."[13] Grierson's definition of wit as "genius . . . showing itself in the discovery of subtle analogies, resemblances" is another way of saying it. The parallel between moving house and dying is, I would argue, a practical instance of it.

Coming even closer to the concerns of pulpit oratory, we find embedded in Emmanuele Tesauro's vast *Cannocchiale Aristotelico* of 1654 a treatise on what he calls "concetti predicabili." These he has already defined much earlier in the book as "un'Argutia leggiermente acennata dall'ingegno Divino: leggiadramente svelata dall'ingegno humano: & rifermata con l'autorità di alcun Sacro Scrittore."[14] This, it seems to me, exactly describes the way Bossuet goes about his *pointes*; it explains why we found St. Paul and St. John Crysostom at the end of the "Sermon sur la Mort." Nor, Tesauro comments, is this a newfangled approach to religious instruction:

Così ancora Salomone, con figurati Emblemi adornò tutto il Tempio di Dio, per allet-
tare il Popolo all'adorazione con la maraviglia. Così Mosè con ceremoniali Misteri,
insegnò documenti morali. Così Iddio con Simboli arguti rivelò i suoi secreti nella
Scrittura. Così il Verbo Divino, con paraboliche Figure predicò il Verbo Evangelico.[15]

Just as the restraints which hold wit in check derive from the Latin tradition of decorum, of the purposes and limits of rhetoric, so the conceit
justifies itself by its appearance in Scripture. "Tu es Petrus, et super hanc
petram aedificabo Ecclesiam meam." There is a renewing of links in the
seventeenth century with the sort of conceit one finds in early medieval
hymnody: Venantius Fortunatus' play on the royal crimson that adorns
the Cross is precisely a "discovery of analogies between extremes," since a
royal robe and blood, though opposites, are connected through their shared
color, and this points up the mysterious paradox of the King of Heaven
dying by a human instrument of torture.[16] Similarly the hymn *Ave Maris
Stella* observes that the Angel's *Ave* at the Annunciation is a reversal of the
name Eve: "Sumens illud Ave / Gabrielis ore, / funda nos in pace, / mutans
nomen Evae."[17] S.L. Bethell, in his pioneering article on the subject, even
claimed (adding to rather than clarifying the "welter of terminology," perhaps) that "the whole European movement of 'baroque wit' or 'metaphysical conceit' originated in a Jesuit revival of patristic wit."[18]

Bossuet, I am arguing, blends that Christian tradition with a classical,
Roman, one. Nor is he unaffected by more modern types of secular and
social wit. The *Oraison funèbre de Henriette de France* begins with a re-
sounding text from Psalm 2: "Et nunc, Reges, intelligite; erudimini qui
judicatis terram." It is, of course, appropriate to the theme he will shortly
develop, but how much more pointed an opening it becomes when we realize that Cromwell had struck a medallion with precisely this text on it.[19]
This is *allusion* in Furetière's second sense. The elegant discretion of it is
paralleled on a larger scale by the fact that Cromwell, whom every listener
or reader knows is the villain of the piece, is never once mentioned by name
in the oration: "Un homme s'est rencontré . . ." (p. 533) is a much more
awe-inspiring periphrasis. Then the oration proper begins: "Celui qui règne
dans les cieux, et de qui relèvent tous les empires, à qui seul appartient la
gloire, la majesté et l'indépendance" (p. 515), and we find an almost exact
transcription of the opening words of the Papal Bull of 1570 which excom-
municated Elizabeth I and absolved her subjects from obedience: "Regnans
in excelsis, cui data est omnis in caelo et in terra potestas."[20] Bossuet has,
by this veiled reference (not so veiled perhaps for those who were preparing to celebrate or execrate the centenary of the Bull's promulgation),

anticipated his central argument, namely that England's woes are the result of her quitting the fold of Peter a century earlier. It is clever, subtle; it does not detract from the argument, but actually strengthens it.

Another sort of *jeu d'esprit* comes close to *jeu de paroles*. Readers of the *Oraison funèbre de Henriette d'Angleterre* quite often feel that Bossuet is rather straining for effect when he builds up his introduction there to his favorite text of *Ecce mensurabiles*:

> Ecoutez à ce propos le profond raisonnement, non d'un philosophe qui dispute dans une école, ou d'un religieux qui médite dans un cloître: je veux confondre le monde par ceux que le monde même révère le plus, par ceux qui le connaissent le mieux, et ne lui veux donner pour le convaincre que des docteurs assis sur le trône. *O Dieu*, dit le Roi-Prophète . . . .[21]

The periphrases for David seem perhaps coy rather than discreet: everyone knows what is going to come. Their use, however, is still functional rather than decorative. He is anxious to speak as directly as possible to the worldly, court-centered audience he has in front of him. A much more successful example occurs in the exordium of the *Oraison funèbre d'Anne de Gonzague*. Bossuet is again addressing a worldly audience. He has listed at great length the elaborate titles of the Princesse Palatine; he has spoken of her repentance as a model for the court. Then, as at the opening of the "Sermon sur la Mort," he takes their reactions into account. He knows (contemporary accounts are full of examples) that people go to funeral orations partly so as to be able to discuss them afterwards. And so he concedes to them that this may be an occasion for using their judgment (Furetière places this critical meaning of *jugement* first in his article on the word) before suddenly turning the tables on them with all the vehemence of an Old Testament prophet:

> Mon discours, dont vous vous croyez peut-être les juges, vous jugera au dernier jour; ce sera sur vous un nouveau fardeau, comme parlaient les prophètes: *Onus verbi Domini super Israel*; et si vous n'en sortez plus chrétiens, vous en sortirez plus coupables.[22]

Everything is pivoted around the play on the word *juger*, but it would be hard to dismiss this as a mere decorative trope. It teases and confounds at one and the same time. Should we be surprised, incidentally, to discover that this technique is also found in English Metaphysical preaching? Eliot, in his essay on Andrewes, quotes a strikingly parallel example:

> I am here speaking to you, and yet I consider by the way, in the same instant, what it is likely you will say to one another, when I have done, you are not all here neither; you are here now, hearing me, and yet you are thinking that you have heard a better sermon somewhere else of this text; you are here, and yet you think you could have heard some other doctrine of downright *Predestination* and *Reprobation* roundly delivered somewhere else with more edification to you.[23]

To this category there also belongs the somewhat less veiled, indeed down-
right derogatory slight, in *Anne de Gonzague*, on the growth of libertine
rationalism and the success of a worldly book Bossuet evidently abhorred:
"Siècle vainement subtil, où l'on veut pécher avec raison, où la faiblesse
veut s'autoriser par des maximes" (p. 321).

Turning from Bossuet's often cutting use of words to his more extended
techniques, one is struck by the use to which he puts the eminently latinate,
Ciceronian, forensic figure of preterition ("I shall not dwell, gentlemen of
the jury, upon the minor crimes of the accused").[24] There is a straightforward example in the exordium of the *Oraison funèbre du Père Bourgoing*:

N'attendez donc pas, Chrétiens, que j'applique au Père Bourgoing des ornements étrangers, ni que j'aille rechercher bien loin sa noblesse dans sa naissance, sa gloire dans
ses ancêtres, ses titres dans l'antiquité de sa famille; car encore qu'elle soit noble et
ancienne dans le Nivernais, où elle s'est même signalée depuis plusieurs siècles par des
fondations pieuses, encore que la grand' chambre du Parlement de Paris et les autres
compagnies souveraines aient vu les Bourgoings, les Le Clercs, les Friches, ses parents
paternels et maternels, rendre la justice aux peuples avec une intégrité exemplaire, je
ne m'arrête pas à ces choses, et je ne les touche qu'en passant.[25]

"Encore qu'elle soit noble et ancienne dans le Nivernais . . ."; many of us
may have guiltily suppressed a fleeting smile at this point, schooled as we
are to a Flaubertian scorn for French provinciality in Parisian writing. Nonetheless, Bossuet here manages to include all the conventional *topoi* of the
panegyric and at the same time give the impression that he has not. Preterition is a powerful tool in his hands both in details of this kind and on a
grander structural plane.

Henriette d'Angleterre is the clearest example. The oration is organized
around the theory of dual time and thus falls into two halves: an account
of Henriette's life in the world, doomed to extinction, and an account of
the moral life which alone determines her, and our, eternity. Into the first
half go all the obligatory commonplaces of the funeral *éloge*, just as for
Bourgoing: the subject's ancestry, birth, actions, nobility of character.
However, because of what is coming (and has already in the *division* been
announced as coming) in the second half of the oration, Bossuet is able to
list these while at the same time emphasizing their ultimate worthlessness:

Et certainement, Messieurs, si quelque chose pouvait élever les hommes au-dessus de
leur infirmité naturelle; si l'origine, qui nous est commune, souffrait quelque distinction solide et durable entre ceux que Dieu a formés de la même terre, qu'y aurait-il
dans l'univers de plus distingué que la princesse dont je parle? (p. 656)

This shows an extraordinary capacity for saying one thing and implying its
opposite. Furthermore, he is able to introduce into this catalogue of qualities a note of pathos which reminds the audience of the dramatic sudden-

ness of their loss and extends the message to their own fate. The passage continues: "Tout ce que peuvent faire non seulement la naissance et la fortune, mais encore les grandes qualités de l'esprit, pour l'élévation d'une princesse, se trouve rassemblé, et puis anéanti, dans la nôtre" (ibid.). The parenthesis "et puis anéanti" is masterly. At the very moment of hyperbolic praise, he undercuts the whole movement of his sentence just as, in the pages that follow, the recurrent image of death is continually juxtaposed to the glittering portrait of a life at court. This balancing of opposites is classical equilibrium at its most controlled, while the use of each element in the equation to highlight its counterpart follows exactly the pattern of metaphysical wit.

Not that the oration dispenses with the other techniques we have been concerned with. There is a moment, just after the famous description of Madame's death, when Bossuet produces a phrase that is almost a textbook illustration of Tesauro's *concetto predicabile*. He expounds the well-known, even tired, funeral verse of Psalm 102 (103 in *A. V.*), "As for man, his days are as grass; as a flower of the field, so he flourisheth." It is directly applied to Henriette: "Madame cependant a passé du matin au soir, ainsi que l'herbe des champs." At first it seems a commonplace. Then it becomes a compliment to her youthfulness, with the *jeu d'esprit* of "fleurissait": "Le matin, elle fleurissait; avec quelles grâces, vous le savez." The insertion of "vous," however, is a direct and painful reminder to the audience of their loss of a beautiful and charming woman whom they will never see again. The next phrase is curt and brutal: "le soir, nous la vîmes séchée," although softened by the "nous" which weaves an even closer bond between preacher and public. And with the dawning realization that the words of the psalm apply only too fittingly to the day on which the princess suddenly died, we have Bossuet at first conceding the general point that Scripture uses imagery we probably consider charming, but rather literary ("et ces fortes expressions, par lesquelles l'Ecriture sainte exagère l'inconstance des choses humaines"), then, with a vigorous release of sounds, turning that judgment on its head: "devaient être pour cette princesse si précises et si littérales!" (p. 663).

A passage like that combines a *pointe* about figurative language with a close awareness of the hearers' tastes and their recently devastated emotions. The shock of suddenly seeing the direct relevance of the psalm marries the pleasure of insight (in which wit largely consists) to the power of feeling. We may be tempted to forget that the companion-word to *plaire* in seventeenth-century French esthetics is often not *instruire*, but *toucher*.

A final example which works on the scale of a complete oration, yet can be discerned in the detailed inspection of a short passage, may suffice, finally, to show the limits of Bossuet's method. The exordium of the *Oraison funèbre du Prince de Condé* of 1687 promises a treatment of the subject of much the same kind as for Henriette d'Angleterre. It ends by announcing a similar extended preterition whereby the worldly glories of the Prince are to be both praised and demolished, a similar stylization of the individual into a symbol of human achievement whether ultimately futile or ultimately substantial:

Mettons ensemble aujourd'hui, car nous le pouvons dans un si noble sujet, toutes les plus belles qualités d'une excellente nature; et, à la gloire de la vérité, montrons, dans un prince admiré de tout l'univers, que ce qui fait les héros, ce qui porte la gloire du monde jusqu'au comble, valeur, magnanimité, bonté naturelle, voilà pour le cœur; vivacité, pénétration, grandeur et sublimité de génie, voilà pour l'esprit, ne seraient qu'une illusion si la piété ne s'y était jointe; et enfin, que la piété est le tout de l'homme.[26]

But everyone who has read the oration knows that it will not turn out like this; the perfect holding in balance of the two visions we find in *Henriette d'Angleterre* is here lopsided, the spiritual crushed under the weight of the historical, the heroic, the parallels with Cyrus and with Alexander the Great. Condé is too unique a figure to become a symbol, too admired a friend to provide a pretext for a sermon on death. And yet, in Bossuet's last great public oration, the wit that can reveal a sudden striking truth, the careful guiding of the audience's understanding and feeling towards a devastating conclusion, is not absent.

Bossuet gives the impression that he is going to end the oration with a deathbed scene (quite a number of critics give the impression that he does). He paints a magnificent picture of the dying prince in bold strokes of dark and light, the battle between faith and unbelief, the triumph of the final revelation that accompanies death. The actual death, however, is replaced at the crucial moment by a sudden generalization of this vocabulary of *chiaroscuro*, and we swiftly move from the imagined bedside to the very cathedral where the funeral is taking place:

Que devinrent alors ces beaux titres dont notre orgueil est flatté? Dans l'approche d'un si beau jour, et dès la première atteinte d'une si vive lumière, combien promptement disparaissent tous les fantômes du monde! que l'éclat de la plus belle victoire paraît sombre! qu'on en méprise la gloire et qu'on veut de mal à ces faibles yeux qui s'y sont laissé éblouir!

Venez, peuples, venez maintenant; mais venez plutôt, princes et seigneurs, et vous qui jugez la terre, et vous qui ouvrez aux hommes les portes du ciel, et vous plus que tous les autres, princes et princesses, nobles rejetons de tant de rois, lumières de la France, mais aujourd'hui obscurcies et couvertes de votre douleur comme d'un nuage; venez voir le peu qui nous reste d'une si auguste naissance, de tant de grandeur, de tant de gloire. Jetez les yeux de toutes parts: voilà tout ce qu'a pu faire la magnificence et la piété pour honorer un héros: des titres, des inscriptions, vaines marques de ce qui n'est plus; des figures qui semblent pleurer autour d'un tombeau, et des fragiles images d'une douleur que le temps emporte avec tout le reste; des colonnes qui semblent vouloir porter jusqu'au ciel le magnifique témoignage de notre néant; et rien enfin ne manque dans tous ces honneurs que celui à qui on les rend. Pleurez donc sur ces faibles restes de la vie humaine, pleurez sur cette triste immortalité que nous donnons aux héros. (pp. 456-57)

The passage is electric with intelligence and feeling. It begins with the movement from the dying Condé to "nous"; the historical military victories which occupy so many of the preceding pages are alluded to and peremptorily dismissed. The very circumstances of a state funeral are then exploited, in the roll call summoning the nation to witness. Bossuet cleverly articulates this appeal according to the constitutional framework of the three Estates: at the bottom the people, then the nobility—d'épée ("princes et seigneurs") and de robe ("vous qui jugez la terre")—then the clergy ("vous qui ouvrez aux hommes les portes du ciel"), finally the royal family, elaborately and wittily addressed in a periphrasis which depends upon the stereotyped image of them as so many planets orbiting around the roi soleil. Bérain's stupendous décor amidst which they are at that moment sitting is itself called to witness, the artificiality of what amounts to a stage set mirroring the deceptiveness of what we merely imagine to be solid ("semblent pleurer," "semblent vouloir"). Just as Bossuet has elsewhere meditated on the transience of language itself, so here he abruptly, cruelly, points out that even the grief he is orchestrating, displaying, is destined to dissolution and decay. At the culmination of this movement he places, as a total surprise, a pointe , an epigrammatic witticism he knows will make his worldly, sophisticated audience sit up (it could come from La Rochefoucauld) and which, in its shockingness, finally brings home the nothingness of what was the Prince de Condé: "et rien enfin ne manque dans tous ces honneurs que celui à qui on les rend." But next one wonders whether the effect of this pointe has not been too much for the preacher's own control of his matter. The response it evokes is not, as in Henriette d'Angleterre, a renewed and lucid vision of the spiritual values underlying the deceptive vaine pompe. It is the simpler human response of tears. Much as he tries to redeem the effect of his radical insight into the nullity of human life by appealing to soldiers to be pious, by encouraging Condé's friends to preserve his memory, by reminding himself publicly that he has other duties and must give up preaching funeral orations, it is no good. Bossuet loses the balance he has so carefully maintained up to now. The wit, playing at a verbal level, has eroded its emotional and moral chains. The wealth of possible implications disclosed by this verbal wit, when they sink in, induces confusion; and so the pendulum swings away from a rigorously controlled thought to the muddled feelings which dominate his final words.

Metaphysical wit, Odette de Mourgues has written, involves "a keen awareness of insoluble problems lurking beneath accepted truths, and a reflective interest in argumentation on such problems."[27] It is, in the majority of religious writers at least, held in check by the public aims of their writing and by the traditions within which they write. If these aims are confused, as seems to me to be the case with Bossuet's last funeral oration, then the *pointe* misfires. The balance of passionate ratiocination is upset. Where the aims are clearly envisaged and squarely faced, Bossuet's achievement can be called, I think, remarkable. Suffused with the Latin qualities of rigorous argument and passionate pleading, it marries the humanist tradition of clarity with patristic wit and biblical allusiveness. The preterition which a Cicero can use to damn a Verres is here employed to hold together the physical and the intangible in a way which allows each to illuminate the other. There is a constant deployment of wit which enables Bossuet to say something and then, instantly, gainsay it.

All this depends on a further quality which, I believe, characterizes many of the writers discussed in this volume and which, for want of a better word, I have had to call "knowingness." A paradox can only be pushed to its limits, the shock of an unfamiliar image in a conventional context, or of a sudden change of register, is effective only in the hands of someone who knows his audience and his genre. One strand in this is naturally an acute and disciplined linguistic awareness, the self-consciousness on which wit inevitably depends. Another is a mature awareness of the inheritance which comes from the past and of the need to cope with it, to create as it were from within it. This involves not the sort of slavish copying which a term like "neo-classicism" often seems to imply, but organic renewal; not the rejection of the past in some childish gesture of iconoclasm, but a highly sophisticated recognition of its limits and of the way in which the literary landscape is constantly modified by more recent new growth. The way these potentially difficult demands are held together, in the literature of seventeenth-century France, is that sense of esthetic balance here called equilibrium. It is the sense that a work of art can explore paradox and conflict, even in the extreme degree to which most human beings experience them, and can nonetheless be coherent. That coherence in its turn depends on the intelligence and tact of writer and reader, securely embedded in the tradition of western literature.

NOTES

1. Donne's "Death Duell" of 1630 is quoted from *Sermons*, eds. G.R. Potter and E.M. Simpson (Berkeley, California, 1953-1962), X, 230-48. Bossuet's "Sermon

sur la Mort" of 1662 is quoted from *Oeuvres oratoires*, eds. Lebarq, Urbain and Lévesque (Paris, 1914-1926), IV, 262-81. All quotations from Bossuet are taken from this edition, henceforward referred to as *OO*; the first mention of a work is followed by a note of the volume and page, and thereafter page numbers are placed in the text in brackets.

2. *Sermon sur la Mort et autres sermons*, ed. J. Truchet (Paris, 1970), p. 32.

3. *A Study of the Prose Works of John Donne*, 2nd ed. (Oxford, 1948), p. 57.

4. For Bossuet's position vis-à-vis French preaching in the early seventeenth century, see my article "Le Raffinement et les ellipses dans le style oratoire de Bossuet," in *Bossuet: La prédication au XVIIe siècle*, eds. T. Goyet and J.P. Collinet (Paris, 1980), pp. 311-28.

5. Mme de Sévigné's correspondence provides some illustration of the way pulpit oratory was dissected and discussed like any other literary product. The very day Bossuet delivered his oration on Condé she was writing to Bussy-Rabutin: "Je viens de voir un prélat qui était à l'oraison funèbre. Il nous a dit que Monsieur de Meaux s'était surpassé lui-même, et que jamais on n'a fait valoir ni mis en œuvre si noblement une si belle matière." Bussy's reply of 31 March 1687 retails the gossip and *bons mots* which have reached provincial ears about it: "Comme j'ai ouï parler de l'oraison funèbre qu'a faite Monsieur de Meaux, elle n'a fait honneur ni au mort ni à l'orateur. On m'a mandé que le comte de Gramont, revenant de Notre-Dame, dit au Roi qu'il venait de l'oraison funèbre de M. de Turenne." Three years later she is recommending it among her current reading to Mme de Grignan and anticipating the latter's fashionable reaction to it: "Nous admirons ce portrait de Cromwell. Ce sont des chefs-d'œuvre d'éloquence qui charment l'esprit. Il ne faut point dire: 'Oh! cela est vieux.' Non, cela n'est point vieux; cela est divin. Pauline en serait instruite et ravie." The phrase "qui charment l'esprit" shows well enough what were the qualities of Bossuet's writing that attracted at least one of his contemporaries. See *Correspondance*, ed. R. Duchêne (Paris, 1972-1978), III, 284, 285, 808.

6. The point is that in the sermon which purports at the start to be an examination of tombs he does not mention tombs, whereas in the more delicate circumstances of Henriette's interment at Saint-Denis he prefaces the same material with an overt reference to the overcrowded conditions of the royal mausoleum. See J. Truchet's ed. of the *Oraisons funèbres* (Paris, 1961), p. 173, n. 3.

7. The impression is reinforced by a glance at the footnotes in *OO*. There are no fewer than thirteen variants, corrections or crossings-out in this single passage, ranging from "corbeaux" instead of "cerfs" to a lengthy marginal quotation from Augustine's *City of God*, copied out in full and then struck through.

8. *Dictionnaire français* (Paris, 1685).

9. *Dictionaire universel* (The Hague and Rotterdam, 1690).

10. *Sermons*, ed. G.M. Story (Oxford, 1967), p. 194.

11. The rather free translations are my own from the text in *Obras completas*, ed. E. Correa Calderón (Madrid, 1944), pp. 55-290: "Entendimiento sin agudeza ni conceptos, es sol sin luz, sin rayos, y cuantos brillan en las celestes lumbreras son materiales con los del ingenio" (p. 62).

12. Ibid.: "Esta urgencia de lo conceptuoso es igual a la prosa y al verso. Qué fuera Augustino sin sus sutilezas y Ambrosio sin sus ponderaciones, Marcial sin sus sales y Horacio sin sus sentencias?"

13. "Consiste el artificio de esta agudeza en levantar misterio entre la conexión de los extremos o términos correlatos del sujeto, repito, causas, efectos, adjuntos, cir-

cunstancias, contingencias; y después de ponderada aquella coincidencia y unión, dase una razón sutil, adecuada, que la satisfaga" (p. 80).

14. Ed. A. Buck (Berlin and Zurich: Bad Homberg v.d.H., 1968), p. 65.

15. Ibid., p. 503.

16. "Arbor decora et fulgida, / ornata regis purpura, / electa digno stipite / tam sancta membra tangere." *Oxford Book of Medieval Latin Verse*, ed. F.J.E. Raby (Oxford, 1974), p. 75.

17. Ibid., p. 94.

18. "Gracián, Tesauro, and the Nature of Metaphysical Wit," *The Northern Miscellany of Literary Criticism*, 1 (1953), 18.

19. *OO*, V; see esp. p. 515, n. 1.

20. *Select Statutes and Other Constitutional Documents*, ed. G.W. Prothero, 4th ed. (Oxford, 1913), p. 195.

21. *OO*, V, 660.

22. Ibid., VI, 291.

23. T.S. Eliot, *Selected Essays*, 3rd ed. (London, 1951), pp. 350-51.

24. The work of the most latinate of English authors contains perhaps the best known example: "Of the three popes, John the Twenty-third was the first victim: he fled and was brought back a prisoner: the most scandalous charges were suppressed; the vicar of Christ was only accused of piracy, murder, rape, sodomy, and incest." Gibbon, *Decline and Fall of the Roman Empire*, ch. 70.

25. *OO*, IV, 405.

26. Ibid., VI, 425.

27. *Metaphysical, Baroque and Précieux Poetry*, p. 47.

LIST OF CONTRIBUTORS

Dorothy Gabe Coleman: Fellow of New Hall, Cambridge

François Rigolot: Professor of French, Princeton University

Richard Griffiths: Professor of French, University of Wales (Cardiff)

Philip Ford: Lecturer in French, University of Aberdeen

Alan Boase: Emeritus Marshall Professor of French, University of Glasgow

Elizabeth Armstrong: Fellow of Somerville College, Oxford

Terence Cave: Fellow of St. John's College, Oxford

Henri Fluchère: Emeritus Professor of English, University of Aix-en-Provence

Frank J. Warnke: Professor of Comparative Literature, University of Georgia

Gillian Jondorf: Fellow of Girton College, Cambridge

Ian McFarlane: Professor of French Literature, University of Oxford

W.D. Howarth: Professor of Classical French Literature, University of Bristol

Michael Black: Publisher, Cambridge University Press

Jean-Pierre Collinet: Professor of French Literature, University of Dijon

Michael Edwards: Lecturer in European Literature, University of Essex

David Lee Rubin: Professor of French, University of Virginia

Alain Seznec: Professor of French, Cornell University

Michel Jeanneret: Professor of French Literature, University of Geneva

Peter France: Professor of French, University of Edinburgh

Peter Bayley: Fellow of Gonville and Caius College, Cambridge

TABULA GRATULATORIA

Dr. Gwyneth Castor, University of Warwick
Vanessa A. Clarke, London
Professor Mervyn R. Coke-Enguidanos, Bloomington, Indiana
Mr. Robert Coleman, Emmanuel College, Cambridge
Dr. T.G.S. Combe, Pembroke College, Cambridge
Professor Marian G.R. Coope, University of British Columbia
Dr. Christine M. Crow, University of St. Andrews
Professor Hugh M. Davidson, University of Virginia
Mrs. E. Davies, University of Glasgow
Dr. Judith Davies, Girton College, Cambridge
Professor Betty J. Davis, New York
Mlle Solange Dayras, Paris
Dr. Madeleine Defrenne, Brussels
Professor Jean Descrains, Bar-le-Duc
Professor Alvin A. Eustis, University of California, Berkeley
Mrs. Yolande Evans, London
Professor Alison Fairlie, Girton College, Cambridge
Professor Leonard Forster, Selwyn College, Cambridge
Mme M.-M. de la Garanderie, Nantes
Professor Robert Garapon, Paris
Professor Claire L. Gaudiani, University of Pennsylvania
Professor Perry Gethner, Chicago
Miss S.M. Gillies, Girton College, Cambridge
Professor Hope H. Glidden, Tulane University
Mr. and Mrs. A.T.K. Grant, Cambridge
Professor Floyd Gray, University of Michigan
Professor Dennis Green, Trinity College, Cambridge
Professor Robert B. Griffin, University of California, Riverside
Mr. Bruce Griffiths, University College of North Wales, Bangor
Miss Elizabeth Guild, Robinson College, Cambridge
Professor C.A. Hackett, Winchester
Dr. H. Hammond, Limpsfield
Mme Wynne Hellegouarch, Caen
Professor Noémi Hepp, Strasbourg
Professor Dame Elizabeth Hill, Cambridge
Professor Frederick Hodgson, Massachusetts Institute of Technology
Professor Catherine Howard, Los Gatos, California

Professor Mitchell E. Imhoff, Columbus, Ohio
Dr. Edward James, St. John's College, Cambridge
Mr. L.W. Johnson, Berkeley, California
Professor Wallace Kirsop, Monash University, Australia
Professor Roy C. Knight, University College of Swansea
Professor Harold Knutson, University of British Columbia
Dr. A.J. Krailsheimer, Christ Church, Oxford
Professor Raymond C. La Charité, University of Kentucky
Professor Virginia A. La Charité, University of Kentucky
Lise H. Leibacher, Greenbelt, Maryland
Professor Ralph Leigh, Trinity College, Cambridge
Professor Raymond LePage, Fairfax, Virginia
Professor Deborah Lesko, New Haven, Connecticut
Professor Margaret McGowan, University of Sussex
Dr. Melveena McKendrick, Girton College, Cambridge
Dr. G. Jonathan Mallinson, Pembroke College, Cambridge
Professor Andrée Mansau, Toulouse
Professor Rose-Ann Martin, Buffalo, New York
Professor Marianne Meijer, University of Maryland
Dr. Sean O'Cathasaigh, Sidney Sussex College, Cambridge
Professor Ray Ortali, State University of New York, Albany
Dr. Robert Pickering, Downing College, Cambridge
M. Guillaume Picot, Paris
Professor George Pistorius, Williams College
Professor Christine M. Probes, Tampa, Florida
Professor Anthony R. Pugh, University of New Brunswick
Dr. Alan W. Raitt, Magdalen College, Oxford
Mr. John M. Recker, Columbus, Ohio
Professor Peter Rickard, Emmanuel College, Cambridge
Professor Tamara Root, Minneapolis, Minnesota
Mrs. P.M.A. Ross, Haslemere
Professor Jean Rousset, Geneva
Mrs. Patricia Roynon, Eton College, Windsor
Professor David Lee Rubin, University of Virginia
Professor Tilde Sankovitch, Northwestern University
Professor Joyce Scott, Laramie, Wyoming
Professor Jean Seznec, All Souls College, Oxford
Professor Isidore Silver, St. Louis, Missouri

Dr. Alison Sinclair, Clare College, Cambridge
Dr. C.N. Smith, University of East Anglia
Mrs. Natasha Squire, Lucy Cavendish College, Cambridge
Professor Arthur Stabler, Washington State University
Mrs. Sheila Stern, Cambridge
Professor Donald Stone, Harvard University
Dr. Elisabeth Stopp, Cambridge
Dr. Graham M. Sutherland, University of Glasgow
Professor Marie-Odile Sweetser, University of Illinois-Chicago
   Circle
Professor Eugene Thompson, Greensboro, North Carolina
Professor Vivien Thweatt, Merion, Pennsylvania
Mrs. Joyce Tyrer, Surbiton
Mr. Hugo Tucker, St. John's College, Cambridge
Professor A. Kibédi Varga, Amsterdam
Professor Claire Verdi, Irvine, California
Mrs. E.M. Vinestock, Warminster
Dr. A. Vlasto, Selwyn College, Cambridge
Professor Henri Weber, Montpellier
Professor Bernard Williams, King's College, Cambridge
Professor Charles G.S. Williams, Ohio State University
Dr. J. Cameron Wilson, Jesus College, Cambridge
Dr. Dennis Wood, University of Birmingham
Mr. T.S. Wyatt, Sidney Sussex College, Cambridge
Professor Zobeidah Youssef, University of Western Ontario
Professor Eléonore Zimmerman, State University of New York,
   Binghamton
Professor Roger Zuber, University of Nanterre

Institutions

University of Aberdeen
Agnes Scott College
The Queen's University of Belfast
Bodleian Library, Oxford
Bowdoin College
Bowling Green State University

Brigham Young University
University of Bristol
Cambridge University Library
Centenary College of Louisiana
Polytechnic of Central London
Charterhouse
Christ Church, Oxford
University of Cincinnati
Downing College, Cambridge
University of Dundee
University of East Anglia
University of Edinburgh
Emmanuel College, Cambridge
University of Exeter
Fordham University
Girton College, Cambridge
Gonville and Caius College, Cambridge
Harvard University
University of Illinois-Chicago Circle
Keble College, Oxford
Kenyon College
Lady Margaret Hall, Oxford
University of Leeds
U.E.R. des Lettres et des Sciences Humaines, Limoges
Lucy Cavendish College, Cambridge
Maison Française, Oxford
Marquette University
Merton College, Oxford
University of Missouri
Modern and Medieval Languages Library, University of Cambridge
Mount Holyoke College
New Hall, Cambridge
Newnham College, Cambridge
University of Nottingham
Pembroke College, Cambridge
Pembroke College, Oxford
Queen Mary College, London

University of Reading
Rijksuniversiteit, Ghent
University of Rochester
University of St. Andrews
St. Anne's College, Oxford
St. Catharine's College, Cambridge
St. Catherine's College, Oxford
St. David's University College, Wales
St. Edmund Hall, Oxford
St. Mary's College
St. Peter's College, Oxford
Selwyn College, Cambridge
University of Sheffield
Somerville College, Oxford
University of South Carolina
University of Sussex
University College of Swansea
University of Toronto
Université de Tours
Universitätsbibliothek, Trier
Trinity College, Cambridge
Trinity College, Hartford
Trinity Hall, Cambridge
University College, London
Victoria University
University of Virginia
Wake Forest University
University of Warwick
Worcester College, Oxford

FRENCH FORUM MONOGRAPHS

1. Karolyn Waterson. *Molière et l'autorité: Structures sociales, structures comiques.* 1976.
2. Donna Kuizenga. *Narrative Strategies in* La Princesse de Clèves. 1976.
3. Ian J. Winter. *Montaigne's Self-Portrait and Its Influence in France, 1580-1630.* 1976.
4. Judith G. Miller. *Theater and Revolution in France since 1968.* 1977.
5. Raymond C. La Charité, ed. *O un amy! Essays on Montaigne in Honor of Donald M. Frame.* 1977.
6. Rupert T. Pickens. *The Welsh Knight: Paradoxicality in Chrétien's* Conte del Graal. 1977.
7. Carol Clark. *The Web of Metaphor: Studies in the Imagery of Montaigne's* Essais. 1978.
8. Donald Maddox. *Structure and Sacring: The Systematic Kingdom in Chrétien's* Erec et Enide. 1978.
9. Betty J. Davis. *The Storytellers in Marguerite de Navarre's* Heptaméron. 1978.
10. Laurence M. Porter. *The Renaissance of the Lyric in French Romanticism: Elegy, "Poëme" and Ode.* 1978.
11. Bruce R. Leslie. *Ronsard's Successful Epic Venture: The Epyllion.* 1979.
12. Michelle A. Freeman. *The Poetics of* Translatio Studii *and* Conjointure: *Chrétien de Troyes's* Cligés. 1979.
13. Robert T. Corum, Jr. *Other Worlds and Other Seas: Art and Vision in Saint-Amant's Nature Poetry.* 1979.
14. Marcel Muller. *Préfiguration et structure romanesque dans* A la recherche du temps perdu *(avec un inédit de Marcel Proust).* 1979.
15. Ross Chambers. *Meaning and Meaningfulness: Studies in the Analysis and Interpretation of Texts.* 1979.
16. Lois Oppenheim. *Intentionality and Intersubjectivity: A Phenomenological Study of Butor's* La Modification. 1980.
17. Matilda T. Bruckner. *Narrative Invention in Twelfth-Century French Romance: The Convention of Hospitality (1160-1200).* 1980.
18. Gérard Defaux. *Molière, ou les métamorphoses du comique: De la comédie morale au triomphe de la folie.* 1980.
19. Raymond C. La Charité. *Recreation, Reflection and Re-Creation: Perspectives on Rabelais's* Pantagruel. 1980.
20. Jules Brody. *Du style à la pensée: Trois études sur les* Caractères *de La Bruyère.* 1980.
21. Lawrence D. Kritzman. *Destruction/Découverte: Le Fonctionnement de la rhétorique dans les* Essais *de Montaigne.* 1980.
22. Minnette Grunmann-Gaudet and Robin F. Jones, eds. *The Nature of Medieval Narrative.* 1980.
23. J.A. Hiddleston. *Essai sur Laforgue et les* Derniers Vers *suivi de* Laforgue et Baudelaire. 1980.
24. Michael S. Koppisch. *The Dissolution of Character: Changing Perspectives in La Bruyère's* Caractères. 1981.
25. Hope H. Glidden. *The Storyteller as Humanist: The* Serées *of Guillaume Bouchet.* 1981.
26. Mary B. McKinley. *Words in a Corner: Studies in Montaigne's Latin Quotations.* 1981.

27. Donald M. Frame and Mary B. McKinley, eds. *Columbia Montaigne Conference Papers*. 1981.
28. Jean-Pierre Dens. *L'Honnête Homme et la critique du goût: Esthétique et société au XVIIe siècle*. 1981.
29. Vivian Kogan. *The Flowers of Fiction: Time and Space in Raymond Queneau's Les Fleurs bleues*. 1981.
30. Michael Issacharoff et Jean-Claude Vilquin, éds. *Sartre et la mise en signe*. 1981.
31. James W. Mileham. *The Conspiracy Novel: Structure and Metaphor in Balzac's Comédie humaine*. 1982.
32. Andrew G. Suozzo, Jr. *The Comic Novels of Charles Sorel: A Study of Structure, Characterization and Disguise*. 1982.
33. Margaret Whitford. *Merleau-Ponty's Critique of Sartre's Philosophy*. 1982.
34. Gérard Defaux. *Le Curieux, le glorieux et la sagesse du monde dans la première moitié du XVIe siècle: L'exemple de Panurge (Ulysse, Démosthène, Empédocle)*. 1982.
35. Doranne Fenoaltea. *"Si haulte Architecture." The Design of Scève's Délie*. 1982.
36. Peter Bayley and Dorothy Gabe Coleman, eds. *The Equilibrium of Wit: Essays for Odette de Mourgues*. 1982.

French Forum, Publishers, Inc.

P.O. Box 5108, Lexington, Kentucky 40505

Publishers of *French Forum*, a journal of literary criticism